The Culture of Merit

STUDIES IN MEDIEVAL AND EARLY MODERN CIVILIZATION
Marvin B. Becker, General Editor

Charity and Children in Renaissance Florence:
The Ospedale degli Innocenti, 1410–1536
  Philip Gavitt

Humanism in Crisis: The Decline of the French Renaissance
  Philippe Desan, editor

Upon My Husband's Death: Widows in the Literatures
and Histories of Medieval Europe
  Louise Mirrer, editor

The Crannied Wall: Women, Religious, and the Arts
in Early Modern Europe
  Craig A. Monson, editor

Wife and Widow in Medieval England
  Sue Sheridan Walker, editor

The Rhetorics of Life-Writing in Early Modern Europe: Forms of
Biography from Cassandra Fedele to Louis XIV
  Thomas F. Mayer and D. R. Woolf, editors

Defining Dominion: The Discourses of Magic and Witchcraft in
Early Modern France and Germany
  Gerhild Scholz Williams

Women, Jews, and Muslims in the Texts
of Reconquest Castile
  Louise Mirrer

The Culture of Merit: Nobility, Royal Service, and the Making of
Absolute Monarchy in France, 1600–1789
  Jay M. Smith

The Culture of Merit

Nobility, Royal Service, and the Making of Absolute Monarchy in France, 1600–1789

Jay M. Smith

Ann Arbor

THE UNIVERSITY OF MICHIGAN PRESS

Copyright © by the University of Michigan 1996
All rights reserved
Published in the United States of America by
The University of Michigan Press
Manufactured in the United States of America
⊗ Printed on acid-free paper

1999   1998   1997   1996   4   3   2   1

A CIP catalog record for this book is available from the British Library.

Library of Congress Cataloging-in-Publication Data

Smith, Jay M., 1961–
    The culture of merit : nobility, royal service, and the making of
absolute monarchy in France, 1600–1789 / Jay M. Smith.
        p.   cm. — (Studies in medieval and early modern civilization)
    Includes bibliographical references and index.
    ISBN 0-472-09638-9 (alk. paper).
    1. France—Civilization—17th century. 2. Louis XIV, King of
France, 1638–1715—Influence. 3. France—Civilization—18th
century. 4. Monarchy—France—Moral and ethical aspects.
5. France—Kings and rulers—Conduct of life. 6. France. Armee—
History. I. Title. II. Series.
DC33.4.S55 1996
944'.033—dc20   96-9992
                                                               CIP

Acknowledgments

For offering the financial assistance without which this book could never have been written, I would like to thank the ITT Corporation, the Rackham Graduate School of the University of Michigan, the National Endowment for the Humanities, the Research Council of the University of North Carolina at Chapel Hill, and the Lilly Foundation. My thanks also to the History Department and the Institute for the Arts and Humanities at UNC for providing a much-needed sabbatical leave in 1993, during which I nearly completed my revisions to the manuscript. In the preliminary stages of my research, the Newberry Library made possible my participation in a summer institute that provided access to rare published sources and stimulated my interest in genealogical histories of the French nobility. During the academic year 1987–88, and then again in the summer of 1992, I received much assistance and helpful advice from archivists at the Archives Nationales in Paris and the Archives de la Guerre at Vincennes. With each trip to the Bibliothèque Nationale, I gained a greater appreciation for the efficiency and generosity of the BN staff; in 1987–88, in particular, they helped make the Salle des Manuscrits my favorite haunt.

This project has consumed more time than I ever could have anticipated, but I have been sustained along the way by many individuals who provided intellectual and moral support whenever I needed it, which was often. I take great pleasure, at long last, in expressing my gratitude to each of them. David Bien, who has long served as the model for the supportive graduate advisor, shaped this book and its author in countless ways. The themes explored in this study echo those found in Bien's work, and the dissertation that led to this book was subjected to Bien's editorial rigor, for which he is famous. But I am most grateful to him for the lessons he imparted by example: to frame broadly meaningful questions with the big picture always in mind, to feel genuine sympathy for the subjects of one's research, and to write accessible and reader-friendly prose.

As I feebly attempt to live up to the standard he set both as a teacher and a scholar, I find that my debt of gratitude to David Bien continues to accrue interest.

I owe a great debt also to William Sewell. Through Sewell's own work I was initially awakened to the exciting possibilities of historical lexicography, and to his inspiring teaching and challenging intellectual standards I owe my sensitivity to theoretical issues. His feedback and encouragement at every stage in the writing of the thesis (and in the years since) were more important to me than he probably knew.

Since my arrival in North Carolina, several colleagues have kindly read and commented on new versions of the manuscript. John Headley has regularly brought to my attention helpful sources and new perspectives on the early-modern European state, and he has consistently and rightly encouraged me to keep one eye on the Renaissance background. In his careful reading of the manuscript, he saved me from many mistakes of style and substance. My colleagues in French history, Lloyd Kramer and Donald Reid, created a stimulating and supportive environment ideal for exchanging ideas and comparing approaches to the past. In their thoughtful reactions to my manuscript, they pushed me to clarify my ideas, but they also emboldened me to carry the argument further. More generally, I'm grateful to Don and Lloyd for welcoming me to Chapel Hill in the first place; our shared interests in cultural studies and new historical methods have made North Carolina an exciting and rewarding place to practice French history.

Stephen Baxter, Marvin Becker, Thomas Kavanagh, Keith Luria, Orest Ranum, Lionel Rothkrug, and Thomas Tentler all read the entire manuscript at one time or another, and I benefited much from their reactions. In the spring of 1993 the Triangle French Studies Seminar treated me to a discussion of two of my chapters. After fielding many probing questions from that relentlessly critical (but unfailingly warm) group, I was forced to rethink my analytical categories. The anonymous readers for the University of Michigan Press, whose identities I hope to discover in the future, were extraordinarily conscientious and offered insightful and sympathetic critiques.

Other friends and colleagues lent their assistance by reading specific chapters, by sharing ideas when the work was in its formative stages, or simply by providing me a reassuring anchor in the real world. I would particularly like to thank William Beik, Richard Bodek, Gail Bossenga, André Burguière, Steven Clay, Robert Descimon, Aaron Fogleman,

Danielle Haase-Dubosc, Michael Kwass, Michèle Longino, Rene Marion, H.-J. Martin, Terence McIntosh, Allan Potofsky, Mary Louise Roberts, Bryan Skib, Leonard Smith, Mike Smith, Steven Soper, and Rochelle Ziskin. This book has been enriched by the talents and insights of all the people here mentioned; the imperfections that remain are the responsibility of the author.

This book is dedicated to the three people who, really for no good reason, made me believe long ago that I could do it: my wife, Debbie, and my parents. Although I know that no apologies are necessary, I'm only sorry that it took so long to justify their confidence.

Note on Translations

All translations are the author's unless othewise indicated. The spelling and accentuation of the titles of seventeenth- and eighteenth-century French texts have been left in their premodern form.

Contents

Introduction: Merit, Nobility, and the French State

This book is partly the result of a felicitous *conjoncture* in my own personal history. A decade ago, while simultaneously studying for general exams and finishing research for a seminar paper, I glimpsed almost by accident a paradox that seemed both fascinating and unexamined. Under pressure to read primary texts from the seventeenth century at the same time that I was reading literature *about* the eighteenth century, I found myself confronting (and even absorbing) contradictory notions about the history of aristocratic culture.

I read with great pleasure Guy Chaussinand-Nogaret's powerful and influential book *The French Nobility in the Eighteenth Century: From Feudalism to Enlightenment* (first published in 1976).[1] Chaussinand-Nogaret boldly set out to demonstrate the surprisingly modern behavior and outlook of the eighteenth-century French nobility. One of his most important claims involved the nobility's new relationship to the concept of merit. His argument made sense intuitively. Having been infiltrated by many upwardly mobile commoners, having imbibed the liberal principles of the Enlightenment, and having recognized that the idea of merit could actually be turned to the advantage of established elites, leaders of the nobility had apparently begun to champion meritocratic values by the middle of the century.

Chaussinand-Nogaret examined letters of ennoblement as well as the cahiers of 1789 and found evidence of the nobility's changing mores. Beginning in 1760, he wrote, "the notions of valor and honor, which had defined what was specifically noble up to that point, were overtaken by a new notion: that of merit, a bourgeois value, typical of the third estate,

---

1. Guy Chaussinand-Nogaret, *La Noblesse au XVIIIᵉ siècle: De la féodalité aux lumières* (Brussels, 1984). For the English translation by William Doyle see *The French Nobility in the Eighteenth Century: From Feudalism to Enlightenment* (Cambridge, 1985).

which the nobility integrated, made its own, and accepted and recognized as a criterion of nobility." By embracing merit, as well as all of the social and professional activities promoted within the new meritocratic culture, the French nobility jumped over the great divide separating tradition from modernity. "From this moment," Chaussinand-Nogaret suggested, "there was no longer any significant difference between the nobility and the bourgeoisie. . . .The bourgeois ideology drove out and took the place of the noble ideology."[2]

Seventeenth-century voices prevented easy acceptance of Chaussinand-Nogaret's thesis, however. In examining a range of sources from the early decades of that century—noble memoirs especially, but also didactic literature for courtiers, political treatises, and the printed cahiers of 1614—I had been struck by the frequent occurrence of the word *merit*. The word was used, moreover, not against but by the nobility, for whom it seemed to have a special meaning.

What to make of this? Chaussinand-Nogaret had pursued a worthy objective; he had intended to show that in the years before the French Revolution aristocrats had been just as progressive and open-minded as their peers in the upper reaches of the third estate, and that the collapse of the old order could not be blithely attributed to the rigidity of a decadent elite oblivious to the winds of change. Yet an abundance of seventeenth-century texts offered clear proof that, if eighteenth-century nobles had indeed possessed an admirably progressive sensibility, their evocation of the concept of merit was neither sign nor cause of it. Nobles in 1760 obviously lived, thought, and wrote in a context very different from that of the early Bourbon era, and they undoubtedly ascribed to merit meanings that would have been unfamiliar to the nobles of 1600, but when they represented themselves as meritorious they actually carried on a venerable tradition.

Comparison of seventeenth-century texts with Chaussinand-Nogaret's own evidence and argument thus threw into relief several vexing analytical problems: How can one write a history of the French nobility that accounts both for its impressive adaptability and for its adherence to established patterns of discourse? How does one describe the long-term evolution of a class mentality while respecting the integrity and resiliency of its traditional forms? More generally, how does the historian identify

---

2. Chaussinand-Nogaret, *La Noblesse*, 53–54.

and elucidate the points of articulation between traditional and modern modes of thought and behavior?[3]

With these large questions in mind, I resolved to look more closely at the meanings of merit in early-modern France. I began, though, by abandoning the assumption—usually expressed only implicitly—that merit itself had been an autonomous product of the age of Enlightenment.[4] Instead I assumed that changes in noble discourse in the eighteenth century reflected a transformation internal to a broad culture of merit whose lines of continuity could be traced back at least as far as the early seventeenth century. To gain access to this culture, and to understand its modification over time, I set out to analyze all the related concepts, associations, and points of reference implied by use of the word *merit* in

---

3. Jonathan Dewald's *Aristocratic Experience and the Origins of Modern Culture: France, 1570–1715* (Berkeley, 1993) also addresses the nobility's relationship to modernity, but Dewald regards the issue from a perspective very different from the one developed in the following chapters. He focuses on new forms of cultural expression in the seventeenth century—e.g., the written memoir, close personal friendships, and the epistolary genre. He suggests that the search for individual self-expression in this period, a search that foreshadowed the modern individualist ethic, reflected the nobles' desire to evade or reach beyond commonly accepted cultural norms. Nobles did not find "unity" in a traditional culture (7); rather, the constraints of tradition encouraged innovative means of self-expression. I maintain, in contrast to Dewald, that old nobles were indeed unified by a common set of assumptions about society, hierarchy, service, and the meaning of merit, and that the roots of modernity can be found in the processes by which those assumptions were transformed over time.

4. This assumption, whose roots lie in the last century of the ancien régime, was enshrined by the French Revolution. Abbé Auger laid out the classical formulation in an educational treatise of 1789. There he congratulated the right-thinking nobles who now aspired toward "an intrinsic and personal merit" that contrasted with the "birth and intrigue" by which they had formerly acquired honors and positions. See *Projet d'éducation pour tout le royaume, précédé de quelques réflexions sur l'Assemblée Nationale* (n.p., 1789), 3. Historians of the eighteenth century have generally accepted the validity of Auger's dichotomy; they differ only over the degree to which the nobility can be said to have recognized and embraced the new value of merit in the years before the Revolution. Chaussinand-Nogaret is one among many who has argued that the upper segment of the eighteenth-century nobility merged with wealthy commoners to form a broad elite based loosely on meritocratic assumptions. Also see, for example, Denis Richet, "Autour des origines lointaines de la Révolution française: Elites et Despotisme," *Annales, E. S. C.* 24 (1969): 1–23; and Marcel Reinhard, "Elite et Noblesse dans la seconde moitié du XVIIIᵉ siècle," *Revue d'Histoire Moderne et Contemporaine* 3 (1956): 5–38. However, in a multivolume collection devoted to French military history, Jean Chagniot recently observed that "merit respectfully laid claim to its rights" beginning in 1767 with the publication of several pamphlets critical of noble privilege in the army. See André Corvisier et al., eds., *Histoire Militaire de la France,* 3 vols. (Paris, 1992), 1:112.

noble discourse. The seventeenth century became the natural starting point. I hoped that by learning the language of merit, and by studying the relationships between the distinct elements within that language, I would be able to relate the long-term evolution of the noble outlook to changes in the social and political conditions that framed and inevitably were reflected in the nobility's culture of merit.

Two features of this early-modern language of merit require some preliminary comment. I quickly discovered that in both the first half of the seventeenth century and the latter half of the eighteenth—and at every point in between—many voices drew attention to the qualities thought to be reflected in birth and lineage. This intriguing sign of cultural continuity reinforced my initial instinct to focus especially on the history of the old nobility, a nebulous group whose members boasted at least several generations of noblesse and who generally saw themselves as constituting the "true" noble order in France. The decision to highlight their experience seemed justified for two reasons. First, the old (or sword) nobility had always been the most prominent and powerful segment of French society. Successive generations of French historians have recognized that close analysis of that group and of the families who comprised it provides critical insight into the many social changes that accompanied the rise of the absolutist state.[5] Second, by paying special attention to those most anxious to articulate the principle of aristocratic distinctiveness, I sharpen the focus of a study whose main objective is to suggest how traditional concepts may coexist with and even spawn recognizably modern concepts.

One other important aspect of the nobility's discourse on merit should be mentioned here. When nobles discussed and represented their merits in written texts, they made frequent reference to the person of the king, in light of whose gaze, they believed, the nobility's unique qualities

---

5. Some representative titles are Pierre de Vaissière, *Gentilshommes campagnards de l'Ancienne France* (Paris, 1903); Jean Meyer, *La Noblesse Bretonne au XVIIIe siècle* (Paris, 1972); Robert Forster, *The House of Saulx-Tavanes: Versailles and Burgundy, 1700–1830* (Baltimore, 1971); Jean-Marie Constant, *Les Conjurateurs: Le premier libéralisme politique sous Richelieu* (Paris, 1987); idem, *La Vie Quotidienne de la Noblesse Française aux XVIe et XVIIe siècles* (Paris, 1985); idem, *Nobles et paysans en Beauce aux XVIe et XVIIe siècles* (Paris, 1981); Arlette Jouanna, *Le Devoir de Révolte: La noblesse française et la gestation de l'Etat moderne (1559–1661)* (Paris, 1989); William Weary, "The House of La Trémoille, Fifteenth through Eighteenth Centuries: Change and Adaptation in a French Noble Family," *Journal of Modern History* 49 (1977): on-demand supplement; James B. Wood, *The Nobility of the 'Election' of Bayeux, 1463–1666: Continuity through Change* (Princeton, 1980).

would inevitably be revealed and rewarded. This correlation between the image of the meritorious individual, on the one hand, and the 'sovereign's gaze'—responsible for judging merit—on the other hand, helped to direct my research. In search of the values and assumptions that lay beneath the optical field to which both kings and nobles often referred, I was drawn ineluctably toward an examination of contemporary conceptions of royal service. Consequently, the world of royal service is the constant backdrop for this investigation—from the consideration in the first chapter of debates over venality of office in the early seventeenth century to the analysis in the last chapter of reformist perspectives within the royal army of the later eighteenth century. The old nobility's changing attitudes toward merit must be seen as part of a larger historical shift involving perceptions of the domain of royal service and of the gaze thought to illuminate that domain.

By emphasizing the contingent character of the sovereign's gaze, this study of the culture of merit also casts an indirect light on the process of state formation and the creation of a new public-oriented politics in the eighteenth century. Historians of the early-modern period have long recognized that in the sixteenth through eighteenth centuries France (and Europe) witnessed a slow transition away from personal forms of authority and toward an increasingly impersonal political culture. The centralizing state is recognized, moreover, as having been a key agent of change throughout this long process. Many fine monographs devoted to French politics in the seventeenth and eighteenth centuries have demonstrated the depersonalizing tendencies inherent in the activities of the growing state.[6]

---

6. The classic account of state centralization and its corrosive effects on traditional forms of authority in France is Alexis de Tocqueville's *The Old Regime and the French Revolution*, trans. Stuart Gilbert (New York, 1955). More recent appraisals abound, however. Roland Mousnier, for example, argued often that Louis XIV sought to invalidate all personal ties other than those linking the king to his subjects. Norbert Elias and Roger Chartier have emphasized, though from somewhat different angles, the depersonalizing impact of court ceremonial and state ritual in the eighteenth century. Sharon Kettering connects the achievement of administrative efficiency in the later seventeenth century with the withering away of clientelism. And Gail Bossenga has shown how the crown's own financial operations encouraged urban corporations to regard the state as an abstract and impersonal entity in the eighteenth century. See Mousnier, *The Institutions of France under the Absolute Monarchy*, trans. Brian Pearce, 2 vols. (Chicago, 1979–84), vol. 1; Chartier, *The Cultural Origins of the French Revolution*, trans. Lydia G. Cochrane (Durham, N.C., 1991), 124–35; Elias, *The Court Society*, trans. Edmund Jephcott (New York, 1983); Kettering, *Patrons, Brokers, and Clients in Seventeenth-Century France* (Oxford, 1986); Bossenga, *The Politics of Privilege: Old Regime and Revolution in Lille* (Cambridge, 1991).

Certain elements in this long and complicated story remain unexplored, however, because for many historians—including the most sensitive—the word *state* continues implicitly to signify the repository of an already-coercive force or a set of a priori ideological, institutional, and historical imperatives. This tendency can have the effect of distorting the narrative of early-modern state formation because it retains the reassuring fiction that the motives, interests, and perspectives of all actors in the great drama can ultimately be explained by reference to some essential historical reality.[7] To resist the temptation to essentialize the concept of the state, one needs to assume that the state itself, at every stage of its development, belonged to a cultural field in which relations and meanings were never fixed.

Analysis of the sovereign's gaze should offer a new and helpful perspective on the developing French state of the seventeenth and eighteenth centuries. In part this is because the concept of the gaze, with its function of finding and affirming merit, makes it possible to incorporate one of Michel Foucault's most important insights, namely, that systems of

---

7. This tendency is perhaps revealed best by one of the studies that comes closest to overcoming it, Sharon Kettering's *Patrons, Brokers, and Clients*. Kettering shows that Louis XIV and his collaborators increased administrative efficiency in part by reworking established patterns of patronage and by relying on regional power brokers linked to the monarchy through personal relations. Her valuable study shows how the traditional practice of patronage shaped the emerging structures of the centralized state in France. The essential nature of her agent of change is never in doubt, however. She finally depicts clientelism as a system that "statebuilders" exploited and then overcame in their drive to expand and consolidate state power: "But as the central government became stronger in the late seventeenth century . . . the inherently divisive aspects of clientelism began to outweigh its integrative aspects"; "As a result *the state* [emphasis mine] began to search for a more impersonal, professional basis for administrative relationships, and a new bureaucratic form of political organization began to emerge." In other words, "the crown used clientelism in statebuilding, then developed a new bureaucratic system of political organization . . . once the establishment of the absolute state was well under way" (206, 237). This approach, which ascribes to statebuilders a kind of transcendent consciousness that allows them to choose between personal and impersonal administrative techniques, overlooks the possibility that kings and ministers may have conceived their own goals and interpreted their own actions *through* the culture that Kettering claims they "used . . . in statebuilding." Similar kinds of interpretive problems emerge, for example, in works by Kristen B. Neuschel, who omits the centralizing state from her analysis of noble attitudes on the grounds that its activities were distinct by definition from the aristocracy's cultural field, and Sarah Hanley, who takes for granted the state-building motives of kings and their councillors. See Neuschel, *Word of Honor: Interpreting Noble Culture in Sixteenth-Century France* (Ithaca, N.Y., 1989), introduction; and Hanley, "Engendering the State: Family Formation and State Building in Early Modern France," *French Historical Studies* 16 (1989): 4–28, esp. 6–7.

power should be studied through their techniques of mastering and ordering knowledge.[8] This study follows the transition from the "personal" state of the early seventeenth century to the relatively "impersonal" state of the later eighteenth century, and it therefore covers familiar terrain. But because it approaches the phenomenon by examining at the same time changing perceptions of merit, the transformation of the sovereign's gaze, and the epistemological assumptions by which these two variables were linked, the reader is reminded always that state power—whether in 1600, 1700, or 1789—was embedded within a process of cultural construction. The meanings of merit elaborated and negotiated by kings and nobles constituted one element, an important element, in that process.

The first two chapters of this book attempt to define with some clarity the common ideals, perceptions, and social values in terms of which the old nobility conceived its self-image, its view of the monarchy, and its definition of the services it rendered kings. Specialists of the period are already familiar with many of the aspects of noble culture discussed in these chapters, and my discussions of honor, generosity, and lineage, for example, are based largely on well-known sources from the period. But I hope to add new meaning to these ideas by stressing the connectedness and coherence of the various aspects of noble culture and by emphasizing the relationship between representations of the old nobility and representations of the monarchy. The values, assumptions, and practices that mediated relations between the king and the old nobility cohered within a loosely organized structure that I call the personal modality of royal service. Within this modality, definitions of merit ascribed great importance to qualities associated with aristocratic birth, and the proper recognition of merit was thought to be dependent on the discriminating power of the king's personal gaze.

I argue in chapter 3 that the early proponents of *raison d'état* confused and alienated important segments of political society—including especially many old nobles—by attempting to articulate and emphasize the other-than-personal dimensions of royal power. The new political arguments, in addition to the controversial policies of Richelieu and Mazarin, called into question the central features of the personal modality of ser-

---

8. A complete listing of the works dealing with this issue would be superfluous since the subject of power lies at the center of all of Foucault's work. The best introduction is Foucault, *Power/Knowledge: Selected Interviews and Other Writings, 1972–1977,* ed. Colin Gordon (New York, 1980), esp. chap. 8.

vice and threw into confusion the terms regulating the meaning of merit. Louis XIV ultimately corrected this problem, I maintain in chapter 4, by joining the new statist ideal of administrative control with more familiar ideals of personal rule. Because he himself recognized and embraced the principles of the personal modality of service, the gradual expansion of diversified, supervisory administrative structures implied to Louis XIV the refashioning of the sovereign's gaze and the creation of a centralized governing apparatus that made sense within the personal conceptual framework traditionally used by kings, nobles, and others. To be sure, tension and episodic conflict continued to mark the relationship between crown and nobility after 1661, but through the construction of Louisquatorzian absolutism, with its theoretically panoptic reach, the old nobility nevertheless found the means to accept and understand its integration into a more powerful monarchical state.

Louis XIV's desire and ability to engage his nobility in a more satisfying relationship points, ironically, to the analytical value of the much-derided term *absolutism*.[9] The adjective *absolute* conveys the novelty and importance of Louis XIV's regime, not because it describes the *intensity* of the monarch's power, but rather because it expresses the monarchy's

---

9. Revisionist historians in the past twenty years have variously emphasized the French monarchy's ideological commitment to aristocratic power, the financial constraints on monarchical action, the material and political benefits bestowed on privileged groups by Louis XIV and other kings, and the considerable autonomy still exercised by local and provincial powers in the seventeenth and eighteenth centuries. Richard Bonney, in his *Society and Government in France under Richelieu and Mazarin, 1624–1661* (New York, 1988), expresses what is now the consensus view when he writes that "no 'absolute' ruler in theory enjoyed absolute power in practice" (xiii). Some have gone further and urged the abandonment of the very word *absolutism*. See, for example, Roger Mettam, *Power and Faction in Louis XIV's France* (London, 1988); and Sarah Hanley, *The "Lit de Justice" of the Kings of France: Constitutional Ideology in Legend, Ritual, and Discourse* (Princeton, 1983), 226–27. For recent assessments of the concept of absolutism see Richard Bonney, "Absolutism: What's in a Name?" *French History* 1 (1987): 93–117; Andrew Lossky, "The Absolutism of Louis XIV: Reality or Myth?" *Canadian Journal of History* 19 (1984): 1–15; and William Beik, "Celebrating Andrew Lossky: The Reign of Louis XIV Revisited," *French Historical Studies* 17 (1991): 526–41. Among the best and most interesting recent works treating seventeenth-century absolutism are William Beik, *Absolutism and Society in Seventeenth-Century France: State Power and Provincial Aristocracy in Languedoc* (Cambridge, 1985); Roger Mettam, *Power and Faction;* Daniel Dessert, *Argent, Pouvoir et Société au Grand Siècle* (Paris, 1984); idem, *Fouquet* (Paris, 1987); James Collins, *Fiscal Limits of Absolutism: Direct Taxation in Early-Seventeenth Century France* (Berkeley, 1988); Albert N. Hamscher, *The Conseil Privé and the Parlements: A Study in French Absolutism* (Philadelphia, 1987); idem., *The Parlement of Paris after the Fronde, 1653–1673* (Pittsburgh, 1976); David Parker, "Sovereignty, Absolutism and the Function of the Law in Seventeenth-Century France," *Past and Present* 122 (1989): 36–74.

ambition to establish the king's spatial and temporal absoluteness. Louis XIV intended to make royal authority at least preeminent in all areas of the realm at all times, allowing no disorderly spaces or temporal gaps; this ambition separates Louis from all earlier centralizing monarchs. Yet the king carried out the construction of this absolute monarchy by asserting his own presence and by expanding the personal idiom through which kings and nobles had customarily communicated. By elaborating and routinizing a language whose specific relevance had once been confined to the relations between king and nobility, Louis XIV extended the king's power (and duty) of surveillance metaphorically. The king's gaze encompassed all the space of the realm, making it theoretically possible for the king to envision and engage all of society in a direct way. In the changing operation of the sovereign's gaze in the later seventeenth century, I argue, one can actually see the traditional personal modality of service become an incipient public modality.

The emerging public modality of royal service had basic features in common with the personal modality from which it evolved: the assumption of an efficacious sovereign gaze; an emphasis on the personal presence of the monarch; and a conception of merit that still accorded high status to honor, generosity, and all the qualities associated with elevated birth. But in projecting the sovereign's gaze through the structures and routines of an expanding administration, the public modality of service also changed the linguistic matrix through which merit had always been defined and represented. The service culture of absolutism actually amalgamated traditional norms of personal service—expectations of noble generosity, courage, self-sacrifice, and so on—and impersonally enforced norms such as talent and discipline. Nobles and others who served French kings after 1661 learned to aspire to the ideals of skillfulness, application, and efficiency as they internalized behavioral norms expressed and measured through institutions.

The steady elaboration of both sets of norms, I argue, eventually tested to the breaking point the compatibility of the notion of hereditary merit, on the one hand, and the expansion of an all-seeing and impartial public authority, on the other hand. The duality of the royal gaze, after all, made it impossible to fix the meaning of merit or of the monarchy responsible for evaluating and affirming it. This basic tension within the service culture of absolutism is explored at length in chapters 5 and 6 of this book, where I examine the evolution of merit's meaning in a very specific context—the eighteenth-century army.

In that vitally important service institution, dominated by the old nobility, the values ascribed to birth, talent, and discipline came together to form an increasingly unstable compound. As military reformers in the last decades of the ancien régime sought to articulate clearly the meaning of merit in the army, they unwittingly confronted the ever more ambiguous nature of the sovereign's gaze. Most army reformers were noble, and all were committed in some way to the idea of aristocratic superiority; but in making an explicit attempt to reconcile the two modalities of royal service that had shaped the meaning of merit since the later seventeenth century, they unleashed a critical rhetoric that would soon be used to attack the very principles of monarchy and aristocracy. In elaborating a logic internal to absolutist political culture, army reformers gave voice to ideals and arguments that would be turned against absolutism in the French Revolution.

1

Merit and the Personal Modality of Service

The years following the Wars of Religion have been widely interpreted as a period of readjustment for the traditional warrior nobility in France. Recent scholarship has shown that the old nobility ultimately adapted well to the new requirements of postfeudal life, but all specialists would agree that the nobility had to respond to several daunting challenges as the sixteenth century gave way to the seventeenth: the resentment of commoners who blamed nobles for the scourge of civil war; a new and systematic questioning of the meaning of noble status; the changing nature of the military art; and the need to redefine its relationship with a monarchy now prepared to resume its centralizing tendencies.[1]

When set against this threatening backdrop, the motives of the nobil-

---

1. The theme of "aristocratic crisis" is common in the historiography of early-modern Europe. For the French case, the best starting point is Davis Bitton's brief but panoramic *The French Nobility in Crisis, 1560–1640* (Stanford, 1969). Bitton's theme of wholesale crisis is also taken up by André Devyver, *Le Sang Epuré: Les Préjugés de race chez les gentilshommes français de l'ancien régime, 1560–1720* (Brussels, 1973). For the European context, see François Billacois, "La Crise de la Noblesse Européene (1550–1650): Une Mise au Point," *Revue d'Histoire Moderne et Contemporaine* 23 (1976): 258–77; and Henry Kamen, *European Society, 1500–1700* (London, 1984), 93–119. Examples of studies that stress the nobility's deteriorating political situation in this period are James Russell Major, "The Crown and Aristocracy in Renaissance France," *American Historical Review* 69 (1964): 631–45; and Richard Bonney's study of the *intendants, Political Change in France under Richelieu and Mazarin, 1624–1661* (Oxford, 1978). For the controversy over noble status in the sixteenth and seventeenth centuries see Jean-Richard Bloch, *L'anoblissement en France au Temps de François Ier: Essai d'une définition de la condition juridique et sociale de la noblesse au début du XVIᵉ siècle* (Paris, 1934); and Ellery Schalk, *From Valor to Pedigree: Ideas of Nobility in France in the Sixteenth and Seventeenth Centuries* (Princeton, 1986). Most recent studies have stressed the perseverance and adaptability of the early-modern aristocracy. In addition to the works cited in the introduction, see James Russell Major's "Noble Income, Inflation, and the Wars of Religion," *American Historical Review* 86 (1981): 21–48; and Robert Harding, *Anatomy of a Power Elite: The Provincial Governors of Early-Modern France* (New Haven, 1978). Classic studies showing the continued

11

ity in the wake of the Wars of Religion are all too easily deduced. André Devyver, in his study of noble *mentalités,* noted the nobility's increasing preoccupation with lineage and family status in the sixteenth century and interpreted noble behavior after 1560 as a general "reflex of social defense." In insisting on the broad social importance of distinguished birth, wrote Devyver, the nobility merely sought "to maintain all its prerogatives" by artificial means.[2]

Much evidence indicates that established nobles perceived the upward mobility of commoners as a serious threat to their own power and status.[3] Beginning at the Estates General of 1560, and continuing through the meetings of the estates of 1576 and 1588, the second estate complained repeatedly about the loss of important functions to what it called the *champignons d'une nuit,* the commoners who had managed to buy their way into judicial, financial, and court offices.[4] To appease the nobility, the monarchy declared in May 1579 that functions traditionally filled by nobles—the *baillis* and *sénéchaux* at local levels; such offices as *gentilhomme de la chambre, maître d'hôtel,* and *écuyer d'écurie* at court— were now reserved exclusively for *gentilshommes.*[5] To insure a fair distribution of such posts, no one person should hold more than one position at a time. Further, the crown announced that whenever offices in *parlement* fell vacant, the court had to include the name of at least one *gentilhomme* on its nomination list, once assuming him competent as

strength of the aristocracy in the eighteenth century are Robert Forster, *The Nobility of Toulouse in the Eighteenth Century: A Social and Economic Study* (Baltimore, 1960); and Jean Meyer, *La Noblesse Bretonne au XVIIIᵉ siècle* (Paris, 1972).

2. Devyver, *Le Sang Epuré,* 56.

3. In principle, however, most everyone agreed that kings had the right to create new nobles on occasion, especially when this mark of recognition came as reward for distinguished valor. For a survey of attitudes about ennoblement in the sixteenth and seventeenth centuries see Arlette Jouanna, "Perception et appréciation de l'anoblissement dans la France du XVIᵉ siècle et au début du XVIIᵉ siècle," in *L'Anoblissement en France XVᵉ–XVIIIᵉ siècles,* Centre de Recherches sur les Origines de l'Europe Moderne, Université de Bordeaux 3 (Bordeaux, 1985), 1–36.

4. This term of derision appeared in a pamphlet of 1614 titled *Advis, remonstrances, et requêtes aux estats généraux tenus à Paris, 1614: Par six Paysans* (Paris, 1614), 15. For a detailed discussion of the old nobility's response to the challenge of social mobility and the rise of the robe nobility in the later sixteenth and early seventeenth centuries see James Russell Major's recent work of synthesis, *From Renaissance Monarchy to Absolute Monarchy: French Kings, Nobles, and Estates* (Baltimore, 1994), esp. 96–112.

5. The word *gentilhomme,* roughly synonymous with *noble de race* and old noble, would be applied to a noble of at least three to four generations. By the end of the seventeenth century, the definition was unambiguous: a *gentilhomme* was at least a fourth-generation noble.

required by law. This last stipulation probably insured that judges followed the procedure only rarely.[6]

In any case, noble opposition to the influx of new men into crown functions did not reach fever pitch until after the 1604 edict on the *paulette,* an edict that made most crown offices in justice and finance fully inheritable.[7] The juridical systematization of venality of office galvanized noble opinion for a number of reasons. First, the new law finalized the "usurpation" of noble functions by non-nobles and nobles in the making; the *gentilhomme* could no longer hope for a gradual reversal of this insidious trend. Second, the *paulette* came just four years after the important edict on the taille that had indicated that many third-generation officeholders could be counted as nobles. Given the dramatic increase in the sale of letters of nobility in the late sixteenth century, nobles had reason to believe that the crown's renewed commitment to venality portended wholesale recruitment into the second estate. Finally, once the crown established in 1604 that offices should be considered property *immeuble,* prices skyrocketed.[8] Rising prices placed offices beyond the reach of many nobles of moderate income—nobles who might otherwise have quietly resigned themselves to the spread of venality—and created the impression that only the wealthy would have access to important legal and financial functions. For all these reasons, the law of 1604 elicited a new wave of noble criticism and protest.

Noble concerns found expression in the cahiers drawn up for the Estates General of 1614. In their grievance lists, noble deputies formulated an ambitious political program. Nobles now sought representation even in those fields not normally associated, either by contemporaries or

---

6. François Isambert et al., *Recueil général des anciennes loix françaises depuis l'an 426 jusqu'à la révolution de 1789,* 29 vols. (Paris, 1822–33), 14:439–40.

7. The *paulette* was the fee venal officeholders paid every nine years to guarantee the inheritability of their offices. The fee amounted to one-sixtieth the original purchase price of the office.

8. Two articles by Ralph E. Giesey explore the uses of office as property in the seventeenth century: "Rules of Inheritance and Strategies of Mobility in Prerevolutionary France," *American Historical Review* 82 (1977): 271–89; and "State Building in Early Modern France: The Role of Royal Officialdom," *Journal of Modern History* 55 (1983): 191–207. On the price of offices see Roland Mousnier, *La Vénalité des Offices sous Henri IV et Louis XIII* (Paris, 1945); Jonathan Dewald, *The Formation of a Provincial Nobility: The Magistrates of the Parlement of Rouen, 1499–1610* (Princeton, 1980); William Doyle, "The Price of Offices in Pre-Revolutionary France," *Historical Journal* 27 (1984): 831–60; and David D. Bien, "Manufacturing Nobles: The Chancelleries in France to 1789," *Journal of Modern History* 61 (1989): 445–86.

by historians, with the traditional nobility. Showing little awareness of anachronism, they requested restoration to their rightful place in offices of law and finance. Deputies from Auvergne called on the king to place nobles in "the courts of *parlement,* in the *cours des aides,* as *maîtres des requêtes de l'Hôtel,* and in other sovereign courts, in the offices of *tré-soriers généraux* and [other] offices of finance, in the *bailliages* and *sénéchaussées* [courts]"—in short, in all royal courts, where nobles should comprise "at the very least" one-third of the membership.[9] A widely circulated pamphlet of 1614, the *Advis et Remonstrances,* echoed the sentiment; it insisted that "the nobility will be restored to its former splendor and will administer justice as it used to."[10]

Nobles coveted other functions, too. The *Advis et Remonstrances* suggested suppressing the influential office of *trésorier général* and replacing it by a single *gentilhomme* treasurer for each province.[11] And in future councils of war, nobles affirmed, membership should be at least two-thirds *gentilhomme,* considering this was the field of their "particular profession and experience."[12] To this they added the call for complete exclusion of roturiers from the king's household and from the military, a demand reiterated at the Assemblies of Notables of 1616 and 1627.[13] There is no mistaking the sharp distinction the nobility drew between *gentilshommes* and everybody else. Everywhere, it seems, nobles hoped to use the criterion of birth as a barrier to the pretensions of the third estate.

It is important to view the noble grievances stated in and around the year 1614 as something other than the predictable complaints of a class suddenly aware of its decline. Insofar as the nobility's reactions to the new challenges of the early seventeenth century are susceptible to generalization, they should be characterized not as transparent expressions of group interest but as expressions of the culture in terms of which nobles conceived their place in the world. Rather than dismiss the noble cahiers of 1614 as tendentious and self-serving, the historian should use them as

9. Bibliothèque de l'Arsenal (hereafter BA), MS 4485, "Cahiers particuliers de la noblesse (des 3 Etats) de diverses provinces de ce royaume, pour estre représentez en l'Assemblée des Etats généraux tenus à Paris. 1615" ("Auvergne"), fol. 143v.

10. *Advis, remonstrances, et requêtes,* 12.

11. Ibid., 18.

12. Charles J. Mayer, ed., *Recueil des Cahiers Généraux des Trois Ordres aux Etats-Généraux,* 4 vols. (Paris, 1789), 4:199.

13. Charles J. Mayer, ed., *Des Etats-Généraux et autres Assemblées Nationales,* 18 vols. (Paris, 1788–89), 18:302.

a point of entry into the language and attitudes that framed nobles' relationships and therefore enabled them to interpret political change.[14] As the political theorist Antoine de Montchrétien remarked in 1615, everyone attending the Estates General hoped to give "legitimate order to the process of providing charges, offices, and benefices" and wanted to establish "equitable" rules for the distribution of "exemptions, immunities, rewards, and gifts."[15] In this chapter I intend to read the cahiers of 1614, and a wide variety of other texts written by or for the nobility, as earnest attempts to rearticulate the "legitimate order" governing the exchange of service and recompense in the early seventeenth century. In doing so, I hope to define with new clarity the common cultural matrix that provided the traditional nobility and the centralizing Bourbon kings grounds for disagreement and, eventually, compromise.

Careful examination of contemporary texts makes one thing very clear: to focus on the nobility's attention to the prerogatives of birth is to miss half the story. Nobles of the early seventeenth century nearly always joined the idea of birth with another personal attribute—merit. It may seem surprising that hereditary aristocrats would argue their case for filling public positions on the basis of merit, but that is precisely what nobles did. The point emerges from the list of what most offended them. The sale of offices; the practice of *survivance*, whereby a designated heir, regardless of qualifications, succeeded a relative in a public function; the influence of court favorites and *grands,* who monopolized the distribution of the king's patronage; and the growing number of *officiers,* who gradually supplanted nobles in the exercise of substantive local authority—all these "abuses" were attacked specifically for denying men of merit fair access to public functions.

Nobles offered the king a simple solution to the problem. He should choose his public deputies from a more qualified pool of candidates; he

---

14. The cahiers (or grievance lists) of 1614 are an especially valuable source because they seem to speak for a representative cross section of the old nobility. Of the 135 noble deputies who attended the Estates General, Roger Chartier has found that about three-quarters of them were a "middling" nobility of barons and knights, that is, "old" but not particularly "great." See Roger Chartier, "La noblesse et les Etats de 1614: Une réaction aristocratique?" in *Représentation et Vouloir Politiques: Autour des états-généraux de 1614,* ed. Roger Chartier and Denis Richet (Paris, 1982), 117. For an account of the Estates General meeting see J. Michael Hayden, *France and the Estates General of 1614* (Cambridge, 1974).

15. Antoine de Montchrétien, *Traicté de l'Oeconomie Politique, dedié en 1615 au Roy et a la Reyne Mere du Roy,* ed. Th. Funck-Brentano (Paris, 1889), 354.

should choose, that is, from among the nobility. Nobles from Orléanais, for example, requested that the king "admit to the governments and lieutenancies of his provinces, the captaincies of cities, places, and châteaux, only *gentilshommes* of race and recommendable merit."[16] The Assembly of Notables issued a more sweeping statement in 1627: "As nobles hold an honorable rank in the state, being endowed with the necessary qualities, they would seem to merit preference for the most elevated charges in the church and in justice."[17] In addition to their obvious fitness for positions in the army and at court, nobles represented themselves as the best-suited to hold important functions in the royal courts, in the church, in the financial hierarchy, and in the king's councils. They told the king to choose men of merit for these lofty positions—that is, to choose nobles.

From a modern perspective, the nobility's reliance on a rhetoric of merit seems only to underscore its naïveté. Surely nobles should have recognized that to compete with "bourgeois" lawyers and merchants for legal and financial office, they had to avoid the criterion of personal merit at all costs. After all, legal training was in principle a prerequisite even to be considered for appointment to the law courts. In theory, and usually in practice, new recruits to judicial office had to submit to a test of their legal knowledge before a standing panel of jurists.[18] The young man of *robin* upbringing would normally be better able to meet these requirements than would nobles of the traditional type.[19] Similarly, the candidate to high financial office had probably spent part of his career in commerce and credit operations or had a father or grandfather who had done so. At minimum, a knowledge of mathematics and bookkeeping strengthened his claim to competency. The typical noble did not have the same experience, nor would he have cared to admit it even if he had.

Nobles knew all this of course. The question is, How could they have overlooked such obvious incongruities in their rhetoric? Their method of attack has certainly been a source of puzzlement to most historians. Davis Bitton, for example, remarked that the nobles' position rested on "a gratuitous assumption that . . . the nobility would benefit if offices

---

16. BA, MS 4485, "Cahiers particuliers . . . Orléans," fol. 30v.

17. Mayer, *Des Etats-Généraux*, 18:303.

18. Jonathan Dewald notes that all officers in royal courts were formally required to have a license from a law school and were also examined before being received into office. Standards were not rigidly enforced, and so not all tests were equally challenging, but the examination requirement was nevertheless universal. Dewald, *Formation*, 22–28.

19. Over the course of the seventeenth century, officeholders in the law courts came to be called *nobles de robe*, or *robins*.

were granted on the basis of merit," an idea that "was never really feasible anyway without a complete social upheaval, for implicit in all arguments for merit . . . was the idea of an elite as opposed to a hereditary aristocracy."[20] More recently, another specialist of the seventeenth century condemned the noble program of 1614 for "clumsily" linking birth and merit in a transparent defense of privilege.[21] How could nobles have been so confused as to use the very word *merit* as a euphemism for inherited distinction?

In the spirit of semiotic methodology, which holds that cultural analysis consists in "construing social expressions on their surface enigmatical" to gain access "to the conceptual world in which our subjects live," one needs to concede to seventeenth-century nobles that *they*, at least, knew what they were talking about, and that the best way to ascertain the meaning of noble discourse is to penetrate the surface contradictions in the rhetoric while shedding our own prejudices.[22] To the modern reader, it is the merit implied in the context of the *robin* world that resonates. Hard work and dedication, experience, educational achievement, demonstrable ability—in short, tangible credentials—these are what constitute merit. But given the persistent, and insistent, association of the ideas of birth and merit in noble discourse throughout the seventeenth century and beyond, is it not important to suppose that nobles indeed lived in a "conceptual world" where birth and merit were thought to be compatible, even synonymous? By reviewing the terms most often used by nobles in their attempts to defend and describe their own merits, we can uncover the peculiarly noble definition of merit in the culture of the seventeenth century. The question to bring to the texts is, What enabled nobles, in their competition with the third estate, to think that merit was on their side?

---

20. Bitton, *French Nobility*, 44, 63. Ellery Schalk betrays similar assumptions in his more recent book on noble attitudes. He judges contemporary pamphlet literature: "Sixteenth-century nobles . . . sound a good deal like their nineteenth-century bourgeois counterparts when they call for ability and merit. If such calls were taken literally and seriously by others in society, they could become dangerous for a social group whose position was in reality essentially a hereditary one. But at least in the 1570s and 1580s . . . [s]uch discussions had not yet become dangerous." See *From Valor to Pedigree*, 69.

21. Erica Harth, *Ideology and Culture in Seventeenth-Century France* (Princeton, 1983), 46.

22. Clifford Geertz, *The Interpretation of Cultures* (New York, 1973), 5, 24.

Merit, Service, and Recompense: The Norm of Obligation

When the Assembly of Notables affirmed in 1627 that nobles "would seem to merit preference" for all offices of importance, "being endowed with the necessary qualities," what qualities did they have in mind? There is little reason to think that they were pointing to the nobility's superior knowledge of letters. For more than a century, individuals both within and outside the corps had been scolding nobles for their ignorance and urging them to take up mathematics, fortifications, languages, rhetoric, history, and geography to ready themselves for public service. In his celebrated treatise from the 1580s, François de La Noue had called for the founding of crown-supported academies for noble adolescents, training centers where they could make themselves qualified for "all public functions."[23] Antoine Laval noted in 1611 that for any noble who hoped to serve as councillor of any kind, a proper education was now essential, since "for the councillor it is not enough to be faithful; I would want him to be prudent . . . [and] where will he learn to be wise if not among the wise and informed?"[24] The sound of alarm had not subsided by the time of the Estates General in 1614. Perhaps in response to the nobles' disgruntled appeals for preference in public positions during that gathering, one pamphlet told the history of how nobles had inadvertently invited other men to take their jobs away from them.

> "Letters" and studies being arduous, long, and costly, and the nobility having abandoned them, it was necessary by and by to relinquish public posts and offices to roturiers. . . . the roturiers knew enough to grab this occasion by the hair and, making the most of their necessity, introduced themselves into offices and dignities and are now recruited for them.[25]

Even members of the third estate warned nobles that any *gentilhomme* who failed to have his son schooled in mathematics and "letters" would live to regret it.[26]

---

23. In the *Discours politiques et militaires* (Lyon, 1599), 121–27.

24. Antoine Laval, *Desseins de professions nobles et publiques* (Paris, 1612), fol. 35r.

25. From a pamphlet titled *Le Paysan Français,* cited in Roger Chartier, Madeleine Compère, and Dominique Julia, *L'Education en France du XVIe au XVIIIe siècles* (Paris, 1976), 168.

26. The cahier compiled by the town of Sens in 1614 provides a typical example: Archives Nationales (hereafter AN), K 675, no. 99. "Mémoire . . . Sens," fol. 3r.

Nobles responded ambivalently to this well-meaning advice. By the seventeenth century more nobles attended *collèges* to do the "cycle" of humanities, and some even took a year or two of law with a tutor or at a university before embarking on their careers.[27] In 1623, the biographer of the maréchal de Lesdiguières could boast about his subject's studies in jurisprudence and canon law at Avignon, which made him "one of the best students in the whole city."[28] Other nobles, however, seemed indifferent to the charge of ignorance.

In answer to the critics who asserted, for example, that nobles, given their meager knowledge of Latin, had no business holding positions in law courts, noble representatives at the estates called that argument a "most subtle means" to justify excluding *gentilshommes* from offices in the judicature. They countered that in the golden age from Charlemagne to Philip the Fair, the king's one hundred *gentilshommes* rendered justice and were never asked to study the "Roman and Greek laws that are so esteemed today." Formerly, nobles had to know no laws or writings other than the king's ordinances and local customs, and these provided the best and "true means to render good and rapid justice to everyone." The deputies from the Île-de-France therefore requested the king to order that *procureurs* and *avocats* that invoked any laws "other than yours Sire" would not be permitted "in any pleading, writing, or other procedure." The king's laws alone were "inviolable."[29]

---

27. A wealth of anecdotal evidence at least suggests this was the case. In describing the progressive regulation of the scholastic life in *Centuries of Childhood,* Philippe Ariès suggested that noble attendance at *collèges* became routine in the seventeenth century. Even the boys "from the greatest families went to school, particularly to the Jesuit college of Clermont which, in the sevententh century, took the place of Navarre College, where the high nobility had hitherto received their training." See Philippe Ariès, *Centuries of Childhood: A Social History of Family Life,* trans. Robert Baldick (New York, 1962), 202. For more evidence that nobles took seriously the need for education in "letters" see Mark Motley, *Becoming a French Aristocrat: The Education of the Court Nobility, 1580–1715* (Princeton, 1990); and Jonathan Dewald, *Aristocratic Experience and the Origins of Modern Culture: France, 1570–1715* (Berkeley, 1993), esp. chap. 3.

28. M. d'Avity, *Panégryique à Mgr Lesdiguières, maréchal de France et lieutenant général pour le roi en Dauphiné* (Lyon, 1611), 7.

29. BA, MS 4485, "Cahiers particuliers . . . Ile de France," fol. 6v. The noble apologist François L'Alouëte also faulted the elaborate system of French jurisprudence for distancing *gentilshommes* from the law courts. He proposed that the corpus of French law be simplified, codified, and produced in a handy three-volume collection. Then "the noble with only a mediocre knowledge of letters would be able to render justice to everyone without much trouble." See François L'Alouëte, *Des affaires d'estat, des finances, du prince et de sa noblesse* (Metz, 1597), 172.

There is much evidence that in the early seventeenth century nobles became more sensitive to the need to educate themselves at least in the rudiments, but most continued to deny that supposed educational deficiencies should block them from public functions. On the contrary, as the notables explained in 1627, the overeducated should themselves be disqualified from royal service, since these people, "having passed their youth in the idleness of 'letters,' become for the most part incapable of serving."[30] Nobles, then, obviously entertained a special definition of service and of the qualities appropriate to that service. Some nobles pursued formal education and others resisted it, but none would have confused schoolroom training with merit. The term *merit* implied something quite different.

To perceive the meaning of the term *merit* in early seventeenth-century France, one should begin by recognizing that there were (and are) two ways to define it. The dictionary of the Académie Française in 1694 expressed the two meanings in the following way: "*Mérite* signifies . . . virtue, excellent quality, or an assemblage of several good qualities"; but also, "It is said 'One creates merit . . . in relation to someone else' as a way of saying, to draw glory or advantage over someone for having done something."[31] Antoine Furetière's *Dictionnaire Universel* (1690) gave the following two definitions for the word *mériter* (to merit): "to have good or bad qualities which attract honor or scorn"; and "to do a good or bad action to which one must give recompense or chastisement."[32] In noble discourse of the early seventeenth century, the line separating the two meanings of *merit*—one signifying personal qualities in an absolute sense, the other implying deserved recompense by others—was consistently blurred. A man of merit had certain praiseworthy qualities to rec-

---

30. Mayer, *Des Etats-Généraux,* 18:304.

31. The distinction between the two kinds of merit had an interesting parallel in contemporary theological discourse. Scholastics distinguished between congruous merit and condign merit. The notion of condign merit, largely rejected by theologians beginning in the later Middle Ages, implied a relationship of necessary reciprocity: the Christian performs a virtuous act that God is obligated to reward with grace. To believe in congruous merit, however, is to see virtue and reward differently. God still rewards virtue when He sees it, but He does so only in recognition of an intrinsic merit, not to satisfy an obligation incurred. On the application of these concepts in Renaissance literature see Ullrich Langer, "Merit in Courtly Literature: Castiglione, Rabelais, Marguerite de Navarre, and Le Caron," *Renaissance Quarterly* 41 (1988): 218–41.

32. *Dictionnaire de l'Académie Française,* 1st ed. (Paris, 1694), and Antoine Furetière, *Dictionnaire universel* (The Hague and Rotterdam, 1690). These works shall be cited hereafter as *DAF* and *DU,* respectively.

ommend him. But more important, perhaps, he had something coming to him in the form of recompense for past "services."

The blending of the two connotations of *merit* broadened its semantic field and gave the term a meaning more pointed than the comparatively narrow term *virtue*. Although both labels referred to a person's superior qualities, *merit* also implicitly assessed relationships between individuals. To give an example, at midcentury the author of the genealogical history of the La Rochefoucauld family lamented the elevation of certain families "of base origin, some by their virtue, some by the favor of our kings, without any merit at all." The writer thereby suggested that virtue of itself was no justification for enjoying the king's *graces* if merit had not also been accumulated in the past.[33] The same thinking is evident in the demand in 1614, by the noble deputies from Auvergne, that all pensions be revoked except for those "given to persons who are qualified and of merit for the good and signal services they will have rendered the state and Your Majesty."[34]

The nobility's understanding of the term *merit* becomes clearer when placed in a broader context. Above all, it is important to recognize that in the early seventeenth century, personal bonds formed within an ethos of gift giving.[35] Exchanges of gifts, in their many forms, tangibly

---

33. Pierre Hutin, *Généalogie de la très-grande, très-ancien* [sic], *et très-illustre maison de La Rochefoucauld* (n.p., 1654), 74.

34. BA, MS 4485, "Cahiers particuliers . . . Auvergne," fol. 14r.

35. In recent years many historians of medieval and early-modern societies have examined practices of gift giving and expectations of reciprocity. Among the most prominent examples are "Pour une Histoire Anthropologique: La Notion de Réciprocité," *Annales E. S. C.* 29 (1974): 1309–80; Georges Duby, *The Early Growth of the European Economy: Warriors and Peasants from the Seventh to the Twelfth Century*, trans. Howard B. Clarke, (Ithaca, N.Y., 1984); Marvin Becker, *Medieval Italy: Constraints and Creativity* (Bloomington, Ind., 1981), esp. the introduction and chap. 1; idem, *Civility and Society in Western Europe, 1300–1600* (Bloomington, Ind., 1988), chap. 1 and passim; Natalie Zemon Davis, "Beyond the Market: Books as Gifts in Sixteenth-Century France," *Transactions of the Royal Historical Society,* 5th ser., 33 (1983): 69–88; idem, "A Renaissance Text to the Historian's Eye: The Gifts of Montaigne," *Journal of Medieval and Renaissance Studies* 15 (1985): 47–56; Sharon Kettering, "Gift-Giving and Patronage in Early-Modern France," *French History* 2 (1988): 131–51; Martine Grinberg, "La Culture Populaire comme Enjeu: Rituels et Pouvoirs (XIVᵉ–XVIIᵉ siècles)," in *Culture et Idéologie dans la Genèse de l'Etat Moderne: Actes de la table ronde organisée par le Centre national de la recherche scientifique et l'Ecole française de Rome (Rome, 15–17 octobre, 1984)* (Rome, 1985), 381–92. For a sociological perspective see Pierre Bourdieu, *Le Sens Pratique* (Paris, 1980), chap. 7; also see Alvin W. Gouldner, "The Norm of Reciprocity: A Preliminary Statement," *American Sociological Review* 25 (1960): 161–78; and George C. Homans, "Social Behavior as Exchange," *American Journal of Sociology* 63 (1958): 597–608.

expressed the affection binding one individual to another. Because an offering of gifts always demanded a reciprocal gesture of affection from the other party, gifts were tools to use in contracting personal obligations. Any offering from one person to another, wrote René de Ceriziers, should take the form of a gift, since

> one who receives a gift feels obligated; one who receives a salary believes he has been paid. . . . One loses the best part of the present when it is given simply as recompense; on the contrary, one wins the entire affection of a man when he is predisposed in one's favor by a pure bounty.[36]

Contemporaries attempted to learn and master the techniques of gift giving.[37] Speaking to ambitious court nobles, in 1616, Eustache Du Refuge advised readers of his treatise to study the art of giving and receiving gifts (*bienfaits*) and compliments, so as to "induce into our confidence" influential court figures "by a declaration or demonstration of honor and obligation."[38] Gifts, he wrote, were "the cement of human

---

36. [René] de Ceriziers, *Le Héros Français, ou l'idée du grand capitaine* (Paris, 1645), 190–91.

37. Some of the linguistic "rules" regulating the exchange of gifts and pledges of personal fidelity are discussed in Arthur L. Herman, Jr., "The Language of Fidelity in Early-Modern France," *Journal of Modern History* 67 (1995): 1–24. In this intriguing article, Herman tries to resolve the apparent contradiction between nobles' altruistic expressions of selflessness and their evident pursuit of interests, by suggesting that their linguistic conventions were merely imposed on them by the "rules" of the game they played. "The language game approach," he says, "allows us to see . . . that participants could describe, evaluate, and justify their individual actions by employing these verbal conventions, quite apart from whether they meant what they said or not" (7). This approach raises some troubling questions, however: What explains the formation and persistence of a normative set of linguistic rules within a society? What is the relationship between these rules and deeper social and cultural structures? Herman notes the late sixteenth-century influence of Christian and Neostoic moralists, and he points to the existence of a traditional "affective political culture," but his insistence on seeing language "in strategic, rather than ideological, terms" oddly implies the separation of language from the social processes that language inevitably reflects (9–10). He asserts, for example, that Richelieu's use of the language of fidelity "was strategic and selective," representing no particular "thought system. It was not a set of beliefs represented by language but a means of representation through language" (16). As my first three chapters will indicate, I prefer to see early seventeenth-century political language as representative of two competing (though entangled) "thought systems."

38. Eustache Du Refuge, *Traité de la Cour ou instruction des Courtisans* (Paris, 1658), 15. Du Refuge's favored word is *bienfait,* which Furetière defined as "gift, or good office that pleases or does someone good." It can be interpreted as "kindness," "benefit," or "service." The words are interchangeable, all of them dealing with personal gestures that func-

society . . . the prisoner's chains . . . with which one can bind and enslave others."[39]

The detailed protocol outlined by Du Refuge deserves a close look. When receiving thanks for a compliment or a small service rendered, for example, one had to take special care not to be overly modest or to give the impression that "it was nothing." By devaluing one's initial gift one ran the risk of insulting the judgment of someone

> who believes he has a more than common pledge of our benevolence, which [impression] we diminish by diminishing the gift too much; and at the same time we slight someone who believes himself to be regarded by us as a friend, putting him on an equal footing with those who are not. That is why, even when duty [alone] has prompted us to accommodate someone, we must show that a particular affection contributed something to our action.[40]

The act of recognizing an obligation to another party for a gift received was no less important and no less delicate an operation. The process unfolded in three stages: receiving the gift with grace; formally "recalling" the gift at a later time ("s'en ressouvenir"); and repaying the gift with dignity at the appropriate moment. Recalling the gift or favor was an especially crucial step, because only by openly acknowledging his indebtedness did the recipient stake his honor on the engagement: "We should do this by making public the favor we have received, not only by setting a high value on it and making much of it, but also in praising our benefactor."[41] As for the means to repay the favor, "they should (if possible) surpass or at least equal the initial favor to indicate that one was greatly obliged. . . . this is not to satisfy the obligation but only to show that one recognizes oneself to be obligated." Conversely, if a gift did not succeed in obliging another party as hoped, Du Refuge advised that "it is prudent to continue [giving], so as to force the ungrateful one, if he is someone we cannot do without, to acknowledge his debt, and by new

---

tioned as gifts. For the sake of clarity and consistency I will translate all the terms used in the context of gift giving—*don, présent, bienfait, grace, service,* etc.—as the all-embracing "gift," except when two or more of the words are used at once or when a different meaning is clearly implied.

39. Du Refuge, *Traité de la Cour*, 19.

40. Ibid., 18.

41. Ibid., 23.

gifts confirm and renew the old ones."[42] Finally, in acquitting oneself of a debt, one should be sure not to repay it too promptly or too carefully, "for fear that it will seem that we are impatient in our obligation to our friend and that we are of the opinion that he performed a favor for us only so as to receive one in return."[43]

This last point was echoed in Claude Pelletier's *Education of the Nobility*. Because personal relationships rested on mutual bonds of affection, one had to preserve at least the veneer of disinterested generosity signified in the act of gift giving. Pelletier instructed young nobles that it was a special type of liberality

> to receive something as a gift on the part of one's friend, and even to give him the satisfaction of believing that he has obliged you by his courtesy, without hastily wanting to pay him back in kind, no more or less than if you felt yourself charged with this obligation as like a heavy burden. Allow his gift therefore to remain in deposit within your hands for a time, so that when you do the same for him, he will believe that your present is offered more as a mutual exchange of friendship than to acquit yourself of what he has given you.[44]

Gifts are still used today, of course, to affirm and solidify private relationships. But as political historians have emphasized time and again, medieval and early-modern societies did not consider the private and the public spheres mutually exclusive. Because they established reciprocal loyalties, gifts were considered "the cement of human society" even in its most "public" expressions. The seigneur recognized the services of his peasant-tenants with occasional displays of liberality, which in turn secured their affections. The lord periodically rewarded his vassals by showering them with gifts and giving splendid feasts, thereby affirming the feudal ties of mutual obligation.[45]

Within this matrix of gift and countergift, the king had a supremely

---

42. Ibid., 22.

43. Ibid., 25.

44. Claude Pelletier, *La nourriture de la noblesse où sont représentées comme en un tableau, toutes les plus belles vertus, qui peuvent accomplir un jeune gentilhomme* (Paris, 1604), fol. 47r.

45. For descriptions of liberality and good lordship, see Duby, *Early Growth*, 56; Felicity Heal, "The Ideal of Hospitality in Early-Modern England," *Past and Present* 102 (1984): 66–93.

important role to play.[46] Since at least the age of Beowulf, one of the chief occupations and responsibilities of a king had been to distribute his bounty liberally to those who served him. Indeed, because kings hoped to secure the loyalty and affections of all their subjects, and since the sources of their bounty were richer than most, magnanimity had always been seen as one of the principal attributes of kingship, and gift giving had been considered sound policy: "As royal dignity surpasses all others, the gifts of princes must also surmount in largesse every other *grace* and liberality, in that . . . a man's gifts increase his means [*les dons de l'homme élargissent ses voyes*] and acquire honor and glory for him who gives them."[47] Conspicuous generosity would earn the king not only honor and glory but also devoted servants. As Ceriziers put it: "A prince who has nothing has everything when he gives everything: the hand of those who receive from him is like the coffers of his treasury. No, it is a fertile ground where the gift increases its value . . . returning him a heart, which returns the man."[48] This was no small return, for as the biographer of the duc de Rohan explained, "the great [*grands*] must learn, above all things, . . . [how] to win men."[49]

For the sovereign, then, liberality represented more than an endearing mark of character. The king's relationships, like those of his subjects, were structured by a mentality of gift giving. In the France of Henry IV and Louis XIII, kings still used magnanimous gestures of royal largesse to acquire new obligations over their most valued subjects. And significantly, the king's bounty was by no means limited to his private resources. Kings rarely gave gifts as private tokens of affection. The king's *grace* more often took the form of "dignities," encompassing not only honorific distinctions but legal and fiscal privileges, pensions, court offices, ecclesiastical sinecures, positions in the army, offices in the sovereign courts—in short, a large portion of the king's grandeur and authority. The king's largesse knew no boundaries: "The liberality of monarchs gives at once duchies, marquisats, governments. . . . they fashion with

46. On the traditional image of the king as gift giver and how it affected conceptions of royal finance in the Renaissance see Alain Guéry, "Le Roi Dépensier: Le don, la contrainte, et l'origine du système financier de la monarchie française d'Ancien Régime," *Annales, E. S. C.* 39 (1984): 1241–69. For contemporary English attitudes see Linda Levy Peck, " 'For a king not to be bountiful were a fault': Perspectives on Court Patronage in Early Stuart England," *Journal of British Studies* 25 (1986): 31–61.
47. L'Alouëte, *Des affaires d'estat,* 107.
48. Ceriziers, *Le Héros,* 205–6.
49. *Histoire de Henry, duc de Rohan* (Paris, 1666), 27.

their own hands from the dirt and silt of the earth creatures that are like new deities."[50]

Even if only a few could ever expect to achieve the stature of "deity," we have seen that nobles nonetheless coveted public positions and "dignities" of all kinds. What is revealing is that their discussions about the granting of these public positions were invariably encased within the language of gift giving and personal affection. All shared the assumption that "from fidelity [to the king] . . . riches and honors are born."[51] In 1618, for example, the eulogist of the noble army officer Medavy noted that Henry IV had had "such esteem for his merit . . . that he treated this subject as a friend and promised him . . . one of the lieutenant generalships of Normandy." Henry showered him with

> so many gifts and presents that (beyond the common duty to serve his king loyally, which had been conferred on him by birth) his heart full of gratitude, and feeling such sentiment all his life, he breathed nothing but fidelity, aspired to nothing but obedience, and conspired . . . only to die for his king and to use his powers, his friends, and his arms in the service of the [the monarchy].[52]

Even discounting the hyperbole, the underlying premise is evident: the king's liberality had the power to oblige. In a like manner, the panegyrist of Lesdiguières emphasized the mutual bond formed when the maréchal offered his "services" to the king in exchange for a public function. After years of faithful service, the king had named Lesdiguières *lieutenant général* of the armies for the provinces of Dauphiné and Provence: "You thereby bound yourselves reciprocally, the one to serve well, the other to recognize it well, just as one sees a river render the tribute of its waters to

50. Pelletier, *La nourriture,* fol. 76r. Pierre de La Primaudaye, in his *Academie Françoise* (Paris, 1580), noted in similar fashion that sovereign princes need to be prudent and just, in order "to distribute liberally and in harmonious proportion their gifts, *graces,* and benefits, whether they be estates, offices, benefices, knighthoods, exemptions, freedoms [*immunitez*], and other recompenses due as rewards to their subjects, according to the merit of each" (fol. 211v).

51. F. F. P. de V., *Tableau Historique, dans lequel sont contenues quelques remarques d'Etat: Et comment le Roy, a fait Monsieur le Mal de Lesdiguières, Connétable de France* (n.p., 1623), 4.

52. G. Le Rebours, *Discours fait aux obsèques de Mgr de Medavy* (Rouen, 1618), 35–36.

the ocean, and the sea not wanting to appear ungrateful, suddenly sends a great abundance back to this same river."[53]

Against the background of the early-modern norm of obligation, and the role of the gift in activating and applying that norm, the nobility's special attachment to the term *merit* takes on new meaning. As part of the discourse regulating the exchange of gifts and the formation of relationships, *merit* very frequently implied "deservedness" and pointed up the prior obligations candidates had acquired over the king with their past service and affection (*merit* meaning "to draw glory or advantage over someone for having done something").[54] As Louis Guyon explained, kings should "bestow goods on those who merit it by their virtues, recognizing the service they have done."[55] Because the king's gifts should create a web of reciprocal obligations, the monarch must indeed weigh the merit of all candidates for public positions. According to the La Rochefoucauld genealogist, history had shown the dangers of elevating new families, "without any merit at all . . . who after having devoured the gifts of our kings, served them but little, and were often ungrateful for them."[56]

But from this perspective, positions in the king's armies, his courts, or his household were more than jobs to be exercised with competence; they were also gifts to be properly appreciated—the cement of obligation: "Kings and the great [*grands*] only possess the goods of the earth in order to distribute them, [and] the principal use of their wisdom is to place gifts where they find merit; otherwise, while thinking they are giving presents, they are only losing."[57] Because public functions could be imagined the gifts of kings, the framework of mutual obligation conditioned the perception of the word *merit* for the monarch and all who served him.

Still, though one cannot overestimate the importance of the culture of gift and obligation in the first half of the seventeenth century, another question needs to be answered. After all, the Académie Française defined *merit* also as an "assemblage of several good qualities." When nobles presented themselves as men of merit, what particular qualities did they highlight? A typical paean appears in a 1624 biography of La Valette, the former governor and *lieutenant général* of Provence. The chronicler notes

---

53. Avity, *Panégyrique*, 13.
54. *DAF*.
55. Louis Guyon, *Diverses Leçons* (Lyon, 1617), 80.
56. Hutin, *Généalogie . . . La Rochefoucauld*, 74.
57. Ceriziers, *Le Héros*, 188.

the family's natural wish to see their hero's accomplishments "appear before the eyes of the public," who will remark in his life "the image of all the most desirable virtues, and particularly of a great generosity and fidelity of a subject toward his Prince."[58] The following pages will demonstrate, through examination of the meaning of *generosity* and related concepts, that even the intrinsic qualities thought to characterize the meritorious individual reflected expectations of mutuality, for they bespoke one's value within personal relationships.

Generosity and the Personal Idiom

All nobles could agree that generosity ranked first among the "assemblage of good qualities" that signaled merit, but what exactly did the word *generosity* mean? Generally speaking, *générosité* implied greatness of soul, as the dictionaries of Antoine Furetière and the Académie Française both indicate. For its first definition of the term *généreux*, the Académie Française stated simply, "Magnanimous, of noble character." *Noble*, when used as an adjective, implied "illustrious, raised above the common level. 'A noble and generous soul.'" Delving further, one finds the definition of *magnanime* under the listings for *âme* (soul). This is only natural, for the word *magnanime* applied to "one who has a great and elevated soul."

In a world where gifts and countergifts cemented all manner of personal relationships, the word *généreux* had a more specific usage, however, for it also described one who gave freely: "The word also signifies Liberal. 'This man is so generous that he bestows great presents in return for the smallest service. He loves to give, he has a generous soul.'" The word *libéral* was in fact nearly interchangeable with *généreux*. It referred also to "one who loves to give, who takes pleasure in giving. 'Generous and liberal, liberal toward men of merit. He has a liberal character, inclination, soul.'" The term *généreux*, then, was most often used to describe one who freely shared his resources with others—and especially with others who "merited" such largesse by showing a similar willingness to give of themselves ("he bestows great presents . . . for the smallest service"; "Generous and liberal . . . toward men of merit)."[59]

---

58. H. de Mauroy, *Discours de la vie et faits héroiques de M. de La Valette, amiral de France, gouverneur . . . en Provence* (Metz, 1624), dedication.

59. DAF.

To appreciate the centrality of generosity to the noble identity, let us pause to define more precisely the word usually given as its synonym, *liberality*. Here the dictionary of Antoine Furetière becomes useful because it defines *libéralité* explicitly as "a feature only of noble and generous souls."[60] Furetière's reasons for associating the quality of liberality with "noble" souls come into view if one reads between the lines of his definition of the term. *Libéralité*, he wrote, is a "moral virtue that occupies the middle ground between prodigality and avarice; the virtue of one who gives when giving is called for, and without self-interest." These qualifications recur in Furetière's treatment of the word *libéral*. The liberal "gives reasonably and with judgment. . . . There are a great many people who give much and yet are not liberal at all. One is liberal only when one gives without self-interest. The inclination to be liberal is often confused with a penchant for spending." For Furetière, then, simple openhandedness did not constitute liberality. Like the Académie Française, which suggested that liberality flowed toward men of merit, Furetière emphasized that the true liberal dispensed bounty selectively, using reason and judgment. Moreover, liberality also implied giving without self-interest, and it thus stood for the opposite of selfishness.

Furetière made these fine distinctions because a social fault line ran through the concept of liberality, a fact that becomes clearer when one considers the word's associations. The term *libéralité* bore an obvious relation to the word *libre* (free), and it thus recalled the ancient distinction between the free and the unfree—a distinction that presaged that between noble and common in Capetian France. The jurist Charles Loyseau, in his *Treatise on the Orders and Simple Dignities* (1610), noted that in the earliest days of the French monarchy, society had been divided between the *gentilshommes* who defended and maintained the state, on the one hand, and the farmers, craftsmen, and merchants who lived in "a condition of partial servitude," on the other hand. This division, he added, "has continued up to the present time."[61] As symbols of their "freedom," nobles still enjoyed in Loyseau's day a wide range of privileges (also known as *libertés*), which included tax exemptions, the right to carry a sword in public, lighter punishments for criminal offenses, and, fittingly, the exclusive right to hunt game—a prestigious leisure activity. Loyseau explained that commoners were "justly denied" this last privi-

---

60. *DU.*
61. Charles Loyseau, *Traité des ordres et simples dignitez,* in *Les Oeuvres de Maistre Charles Loyseau, avocat en Parlement* (Lyon, 1701), 24.

lege by law, "for fear that it would lead them to abandon their ordinary employment to the public detriment."[62] Nobles in the seventeenth century remained quite conscious of the freedom that separated them from common subjects, and this explains why the author Claude de Marois would describe the sons of *gentilshommes* in 1631 as "children of free condition."[63]

That the dichotomy free/unfree (and noble/common) informed the contemporary understanding of liberality is apparent in several ways. As the primary connotation of the word *libre*, Furetière listed the following: "One who has freedom of choice. Only the free man is a free arbiter." Furetière no doubt had this condition in mind when he emphasized that the liberal gives only when giving is called for. Since liberality presupposed freedom, one could express it only by choosing "freely" the recipients of one's largesse. But free individuals belonged to an exclusive category. Furetière ruled out not only those held captive or dominated by others; more particularly, he excluded those who, like animals, "act from necessity." Furetière's distinction between those who did or did not act from necessity corresponded to the contemporary division between those engaged in common trades and occupations (businesspeople, farmers, shopkeepers) and those excluded from such vile occupations by law and custom (the nobles).[64] As Loyseau pointed out, one of the conditions characterizing the "servitude" of commoners was that they were constrained "to sell their toil and labor." Nobles, by contrast, earned exemption from such "mercenary" concerns and therefore shunned all exercises leading to "vile and sordid profit."[65] Furetière followed convention in assuming that people forced by necessity to work for their subsistence lived captive to material interest and therefore could not make the free choices true liberality required. Hence he insisted that the liberal give "without self-interest." The word *libéralité* implied freedom from selfishness, and Furetière instinctively associated this type of freedom with "noble" souls.

By exposing the more subtle meanings of *generosity* and the terms

---

62. Ibid., 29.

63. Claude de Marois, *Le Gentilhomme Parfaict ou tableau des excellences de la vraye noblesse: Avec l'institution des jeunes gentilshommes à la vertu* (Paris, 1631), 491.

64. On the rules of derogation see Etienne Dravasa, *Vivre noblement, recherches sur la dérogeance de noblesse du 14e au 16e siècles* (Bordeaux, 1965). For the later period see Marcel de La Bigne de Villeneuve, *La Dérogeance de la noblesse sous l'Ancien Régime* (Paris, 1971).

65. Loyseau, *Traité des ordres*, 31.

often used in conjunction with it, the contemporary dictionaries make it easier to understand why nobles considered these qualities the most desirable virtues. Two points stand out. First, the conditions implied by the concepts of generosity and liberality indicate that nobles took pride in their a priori status as free individuals. The terms *generous* and *liberal* identified the noble not only as one who loves to give but also as an autonomous individual who gave only when called for. The *gentil-homme*'s freedom to determine the conditions of his largesse qualified him as truly generous and increased the value of the gifts he gave, whether these came in the form of presents, favors, or personal loyalty. As Kristen Neuschel has already shown, one must keep in mind the nobles' strong sense of autonomy when studying the relationships of fidelity that entangled them in a web of personal and family alliances in the early-modern era.[66] The unspoken understanding that nobles *chose* to enter their relationships is what made them such valuable personal allies, even though this also implied the right to dissolve mutual ties when giving was no longer called for.[67]

The second point to note about the self-perception of the nobility is really the inverse of the first. Nobles trumpeted their reputation for generosity not only because the word implicitly signified freedom but because it signaled at the same time one's capacity to give selflessly to other individuals and to make selfless commitments to them. Personal freedom and the formation of personal ties were linked symmetrically in the noble mind. Jean Savaron expressed this assumption when he lauded the nobility's "franchise et fidélité" in his *Treatise concerning the Sword in France* (1610).[68] He explained that the reason kings had granted *gentilshommes* the privilege of "being near the king in his sacred Majesty

---

66. Kristen B. Neuschel, *Word of Honor: Interpreting Noble Culture in Sixteenth-Century France* (Ithaca, N.Y., 1989). See especially the insightful historiographical introduction, "The Problem of Clientage."

67. In his treatise *Le Gentilhomme* (Paris, 1611), Nicolas Pasquier articulated this principle in a discussion of liberality. He noted that the noble must use liberality with some discretion: "To give to just anyone is harmful; it means that chance rather than choice governs one's liberal hand, and this only attracts disdain" (103).

68. *Franchise* sometimes signified sincerity, but it just as frequently implied *liberté*, as the dictionaries of Furetière, the Académie Française, and Pierre Richelet all indicate. In his *Dictionnaire Français tiré de l'usage et des meilleurs auteurs de la langue* (Geneva, 1679–80), Richelet lists *liberté* as the first connotation of *franchise*, and places *sincerité* second; Furetière reverses the order and notes that *liberté* is the meaning most often implied "chez les Poëtes" *(DU)*.

and entering into his bedchamber with swords at their side" was because they wished to recognize the nobles' "generosity, to which the king entrusts his own well-being and the security of his person."[69]

The two meanings of *merit* in seventeenth-century thinking intersected, then, at the concept of generosity. Nobles could be admired from afar for possessing "an assemblage of good qualities," generosity foremost among them; but generosity derived its real value from the culture of gift and obligation that served as its context. As Savaron's description of noble generosity aptly illustrates, everyone took it for granted that affective bonds underlay the most formal service relationships, and that judgment of a person's merit must take into account his capacity for selfless commitment. The author Avity, after describing the reciprocal tie formed by Lesdiguières and Henry IV, composed an axiom to be remembered by princes: "Learn from this, Princes, first to weigh and then to reward the merit and affection of those who serve you."[70] Other texts reveal the same attitude. When Henry IV had to select a new *maître de camp* in the Brittany regiment, he chose the baron de Molac, explained Augustin Du Paz, because he needed "someone of merit, of quality," someone in whom he could have "belief in his person."[71] The eulogist of another noble army officer, Mandelot, lamented that Henry III "was assured of having lost in [Mandelot] one of the best and most faithful servants he had in all the realm, and one of the most affectionate . . . for the good of his person."[72]

A *personal* idiom governed discourse on merit throughout the seventeenth century. Since generosity, liberality, and fidelity could be visibly validated only through personal interaction, nobles naturally articulated their merit through discussion of personal relations, especially those involving the king and the *grands* of the realm. A passage from a 1617 history dedicated to the heirs of the Chabannes family is typical. The author focused on the abiding personal trust that bound Charles VII and Antoine de Chabannes, comte de Dampmartin, the king's *grand maître*. It seems that in the days preceding his death, the king lay in his bedchamber refusing to eat. Dampmartin paid the king a visit to try to persuade him to accept the meals prepared for him "and not to mistrust any-

---

69. Jean Savaron, *Traicté de l'Espee Françoise* (Paris, 1610), 36.
70. Avity, *Panégyrique*, 13.
71. Augustin Du Paz, *Généalogie de la maison de Molac* (Rennes, 1629), 110.
72. *Discours de la vie, mort et derniers propos de feu Mgr de Mandelot* (Lyon, 1588), 33–34.

one." The king cynically replied that he trusted God would avenge his death. Undeterred, Dampmartin responded by "begging the king once again to eat. 'Very well,' the king said, 'I will do so, provided that you yourself go to fetch me a broth, and that you see it prepared in front of you. . . . you I do not distrust.'"[73] Here was an achievement worthy of note in a family history: having gained the trust and esteem of the king himself.

Biographies, memoirs, and family histories of the nobility especially highlighted evidence of the king's personal recognition. Du Paz, historian of the Molac family, bragged that Henry IV personally appreciated the services of Sebastien de Rosmadec, baron de Molac: "His Majesty recognized it and said it with his own mouth several times," at one point assuring him in a letter that "in continuing to serve me as well as you have done, you will find in me a good master."[74] In a later history of the same family, Vulson de la Colombière wrote that "the esteem the king had for the baron and the knowledge he had of his services and fidelity" were such that in 1602, "at the appearance of trouble in the state," the king commanded Molac "with his own mouth" to raise a regiment of twenty companies.[75] Praising the merits of the privy councillor François de Montholon in an *oraison funèbre* in 1626, Jacques Brosse lamented that Montholon had "wanted to be hidden in the world" (meaning the world of the court and the king's affairs), and that

to his credit, his accomplishments in the world, although singular and almost without example, will be hidden in my discourse. . . . [But] you only have to see the letters among his papers, where the great Henry IV, . . . writing in his own hand, began with these words, "M. de Montholon my friend," signing the letter in these terms, "Your good friend Henry."[76]

In these and many other texts, professions of friendship and personal approval by the king are often invoked as a testament to merit. Of course

73. Du Plessis, *Les vies de m. Jacques et Antoine de Chabannes, tous deux grands maîtres de France* (Paris, 1617), 63.

74. Du Paz, *Généalogie de la maison de Molac*, 109, 122.

75. Marc Vulson de La Colombière, *Généalogie de la maison de Rosmadec* (Paris, 1644), 24.

76. Jacques Brosse, *Tableau de l'homme juste, sur les vertus et à la mémoire de François de Montholon* (Paris, 1626), 21.

one should not infer from this language that kings wished to be served only by friends. Although the family historian Guy Bretonneau could identify "the friendship of kings" as one of the qualities that lent celebrity to a noble house, no one imagined that all nobles qualified as friends of monarchs.[77] Still, though few nobles could aspire to personal friendship with kings, everyone seemed to accept that the king was most likely to detect merit in a service performed near his person, one praised with his own mouth. Kings often reinforced the assumption by singling out services performed before their own eyes as justification for elevating someone to noble status. Henry IV, for example, granted a typical letter of ennoblement to Jehan d'Armaignac in 1605. The man's father had been "killed by a cannon shot while fighting next to our person." But the loss of his father had not dampened Jehan's ardor for the king's service. He "has always been armed and well-equipped near our person in every battle, siege, and encounter that has presented itself."[78]

The emphasis on proximity to the king is no mere rhetorical device. On the contrary, in this recurring theme of intimacy and familiarity, one glimpses the unique epistemological assumptions entwined with the personal idiom. Since merit was determined through personal and subjective judgments, not through abstract standards, nobles naturally assumed that their qualities should be displayed visibly for the prince. Burgundian deputies to the Estates General could have been speaking for all French nobles in 1614 when they advised Louis XIII that "nothing pleases us more, Sire, than our sovereign's gaze—and any time spent beyond his presence or his service we consider lost time. . . . the glory of being recognized in Your Majesty's presence is much dearer to us than any other advantages that might befall us elsewhere."[79] Nobles from Champagne felt the same way, and they reminded the king that "the honor of approaching your person . . . is so dear to [us]."[80] The author of a 1649 guide for the "generous courtier" developed the theme. He explained that "the grandest actions of courtiers are of little merit if they are not considered by the prince." Echoing the noble deputies of 1614, he emphasized that the courtier must "at an early point manage to be seen." To this end, it is advisable to "follow in the prince's train at court, to be

---

77. Guy Bretonneau, *Histoire généalogique de la maison des Briçonnets* (Paris, 1620), 7.

78. AN, Z[1A] 537, Armagnac, 1605.

79. BA, MS 4485, "Cahiers particuliers . . . Bourgogne," fol. 212v.

80. BA, MS 4485, "Cahiers particuliers . . . Champagne et Brie," fol. 164v.

looked at in this theater, where the . . . most noble, most generous souls appear with brilliance." The noble who chose to live in obscurity ("demeurer inconnu") in his château not only concealed his merit but forfeited it.[81]

Moreover, it was incumbent on the king, the supreme judge of merit, to remain accessible to his nobility; for without personal contact, how would he find his meritorious men? Louis Guyon enjoined princes to "take pleasure in visiting and receiving visits, in seeing and being seen, in communicating and being communicated with." In this regard princes should emulate Julius Caesar, who, Guyon admiringly reported, "knew each of his soldiers . . . and could identify all of them by name." Direct contact was most useful, since "we cannot love perfectly what we do not see or know."[82] Guyon conceded that kings could not hope to know intimately every noble in the realm. Even so, they should never choose to leave the determination of merit to underlings. Guyon offered the good example of the Roman emperor Alexander Severus, for

> among the things for which he was most praised was that he kept in his bedchamber a secret book in which were written the names of all the nobles of the empire; & when an office fell vacant, he never filled it simply according to the recommendation someone gave of the person, but because of what he found in his secret paper.[83]

A proposal by the nobles of the Orléanais on the eve of the Estates General expressed the same concern. Although the second estate did not include the plan in the general cahiers sent to the king in 1614, the spirit of the project must have earned it a sympathetic hearing. The objective was to reinforce the personal link between monarch and nobility by proxy.

> Inasmuch as Your Majesty does not yet know the majority of the *gentilshommes* who live in the provinces of the realm and who do not

---

81. *La véritable conduite du courtisan généreux* (Paris, 1649), 4. The passage in the original (after the author has mentioned that it is imperative to be "known") reads: "C'est pour cette raison sans doute que les Courtisans fréquentent ordinairement la Cour, & se rendent sujets à la suitte du Prince, afin de se faire regarder sur ce Théâtre, où les plus beaux, les plus nobles, les plus généreux esprits paroissent avec éclat."

82. Guyon, *Diverses Leçons,* 77.

83. Ibid., 80.

come to court; so as to gratify them and reward their services as the occasion arises . . . we beg Your Majesty to keep near you one *gentil-homme* from each province of the realm, as much to inform you of the condition of the said province as of the number of the said *gentil-shommes,* of the antiquity of their houses, the services they or their predecessors have rendered, the places where they [presently] command . . . and their capacities.[84]

For each province, the king would choose one *gentilhomme* informant from among three candidates nominated by the local nobility. The process could be repeated annually. In this way, the king would be apprised of the qualities and merits of every noble in the realm, a clear benefit to the king's service. In the end, the general assembly of the nobility opted for a more practical solution. They instead urged the king to compile comprehensive catalogs of nobles.[85]

The idea for a general catalog of nobility may have been inspired by the writings of Blaise de Monluc. The renowned captain had urged Charles IX in the 1570s to take advantage of the nobility's desire for royal attention. He addressed the king in his *Commentaires:* "[You] know, Sire, that those who wish to advance in your service by way of arms will do all it takes to be placed under your consideration." The king therefore should make lists of all "the men of valor of whom you have heard spoken, together with their qualities." This "book of honor," which would contain chapters for each province, should be consulted frequently so that "you may use it to refresh your memory of these men" when offices needed to be filled. Monluc suggested that, as an added incentive for all men of arms, the king, after being well informed of someone's accomplishments, should "declare for all to hear that he is to be placed on your roll." The mere existence of a royal honor roll would incite men of arms to increase their efforts: "Those who know they are on your list will take heart and push themselves to do you some service, and the others, not yet placed on the list, will expose themselves to a thousand dangers in order to be placed there."[86] Monluc shared with others, then, the conception of the all-knowing monarch. And as we shall see, he was not the last to recognize that kings could at once satisfy

---

84. BA, MS 4485, "Cahiers particuliers . . . Orléans," fol. 33v.

85. Mayer, *Recueil,* 4:199. This request is discussed also in chapter 2.

86. Blaise de Monluc, *Commentaires et Lettres de Blaise de Monluc, Maréchal de France,* ed. Alphonse de Ruble, 5 vols. (Paris, 1864–72), 3:485–86.

nobles and improve the quality of their service by working to stay informed of their merits.

Monluc's proposal casts light on another assumption expressed through the personal idiom: one best displayed generosity for the king by risking life and limb on the field of battle. Here the sixteenth and seventeenth centuries begin to look rather exotic to the modern reader, because the assumption that one showed generosity through martial prowess implies that contemporaries actually appraised military exploits by reference to the norm of obligation. Although the idea seems odd from a modern perspective, it certainly helps explain why Furetière included *courage* and *bravery* among his synonyms for *generosity*, and why the dictionary of the Académie Française pointed out that *généreux* "sometimes particularly signifies valiant, bold in combat."

The appearance of *bravery* and *courage* in lists of synonyms for *generosity* is really not so strange, because boldness in combat signified more than a willingness to face perilous circumstances. *Courage* also expressed selflessness in the service of another. The Académie Française defined *courage* as a "disposition of the soul that inspires it to repel or suffer something." But the dictionary also noted that "it is sometimes taken to mean affection." Furetière defined *courage* similarly. After calling it "a virtue that elevates the soul, and that inspires it to scorn perils when there are opportunities to exercise one's valor, or to suffer grief when there is opportunity to show one's constancy and firmness," he wrote that *courage* "also sometimes signifies ardor, affection. . . . [One says,] He serves his friends with great courage. He works with great courage, in order to say great affection."[87] The term *courage* derived from the French word for heart (*coeur*), and it implied that the soldier who braved "a thousand dangers" served his master affectionately as well as fearlessly. The battlefield, like the court, was a theater where the "most

---

87. *DAF* and *DU*. By recognizing the dual meaning of the word *courage*, one can make better sense of a statement by Ceriziers that seems, at first glance, quite peculiar. He opined, in his biography of the comte d'Harcourt, that princes should hire spies to "discover hidden merit," since "there are some men who have too much courage to present themselves and the bad luck not to be presented by anyone else" (*Le Héros*, 189). Today, a failure to present oneself before some eminent personage might be looked on as evidence more of cowardice than of courage. But because it implied a sign of one's affection *and* of one's capacity for suffering and sacrifice, the word *courage* functioned in the seventeenth-century as a synonym of *generosity*. When Ceriziers writes that some nobles have too much courage to appoach princes, he means that some are too selfless.

noble, most generous souls" showed their capacity for self-sacrifice and earned the attention of their peers and the king.

The assumption that nobles should endeavor to attract the sovereign's gaze even on the field of battle had been spelled out explicitly a century earlier by Castiglione. In his seminal treatise of the sixteenth century, the expositor of court manners had instructed his readers that one could "take it to be implied" in his rule that

> whenever the courtier chances to be engaged in a skirmish or an action or a battle in the field, or the like, he should discreetly withdraw from the crowd, and do the outstanding and daring things that he has to do in as small a company as possible and in the sight of all the noblest and most respected men in the army, and especially in the presence of and, if possible, before the very eyes of his king or the prince he is serving, for it is well indeed to make all one can of things well done.[88]

One finds essentially the same idea behind Monluc's plan for the book of honor. Since not everyone had opportunities to perform acts of daring in the presence of the king, Monluc would settle for the next best thing—insuring the king's awareness of such actions.

The impulse to display courage for the king suggests that the nobility's martial inclinations helped to reinforce the personal character of all political bonds. Nobles uniformly considered the military profession "noble in its cause," and this was because valor seemed "the most generous and heroic of all the virtues."[89] But nobles aspired to heroism for more than personal satisfaction alone. By acquiring glory on the battlefield, they dramatically represented their merit for the king, for princes, and for whoever else might take notice. In fact, François L'Alouëte contended that only the soldier who "made proof of his person" through feats of arms truly deserved the status of "noble."[90]

The urge to establish "proof of person" makes it easier to understand why graphic accounts of battles and *combats singuliers* figured so prominently in literature written by or about the nobility. The *Portrait of Marshal Schomberg* (1633) gives a typical example.

---

88. Castiglione, *The Book of the Courtier*, trans. Charles S. Singleton (Garden City, N.Y., 1959), 99.

89. Marois, *Le Gentilhomme Parfaict*, 553.

90. L'Alouëte, *Des affaires d'estat*, 190.

A hundred times in the view of his king (the most glorious reward of virtue) he charged and sallied when anyone else would have remained behind; there his body sustained glorious wounds, which then only served to urge him onward amid the blows, where the fire was most furious. . . . How many times have we seen his thunderous sword bloodied at the tip, thrusting right and left and withdrawing again, frightful in its furor, terrifying in its carnage . . . ?[91]

Since nobles viewed all armed combat as an opportunity to be seen and judged worthy by others, even their well-known penchant for dueling should be seen as a natural expression of the personal idiom.[92] To reiterate an important point, personal honor had less to do with glorifying the individual in isolation than with guaranteeing relations *between* individuals; the social value of honor was what made it worth fighting for.[93] Nobles engaged in duels not merely to satisfy hubris or relieve boredom but to project the two seemingly contradictory attitudes bound together in all generous people: high self-regard (as befitting a free person) and scorn for one's own life. This is why the duel, an audacious act of self-affirmation, required the presence of spectators. As Ceriziers remarked, "when a man exposes his life, he justifies it."[94]

Dueling became a popular subject of comment and debate in the early seventeenth century, as kings and other interested observers tried to bring under control a practice that took the lives of dozens, perhaps hundreds, of nobles each year.[95] Some considered dueling a waste of time and blood and argued for its abolition, while others hoped to preserve the practice by subjecting it to stricter rules. Regardless of their personal perspectives,

---

91. E. Bachot, *Tableau de Mr le Mal de Schomberg* (Paris, 1633), 22.

92. The best study of dueling in early-modern France is François Billacois, *Le Duel dans la société française des XVIe–XVIIe siècles: Essai de psychosociologie historique* (Paris, 1986), translated as *The Duel: Its Rise and Fall in Early-Modern France*, trans. and ed. Trista Selous (New Haven, 1990).

93. Arlette Jouanna discusses "the social role of honor" in volume 3 of her *L'Idée de Race en France au XVIe siècle et au début du XVIIe siècle (1498–1614)*, 3 vols. (Paris, 1976). The most sensitive and thorough analysis of noble honor is in Neuschel, *Word of Honor*. For other perspectives see Jouanna, "Recherche sur la Notion d'Honneur au XVIe siècle," *Revue d'Histoire Moderne et Contemporaine* 15 (1968): 597–623; and Léon Halkin, "Pour une histoire d'honneur," *Annales, E.S.C.* 4 (1949): 434–44.

94. Ceriziers, *Le Héros*, 176.

95. According to one estimate, for example, as many as eight thousand nobles died in duels between 1588 and 1608. See Richard Herr, "Honor versus Absolutism: Richelieu's Fight against Dueling," *Journal of Modern History* 27 (1955): 281–85.

however, the contemporary writers make clear in their discussions that the presumed function of the duel was to make one's character visible and open for inspection. In the incident that typically led to a duel, one noble publicly challenged another's honesty and trustworthiness.[96] The *démenti* (from the French *mentir*, "to lie"), as described by Marc de La Béraudière, was an open and defiant rejection of an accusation of cowardice, of disreputable behavior toward a woman, or, in the most egregious case, of lèse-majesté.[97] The accused took offense because such charges left one's reputation shrouded in doubt. As Scipion Dupleix put it, "in whatever manner one hides, falsifies, or disguises the truth, this always amounts to a lie. . . . [the truth] must never be covered, disguised, masked, glossed, or veiled, but rather known openly and exposed to everyone's view in all its simplicity and candor."[98] The aggrieved noble, explained Nicolas Pasquier, "willingly risks his life so that, by his valor, he may avoid being stained by the charge of dishonesty." Pasquier noted another important objective of the duelist. He wishes "to display valor and courage . . . giving assurance that in a weightier matter he would certainly give proof of his valiance since, in an affair of lesser importance, he displayed his virtue without giving a thought to the danger involved."[99]

If performed under the right conditions, then, the duel enabled the noble to earn the recognition of the king and to display his veracity and valor in the presence of witnesses. That this assumption motivated duelists is confirmed by the arguments both for and against the practice. Henry IV, for example, intended to stop all duels except those specifically sanctioned by the king, and a royal edict of 1609 provided a most fitting penalty for offenders. They would be stripped of their honors and offices and, more to the point, deprived of the visibility they craved. Those found guilty of fighting in unauthorized duels were forbidden to come "within ten leagues" of the royal court for a period of six years.[100]

Marc de La Béraudière, writing in 1608, agreed that only the king could decide when a dispute over honor should be resolved by a duel. But once having obtained the king's permission, the principals must settle their quarrel on an appropriate stage. The duel should therefore take

---

96. On the significance of the *démenti* and the other circumstances that typically led to a duel see Billacois, *The Duel*, 8–14.

97. Marc de La Béraudière, *Le Combat de Seul a Seul en camp clos* (Paris, 1608), 6.

98. Scipion Dupleix, *Les Loix Militaires Touchant le Duel* (Paris, 1602), 108.

99. Pasquier, *Le Gentilhomme*, 111, 128.

100. The edict of 1609 is discussed extensively in ibid., 139.

place in a field large enough to allow the opponents freedom of movement. The field, resembling a modern boxing ring, should be enclosed on four sides by rope barriers twenty to twenty-four feet long. La Béraudière specified that these barriers should never exceed a height of five feet, for "in this way, those who attend the battle can see it better and speak about it more truthfully."[101]

An antidueling treatise of 1650 also recognized the duel's function as a mechanism for display. In an imagined dialogue between a "governor" and the "king," the governor attempts to persuade the king that dueling must gradually be abolished. The king, however, understands the difficulty involved: "What you say is all well and good; but if we ban duels, how will the nobility display its courage?" The governor replies that nobles must learn to be content to demonstrate their courage "in your armies, Sire."[102]

Marc Vulson de La Colombière tried to find a way around this problem. He implored the king in 1648 to restore the *combat singulier* as a regular court event.[103] La Colombière distinguished between "the horror of the duels that are prohibited" and properly regulated duels that could serve their purpose admirably.

> I dare to ask the king to reestablish those that were formerly allowed. ... The former combats were performed by ordinance of the courts of *parlement;* & the recent ones in spite of [*parlement's*] proclamations; the former in the presence of the king, the connétable, the maréchaux de France, and in view of women and all the people; the recent ones secretly in out of the way places, in forests, out of sight of the whole world . . . ; the former in closed fields, marked by barriers and boundaries, with pavilions and tents; the recent ones in whatever place pleases the challenger, however unsuitable.[104]

Vulson knew that his plan to have the king sponsor duels at court, thus reviving the tournament, would appeal to the nobility. Designed to call attention to the performance of individuals in battle, the new *combat*

---

101. La Béraudière, *Le Combat,* 26.

102. *Catéchisme Royal* (Paris, 1650), 21.

103. The last officially sanctioned duel had been performed before the king and court in 1547. For a description see Billacois, *The Duel,* 49–56.

104. Marc Vulson de La Colombière, *Le Vray Théâtre d'Honneur et de Chevalerie ou le Miroir héroique de la Noblesse,* 2 vols. (Paris, 1648), 2: preface.

singulier would give nobles valuable opportunities. Through these "glorious" exercises "you can better display your skill and your courage, in the presence of your king and of his princes."[105]

Royal Service and the Personal Modality

To bring together the threads of my analysis as presented thus far, let me summarize the most important points of my argument. I have noted that, in the minds of traditional nobles, the word *merit* evoked a context of personal relationships predicated on mutuality. It sometimes pointed directly to obligations of mutuality, for it frequently implied "deservedness." But the norm of obligation shaped the meaning of *merit* even in its absolute sense, for the qualities deemed central to merit were the ones most valued in interpersonal relations—generosity, fidelity, courage, and affection. Moreover, because the signs of merit represented one's value within personal relations, nobles sought whenever possible to display merit before the very eyes of the king or the person they served. Many shared the ideal that every noble and his merit should be exposed to the king's view.

These assumptions permeated the noble mentality, and their interconnectedness requires special emphasis. Together they comprised a coherent system of meaning, a personal modality, which mediated the relationship between king and nobility in early seventeenth-century France. This modality determined not only the nobility's view of specific concepts, such as merit, generosity, and courage; it determined the meaning of royal service itself. To underscore that point, this section will probe more deeply into a set of attitudes that, to this point in the analysis, has only been implicit. When contemporaries thought about "professions," what categories came to mind? How did they conceive of professional qualifications and duties?

For most nobles, the classic division between the three estates of the realm—separating those who worked from those who prayed and those who fought—still seemed a reliable guideline for explaining occupational divisions within society. The traditional social hierarchy, based on principles of spirituality, assigned a moral value to the objectives of one's work.[106] The life of worship and religious service best expressed the ideal

---

105. Ibid., preface.
106. The following discussion owes much to William H. Sewell Jr.'s lucid account of old regime social structure. See *Work and Revolution in France: The Language of Labor from*

of self-denial, and it stood out as the most dignified calling. But other occupations also enjoyed honorable status. Warriors especially deserved high esteem because they protected the state and insured its general welfare. Next, in descending order of dignity, came judges, doctors, men of letters, financiers, court functionaries, merchants, farmers, and artisans.[107] All these occupations exercised the mind, in varying degrees, and they entitled those who practiced them to a degree of respect commensurate to the level of mental activity their work required. The least dignified, the men whose work lacked even the hint of spiritual purpose or mental discipline, were the manual laborers who earned their living by "la sueur de leur corps" [by the sweat of their brow].[108]

Ideals do not always mirror reality, of course, and the rigidity of this hierarchy should not be exaggerated. A wealthy merchant or a renowned physician might claim as much respect in his community as a noble army captain. Nevertheless, the traditional vision of society was pervasive, and it implied that intangible moral qualities were as important to one's occupation as were training and skill.

The traditional noble view of royal service certainly reflected this assumption. As construed by the nobility, the social order distinguished between those who served God (the first estate), those who served the king (the second estate), and those who served themselves (the third estate);[109] and the professions of the king's service required above all a disposition to selflessness. To help the king govern the realm, to serve him well in whatever capacity he required, one had to be endowed with the necessary qualities—the capacity for generosity, courage, and fidelity that commoners could not be expected to possess. Ceriziers observed that "anyone can understand without being much of a philosopher, that courage . . . is necessary to those who govern. . . . It is the stuff of which

the Old Regime to 1848 (Cambridge, 1980), chap. 1; idem, "Ideologies and Social Revolutions: Reflections on the French Case," Journal of Modern History 57 (1985): 57–85. The medieval background for the society of "orders" is treated in Georges Duby, Les trois ordres ou l'imaginaire du féodalisme, (Paris, 1978).

107. The source for this occupational ranking is Loyseau, Traité des ordres, chap. 8. See Sewell's discussion of the dichotomy between "art" and "labor" in Work and Revolution, 21–25.

108. Loyseau, Traité des ordres, 52.

109. M. de Grenaille characterized the function of the third estate in a slightly different way: "The clergy is properly destined to serve God, the nobility to serve the king, and the third estate to serve the other two orders." See L'Honneste Garçon, ou l'Art de bien Elever la Noblesse à la Vertu, aux Sciences, & à tous les exercices convenables à sa condition (Paris, 1642), 93.

extraordinary men are made. . . . this is particularly true in our nation; none tolerates less being governed by persons who are base and roturier."[110] Claude de Marois echoed the sentiment: "The people of the state who take their origin from roturiers and plebeians cannot have honor imprinted vividly in the soul. . . . those of the third estate always have weak constitutions . . . and never elevate their thoughts [above] infamous and dishonest gain. . . . their courage is timid."[111]

It is in this context, for example, that one can understand the nobility's contempt for ambition, a quality that self-respecting professionals in the modern world claim with pride. Contemporary dictionaries defined the word *ambition* as "an uncontrolled passion for glory and fortune," "an excessive desire for honor and greatness. 'Great, unregulated, furious, horrible, execrable, pernicious ambition.'"[112] The term assumed a favorable connotation only when context altered its usual meaning. Pierre Richelet, in his *Dictionnaire Français* (1679–80), explained that the word "is taken positively when accompanied by some favorable modifier. One says, 'a noble ambition,' 'a glorious, ingenious ambition.'"[113]

Insofar as nobles possessed a professional identity, it could not have included a sense of ambition, because that characteristic epitomized the selfishness and cupidity of roturiers. Like lust for wealth, the desire to rise above one's natural station in life betrayed an unseemly acquisitive spirit. Jean-Antoine de Baïf, writing in 1597, represented ambition as the trait of an "âme vicieuse" [vicious soul].[114] Pierre de La Primaudaye called "ambition and avarice" the main elements of mischief, and he observed that the two qualities "are found together for the most part in the same persons."[115] Ambition, dismissed as a "vice of excess," stood in contrast to generosity, which signified "contempt for all things mortal and perishable" and freedom from "earthly cares."[116]

The importance of moral credentials in the culture of royal service

---

110. Ceriziers, *Le Héros*, 66–68.

111. Marois, *Le Gentilhomme Parfaict*, 539–40.

112. *DU* and *DAF*, respectively.

113. Pierre Richelet, *Dictionnaire Français*. Jonathan Dewald writes that nobles "placed ambition at the center of their lives," but by *ambition* he means simply the desire to do well, to makes one's "fortune" in life. This ambition nobles certainly had. For examples showing how nobles framed their personal ambitions, see Dewald, *Aristocratic Experience*, 16–20.

114. Jean Antoine de Baïf, *Les mimes, enseignements et proverbes,* ed. Prosper Blanchemain (Paris, 1880), 128.

115. La Primaudaye, *Academie Françoise*, fol. 108r.

116. Ibid., fols. 107v, 142v, 143r.

emerges even more clearly when one examines the nobility's outlook on their favored form of service, the military. Of course it is well known that France, like every other European state, witnessed a military revolution in the seventeenth century, a revolution driven largely by tactical innovation.[117] The successes of Maurice of Nassau, Gustavus Adolphus, and other creative generals accelerated the movement away from slow, compact infantry units, typified by the Spanish *tercio*, toward expansive linear formations that increased mobility and maximized firepower. The new tactics placed a premium on discipline, flexibility, and order. As a consequence, army officers had to train more intensively, master a variety of skills, observe precise performance standards, and exact prompt obedience from their troops. By the end of the seventeenth century, French nobles emulated a new ideal: that of the accomplished, highly skilled, and well-trained officer.

Both the definition of merit and the self-perception of the nobility were caught up in this transformation of the warrior ethos, as we shall have occasion to see in later chapters. But in the age of Henry IV and Louis XIII, descriptions of the ideal *militaire* still ran parallel to common representations of the *noble généreux*. Influenced in part by a blossoming Neostoicism, but also by prevailing assumptions concerning the essence of service relationships, observers of the military generally emphasized the importance of moral qualities over intellect, technical proficiency, or skillfulness.[118] The historian of the Rantzow family, for example, dis-

---

117. The chronology of the transformation has been debated by Michael Roberts in *The Military Revolution, 1560–1660* (Belfast, 1956); and by Geoffrey Parker in "The 'Military Revolution' 1560–1660—A Myth?" *Journal of Modern History* 28 (1976): 195–214. Geoffrey Parker extended his interpretation in *The Military Revolution: Military Innovation and the Rise of the West, 1500–1800* (Cambridge, 1988). Roberts sees a sudden revolution propelled mainly by Dutch and Swedish innovations; Parker sees the transformation occurring in a drawn-out evolutionary process involving all continental military powers. For a recent reconsideration see John Lynn, "Tactical Evolution in the French Army, 1560–1660," *French Historical Studies* 14 (1985): 176–91.

118. Gerhard Oestreich, in charting the influence of the writings of Justus Lipsius after about 1584, notes that the Dutch Neostoic thinker made an important contribution to military science throughout Europe. See Oestreich, *Neostoicism and the Early Modern State*, trans. David McLintock (Cambridge, 1982), esp. chap. 5. Apart from military organization and the arts of war proper, writes Oestreich, "Lipsius had called for military ethics to be treated as an equally important ingredient of reform" (79). Lipsius and his disciples (including Jean de Billon in France) repeatedly stressed the qualities of constancy, self-control, and obedience, and they sought thereby to make the army a disciplined and pliant tool of state power.

cussed the attributes of the *capitaine*—the generic term used to designate a military leader.

> Among the properties that are necessary to the perfect captain, the military art emphasizes generosity and prudence, or courage and conduct; in that the one without the other cannot elevate a captain to such perfection as the ancients desired; courage causes us to esteem and recognize a generous heart born for war, prudence shows its excellence in its conduct.[119]

Despite its acknowledged value in time of war, intelligence seemed an ancillary quality for the *chef de guerre*. Ceriziers explained why other features took precedence.

> Judgment is admittedly a useful quality in a leader, but belonging more properly to the *politique* than to him, I believe that it does not compose the essence of the hero. . . . Nothing is more dangerous for a general than fear; nothing better excludes fear than courage; thus courage is [most] necessary to the general.[120]

This theme reappears in a noted military treatise first published in 1612, Jean de Billon's *Principles of the Military Art*. In his preface, titled "In Praise of the Profession of Arms," Billon first remarks that the successful captain continually exercises both mind and body, and that this proclivity "is rarely found among other men." But Billon places more emphasis on another characteristic. Since the captain "is always surrounded by dangers and death, it is essential that he use his reason and magnanimously rise above all fear: for wherever one finds the most magnanimous actions, one also finds the most virtue."[121]

Magnanimity often functioned as a synonym for *generosity* (as noted earlier in this chapter, in the discussion of the lexicon of the personal idiom), and the performance of magananimous actions therefore required not only fearlessness but a noble and generous demeanor. La Primaudaye had this in mind when, in his own discussion of military principles, he observed that since a general "needs to be served faithfully

---

119. Claude Malingre, *Eloge historique de la noble et illustre maison de Rantzow* (Paris, 1641), 5.

120. Ceriziers, *Le Héros*, 43.

121. Jean de Billon, *Les principes de l'art militaire* (Rouen, 1626), preface.

by his men," he must not rely on "authority and rigor" to win their loyalty. Rather, he must first establish a "well-recognized reputation for valor, generosity, and courage"—here La Primaudaye especially stressed the "great importance" of "exposing oneself to peril," of "fighting with one's own hands, one's own person, without regard to safety."[122] Once the soldiers had a "good opinion of [his] merit and valor," the general could attract their loyalty and obedience through "gentleness and benevolent gestures [par douceur & bien-faicts] . . . liberality and a gracious manner. For, after all, [only a general's] good friends and affectionate servitors will set aside all possible excuses and fight for him."[123]

These theorists of the military vocation emphasized courage, magnanimity, and liberality because men of war had to sustain the bonds of affection that underlay relationships of service in the king's armies. The maréchal de Lesdiguières explicitly recognized this need in his *Discourse on the Military Art*. He stressed that the sovereign who does not personally lead his army must "elect a good general and other officers who are above all faithful, desiring to accomplish his commands." Similarly, "a general must always have on hand chosen and experienced captains, artful in the ways of war, faithful and feeling affection for his service."[124]

Even the terms *discipline* and *obedience,* which became watchwords for the professionalizing army of the eighteenth century, were regarded from a unique moral perspective. The language used to discuss the qualities these words represent often seems familiar. Jean de Billon called obedience "the cause of all good things." Since it preserved "order in the ranks," and therefore led to victory, obedience was the soldier's first duty. But for Billon the word *obedience* meant many other things as well. Obedience to superiors "conserves virtue and good morals: it maintains friendships. . . . It earns a man esteem and brings him recompense once his patience in serving has been recognized. . . . It upholds the courage that our captains require of us at all times. . . . It instructs us in the glorious virtue of fidelity."[125]

Discipline, too, implied something other than subordination or repression. As John Lynn has indicated, when contemporaries called for discipline among the troops, they most often referred to the need for "control

---

122. La Primaudaye, *Academie Françoise,* fols. 367v, 369r–v.
123. Ibid., fol. 368r.
124. Bibliothèque Nationale, MS fr. 23042, [Lesdiguières], "Discours de l'art militaire, faict par Msr le Connétable de Lesdiguières," fols. 6, 10.
125. Billon, *Les principes,* 12.

and restraint." Commanders imposed discipline by limiting the soldier's propensity to pillage and by enforcing civilized behavior.[126] But the concept of discipline also incorporated a specific moral component. As La Primaudaye made clear in a chapter on "the ancient discipline and order of war," one did not acquire discipline through subjection to severe regulations and measured punishments. As he understood it, discipline removed "all fear of enemies" and led inevitably to "honor and immortal glory"; it prepared the soldier to "sustain all travels, confront all perils, and hold the opinion that it is more desirable to die fighting in a good and just quarrel than to save oneself by fleeing away."[127] This "discipline of virtue," which instilled "knowledge of fortitude and magnanimity," and which had to be implanted "in the hearts of persons," could only be absorbed through "good nurturing and instruction in one's youth." Like obedience, discipline implied above all a rigorous commitment to generous values. Those trained in the "discipline of virtue," wrote La Primaudaye, "may bring to pass their generous enterprises."[128]

The common emphasis on the moral qualifications necessary to the military profession is quite revealing when considered in context. Keeping in mind contemporary ideas about social classification, one detects in these discussions of the military art an elastic notion of "profession." After all, the qualities exemplified by military service—courage, generosity, magnanimity, affection, and fidelity—were hardly unique to the profession of arms.[129] In fact, nobles used precisely the same language when describing the reasons they merited all manner of nonmilitary jobs. One reads in a Du Chesne family history that Philippe de Béthune "negotiated so generously" in his role as *ambassadeur extraordinaire* to the duc de Savoy in 1617 "that finally peace was concluded." Nobles are found complaining in 1614 that venal officeholders did not demonstrate the "courage required of good magistrates and officers," by contrast to the nobility that would render "as much . . . fidelity in the exercise of justice as it does in the armies." In 1649 "the generous courtier" is offered as the

---

126. Lynn, "Tactical Evolution," 188.
127. La Primaudaye, *Academie Françoise*, fol. 362v.
128. Ibid.
129. Arlette Jouanna has also drawn attention to the nobles' belief that valor and generosity should be the principal prerequisites for candidates to all public positions. See "Les Gentilshommes Français et leur rôle politique dans la seconde moitié du XVIe et au début du XVIIe siècle," *Il Pensiero Politico* 10 (1977): 22–40.

ideal royal councillor, since "it is only the generous and prudent soul that can counsel kings well."[130]

The evidence suggests that mental barriers segmenting the different professions of royal service had not yet been erected in the early seventeenth century. This point is important, because it helps explain why nobles petitioned for legal and financial offices despite their clear and admitted preference for military careers. The qualities of generosity, courage, and fidelity were indeed important to the army because they enabled the soldier to make proof of his person. But proofs of person underlay the whole pervasive culture of gift and obligation, and the personal modality refracted the same vision of merit throughout all the institutions of royal service. In juxtaposing such terms as *courage* and *generosity* with the seemingly unheroic professions of councillor or judicial magistrate, nobles simply brought the entire world of royal service within the personal idiom and articulated their merit in the way most familiar to them. To the nobles' way of thinking, they were "endowed with the necessary qualities," the intangible personal qualities thought to be the grounds for determining who merited the king's favor and bounty. Nobles expressed confusion at the Estates General of 1614 and after precisely because kings now seemed ready to award *graces* on the basis of some other understanding of merit.

Merit at the Estates General (1614)

Having explored in some depth the nobility's understanding of royal service and merit in the early seventeenth century, we are now in a better position to assess the rhetoric and intentions of the second estate at the Estates General of 1614. Nearly all the provincial cahiers of the noble order placed the *paulette* edict at the top of the list of abuses to be abolished, and one is struck by the force of the nobility's indictment of venality.[131] Nobles attacked what they called the "hideous monster of venal-

---

130. Respectively, the references are from André Du Chesne, *Histoire Généalogique de la Maison de Béthune* (Paris, 1639), 501; Mayer, *Recueil*, 4:207; Bitton, *French Nobility*, 58; and *La véritable conduite du courtisan généreux*, 14.

131. Venality was a principal theme of the Estates General, so it is of course not surprising that it held a prominent place in the provincial cahiers. Of the eleven provinces represented in the Bibliothèque de l'Arsenal's collection of "Cahiers particuliers" (Ile de France, Orléans, Dauphiné, Normandie, Provence, Guyenne, Auvergne, Champagne et Brie, Bourgogne, Bretagne, and Picardie), ten call for the abolition of venality of office. The

ity" that threatened "honor, security," and "the public faith." The "shameful" practice would in time lead to "anarchic confusion" and "the total ruin of the state."

The noble critics of venality were eventually proven wrong. The sale of offices, far from leading to the total ruin of the state, provided a new foundation for the expanding monarchical state in the seventeenth century. By tying the interests of officeholders and their families to the various branches of royal administration, venality promoted an ethic of public service that supported the growth of monarchical authority in the decades following the Wars of Religion.[132] Venality also encouraged a corporate solidarity that would later complicate and impede centralization of the state's fiscal and judicial apparatus, but the new class of officers nevertheless provided kings useful services and lessened their dependence on the great nobles who had so often proved unreliable in the past. On balance the monarchy benefited from its sometimes uneasy alliance with the officers of *robe longue.*

Moreover, despite the claims of its critics, venality of office in some ways reinforced the theoretically personal nature of the king's service relationships. As one defender of the practice noted in 1614, venality helped the king to secure the affections of officials whose own well-being now depended "entirely on the prince's good fortune." This writer freely accepted the argument that royal servants should feel a deep personal commitment to the king, but he rejected the notion that only martial servants were capable of such commitments: "[Historians] have gone so far to say that the king's officers, in their various capacities, have done more to preserve the safety of his sanctified person than even his *gardes du corps.*"[133] The exchange of money for office, in other words, did not

---

one that makes no mention of it—BA, MS 4485, "Cahiers particuliers . . . Provence"—limits itself to local concerns and makes no general proposals.

132. As Ralph E. Giesey persuasively argued some years ago, venality assisted the process of state centralization because it "created a class of families that [had] a perpetual commitment to national public service which feudal seigneurs could never have qua seigneurs" ("State Building," 198). Sarah Hanley has explored further the alliance between monarchy and venal officeholders in a number of works emphasizing the patrimonial assumptions shared by kings, administrators, and officeholders. For the essentials of her argument see "Engendering the State: Family Formation and State Building in Early Modern France," *French Historical Studies* 16 (1989): 4–28.

133. AN, K 675[2], no. 143, "Offices," [1614], fol. 1r: "[Les historiens] ont osé dire que les officiers du Roy de toutes qualités tenoient sa personne saincté en plus seur garde que les gardes mesmes de son corps."

negate or override the reciprocal bonds of loyalty linking the king and his men.

One could say that noble opposition to the sale of offices around the turn of the sixteenth century stemmed in part from an initial misreading of the impact of venality. Contrary to what one would conclude based on the reaction it provoked among much of the nobility, the system of venality actually belonged to the political culture it ostensibly threatened. The sale of offices continued to blur distinctions between public powers and private interests; the new forms of patronage it inspired prevented, rather than encouraged, the depersonalization of political relations; and the requirement that one purchase one's office—a requirement that expanded to include many posts at court and in the military—in no way displaced the affective bonds thought to suffuse the hierarchy of royal service from top to bottom. This helps to explain why most nobles eventually found it possible to accept, and even to profit from, the venal system they once condemned.[134]

Still, it would be unfair to view the nobility's expressions of opposition to venality in 1614 as naive, disingenuous, or desperate. That most nobles ultimately accommodated themselves to venality in all its forms should not lead the historian to dismiss retroactively earlier denunciations of the practice. When the sale of offices hardened into a system in the early seventeenth century, the change seemed to signal a whole new conception of merit and recompense in the context of the king's service. In theory, it now became possible for wealthy roturiers to buy for themselves a portion of public power—even without the patronage or formal endorsement of a noble whose merits were known by king and court. Moreover, venality insured that money could now serve as a substitute for the proofs of person formerly required of one who sought royal recognition and reward. Noble opponents of venality called forth many

---

134. Like other segments of elite society, nobles found that they could use to their own advantage the crown's ever increasing need for money. Not only did many nobles buy offices in the army and at court, but the wealthier and well-connected nobles also formed alliances with officeholders and financiers who regularly floated loans to the king at high rates of interest. In the seventeenth century these credit syndicates (or "lobbies") rapidly infiltrated the organs of the central government and, as Daniel Dessert has shown, exercised a powerful influence over royal policy. On the system of crown finance in the seventeenth century, see especially Dessert, *Argent, Pouvoir et Société au Grand Siècle* (Paris, 1984); and idem, *Fouquet* (Paris, 1987). See also Françoise Bayard, *Le Monde des Financiers au XVIIᵉ siècle* (Paris, 1988); and James Collins, *Fiscal Limits of Absolutism: Direct Taxation in Early-Seventeenth Century France* (Berkeley, 1988).

different arguments—the practice undermined hierarchy, it represented a challenge to royal authority, it opened the door to corruption. But the atmosphere of protest in the first decades of the seventeenth century is captured best by a word that appears often in the cahiers of the Estates General: *confusion*. Beneath all the rhetoric lay a deep anxiety over the ways in which merit should be recognized, rewarded, and defined. Determined to establish what Montchrétien later called the "legitimate order" for distributing royal *graces,* noble deputies to the Estates General reacted to the challenge of venality by reemphasizing the personal character of royal service and by staking their claim to the merits long valued in the context of personal relations.

The cahiers of Orléans drew a sharp distinction between the past, when the nobility's merits were always rewarded, and the present, when they suddenly found their merit being overlooked. Nobles, "Sire, were honored, esteemed, cherished, and advanced in all the honorable posts of this monarchy, political as well as military," but now the nobility is "overtaken, deprived of positions" by people "who are much inferior to them," the newcomers having acquired their posts "by money rather than by merit."[135] The nobles of Dauphiné repeated these concerns and invoked historical precedent to point out the inevitable consequence of valuing money over true merit: when "venality entered the city of Rome by one door, honor, security, and public fidelity left by the other." The *paulette* would lead to anarchy, charged the nobles from Normandy, because it would eventually leave the king "without officers or without fidelity." Venal officeholders could not possibly demonstrate for the monarchy "the faithful and continual attachment that all true *gentilshommes* have always displayed."[136]

Some noble deputies went to extreme lengths and represented the sale of offices as an imminent danger to the king. Venality, in permanently removing offices from the king's store of gifts, "takes away from Your Majesty the means of fastening, by new obligations, the sons of those who have served with dignity."[137] Some thought it "perilous for the person of the king, and for the state, that offices . . . even including the ones

135. BA, MS 4485, "Cahiers particuliers . . . Orléans," fol. 26v.

136. The first two citations are from BA, MS 4485, "Cahiers particuliers . . . Dauphiné" (fol. 49v) and "Cahiers particuliers . . . Normandie" (fol. 71r). The last is from AN K 118ᵃ 26, no. 4, "Requête faite au Roy par le corps de la Noblesse," 1649, 3–4. The petition repeated many of the themes pressed in 1614.

137. Mayer, *Recueil,* 4:172.

that serve his person are put publicly on sale . . . and that the said offices are in the hands of persons whose only obligation is to their purses."[138] Through venality, they charged, the king invited the wrong kind of men into his service and rewarded all the wrong qualities, thereby making it impossible to create and reinforce bonds of obligation with his servants. If the prince expected to give a gift that "returns [to him] the man," above all he must choose someone whose heart would respond appropriately to a generous offering. Yet the wealthy commoners who now overran the *bureaux des finances* and the law courts rose to their positions in the king's service not by proving generosity but "by scaling their mountains of gold."[139] They certainly had rendered no "signal services" to demonstrate "honor and obligation" to the king. Such demonstrations were above them, for they had been shaped by "a narrow and mechanical life" and were marked by "avarice."[140]

Nobles argued that the king needed only to "place gifts where he finds merit." He should distribute offices not to those who have the most money, which is often acquired dishonestly (*souvent malacquise*), but in recognition of "valor, generosity, and blood spilled by one's predecessors in the service of kings."[141] The recent assassination of Henry IV had made it all the more obvious that posts should only be given to "persons of merit and whose fidelity will be well recognized by proofs and not by words."[142] Nobles from Burgundy observed that honors, in a state as populous as France, should "come directly from the hand of the king, so that he holds the balance of his subjects' affections." Deputies from Normandy insisted that "the provisions to all military offices," instead of being sold, should "be granted in pure liberality and [as] gratification." This was so that "the nobility and those who are placed in positions will hold them solely from the hand and by the liberality of Your Majesty as recompense for services," thereby creating "a special obligation to render [the king] more services in the future."[143] The king should abolish venal-

---

138. Mayer, *Des Etats-Généraux*, 18:84.
139. *L'Hercule François. Harangue au Roy Pour la Noblesse de France en l'assemblée des Notables tenuë à Rouen. Par le Sieur D. B.* (n.p., n.d.), 5.
140. Ibid.
141. BA, MS 4485, "Cahiers particuliers . . . Ile de France," fol. 9r.
142. AN, K 675, no. 99, "Mémoire . . . Sens," fol. 3v.
143. BA, MS 4485, "Cahiers particuliers . . . Bourgogne" (fol. 212r) and "Cahiers particuliers . . . Normandie" (fol. 65v).

ity and preserve the practice of personally choosing "the most powerful instruments of his domination."[144]

Whom should the king choose if not nobles? They had shown time and again their devotion to the king's person. As the *Advis et Remonstrances* stated it in 1614:

> Where better to allocate pensions than to those whose greatest desire . . . is to serve the king, and to put at risk their property and lives for His Majesty, and by consequence, for the state? . . . The king will find a good number of this type among our nobility. Is it not the most willing and most generous in the world?[145]

In order that all "offices . . . posts, dignities, [and] governments" be filled by men of appropriate quality and capacity, the nobles of Guyenne demanded that the king choose exclusively from the *gentilshommes* who had served the king in the past. Even more, "it is necessary that a number of great and signal services should precede this honor, and that one's fidelity has been well recognized."[146] The nobles of Normandy neatly summed up the argument.

> The nobility has rendered signal services and hopes to make itself recommendable to Your Majesty by its generosity and obedience, so that as offices become vacant, in the army and elsewhere, you will provide them gratuitously and liberally . . . without having any regard for this shameful venality that has even been introduced in the offices of your household, to the confusion of all men of courage.[147]

I have emphasized that a personal understanding of merit and an equally personal epistemology characterized the culture of royal service in the first half of the seventeenth century. All service relations were construed through the prism of personal obligation, and the gaze that judged and confirmed merit inevitably sought the all-important proofs of person that bound individuals to one another. These assumptions traced their origins to a time when centrifugal forces had diminished the powers of kings and reinforced the personal nature of all authority; thus, they operated far

---

144. Mayer, *Des Etats-Généraux*, 18:111.
145. *Advis, remonstrances, et requêtes*, 26.
146. BA, MS 4485, "Cahiers particuliers . . . Guyenne," fol. 90r–v.
147. BA, MS 4485, "Cahiers particuliers . . . Normandie," fol. 64v.

beyond the confines of the royal court or any other single location. Those who acted as intermediaries between the king and his provincial servants in the seventeenth century—princes, governors, military commanders, the patrons and brokers studied by Sharon Kettering[148]—embodied the moral merits of the personal modality and judged and rewarded those merits in others.

Because it reflected and incorporated basic principles of social organization in early-modern France, the personal modality naturally implicated many persons outside of the old nobility. For everyone, it filtered perceptions of royal government; and for monarchs, it defined the services expected of all subjects—a point that will be further demonstrated in chapter 2. Nevertheless, the personal modality of service had special relevance for the king-noble relationship, because in it nobles saw both the rationale for their own social and political status and the meaning of monarchical power. Their vision of the social order, their belief in the special qualities of the nobility, and their understanding of the king's authority all found ultimate affirmation in the light of the sovereign's gaze. These assumptions emerged fully into view in the course of debates over venality of office in the early years of the seventeenth century. To many the rapid growth of venality seemed alarmingly inconsistent with the ideal exchange of noble service and royal recompense. Hence, to clear up the "confusion" besetting "all men of courage" in 1614, nobles used the occasion of the Estates General to remind the king of the proper definition of merit and of the values reflected in that definition.

Indeed, because the noble cahiers at the Estates General articulated a view of merit expressed reflexively, and somewhat less self-consciously, in countless other contexts both before and after 1614, they provide a useful standard against which to measure and assess the evolving political culture of the ancien régime. To understand how the construction of absolute monarchy in the seventeenth and eighteenth centuries related to the evolution of the nobility's basic assumptions—to understand, that is, how the two processes shaped each other—one needs to follow over the long term the transformation of the conceptual triad on which the definition of royal service was implicitly based: the mutually recognized images of "service," the "servants," and the "served." How did kings and nobles understand merit in the seventeenth and eighteenth centuries?

---

148. Kettering, *Patrons, Brokers, and Clients in Seventeenth-Century France* (Oxford, 1986).

Through what processes was it represented and judged? How did nobles come to reinterpret their role as servants of the crown? In short, how did the personal modality of service change, and how were those changes expressed semantically? I will suggest in subsequent chapters that one can answer these questions, and thus can better perceive the lines of transformation leading to the society and culture of the eighteenth century, by closely examining changes in the conception and operation of the sovereign's gaze.

As the nobility's increasingly self-conscious elucidation of the personal modality suggests, one can already find in the early seventeenth century a growing tension between new political imperatives and the nobles' customary understanding of service, merit, and the criteria by which these were judged. But before seeking a fuller explanation of this tension, we need to take a closer look at one element of the nobility's conceptual world. It seems puzzling at first that nobles proposed to remedy the ills of venality by directing the king's attention not only to merit but to birth. One remonstrance of 1614, for example, expressing doubt that the king could ever completely eradicate "this confusion . . . venality," proposed that the king fill simply half of all offices in the *parlements* with legitimate nobles who would have to verify their nobility with authentic letters or proofs of some kind.[149] In discussing the selection of officers for the royal households, noble deputies to the Estates General were even more insistent. They asked the king to "remove this usage [venality] entirely and declare . . . that the said offices can be possessed only by *gentilshommes* of extraction."[150]

What justification did nobles have for asserting that in the search for merit the king should favor those with the longest genealogies? We know that the qualities of courage, generosity, and fidelity shaped the nobility's definition of merit, but why did nobles have a monopoly on those personal qualities? Why did birth indicate merit? The manner in which nobles made the connection is the focus of chapter 2.

---

149. AN, K 675², no. 193, "Remonstrance," [1614], fol. 2r.
150. Mayer, *Recueil*, 4:171.

2

Family and the Personal Modality

For old nobles, lineage became ever more important in the early years of the seventeenth century. Evidence of the new attention to birth is not hard to find. As the growing number of arrivistes diluted the corps of noblesse, *nobles de race* tried hard to preserve the special identity of the *gentilhomme*. At the Estates General in 1614 the second estate condemned usurpers of noble status and asked the king for measures to stem the tide of undeserving newcomers flowing into the order of nobility. Nobles also demanded stricter regulation of the identifying marks of noblesse. To prevent the use of crested armorial bearings by *anoblis*, for example, old nobles asked the king to name a *juge d'armes*. That official would compile

> a universal register of the noble families of your realm, in which he will place their names and arms . . . and with the help of the *baillis* and *sénéchaux*, inquiry will be made of those who have usurped [their status] . . . all [verified] in the presence of four *gentilshommes* of each *bailliage*.[1]

Louis XIII responded by creating a *juge général des armes* in 1615.

But the most obvious sign of the nobles' strengthened emphasis on birth in the first half of the seventeenth century is the wave of family histories and genealogies that began to appear after the turn of the century.[2] Although relatively few were produced in the sixteenth century, the production of these family monographs rose dramatically in the seventeenth

---

1. Charles J. Mayer, ed., *Recueil des Cahiers Généraux des Trois Ordres aux Etats-Généraux,* 4 vols. (Paris, 1789), 4:199.

2. The many family histories written by or for the nobility in seventeenth-century France have received little scholarly attention. Orest Ranum, however, does stress the importance of the family history genre in shaping seventeenth-century historical scholarship in general. See his *Artisans of Glory: Writers and Historical Thought in Seventeenth-Century France* (Chapel Hill, 1980), esp. 3–12.

century, as table 2.1 indicates.[3] Obviously, many more noble families were writing their histories, or having them written, in the seventeenth century. Comparing only the last three decades of the sixteenth century with the first three decades of the seventeenth, the latter period shows a threefold increase in the number of genealogical works. If we extend the chronology of the comparison and add those works for which the exact date of writing is not known, we find that 99 formal genealogical histories appeared in the sixteenth century. By contrast, the seventeenth century produced 633. Moreover, the interest in genealogy did not soon wane. It continued on through the eighteenth century, as table 2.2 indicates. Adding those histories that cannot be dated precisely, a total of 473 appeared between 1700 and 1789.

TABLE 2.1   Production of Family Histories, 1550–1659

Decade	Printed	Manuscript	Total
1550–59	2	2	4
1560–69	9	2	11
1570–79	4	2	6
1580–89	10	0	10
1590–99	6	1	7
1600–1609	9	3	12
1610–19	17	3	20
1620–29	35	9	44
1630–39	27	14	41
1640–49	44	9	53
1650–59	35	12	47

3. Gaston Saffroy's *Bibliographie Généalogique, Héraldique et Nobiliaire de la France: Des Origines à Nos Jours*, vol. 3, *Recueils généalogiques généraux, Monographies Familiales et Etudes Particulières* (Paris, 1974), gives a complete listing of extant genealogical histories (in print and in manuscript) held in French libraries and archives. My tables 2.1 and 2.2 are actually far from exhaustive. They represent only the works Saffroy was able to date accurately. When one takes into account histories and genealogies for which only the century is known, the rising interest in family history after about 1600 is underscored even more strongly. Sixty-one such undated histories were composed in the sixteenth century, sixteen of which were devoted to either Godefroy de Bouillon or the chevalier de Bayard—two especially popular heroes. By contrast, an impressive 205 of these undated histories were produced in the seventeenth century, and 162 in the eighteenth. Also, because the object here is to illustrate the rise in the nobility's own interest in genealogical history, I have excluded genealogies that were written expressly for legal purposes. I omit hundreds of *factums*, for example, because these were generally used to help decide land disputes and the like. For similar reasons, I leave out dozens of genealogies submitted to officials who headed provincial *recherches de la noblesse*. It could reasonably be argued that the inclusion of *factums* and genealogies composed at the crown's request would only inflate artificially the numbers for the middle decades of the seventeenth century.

TABLE 2.2   Production of Family Histories, 1660–1789

Decade	Printed	Manuscript	Total
1660–69	49	40	89
1670–79	21	21	42
1680–89	31	14	45
1690–99	20	15	35
1700–1709	22	19	41
1710–19	16	11	27
1720–29	13	5	18
1730–39	19	12	31
1740–49	11	9	20
1750–59	28	8	36
1760–69	29	4	33
1770–79	49	7	56
1780–89	40	9	49

Source: Gaston Saffroy, *Bibliographie Généalogique, Héraldique et Nobiliaire de la France: Des Origines à Nos Jours,* 4 vols. (Paris, 1968–79), vol. 3, *Recueils généalogiques généraux. Monographies Familiales et Etudes Particulières.*

Of course, focusing on ancestry and genealogical trees seems quite characteristic of an aristocratic frame of mind. One explanation for the nobility's fascination with family history in ancien régime France is in fact ready-made: aristocrats in all ages inevitably base their status and identity on their birth. But that explanation implies that the noble outlook was unchanging—a premise the evidence does not sustain. In a 1645 family history, for example, Jules Chifflet considered the nobility's use of genealogy from a historical perspective. In previous generations, he noted, families had looked at history and genealogy differently. Formerly, the habit was to record the glorious history of one or two individuals from the family's past, a history that would then serve as an example for the descendants of the line: "In this way, the work always remained in the hands of those born afterwards." But now, Chifflet noted, "it is done otherwise." Families had become ever more meticulous in their record keeping: "One writes in fine order not only that which concerns an individual lord of the House but generally all [details] that might give heart to those who bear the name." Finally, many of these works, which had once "remained in the hands" of the family, now found their way into print.[4]

What was new, it seems, was the common desire to make the family's history public. The nobility's shift toward what one historian has termed

4. [Jules] Chifflet, *Les Marques d'Honneur de la Maison de Tassis* (Antwerp, 1645), 1.

"genealogical consciousness"[5] is shown clearly by the numbers. The first chart indicates that the turning point came sometime in the second decade of the seventeenth century. What had happened to make nobles more aware of their family past and more anxious to share it with everyone else?

Actually, there were several motives for recording one's family history. With the arrival of "new" men who did not boast long histories themselves, older nobles emphasized their family's antiquity for pride's sake. Everyone held old nobility in high esteem. Many noble families whose origins dated back to the fifteenth century, or further, naturally found in genealogy the means of reinforcing their special status in the eyes of their peers.

But genealogy could also perform a more practical function. Beginning in 1463, the monarchy conducted periodic *recherches* to check the credentials of all the nobles in a given *généralité* (the largest administrative unit at the provincial level).[6] The crown wished to single out those who did not have a legal claim to tax exemptions, and to do this investigators had to separate the true nobles from the pretenders. In Normandy, where most of the *recherches* took place before the seventeenth century, the initial investigation of 1463 led to similar proceedings in 1523, 1540, 1555, 1576, and 1598. In each case, genealogical evidence was central to the verification process. To prove its nobility, a family had to produce documents showing its line of descent and proving the nobility of individuals belonging to each generation.[7] For old nobles, the commissioners sought evidence for the possession of noble status over four generations. An *anobli,* however, would have to present his "principle" or origin of noblesse, that is, normally his letters of ennoblement given by the king, with written proof of their registration in the sovereign courts. Although neighbors and acquaintances could sometimes testify to the status of

---

5. Harold A. Ellis, "Genealogy, History, and Aristocratic Reaction in Early-Eighteenth Century France: The Case of Henri de Boulainvilliers," *Journal of Modern History* 58 (1986): 414–51. See also, idem, *Boulainvilliers and the French Monarchy: Aristocratic Politics in Early Eighteenth Century France* (Ithaca, N.Y., 1988). The following discussion of the nobility's understanding of genealogy and family history owes much to arguments already developed by Harold Ellis.

6. This section closely follows James B. Wood's detailed description of the *recherches* conducted in the *élection* of Bayeux between 1463 and 1666. See the chapter titled "Defining the Nobility" in his *The Nobility of the 'Election' of Bayeux, 1463–1666: Continuity through Change* (Princeton, 1980).

7. Wood, *Nobility*, 29.

older nobles, especially at the early *recherches,* families could establish an irrefutable claim to nobility only by submitting proper documentation. Perhaps to encourage good record keeping, or to speed the verification process, commissioners in succeeding *recherches* accepted the genealogies certified in previous ones as adequate proof of a family's nobility.[8]

By the late sixteenth century, much of the French nobility would have seen the implications of the Normandy *recherches.* The monarchy's fiscal needs provided a practical reason for families to review their past. For the security of a family, well-organized records of its history should be on hand. Although the monarchy had not yet launched a comprehensive *recherche de la noblesse* (investigation of the nobility) extending to every province, it obviously could do so at any time. And nobles anxious to weed out usurpers from their ranks would have welcomed that prospect. Noble deputies to the Estates General themselves called for the general *recherche* in 1614.[9] Noble families were never compelled to present printed genealogies to local fiscal officials, it is true, but after family members had taken the trouble to collect and record the family's genealogical history, publication of that record might have seemed the obvious final step for those who could bear the added expense. Noble interest in genealogy in the seventeenth century, then, is explained in part by the *recherche,* which had become something of an administrative habit by the end of the sixteenth century.

To explain the nobility's greater interest in genealogical history at the turn of the seventeenth century, however, many historians assert that nobles were beset by fear and anxiety. In their view the old nobles, having long since lost their position as sole defenders of the realm, and facing imminent decline, resorted to using an ideology of birth to bolster their sagging social and political fortunes. Ellery Schalk has argued, for example, that the chaos of the Wars of Religion severely damaged the reputation and social standing of the warrior nobility. Frightened by the violent peasant uprisings of the 1590s, and startled by the "anti-upper-class overtones" marking the literature of lower-class supporters of the League in Paris, the nobility, says Schalk, slowly adopted a "less 'dangerous' idea of nobility"—one that abandoned virtue as a sign of nobility and left noble status to rest squarely on birth. Compelled by circumstance to redefine their identity, nobles traded in the troublesome

---

8. Ibid., 30.
9. Discussed at the beginning of this chapter.

obligation of "virtuous action" for the security guaranteed by "pedigree."[10] Schalk's analysis actually extended and refined that presented by André Devyver some years earlier.[11]

It may well be right to assume that the nobility's growing emphasis on pedigree reflected its impression of an increasingly fluid, and thus less certain, social order. To interpret this response as defensive resistance to change, however, one must assume that seventeenth-century nobles subscribed to an inferior and obsolete belief system, and that they somehow sensed that their values were being overtaken by others whose superiority they could not deny. This chronological and conceptual dichotomy is problematic both because it implies that an older mentality is somehow less legitimate than a newer one and because it exaggerates the semantic distance that separated the concepts of birth, virtue, and merit in the early-modern period. An examination of the vocabulary contemporaries used when discussing nobility—*birth, blood, race*—will indicate more clearly the coherence of the noble outlook. More important, by peeling away the layers of meaning in this terminology, I hope to lay bare the connection between the increased attention to genealogy and noble discussions about merit in the early seventeenth century.

Understanding what *naissance* (birth) actually meant in the seventeenth century requires a bit of decoding, for definitions of the word referred to other loaded terms whose meanings were usually taken for granted by lexicologists and laymen alike.[12] The Académie Française, for example, listed *noblesse* as one of its definitions of *naissance*. But one of the words most frequently utilized in discussions of birth, *qualité* (quality), provides the key to penetrating the code. *Naissance,* again according to the Académie Française, "is also used with respect to the good or bad qualities with which one is born."[13] The word *condition* often functioned as a synonym for *naissance* ("One says 'of condition' to mean 'of good birth'"), so it is not surprising that the idea of *qualité* also held a promi-

---

10. Ellery Schalk, *From Valor to Pedigree: Ideas of Nobility in France in the Sixteenth and Seventeenth Centuries* (Princeton, 1986), 109.

11. André Devyver, *Le Sang Epuré: Les Préjugés de race chez les gentilshommes français de l'ancien régime, 1560–1720* (Brussels, 1973). On Devyver, see chap. 1.

12. As in chapter 1, the two dictionaries consulted here are the *Dictionnaire de l'Académie Française,* 1st ed. (Paris, 1694); and Antoine Furetière, *Dictionnaire universel* (The Hague and Rotterdam, 1690). These works shall be hereafter cited as *DAF* and *DU,* respectively.

13. *DAF.*

nent place in its definition: "The nature, estate, or quality of a thing or person. It also signifies the quality given by birth."[14]

A notion of quality was therefore implicit in discussions about inherited status. What, in turn, did it mean to be marked by a certain quality? The Académie Française pointed out that *qualité,* as a near synonym of *naissance,* often implied "nobility of extraction." But in its widest connotation, the word referred to one's moral disposition. Both Furetière and the Académie Française observed in their first definitions of *qualité* that "it is said figuratively of spiritual and moral things." The dictionary of the Académie duly noted that the word could be used in describing an individual's personal characteristics and status or the properties of a given object ("Accident according to which a thing or person is said to be such and such"). But "more particularly," it was noted, "it signifies inclination, habit." *Inclination,* according to Furetière, "signifies a leaning or natural disposition to do something."

By following the trail of implied meanings, one finds that the word *naissance* did more than establish a biological fact. The term sometimes evoked "moral" inclinations and the set of behaviors appropriate to those inclinations. For illustration, one need only look again at the definition of *naissance* as given by the Académie Française—this time substituting the definition of *qualité* where the word *qualité* itself appears: *Naissance* "is also used with respect to the good or bad [inclinations, habits] with which one is born. . . . 'He has a great soul and noble inclinations.'" The same nuances are found in related terms. For example, the concepts *race* and *sang* (blood), which clearly signified pedigree, implied at the same time a set of behavioral expectations. *Race* referred to "lineage, extraction, all those who come from the same family." But the word could also be taken in a figurative sense: "One says . . . that 'Good dogs are hunters due to their race,' as a way of saying that children have the morals [*moeurs*] and inclinations of their fathers. In the same sense, one can say that 'A man hunts due to his race.'"[15] Furetière explained *sang* in much the same way. After giving all the literal definitions of the term, he added that "one says proverbially, 'Good blood never lies,' as a way of saying that children ordinarily have the good qualities of their fathers and mothers."[16]

---

14. *DAF.*
15. *DAF.*
16. *DU.*

At first glance it seems reasonable to conclude that, in contrast to their sixteenth-century counterparts, commentators on nobility in the early seventeenth century described noble status as the result not of virtue but of birth and pedigree.[17] When its ambiguities are closely examined, however, the contemporary lexicon reveals that the concepts of birth and virtue could communicate similar ideas, and that emphasis on pedigree may have been a way of affirming a specific and traditional set of moral qualities. Even those who saw nobility purely as a product of biology stressed the spiritual and moral things associated with elevated birth. Pierre de Sainct-Julien, writing in 1588, stated explicitly that nobility passed from father to son as a "substance" in the blood. But how did he describe this substance? He explained that nobility is derived from "virtuous habits, continued excellence," and that the habits themselves, once hardened into something *substancielle,* are transmitted from one generation to the next. Elite societies in the past had diligently researched the "origin and extraction" of prospective members, Sainct-Julien asserted, because of the assumption that "modesty, an agreeable disposition, as well as magnanimity, courage, prowess, and polished gentility all have their source . . . in the seed of one's progenitors."[18]

In linking the habits of virtue directly to heredity, Sainct-Julien took an exceptional position—as he himself recognized.[19] In 1611 Nicolas Pasquier expressed an opinion more typically ambivalent. On the one hand, nobility seemed to Pasquier a kind of genetic mystery; noble children follow in the footsteps of their ancestors because of a "secret seed" planted in their hearts at birth. But on the other hand, he noted that the young *gentilhomme* must himself work to insure "that the virtue that he derives from his family descent is truly hereditary." Why should virtue require effort if genealogy determined one's character? Pasquier compared the noble family to a fertile field where wheat is grown. One normally expects the field to produce a rich and bountiful harvest, but everyone knows that unfavorable conditions sometimes lead to crop failures.[20]

---

17. See Schalk, *From Valor to Pedigree,* esp. 115–44.

18. Pierre de Sainct-Julien, *Meslanges Historiques et Recueils de diverses matieres pour la plupart paradoxales, & neantmoins vrayes* (Lyon, 1588), 631, 626.

19. Sainct-Julien noted that most writers considered nobility not a substance, but "an accidental thing" (ibid., 630). Arlette Jouanna has noted that when nobles or other writers approached the issue of heredity, "imprecision reigned in their minds." See Jouanna, *L'Idée de Race en France au XVIᵉ siècle et au début du XVIIᵉ siècle (1498–1614),* 3 vols. (Paris, 1976), 1:112–13.

20. Nicolas Pasquier, *Le Gentilhomme* (Paris, 1611), 2–3.

Pasquier's metaphor pinpoints the connection contemporaries saw between family background and individual character: distinguished birth furnished the all-important soil in which the seeds of virtue were sown. As Furetière implied in his definition of the term *race*, the family served as an important reference point when assessing individuals, precisely because children were expected to "have the morals [*moeurs*] and inclinations of their fathers." Why? Because *moeurs*, the "natural or acquired habits according to which a people or individuals live their lives," shaped the family's identity and determined the context for a child's development.

All this suggests that contemporary debates about the basis of nobility—Was it the product of virtuous action or well-recognized birth?—may have been less important than the widely shared expectation that those born into a distinguished race would conform to moral and behavioral patterns set by the family. Nobles (and others) may indeed have been divided on the question of whether *moeurs* were essentially natural or necessarily acquired, but all recognized that the family was more than the source of one's genes; it also was the source of those habits according to which individuals live their lives. This helps explain why *naissance*, as Furetière noted in his last entry for the term, sometimes functioned "with regard to the first years of life."[21] As the following discussion of genealogical histories should indicate, the nobility's heightened sense of ancestry in the seventeenth century did not signal their flight from virtue or their defensiveness about merit. On the contrary, the merits implied by the personal modality demanded consciousness of family values.

Education, *Moeurs*, and Family History

It is well established in the historical literature that the old nobility only slowly awakened to the need for conventional schooling.[22] Few nobles cared to spend time in a classroom learning dead languages and poring over ancient texts under the supervision of indolent monks—their picture of life in the *collèges*. It would be wrong to assume, though, that nobles instinctively resisted all forms of education. They had fixed ideas con-

---

21. *DU.*

22. For a review of educational attitudes and practices among court nobles in this period see Mark Motley, *Becoming a French Aristocrat: The Education of the Court Nobility, 1580–1715* (Princeton, 1990).

cerning both the form of education appropriate and desirable for young nobles and the content to be learned. In truth, many immediately recognized that instruction given in an institution could supply young nobles with important and useful skills—provided the subject matter and the setting were suitable to the noble condition. It seems, for example, that a fair number of academies designed to train young, aspiring military officers were established in France beginning as early as the 1560s, the most famous being Antoine Pluvinel's riding academy in Paris, founded in 1594. Pluvinel introduced a broad curriculum, including classes in dancing and music as well as horsemanship and fencing. Here, beginning at about age twelve, nobles learned to be "nobles" rather than simply military men.[23] Later, in 1627 the Assembly of Notables requested that the king establish *collèges militaires* in each province or the archdiocese, where young nobles would avoid "l'oisiveté des lettres" while being "nurtured, supported, and instructed" in a number of useful subjects. By studying a range of topics ("the laws of war," mathematics, history) they would elevate their minds "according to the force and talent given them by nature."[24]

In the mind of the typical noble, however, classroom instruction did not impart the most important lessons of youth. Nicolas Pasquier wrote that "knowledge of *moeurs* is the first thing [the young noble] must learn; it is the basis for all he will learn in the course of his life."[25] The royal chancellor Cheverny elaborated this idea by linking the very meaning of nobility to the cultivation of *moeurs*. He noted that the public admired nobility only because "we assume that the children of men who are better, more virtuous and generous, will also have more courage and valor than others." This meant that the young noble effectively sustained his

23. For a brief account of the rise of the academies see Philippe Ariès, *Centuries of Childhood: A Social History of Family Life,* trans. Robert Baldick (New York, 1962), 203–9. For a more thorough account see Motley, *Becoming a French Aristocrat,* chap. 3. For comparisons of French and German academies see Norbert Conrads, *Ritterakademien der Frühen Neuzeit* (Göttingen, 1982). A broad, contextual picture of the academies' place in the educational history of early-modern France is provided in Roger Chartier, Madeleine Compère, and Dominique Julia, *L'Education en France du XVIᵉ au XVIIIᵉ siècles* (Paris, 1976).

24. Charles J. Mayer, ed., *Des Etats-Généraux et autres Assemblées Nationales,* 18 vols. (Paris, 1788–89), 18:305.

25. Pasquier, *Le Gentilhomme,* 27.

nobility only if he did not "degenerate from the good *moeurs* and merits of his predecessors."[26]

More than schooling alone, then, education implied to the nobility a "good and generous nurturing" of the proper *moeurs*.[27] Noble children had to become attuned to the values of selflessness that suffused the second estate. Claude Pelletier remarked, for example, in his *Education of the Nobility*, that the nobility "must become inflamed with the love of [valor] from childhood so as never to abandon it."[28] Similarly, Claude Le Laboureur maintained that the noble's education should inculcate a willingness to die for one's prince. For the future warrior, psychological preparation seemed more basic even than practical skills, such as good horsemanship: "Before you become engaged in an undertaking that demands more strength than you have at your age, work seriously to fortify your mind and render yourself intrepid and unshakeable in the face of peril." Le Laboureur knew of no better method to achieve that than the one used by the ancient Gauls, who, in the "nurturing of the young nobility of their nation," instilled a scorn for life itself. They took this as their "greatest and almost only goal": "Death, armed with fire and iron, may appear before your eyes in order to intimidate you. . . . But those who have been taught to scorn life will not dread death or any of its faces."[29]

To instill the values of generosity and selflessness, noble parents knew that they had to shape their children's thoughts from the very beginning. In his memoir written in the 1590s, Cheverny discussed with his son the proper methods of child rearing.

---

26. Philippes Hurault, comte de Cheverny, *Les Mémoires d'Estat de m. Philippes Hurault, comte de Cheverny, Chancelier de France, Avec une Instruction à Msr son Fils, ensemble la Généalogie de la Maison des Huraults* (Paris, 1636), 491.

27. The phrase is taken from the title of a noble biography. See [H.T.S.] de Torsay, *La vie, mort, et tombeau de Philippe de Strozzi . . . où par occasion se voit la bonne et généreuse nourriture de la jeune noblesse française, sous les roys Henry et François second, pendant son bas aage et plusieurs notables points de l'histoire de nostre temps non touchez, ou si particulièrement déduis ailleurs* (Paris, 1608).

28. Claude Pelletier, *La nourriture de la noblesse où sont représentées comme en un tableau, toutes les plus belles vertus, qui peuvent accomplir un jeune gentilhomme* (Paris, 1604), fol. 67r.

29. Claude Le Laboureur, *Histoire généalogique de la maison de Sainte-Colombe et autres maisons alliés* (Lyon, 1673), dedication.

My son, I have always thought that the principal fortune a father can leave to his child consists not of the goods of his inheritance but in good nurturing, instruction, and teaching. . . . And if you do not start on this route from his earliest youth, it is most difficult to do so afterward; because it is necessary to form and regulate his mind, his will, and his *moeurs* beginning with his earliest and tender youth.[30]

Cheverny's concerns were echoed by the biographer of an illustrious *parlementaire* in 1617: "If you do not water these young plants and see that they take in the essence of virtue at an early stage, while they are still tender and delicate, you will work in vain to that end once they have reached their full size."[31] Claude de Marois, author of *Le Gentilhomme Parfaict,* cited as a shining example of intelligent child rearing one of the customs of the ancient Persians: "As soon as the children of their kings were born, they had them nurtured not by just any nurse but only by eunuchs judged the best at the king's court, so they could fashion and form their *moeurs* from birth, much like you see good gardeners drive a large stake next to young plants to keep them straight."[32] Perhaps Marois would have approved of the education received by the comte d'Harcourt, who, his biographer claimed, had been unsurpassed in his precocious application to the study of soldiering. His mother was "not timid" and had always insured that he did not lack the "wisdom and generosity" of a governor who could teach him the art of command: "Not even his childhood was exempt from this noble activity."[33]

The need to condition a child's morality even required close attention to his physical development. In his concern for nutrition, Cheverny showed how nobles could attribute great weight to both biological and environmental determinants of character.

The mother must take care to have good wet nurses who eat good food, inasmuch as it is from this source that the milk is created and retains its substance, and they must abstain from drinking wine, which heats the milk and harms the child, who himself becomes too flushed;

---

30. Cheverny, *Les Mémoires d'Estat,* 365–66.

31. Charles Paschal, *La vie et moeurs de m. Guy Du Faur, sr. de Pybrac* (Paris, 1617), 27.

32. Claude de Marois, *Le Gentilhomme Parfaict ou tableau des excellences de la vraye noblesse: Avec l'institution des jeunes gentilshommes à la vertu* (Paris, 1631), 506.

33. [René] de Ceriziers, *Le Héros Français, ou l'idée du grand capitaine* (Paris, 1645), 141.

and when male children leave the hands of the women who nurse them, fathers must be diligent in seeing that they are well instructed and governed by wise and virtuous preceptors . . . because the marks of this first institution remain forever imprinted in the minds of children. [34]

Claude de Marois instructed female readers to be equally sensitive to their children's environment. Mothers, he wrote, should be wary of entrusting to women of inferior quality the care of infants, who, after all, are "tender and disposed to receive all sorts of impressions." They should insure that "the nurses, or those who frequent the children, should not recount indifferently all sorts of fables, for fear . . . that their souls will drink in folly and false opinion from the beginning."[35] From the moment of birth, parents had to work hard to provide their children only edifying experiences, for, as Cheverny noted, "if there is any defect in this first nurturing of the child, it is always attributed to the father; because it is commonly said that the son is like the father who formed him."

Naturally disposed to receive all sorts of impressions, the noble child had to be insulated from corrupting influences while surrounded by models of virtue to study and emulate. Cheverny, for example, even advised assigning children an illustrious namesake. "It is the father's duty to insure that the children are given some *honnête* name at their baptism— by *honnêtes* Godparents—respected people of honor, because the dignity of the name . . . gives them an example, [and] they can imitate the virtue of the one whose name they bear."[36] One fine example would hardly prove sufficient, however; instead there must be a multiplicity of examples, all conveying the same impressions and teaching the same lessons. The proper moral habits could be instilled only through repetition. As Guillaume Chevalier remarked, "if valor were inborn, everyone might have it—the same with all the other virtues; but it is acquired with knowledge and habit." Chevalier explained that three "columns" supported the virtuous man: a familiarity with the nature of virtue, the will to be virtuous, and *"habit,* that is to say, *An action that is repeated and done many times"* (Chevalier's emphasis).[37]

Nobles found that the most powerful lessons in the habits of virtue

---

34. Cheverny, *Les Mémoires d'Estat,* 529.

35. Marois, *Le Gentilhomme Parfaict,* 505–6.

36. Cheverny, *Les Mémoires d'Estat,* 529–30.

37. Chevalier, *Discours de la Vaillance* (Paris, 1598), 23, 36.

came from family histories that showed the same virtues in practice for generation after generation.[38] As one of the most celebrated genealogists of the first half of the century once declared, "virtue knows how to elevate to the heights of honor those who know how to prefer it above all other things."[39] He and the rest of the old nobility assumed that to know how to prefer virtue one needed to heed the examples of those who already knew how—those for whom it seemed to come naturally in the past. Stories retelling the exploits of one's ancestors could be counted on to "incite" children "and give them the desire to resemble" their predecessors in all their virtue.[40] As one author who compiled the history of his own family wrote,

> those who write good genealogies raise up models of virtue and perfection for posterity, furnish all the descendants of a given family with an *honneste* dialogue [with the past] in order to persuade them gently and powerfully to follow the piety and generosity of their ancestors, as it is beyond doubt that domestic examples touch us more than any other.[41]

Genealogy, used as a pedagogical tool, effectively dissolved any distinction between pedigree and the nurturing process. Why else had the kings of France chosen to make nobility a hereditary quality all those centuries ago, asked Chevalier, if not so that they could "choose from those who are moved by domestic objects and examples from their youth?"[42] These examples had such power that the biographer of the maréchal de Souvré portrayed "the memory of his fine and glorious actions" as "the only school where all of this illustrious race shall be instructed from father to son."[43]

38. Others have noted that nobles prized family history for its educational value. David D. Bien has shown that nobles in the army in the eighteenth century viewed the power of "domestic examples" from a perspective that conformed easily with prevailing "Enlightenment" ideas. Harold Ellis has examined the importance of the presumed didactic function of history in the thought of that noted noble "reactionary" Boulainvilliers. See Bien, "The Army in the French Enlightenment: Reform, Reaction, and Revolution," *Past and Present* 85 (1979): 68–98; and Ellis, "Genealogy, History, and Aristocratic Reaction."

39. Bibliothèque Nationale (hereafter BN), MS fr. 32621, Pierre d'Hozier, "Généalogie de la maison d'Aumont," 1627, fol. 3.

40. Guillaume Chevalier, *Discours des Querelles et de l'Honneur* (Paris, 1598), 27.

41. BN, MS fr. 18670, Georges Viole, "Généalogie de l'ancienne maison des sieurs de Viole," 1660, fols. VI–VII.

42. Chevalier, *Discours des Querelles,* 27.

43. [Claude Pelletier], *Discours sur la mort de feu M. de Souvré, Mal de France* (Paris, 1626), 12–13.

In concentrating heavily on the family's past greatness the young noble risked becoming self-satisfied and arrogant, a problem noted by writers of the time, but none doubted that the benefits of family consciousness far outweighed the costs. Marois, for example, after railing, on one page, against the "deceit and folly of nobles who glorify in their nobility and in the courage and virtuous actions of their predecessors to elevate themselves . . . above the common people," calmly discussed, on another page, the built-in educational advantages that noble children possessed.

> Now the *gentilhomme* & the children of free condition, those principally who are born of honorable mothers and fathers without reproach, have this advantage over those who do not enjoy such a brilliant origin, that they have, in the contemplation of the fountain from which they derive, luminous lights, or rather sharp spurs, to excite their nature and make them aspire to elevated things, however stupid or dull they may be.[44]

However ordinary his intellectual capacities, the son of noble parents received a moral formation that prepared him for great things. Genealogical history played a key role in insuring this outcome. Under the careful guidance of parents and preceptors, the inculcation of the family's traditions into the young noble allowed virtue, in the words of François L'Alouëte, to "flow from father to son and, by an accustomed fashion of living, to become in the lineage a habit causing its descendants to shine above others."[45]

The nobles' assumptions about the nature of education suggest why they saw no paradox in associating the concepts of birth and merit. As I argued in chapter 1, nobles knew that they had to prove merit by exhibiting a specific assemblage of good qualities. They also knew that those qualities reflected an accustomed fashion of living rooted in the habits of the family.[46] Raised in noble surroundings, where examples of the family's past generosity weighed constantly on his mind, the young noble

---

44. Marois, *Le Gentilhomme Parfaict,* 10, 491.
45. Francois L'Alouëte, *Des affaires d'estat, des finances, du prince et de sa noblesse* (Metz, 1597), 184.
46. Other seventeenth-century communities concerned with the "moral formation" of children showed a similar tendency to superimpose the notions of lineage and domestic nurturing. See Edmund Morgan, *The Puritan Family* (New York, 1966), for an especially striking parallel to French noble attitudes.

learned to "employ all his time and fortune in the service of the king and to feel an inviolable fidelity toward him, in imitation of his ancestors."[47] His inclinations differed from those of other young men who, by contrast, "are constrained to abase themselves in activities we may call servile, where the virtue of generosity is so obscured that it is only known as something up in the clouds, or as something others talk about."[48]

Genealogy stood as a metaphor for moral as well as biological continuity, and families therefore recognized and exploited its educational value. But nobles also used genealogical histories to represent their merits to other interested readers. In embracing this practice, nobles followed the lead of the royal family. During the Wars of Religion, rebel factions led by Guise and Mayenne had tried to stain the reputation of the Bourbons to cast doubt on their fitness for the French throne. Apologists for the Bourbon family chose to defend them by referring to the centuries of continuous sacrifice they had rendered in the service of the monarchy. The author of one widely read Bourbon family history (1587) "wanted to write a memoir of their services and the posts each member [of the family] has held," to refute falsehoods circulated by rebel propagandists. He noted that "For three hundred and forty years, ever since M. Robert de France, almost all the princes of Bourbon who have carried arms have died in the service of the crown." The Guise pretenders, by contrast, "have only had positions of command in France for thirty-five years," an empty record that did not inspire trust. Belloy intended to show that Bourbons had always been

> great, excellent, & brave captains, exposing their lives, & conducting themselves wisely with arms in hand, striking fear into the hearts of the enemy by their prowess & generosity—nothing great or outstanding ever having occurred when they were not to be found in the service of the king and of the crown of France.[49]

---

47. As presumably did the man in whose honor this eulogy was given at the *parlement* of Rouen in 1658: Sieur de Prefontaines, *Eloge de m. Henry de Matignon . . . Cte. de Thorigny . . . prononcé au parlement de Rouen, le 9 avril 1658* (n.p., [1658]), 31.

48. Chevalier, *Discours des Querelles*, 27.

49. [Belloy], *Mémoires, et recueil de l'origine, alliances et succession de la royale famille* [sic] *de Bourbon, branche de la maison de France; ensemble de l'histoire, gestes et services plus memorables faictz par les princes d'icelle aux rois et couronne de France* (La Rochelle, 1587), 397–98.

Another Bourbon history in 1609 portrayed the family as a "warlike and generous race," one that had flourished honorably since the year 359. "Blood never lies," the author wrote. "If valor and gentility are the virtues that most recommend the majesty of a monarch, where better to find them than in these heros of royal extraction who suckle them, in a manner of speaking, with the milk of their nurses, and who maintain them by communication with their ancestors?"[50]

Because genealogical history highlighted the generous qualities found in the family's record, it could be used as a résumé. Nobles hoping to impress the king and other dignitaries quickly learned this lesson. Had not kings since the Middle Ages valued the heroic qualities of generosity and fidelity above all else? To find those qualities, kings need only look to noble family histories, since "it is to be believed that . . . a long line of nobles in one lineage . . . [can] bring maturity and accomplishment to their quality, and their courage, fidelity, and affection toward their prince . . . are, so to speak, consolidated."[51] As Jules Chifflet put it, family histories offer examples of courage and generosity that "never die in our sovereign's memory." After these familial qualities have been affirmed, "[the sovereign] takes heart in knowing, once he sees you carrying on the family name, that the virtues of your ancestors will be reborn in your person."[52] The line separating family merit from personal merit seemed very thin indeed.

In the previously noted history of the lives of Jacques and Antoine de Chabannes, for example, the author, Du Plessis, dedicated a preface to the king. In it he wrote that

after having pondered many times what service I might render Your Majesty, from which you could draw the most utility, . . . seeing the corruption of this century where fidelity is so remote and so hard to find, [and] principally in your realm where money is almost everywhere the master of honor and reason, I thought it appropriate to show you the lives of some of those from the Chabannes family.

50. Henry de Montagu, sieur de La Coste, *La Descente généalogique depuis St. Louis de la maison royale de Bourbon; enrichie de l'histoire sommaire des faits, vies et morts de tous* (Paris, 1609), 2, 11.

51. David de Rivault de Flurance, *Les Etats, èsquels il est discouru du prince, du noble, et du tiers état* (Lyon, 1596), 279.

52. [Jules] Chifflet, *Histoire du bon chevalier, m. Jacques de Lalain, frère et compagnon de l'ordre de la Toison d'or, par Georges Chastellain*, (n.p, 1634), dedication.

The author's purpose was really twofold.

> This will serve two ends, one to animate those who presently bear the name [of Chabannes] to imitate their ancestors, the other to prompt Your Majesty to honor them with commands and offices and to be certain of their fidelity, in which if ever they were found lacking, they would be more culpable and doubly worthy of punishment than others who are not descended from people so generous and full of merit. . . . It is so important that you elect good and faithful servants, since the security of your state depends on it.[53]

In his first pages, Du Plessis is found assuring his readers that the Chabannes "can boast (up to the present) of always having been men of great probity & valor, good Catholics, faithful servants of kings . . . all generous and filled with virtue, the kings having placed them in the finest and greatest posts they possessed."[54] At the end of his history, which is devoted to two fifteenth-century luminaries, Du Plessis brings his readers up to date. On the final page, he passes rapidly through the genealogical history of the Chabannes and concludes with the living descendants. Apparently, the accomplishments of the two illustrious ancestors spoke for the quality of the entire family.

More than an exercise in vanity, then, the elaborate family history served as a recommendation for present-day descendants by illustrating merit's cyclical pattern. The biographer of the maréchal de Matignon, for example, spent the first pages of his lengthy eulogy displaying the virtues of the maréchal's ancestors, thinking to explain in that way the source of Matignon's own merit.

> So many illustrious examples of the piety and of the valor of his ancestors, so much glorious testimony to their inviolable fidelity toward their prince, so much assiduity in the service of the king, so many glorious deaths, so much blood courageously spilled . . . seeing this in his family pushed him strongly to follow the brilliant glory of his ancestors.[55]

---

53. Du Plessis, *Les vies de m. Jacques et Antoine de Chabannes, tous deux grands maîtres de France* (Paris, 1617), 3–5.

54. Ibid., 3.

55. Prefontaines, *Eloge de m. Henry de Matignon,* 26–27.

The subsequent success of his own career—the king named him maréchal de France "at a time when there were only three or four"—proved that "his fidelity and valor had been put to every kind of test, and that his blood had been judged to be among the most pure and generous in France."[56]

The descendants of the line of Vergy had been so consistently characterized by their valor, wrote the famous genealogist André Du Chesne, that the lords of this house had earned the epithet *les Preux* (the worthies): "And especially, they have always remained so firm in their fidelity to the service of their princes, WITHOUT VARIATION, that this has always been their motto."[57] Indeed, at the death of François de Vergy in 1592, Henry IV sent the letters patent naming his successor as governor of Burgundy directly to his son Claude, "without any delay, so much had the virtues of his predecessors made him recommendable to the king."[58] Proof of past fidelity and generosity had earned for all those named Vergy "a perpetual esteem."[59]

From the perspective of the nobility, the perpetual esteem or perpetual recommendation reflected in a family's history enabled the king to predict the quality of a candidate's performance in important functions. If kings had rewarded one's ancestors with "the greatest and most honorable positions in the realm" for their "rare merit" and the "esteem [the kings] had for their fidelity," then it only made sense to assume, as did Du Plessis, that the descendants should be in line for similar honors.[60] The author of a history of the lords of Montauban clearly expected it. In his opening epistle to the current lord of Montauban, he explained his purpose for writing.

> I offer you [this work] which I am sure your successors and the heirs to your honor and fortune will study so as to follow your footsteps and those of your predecessors . . . so that you will have the satisfaction of seeing them grow . . . [and] by their own merit arrive at offices

56. Ibid., 16.

57. André Du Chesne, *Histoire Généalogique de la maison de Vergy* (Paris, 1625), epistle.

58. BN, MS Collection Duchesne 42, André Du Chesne, "Histoire de la maison de Vergy," [seventeenth century], fol. 17.

59. Du Chesne, *Histoire Généalogique . . . Vergy,* epistle.

60. Pierre d'Hozier, *Généalogie et alliances de la maison des sieurs de Larbour dite depuis de Combauld* (Paris, 1629), epistle.

and honors next to kings and princes, where those of their condition are normally called.[61]

Other histories appealed openly to the king's benevolence—after reminding him of the family's hereditary virtues.

> It is not to be doubted that Your Majesty, feeling much regret at the loss of [the maréchal de Souvré], will continue to show toward his children the great affection that you always harbored for the father (which led you to honor him with the charge of maréchal de France and shower him with goods and favors), since they are true imitators of the virtue of this valorous lord. . . .They will all do their best to merit the honor of your good graces . . . by the generosity of their courage.[62]

The same technique appears in a history of the La Rochefoucauld family. The author described first the "entire and continual fidelity toward our kings" always exhibited "by the eldest as well as the youngest of this house, most of whom served the king at their own expense." Then he insured his readers that "M[onsieur] le Duc de La Rochefoucauld, who is presently the head of this illustrious house . . . confirms well what I say, without forgetting the expectations we have for M[onsieur] his son, who has already shown signs of his valor."[63]

Nobles seem to have been stung by criticism that many of them relied on the exploits of ancestors to maintain their position "above the common people," as Marois had put it. Consequently many histories and genealogies also displayed pride in individual achievement, and some even refuted the most extreme implications of family consciousness. The genealogist Valles, for example, did not think it adequate to praise the virtues of the family without duly noting the merit of the current head of the house.

---

61. Bibliothèque de l'Arsenal (hereafter BA), MS 4920, Valles, "Généalogie des très illustres et très anciennes maisons de Montauban et d'Agoult, comtes de Sault," 1632, fol. 3v.

62. [Pelletier], *Discours . . . Souvré*, 10–11.

63. Pierre Hutin, *Généalogie de la très-grande, très-ancien* [sic], *et très-illustre maison de La Rochefoucauld* (n.p., 1654), 6–7.

Not only are you [Ferdinand de la Baume] descended from a race whose old nobility is noted by everyone, and whose incomparable virtue has won them the most eminent posts and dignities. . . . But also your own merit and integrity in the springtime of your age shows us that you do honor to your fathers no less than they do honor to you.[64]

Antoine de Ruffi considered family upbringing and individual exertion as two sides of the same coin. "I do not deny that it is a great advantage to come from an illustrious stock, in that it often inspires in the soul of those who descend from it high and generous thoughts and assures a magnanimous upbringing." But the merits of Cardinal Grimaldi resulted from his own effort more than anything: "All these great advantages of birth have not served at all to acquire you your glory; you owe this to nothing but your own virtue."[65] A member of the distinguished family of La Rochefoucauld represented emulation—the desire to replicate and even improve on the examples set before you—as the most important "hereditary" characteristic. "There is a remarkable thing found in few families," he noted: that for year after year over the course of six centuries, everyone in his family "has had the same emulation to surpass everyone else, so much are excellence, courage, and virtue hereditary in this illustrious House."[66]

Some chroniclers came close to asserting that individual merit owed nothing to heredity. In a *harangue funèbre* printed at the end of the history of the maréchal de Toiras, the author refused to do in this place "what most men do," which is to focus on "the names of ancestors and the ashes of grandfathers." "The antiquity of families" is but "a borrowed beauty." It is better to highlight the personal merits of Toiras himself.

The virtue so characteristic of M. the Maréchal de Toiras, is it not more considerable than the blood he received from his father? The qualities that his virtue acquired for him, are they not more precious than those given to him by his birth? The glory that his merit left to him, is it not more brilliant than that which he draws from his House?

---

64. BA, MS fr. 4920, Valles, "Généalogie des très illustres et très anciennes maisons de Montauban et d'Agoult, comtes de Sault," 1632, fol. 2v.

65. Antoine de Ruffi, *La vie de M. le chevalier de La Coste* (Aix, 1659), epistle.

66. Hutin, *Généalogie . . . La Rochefoucauld*, 7.

The nobility of his heart, is it not more illustrious than that of his blood?[67]

Nevertheless, in Toiras's biography we are still very far from the ideal of the self-made man. The history of the maréchal's life is prefaced by a "Discourse on the Genealogy of the Maréchal de Toiras," which emphasizes his sixteen degrees of nobility. The nobility of his heart may have seemed even more illustrious than that of his blood, but Toiras's biographer did not doubt that credit for much of the maréchal's virtue belonged to his family background and that his birth and his merit were closely intertwined. The noble of the seventeenth century certainly became more conscious of the difference between family glory and personal achievement, but he always wished to present himself, as would Lesdiguières, as "a man of heart and of birth."[68]

Merit, Family, and the Robe Nobility

One finds, in reading early seventeenth-century texts, that authors invariably included genealogical references when writing either to praise or to criticize an individual or a family. Claude Malingre, for example, composed a detailed biography of the maréchal de Rantzow in 1641. Despite his focus on the life on the maréchal, Malingre titled his book the *Historical Eulogy of the Noble and Illustrious House of Rantzow*. He appended to his work a genealogical table of the Rantzow house and thus pointed out that Rantzow, in demonstrating his "valeur toute généreuse," had shown the "natural" generosity "hereditary" in his lineage.[69] The very personal memoir of chancellor Cheverny, quoted earlier in this chapter, ended similarly with a lengthy family genealogy.

Conversely, efforts to smear an individual's character usually involved attacks on the family. The widely shared assumption that genealogy symbolized an individual's merit gave rise to an interesting polemical

67. [Baudier], *Histoire du Maréchal de Toiras* (Paris, 1644), *harangue funèbre*, non-paginated.

68. F. F. P. de V., *Tableau Historique, dans lequel sont contenus quelques remarques d'Etat: Et comment le Roy, a fait Monsieur le Mal de Lesdiguières, Connétable de France* (n.p., 1623), 15. On the growing awareness of the difference between family identity and the exploration of selfhood see Jonathan Dewald, *Aristocratic Experience and the Origins of Modern Culture: France, 1570–1715* (Berkeley, 1993), chaps. 1, 3, and 4.

69. Claude Malingre, *Eloge historique de la noble et illustre maison de Rantzow* (Paris, 1641), 26–29.

exchange during the Fronde. A vituperative tract celebrating the arrest of Condé in January 1650 sought to show that Condé's misdeeds, as leader of the Fronde of the princes, were entirely in keeping with his family's history, as "impiety and tyranny have been vices so common to all of their race, that one need only read the history of France to become perfectly well instructed of this truth." Condé's sympathizers later published their own libel, a *Genealogy of the First President,* after the *parlementaire* Mathieu Molé, who had vacillated between support for the crown and support for the Fronde of the princes, became Keeper of the Seals. One called to this dignified position, argued the author, should be endowed with something "beyond a capable mind." He should also demonstrate "an exemplary probity . . . and incorruptible *moeurs.*" Molé's family and personal history, however, should tell the king "what he can expect" from him—treachery and self-interest.[70]

This seemingly automatic linkage between descriptions of personal virtue (or vice) and references to family history can be found in works other than those devoted to the old nobility. Highly placed men in the professions of law and finance, the nobles of *robe longue,* also commissioned dozens of histories, genealogies, and biographies in the first half of the seventeenth century, and these works always framed their subjects' "merits" around familiar points of reference: notable acts of generosity, moral qualities, and family background. The new office-holding nobility and the old, predominantly military nobility generally followed different vocations, but on the basis of these texts, one would assume that both groups defined merit within a moral and familial framework.

In 1617, for example, a biographer who described the exploits of a *parlementaire* from the Du Faur family used an anecdote to draw attention to the judge's bravery and fidelity. The future Henry III, after being elected to the throne of Poland, had chosen a number of French notables to accompany him to his coronation. Among them was Guy Du Faur, "whose good counsel and fidelity the king trusted entirely": "This was a happy day for him, the beginning of the honor and influence he was subsequently to enjoy near the king." But the selection of Guy Du Faur also proved fortunate for the king himself: "We will see that an action followed this [choice] that you will judge to have been the result of a brave and generous courage." According to Paschal's narrative, Polish nobles

---

70. *La généalogie du Prince, et comme tous ceux de cette maison ont été funestes au roi et au peuple* (Paris, 1650), 1; *La généalogie du premier président* (Paris, 1652), 3.

unhappy about the election of a foreign king disrupted the coronation ceremony. Sensing crisis, the hero of the story sprang into action. Du Faur rose and, "turning toward the Archbishop, said to him, 'Reverend sir, why are we waiting? The king commands [you] to proceed; is this not why we have all come here? As for the others, the king himself will restore order as soon as he is given the authority.' " Because of Du Faur's courageous eloquence, the ceremony proceeded without incident.[71]

The hero who can no longer conceal his true heart and courage behind his robe of civil office is a character common to many of the family histories and biographies of the office-holding nobility. If one prescriptive treatise is any indication, jurists learned to view the adjudication of cases "as a kind of war that, though not so bloody as that which takes place on the field of battle, nevertheless offers its snares and its dangers."[72] One is not so surprised to hear, then, that the virtue of the *parlementaire* Jean de Gassion "was never so enveloped within his robe that he did not acquire much glory in numerous occasions where he brought attention to his courage and his valor." His heroism during the Wars of Religion deserved special notice.

> The moment he got word that certain Spaniards aiding the rebels had taken Navarrins, catching it by surprise, without men or munitions [to defend it] . . . Gassion became like a man of war . . . and pursued the enemy on horseback with sword in hand all the way to the city of Hortez, where he . . . forced them to surrender soon after.[73]

Claude Expilly, noted *président* of the *parlement* at Grenoble, also had opportunities to display his uncommon generosity during the Wars of Religion. After the omnipresent Lesdiguières had retaken Grenoble from the forces of the Catholic League in 1590, he tried to gain the cooperation of urban notables, some of whom had been league sympathizers, and he turned to Expilly for help.

---

71. Paschal, *La vie . . . Du Faur*, 89.

72. A. G. E. D. G., *L'idée du bon Magistrat* (n.p., 1645), 3–4: "Les procès sont une espèce de guerre qui, pour n'etre pas si sanglante que celle qui se fait à la campagne, ne laisse pas d'avoir ses malheurs & sa corruption autant ou plus pour ceux qui les jugent."

73. Abbé de Pure, *La vie du Maréchal de Gassion* (Paris, 1673), prefatory, "Généalogie de la Maison," nonpaginated.

In fact, from that moment, he took Expilly into his most intimate confidence and continued to call him into secret deliberations . . . because he knew of the liveliness of his mind, the solidity of his judgment, and the firmness of his courage; which obliged him in fact to take him along on most of his military expeditions, where Expilly, though he belonged to a profession other than that of arms, always carried himself as a man of heart and of virtue, showing that he was a worthy heir to his father.

Indeed, Expilly's generosity was battle-tested several times. At Pontcharra, for example, he accompanied Lesdiguières,

armed with every weapon, [serving] under the white cornet with the volunteers . . . and on more than one occasion he jumped very courageously into the thick of the melee, which was noted by all the commanders of the troops, who gave him infinite praise, but especially [it was noted] by Lesdiguières, who after the combat praised him aloud, saying that in the bitterest heat of the battle he had recognized in him a veritable valor that came from a generous heart.

None could fail to perceive the moral of the story: that "an *honnête* man can make equally good use of an excellent pen or a good sword."[74]

Even officers of finance, the men presumed least likely to have imbibed the old nobility's culture of selflessness, are sometimes shown behaving like men of heart and of birth. A genealogical history of the Bertrand family written in 1635 details the glorious exploits of one Marc Bertrand, a *trésorier de l'Epargne* under Louis XIII. Marc, says the author, had always shown "by his fine virtues and rare qualities that he did not degenerate at all from the merit and the courage of his predecessors." His courageous and generous qualities burst into the open during the siege of La Rochelle. The family historian described Marc Bertrand's state of mind at the commencement of the siege.

He believed that this [event] was so important to the interests of the king and of his country that, in the distribution of finances, which was his calling, he felt he must do something above and beyond the others in the effort to overcome the rebels; this explains why, although he

---

74. Antoine Boniel de Catilhon, *La vie de m. Claude Expilly* (Grenoble, 1660), 41.

was in Paris trying beyond his powers to acquire loans and provide for the expenses of the war, his mind was at the siege, where he had his office and where his deputies were working to exhaustion on his orders in order to distribute this money without which the God Mars himself would be powerless.

With his mind at the siege, Bertrand apparently found it difficult to concentrate fully on the task at hand. And his concerns were well founded, because the siege seemed on the verge of failure in September 1628, "for lack of money." At that moment Marc Bertrand, "redoubling his strength and his courage," performed an extraordinary feat.

His heart burning with zeal for the king and for the honor of the state, [he] displayed all the more his influence and his vigilance. Because with less than four thousand livres in the coffers of the Treasury, it seemed that the siege was lost and the soldiers about to disband, when he, going generously everywhere ... searching for everyone who might blindly give him assistance in this occasion based on his own obligations and his own private promises, including those who make it more their business to spend than to lend, ... was able in forty-eight hours ... to gather forty-five thousand livres, which were then dispensed to the militia.

The militia, "finding its courage again," proceeded to take La Rochelle from the Huguenots. Bertrand the treasurer had saved the day.[75]

The desire on the part of robe nobles to compile genealogies and family histories is not hard to explain. In a society sensitive to the symbols of status, a written record of one's lineage may have seemed an indispensable sign of assimilation into the established corps of nobility. *Robins* also knew that creative history could be used to obscure the family's humble origins or to give the impression of a slow and honorable transition from military service to civil service.[76] Competition for status within

75. BN, MS fr. 11465, "Généalogie de l'illustre maison de Bertrand, de Bricquebec et de La Bazinière," [seventeenth century], fols. 56–60.

76. Actually, few *robin* families had exclusively "civil" pasts. James B. Wood has suggested that in the sixteenth and seventeenth centuries as many as half of the officeholding nobles were themselves products of the old nobility, at least in the section of Normandy he investigated. An old line is defined as one covering four or more generations. See Wood, *Nobility*, esp. 73–77.

robe circles no doubt provided another incentive. Some families may have wanted to distinguish themselves from recently ennobled officeholders by producing impressive genealogies of their own.

Still, how should attempts to emphasize the courage, valor, fidelity, and generosity of jurists and financiers be understood?[77] After all, one would not normally expect that handling money and deciding on points of law would entail much "generous" personal sacrifice. Yet the imagery of the heroic tale appears so often in chronicles devoted to officeholders that the language cannot be dismissed as frivolous or accidental.

The apparent incongruity becomes less perplexing when one considers hypothetical alternative strategies for representing the virtues of officeholders. When a modern observer of the seventeenth century compares the old nobility and the new, the special advantages of the latter stand out clearly. *Robins,* as a group, generally received a better education and possessed more diverse talents than their more esteemed counterparts. Some recognized this and noted it at the time.[78] Why did robe nobles not accentuate the distinction more aggressively and thus base their claim to prestige on established skills and an ability to accomplish

---

77. If George Huppert is right, the robe nobility's reliance on the old nobles' language of self-definition may have been a new phenomenon in the early seventeenth century. Huppert has analyzed the social and intellectual milieu of sixteenth-century officeholders in *Les Bourgeois Gentilshommes: An Essay on the Definition of Elites in Renaissance France* (Chicago, 1977). The group defies easy social classification. Usually pursuing tacit ennoblement, they were caught between the upper reaches of the third estate and the established *gentilhommerie.* Huppert argues that this "class" became increasingly self-conscious of its detachment from both the second and third estates, and that by the late sixteenth century it had forged a novel "gentry" identity based on the values of civility, education, prosperity, and profession. By the early years of the seventeenth century, however, this gentry had become frustrated both by its alienation and by its failure to impose its own vision of the good life on French society. From then on, Huppert suggests, *officiers* were forced to decide either to retreat from society altogether or mimic the ways of the old nobility: "The virtues of that ephemeral Fourth Estate, as enumerated by Montaigne—peace, profit, learning, justice, and reason—were not, after all, to take precedence in public opinion over the virtues of the nobility: war, honor, action, valiance, force. In order to achieve the highest honors, it became necessary, once again, to embrace the values of the enemy" (170). Donna Bohanan, who has studied old and new nobles in Aix-en-Provence, disputes Huppert's claims. Even in the sixteenth century, she writes, *anoblis* "were not a world apart from the old nobility, nor did they strive to achieve cultural distance from it." See Bohanan, *Old and New Nobility in Aix-en-Provence: Portrait of an Urban Elite* (Baton Rouge and London, 1992), 137.

78. For examples of sixteenth-century magistrates who celebrated "a style of life very different from that of the warrior," see Arlette Jouanna, "Des 'Gros et Gras' aux 'Gens d'Honneur'," in Guy Chaussinand-Nogaret, ed., *Histoire des élites en France du XVIe au XXe siècle: l'honneur, le mérite, l'argent,* 17–141 (Paris, 1991), esp. 36–37.

specific tasks? The answer lies in the seventeenth-century perception of utility. Even if *robins* had been inclined to stress their special talents, the argument would have had little effect given the prevailing tendency to see attributes like talent and wealth as qualities secondary to a person's value and identity. When Pierre de Sainct-Julien explained the differences between nobles and commoners in his 1588 treatise, he casually conceded that members of the third estate had talents. But talent, far from entitling commoners to special consideration, only helped illustrate their inferiority. People of common origin, lacking a mind "inclined toward magnanimity," could not follow the path of "dignity"; "Their only goal is to use their talent for profit, and thus fill their purses."[79] The mere possession of talent did not make one meritorious any more than the possession of riches made one wealthy, because assets like talent and wealth, though not irrelevant, mattered less than the moral inclinations that determined how one used one's personal resources.[80] The talented commoner, accustomed to pursue profit and personal gain, could be counted on to do one thing: exploit his talent for personal advantage.

Thus, even robe nobles who took pride in their acquired skills and mental acuity sought to establish that they resembled traditional nobles in their inclination toward magnanimity. His panegyrist described Claude Expilly as being torn in his early years between his own wish to follow in the footsteps of his father, who had met a violent end in the army when Claude was young, and his mother's desire that he lead a more tranquil life. His mother persevered, and she sent Claude off to the *collège* of Tournon, where "he gave extraordinary signs of the excellence of his mind." He went on to study at the Universities of Paris, Turin, and Padua, where he became expert in law. Nevertheless, "he employed his leisure time in learning to handle arms, [in learning] to ride a horse, and in [learning] all the virtuous and *honnêtes* exercises that the French nobility generally studied in the Italian academies in those days."[81]

79. Sainct-Julien, *Meslanges Historiques*, 634.

80. Cosimo Bartoli typified the tendency to see wealth as a mere ornamental quality when he wrote, in an influential treatise on honor and warfare, that "I would like us to realize that the possession of gold or riches is not what makes a man rich, but rather his knowledge of how to spend his wealth, how to use it when needed." See Bartoli, *Conseils Militaires, fort utiles a tous Generaux, Colonels, Capitaines & Soldats, pour se sçavoir deuëment & avec honneur acquitter de leurs charges en la guerre*, trans. Gabriel Chappuys (Paris, 1586), fol. 194r.

81. Catilhon, *La vie de m. Claude Expilly*, 16.

Assuming, though, that robe nobles shared the old nobility's conviction that one's general moral disposition mattered more than one's ability to perform specific tasks, why did they not make a case for their superiority precisely on those grounds? Everyone knew that, despite their claims of generosity and inviolable fidelity toward the king, old nobles often behaved cynically in their own self-interest. Moreover, the recent civil wars had demonstrated all too clearly the conditional nature of the nobility's fidelity to the king. Why not criticize the old nobility on this score and argue that the new robe nobility, as a class, could do better?

In fact, the failings of the traditional nobility did not go unnoticed at the time. Old nobles heard much criticism in the late sixteenth and early seventeenth centuries for deviating from their habits of virtue during the civil wars.[82] But it is important to realize that everyone soon came to regard the last decades of the sixteenth century as an anomalous time, a dizzying period marked by an inexplicable and general lapse of civility. One finds the occasional mea culpa in seventeenth-century recollections, but more striking is the willful forgetfulness that overcame most of those who took part in the wars. Indeed, the general amnesty awarded by Henry IV in the Edict of Nantes might be understood more properly as a general amnesia. The king declared in that edict "that the memory of all the events since the beginning of March 1585 until my accession to the throne, as well as the troubles preceding and incidental to these events, shall be extinguished and laid to rest, [regarded] as things that never happened." Moreover, subjects "of every profession and status" were forbidden "under any pretext" to "stir up memories, to attack, insult, or provoke one another in reproach for what has happened."[83] The Edict of Nantes of 1598 officially relieved nobles of the burden of reconciling their recent behavior with their image as faithful servants of monarchs.

At the same time, it is also important to remember that the old nobility's own sense of self-worth depended in part on its cherished freedom to react to circumstances. Nobles who resisted the plots of royal favorites or wicked ministers did not see themselves acting unfaithfully toward the king—a charge nobles always denied. Instead, they believed that their

---

82. Schalk captures much of this criticism in *From Valor to Pedigree*, esp. chaps. 4 and 5.

83. François Isambert et al, *Recueil général des anciennes loix françaises depuis l'an 426 jusqu'à la révolution de 1789*, 29 vols. (Paris, 1822–33), 15:172–73.

independent judgment and freedom of action enabled the king to overcome the evil designs of manipulative, power-hungry advisors.[84]

Thus, old nobles would not have acknowledged that occasional errors
in judgment could be used to challenge their social and moral supremacy.
The personal modality of service did not call for slavish personal commitment at all times, and old nobles did not profess to provide it. The
gentilhomme claimed only that his personal and family background
determined and signaled his generous inclinations, and that on the basis
of those inclinations one could reliably predict his moral choices. No one
denied that commoners sometimes acted virtuously. But because of the
noble's good and generous upbringing, he would shine above others
more often than not. As Florentin de Thierriat wrote in 1606, "it has
always been assumed that fidelity arises rather from the courage of a *gentilhomme* than from that of a roturier." Consequently, "to place complete trust . . . in a newly created noble, without any other proofs of his
virtue and fidelity, is hazardous."[85]

Conventional wisdom held that familial habits molded the individual's
moral outlook and that these habits easily outweighed evidence of occasionally reckless behavior. Thus it would have seemed unnatural even for
solidly established *robins* to represent themselves as more courageous,
generous, and magnanimous than *gentilshommes.* Instead, as a way of
offering "other proofs of [their] virtue and fidelity," they showed that
their inclinations to magnanimity came from a familiar source. *Robins*
paid increasing attention to their own family backgrounds in the seventeenth century to distance themselves from the status of roturier and the
stigma of moneygrubbing. In establishing through their own family histories that they had never been "constrained to abase themselves in activities we may call servile," robe nobles associated themselves with the culture of generosity that mere commoners knew only as "something up in
the clouds."[86]

A member of the *robin* dynasty of Du Faur asserted typically in 1649,

---

84. On the nobility's sense of political independence and their ways of rationalizing
rebellion see Kristen B. Neuschel, *Word of Honor: Interpreting Noble Culture in Sixteenth-
Century France* (Ithaca, N.Y., 1989); and Arlette Jouanna, *Le Devoir de Révolte: La
noblesse française et la gestation de l'Etat moderne, 1559–1661* (Paris, 1989).

85. Florentin de Thierriat, *Trois Traictez* (Paris, 1606), 41–42. Princes are advised "de
faire chois de Gentilshommes, dont la foy & la probité soit cogneuë par les actions prece-
dentes. Car de confier de plein abord, chose de si grand prix à une noblesse originelle sans
autre preuve de vertu & fidelité est un hazard."

86. Chevalier, *Discours des Querelles,* 27.

for example, that his family was "so old that it has always been seen as noble and never as roturier." Moreover, like nobles of the sword, his family turned its back on selfishness and embraced generosity.

> Those of this house have carried generosity to the highest point it can go; not only have they never acquired great dignities with money, but not even through the right of *survivance* . . . believing it better to merit them than to inherit them. . . . Each of us . . . has no obligation for our good fortune except to our own skill and courage. What an admirable generosity to renounce the interests of blood in order to attach oneself only to the interest of virtue![87]

The unquestioned link between personal character and intergenerational habits even gave rise to a novel kind of genealogy in the seventeenth century—the genealogy of an office. In 1645, François Blanchard and Jean-Baptiste l'Hermite de Souliers collaborated to produce *Eulogies of All the First Presidents of the Parlement of Paris,* a work written in praise of every known *premier président* in the annals of the first sovereign court. With brief genealogies of each family involved, the book is designed to glorify at the same time the history of the officers and their families and the history of the office itself. All of the officers seem to have possessed the qualities associated with a noble upbringing. The famous sixteenth-century *président* Achille de Harlay, for example, is noted for his "generosity" and his "immortal courage." But perhaps the best example of the virtues represented by this office were those of the standing *premier président,* Mathieu Molé, whose "ancestors had prepared [his] glorious route for him as much by their great knowledge as by their hereditary virtues and the particular affection they always had for the crown."[88]

The *premiers présidents* were not the only officers to be treated to their own genealogy. Two years later, Blanchard wrote a similarly conceived history touting the merits of all the *présidents au mortier* in the history of the Parisian court. The book, which also included a catalog of all past *conseillers,* outlined the notable distinctions of each individual—their

---

87. Du Faur, *La Généalogie de la maison Du Faur, divisée en trois branches, ou trois chefs de famille* (Toulouse, 1649), 17.

88. François Blanchard and Jean-Baptiste l'Hermite de Souliers, *Les Eloges de tous les premiers présidents du Parlement de Paris depuis qu'il a esté rendu sedentaire jusques à présent, ensemble leurs généalogies, épitaphes, armes et blasons . . .* (Paris, 1645), dedication.

coats of arms and blazons, the positions they had held, their qualities and genealogies, "with several remarks concerning their families."[89] The genealogies served to connect the current presidents with history and with proper values: "I have inserted the genealogies in consideration of the families who have produced men of such high merit, and whose descendants, by their generous actions and the honorable charges that they have well-merited and exercised virtuously, have acquired for themselves immortal praise." Blanchard's language suggests that the *présidents* had won "immortality" in traditional fashion.

> The Parlement of Paris being the first and oldest in the Realm, . . . those who have had the honor to preside over it since its establishment have been chosen for their merits, abilities, and capacities. This is why this sovereign company has always been the breeding ground for many great persons of distinction who, for three centuries, have conserved this state's ancient splendor and maintained its fundamental laws at the peril of their own lives, generously opposing the ambitious designs of foreigners.[90]

The episodes of *robin* bravery recounted in this chapter, as well as the general collections by Souliers and Blanchard, help to reinforce several points important to the argument I am making. First, these texts underscore the obvious but easily neglected fact that the meaning of merit is always embedded in a broad cultural system. In comparison to the warrior nobility, it is true, new nobles of *robe longue* received more praise for their great knowledge and excellence of mind. Moreover, they emphasized the value of education in the *bonnes lettres* and scorned military nobles who reveled in brutishness and ignorance. In their greater attention to the signs of learning, one may even be justified in seeing the makings of a new paradigm for defining and judging merit. Nevertheless, the texts reviewed here indicate that many, and perhaps most, *robins* still understood that the relationship between the king and the men who served him was mediated through a personal modality. In the first half of

---

89. François Blanchard, *Les Présidents au mortier du Parlement de Paris, leurs emplois, charges, qualitez, armes, blasons et généalogies, depuis l'an 1331 jusques à présent: Ensemble un catalogue de tous les conseillers selon l'ordre des temps et de leurs receptions, enrichy du blason de leurs armes et de plusieurs remarques concernans leurs familles* (Paris, 1647), epistle to Séguier.

90. Blanchard, *Les Présidents*, preface.

the seventeenth century, robe nobles sought to display their merits and justify their status, both to themselves and to the readers of their histories, by showing that they too possessed the capacity for generosity and magnanimity important to all professions, that they, like the *noblesse d'épée,* placed their own lives in peril for the service of the king and his state.

The *robins'* habitual and somewhat surprising use of the personal idiom also underlines the importance of studying political and social change through culture. In publishing genealogical histories and emphasizing the past services of their families, *robins* not only signaled their own acceptance of the assumption that family traditions produced the intangible moral qualities central to the king's service; they also laid claim to the privileged position assigned to the old nobility within the personal modality of service. The old nobility was defined, after all, not so much by proofs of antiquity as by its association with a specific set of values, beliefs, images, and practices—an association that people of relatively ambiguous status could also aspire to establish. The *robins'* identification with values most often linked to the old nobility, and their at least partial acceptance of the definition of merit implied by those values, thus illustrates the limitations of analyses that essentialize social groups and their interests. To understand the changing relationship between the king, the nobility, and other groups in society in early-modern France, one needs to focus not on kings or old nobles as such but on the culture in terms of which their respective roles were articulated. Discourse exercises a wide normative power, but it always remains subject to transformation by actors who exploit its potential in new ways. Changing power relations in the seventeenth century should therefore be studied not to gauge their effect on the privileged nobility but rather to gauge their effect on the system of meaning—manifested in the personal modality—that had always privileged nobles and their values.

In closing this chapter, let us return to our original query. What explains the timing of the nobility's rising emphasis on birth and its expressions? It is no doubt true that some nobles were drawn to genealogy because they imagined it showed their innate superiority. But the number of written genealogical histories increased more than sixfold from the sixteenth to the seventeenth centuries. One must look beyond arrogance to find the impulse for such a widespread and seemingly spontaneous shift in sensibility.

Remarks by Chifflet again seem relevant. Assessing the advantages of the recent emphasis on published works, he pointed first to the legal benefits to the families. It was better that they have their records in one place to consult as needed, "without having to recover them from archives and libraries." Chifflet also thought the researching and publication of noble histories proved beneficial in another way. Since "many of these good Houses" had repeatedly served kings in important functions, he wrote, the public would inevitably draw "great utility" from a knowledge of their past.[91]

The latter comment by Chifflet is revealing because it unwittingly evokes a context in which continuity of service could be considered of the greatest utility. Since the distant feudal past, the king had resembled all other nobles in one important respect: his first need was "to win men."[92] In this culture, where the obligations of one person to another could still be envisioned as the basis of public life, the likelihood of personal reliability and mutual commitment took precedence over acquired skills and other ephemera. And since Marc Bloch's first feudal age at least, when the fief became inheritable, lineage had seemed the best guarantee of fidelity and mutual obligation across generations.

As old nobles articulated their vision of the personal modality of service in the first decades of the seventeenth century, they explicitly reaffirmed this implicit connection between lineage and personal merit. They assumed that the king, when looking for the signs of true merit, would ignore learning, law degrees, and money to focus his gaze on brilliant genealogies. He would do this for obvious reasons. Men who came from "noble and illustrious houses" were "honorably elevated and instructed" in their youth. From the moment of birth young nobles absorbed the intangible qualities so basic to the personal service the king required. Evidence of their moral formation shone through in everything they did, so much that "when viewing an accomplished knight, one takes it for granted that he is born to perform well in other honored activities."[93] To use the words of Castiglione, aristocratic upbringing allowed

---

91. Chifflet, *Les Marques d'Honneur*, 1–2.

92. *Histoire de Henry, duc de Rohan* (Paris, 1666), 27. Rohan's biographer noted that in the aftermath of the assassination of Henri IV, the duc was reminded that "the Great must learn above all . . . [how] to win men."

93. Salomon de la Broue, *Le Cavalerice François* (Paris, 1628), 3–4.

the noble to "feed his spectators' eyes with all those things that . . . give him added grace."[94]

It may be no coincidence, then, that the decisive turn toward the increasing use of genealogical history came in the decade of the Estates General (1614), when old nobles simultaneously elaborated their opposition to laws that encouraged commoners to buy royal offices. Genealogical history reinforced a traditional hierarchy of virtues. It placed generous values at the top and explained why nobles held the privileged position at the top of that hierarchy. In writing detailed family histories or having them written, nobles reminded themselves and everyone else who listened that they rendered the king personal service and that the merits most essential to that service came from a culture to which only some families belonged.[95]

That many nobles were aroused to such self-conscious analysis of their identity and their relationship to the monarchy in the early seventeenth century indicates that new circumstances now tested their assumptions. In this chapter we saw that a belief in the importance of elevated birth was an integral part of the traditional personal modality of service and that nobles in the early seventeenth century anxiously restated the connection between lineage and personal merit. In chapter 3 let us examine more closely the subtle changes that had raised the nobility's level of concern.

---

94. Baldesar Castiglione, *The Book of the Courtier*, trans. Charles Singleton (Garden City, N.Y., 1959), 99.

95. Carolyn C. Lougee shows that issues of social stratification also became intertwined with ideas concerning the roles of women in aristocratic society in the seventeenth century. See *"Le Paradis des Femmes": Women, Salons, and Social Stratification in Seventeenth-Century France* (Princeton, 1976).

3

State Formation and the Culture of
Royal Service in the Age of Louis XIII

In France, as elsewhere in Europe, the Wars of Religion that ravaged the country in the second half of the sixteenth century gave rise to feelings of insecurity and pessimism. The constitutional theorist Jean Bodin, for example, once regarded Europe as a naturally harmonious Christian community. By the 1570s, in the wake of the Saint Bartholomew's Day massacre and other atrocities, his perspective had changed. Now the world seemed inherently vicious and unstable, divided among competing groups who pursued narrow interests.[1] Ironically, though, the sense of social disintegration that fueled Bodin's pessimism also engendered a new national consciousness and patriotic awareness in late sixteenth- and early seventeenth-century France.[2] Years of divisive religious conflict had led to a greater appreciation for the advantages of unity and social order.[3] This subtle change in attitude had far-reaching political consequences, not only in France, but throughout Europe. Neostoic thinkers,

---

1. Bodin's transformation is discussed by Lionel Rothkrug, *Opposition to Louis XIV: The Political and Social Origins of the French Enlightenment* (Princeton, 1965), 22–30.

2. See, for example, Myriam Yardeni, *La Conscience Nationale en France Pendant Les Guerres de Religion (1559–1598)* (Paris, 1971). William Church considers the upsurge in "patriotic awareness" during the Wars of Religion in his chapter titled "France" in *National Consciousness, History, and Political Culture in Early-Modern Europe*, ed. Orest Ranum (Baltimore, 1975), 43–66.

3. On the correlation between the search for stability and the growing power of the monarchy in France see Nannerl Keohane, *Philosophy and the State in France: The Renaissance to the Enlightenment* (Princeton, 1980), pt. 2; Quentin Skinner, *The Foundations of Modern Political Thought,* 2 vols. (Cambridge, 1978), vol. 2; William Church, *Constitutional Thought in Sixteenth-Century France* (Cambridge, Mass., 1941); idem, *Richelieu and Reason of State* (Princeton, 1972), chap. 1; J. H. M. Salmon, *Society in Crisis: France in the Sixteenth Century* (London, 1975); Roland Mousnier, *The Assassination of Henry IV: The Tyrannicide Problem and the Consolidation of the French Absolute Monarchy in the Early Seventeenth Century,* trans. Joan Spencer (London, 1973), conclusion; and Mousnier and Fritz Hartung, "Quelques problèmes concernant la monarchie absolue," in *Relazioni del X congresso internazionale de scienze storiche* (Florence, 1955), 1:1–55.

such as Justsus Lipsius, with their emphasis on personal discipline and the need to obey princely authority, found a newly receptive audience among Europe's political classes. "Reason of state," a phrase that appeared in France in the first decade of the seventeenth century, came to be recognized as a guiding principle of government. As Gerhard Oestreich has written, "the ideology of the powerful, centralized state had its origins in the crisis of the religious wars, with all their consequences for the individual and society."[4]

That is not to say that the character of the French monarchy or the distribution of power in French society changed suddenly or dramatically in the decades following the civil wars. On the contrary, many recent studies of political change in the period between the death of Henry IV and the personal rule of Louis XIV have rightly emphasized the enduring partnership between crown and aristocracy and the limits still placed on the authority of kings.[5] Under Louis XIII and Louis XIV the size of the central government remained small. Kings and ministers continued to rely on relatives and networks of personal clients to insure order in the provinces, to raise armies, to procure loans and collect taxes, to bargain with local notables, and to implement policy. After the disturbances of the 1630s and 1640s—disturbances created or made possible for the most part by jurisdictional squabbles—the monarchy restored order mainly by performing its traditional roles more effectively. Louis XIV and his collaborators balanced and served the interests of established elites while creating at Paris and Versailles an exalted image of monarchy that stirred aristocratic pride and reaffirmed conservative values.[6]

This revisionist account of the development of absolute monarchy in France, now widely accepted, has much to recommend it. Its emphasis on the vitality of the hereditary aristocracy, and on the monarchy's continued responsiveness to traditional values and interests, neutralizes older tendencies to exaggerate the power of the absolutist state and to anticipate too quickly the state's detachment from the society in which it was embedded. In this chapter and the next, however, I intend to supplement the revisionist account of seventeenth-century absolutism by reassessing the relations between crown and nobility from a somewhat different

---

4. Gerhard Oestreich, *Neostoicism and the Early Modern State,* trans. David McLintock (Cambridge, 1982), 70.

5. For references to the major works in this tradition, see the introduction.

6. For the most complete and persuasive statement of this argument see William Beik, *Absolutism and Society in Seventeenth-Century France: State Power and Provincial Aristocracy in Languedoc* (Cambridge, 1985).

angle. Analysis of the evolution in perceptions of merit over the course of the century certainly confirms revisionist assumptions about the vitality of the noblesse and royal responsiveness to aristocratic needs and tastes. But contemporary discussions about the meaning of merit also cast a revealing light on some of the more novel features of the political landscape in the age of absolutism. Specifically, the informal and largely unconscious negotiations about the meaning of merit in this period reflect new perceptions about the nature of monarchical power and the nobility's need to meet the cultural challenge represented by those new perceptions.

The emergence of reason of state and the growing emphasis on the absolute power of monarchs following the Wars of Religion indicated a new tendency to conceive of royal government and society in dichotomous terms.[7] When set in a wide chronological context, this new desire to make the powers of government commensurate to society's capacity for disorder sets apart the centralizing impulses of the seventeenth century from all earlier efforts of monarchical centralization, stretching back to the fourteenth century. Few immediately perceived the implications of this subtle change in political thinking, but over the course of the seventeenth century it gradually became possible for all subjects of the monarchy to regard the state as an objective administrative entity responsible for maintaining and regulating the social body.

This new reality entailed a whole set of adjustments to the conceptual world that framed the nobility's thoughts, motives, and self-perception. The king, as the crowning figure in a hierarchy of authorities extending to the remotest locality, still served as the center of gravity in the French political universe. But changes in the idea of merit indicate that the growing prominence of the state as a point of reference in political thought and action posed new problems for the relationship between king and nobility. By shaping and explaining crown policies always by reference to abstractions—reason of state, the interests of the state, considerations of state—Louis XIII and his councillors indirectly raised questions about

---

7. Nannerl Keohane describes the "dichotomous temper" of the age in her analysis of seventeenth-century political and moral philosophy. The relationship between the "private" individual and the exercise of "public" power now became the central preoccupation of moralists and theoreticians of sovereignty: "Frenchmen during these decades worked out two moralities: one for political behavior, the other for the individual." See Keohane, *Philosophy and the State in France*, 124, 119. The most thorough intellectual history of reason of state in the age of Richelieu remains Etienne Thuau, *Raison d'Etat et Pensée Politique à l'Epoque de Richelieu* (Paris, 1966).

the nature of the gaze that assessed service, judged merit, and assigned or affirmed social status. The expressions of anxiety emanating from the apologists of old nobility in the first half of the seventeenth century suggest that cultural dislocation contributed to the climate of apprehension and mistrust that marred the ministerial regimes of Richelieu and Mazarin. This climate of mistrust only gave way to a spirit of cooperation during the personal rule of Louis XIV, when the Sun King established a mutually acceptable cultural basis for the evolution of the French monarchy.

Reason of State and the Old Nobility

That the inclination to establish a new rationale for political order also involved new ways of imagining the social order is evident in two treatises on government published in the first decade of Louis XIII's reign, Louis Turquet de Mayerne's *La Monarchie Aristodemocratique* (Aristodemocratical monarchy) and Antoine de Montchrétien's *Traicté de l'Oeconomie Politique* (Treatise on political economy).[8] Neither writer can be seen as a theorist of "statebuilding"; indeed, when the word *state* appears in their texts it refers in the customary way to the king's realm, the "société humaine" placed under the king's governance.[9] Nevertheless, both writers urged monarchs to act more self-consciously as the guarantors of the public weal. What is most interesting is that their advice literally required a change in the king's point of view as much as a change in policy, for government and society now appeared as distinct entities. In bringing the government's role into sharper focus for society, Montchrétien and Turquet de Mayerne simultaneously showed the king a society defined by its available resources.

No doubt reflecting the widespread disillusionment brought by the Wars of Religion, Montchrétien argued that social and economic policies—what he precociously termed "political economy"—must be removed from the shadow of religion. None could deny that the "contemplative life" brought the individual closer to God. But he pointed out that if people ignored the duties of "the civil occupations" in favor of contemplation, "the republic would necessarily collapse in ruins." He

---

8. Louis Turquet de Mayerne, *La Monarchie Aristodemocratique* (Paris, 1611); Antoine de Montchrétien, *Traicté de l'Oeconomie Politique, dedié en 1615 au Roy et a la Reyne Mere du Roy,* ed. Th. Funck-Brentano (Paris, 1889).

9. The phrase is Turquet de Mayerne's (*La Monarchie*, 16).

urged Louis XIII to keep in mind this distinction between religious and civic duties: "Remember always that the church exists within the state, and not the other way around; that the church derives its wealth and splendor from you, after God; that only through you can the church maintain its position."[10]

"Good political administration" insured the health of "the entire body of the state." To Montchrétien this implied that the king, in monitoring the well-being of his people, must extend his field of vision to assess the value of "each individual member" of the realm: "It is important to consider the basest individuals as well as the most noble, the obscure in addition to the well known. . . .This serious consideration should induce Your Majesty to study diligently the common classes of your state."[11] The king should study all his subjects with one question in mind: In what specific ways do they contribute to the general welfare? "The riches of a state," according to Montchrétien, "consist not only in its size or the number of its people but also in leaving none of its lands uncleared, in judiciously assigning each person to his proper function."[12]

Montchrétien informed Louis XIII and the queen regent that simply by strolling through the streets of Paris they could see that France possessed all the human resources it needed—distinguished thinkers and writers, artisans of all types in great number, merchants trading every article imaginable. Montchrétien lamented, "You lack only one thing, O great state: knowledge of yourself and the full use of your strengths!"[13] The king therefore had to direct his attention to people who usually escaped royal notice: those who provided the necessities of life. It made sense, for example, for the king to establish workshops devoted to the production of popular items. These shops could be supervised by specialized craftsmen chosen by the king, "so that they may distribute tasks and labors among the artisans according to their capacity and potential." By showing attention and affection for the mechanical arts, the king would infuse them with honor and thus increase their vigor. Montchrétien exhorted the king and his mother to "show favor to capable men, extend your hands to pull them from the crowd that restricts and hides them," for in doing so they would "uncover a thousand sources of profit, overflowing with glory and utility."[14]

---

10. Montchrétien, *Traicté*, 21, 341.
11. Ibid., 18.
12. Ibid., 31.
13. Ibid., 34.
14. Ibid., 38, 35.

Like Montchrétien, Louis Turquet de Mayerne wrote his piece in response to the horrors of internecine religious conflict.[15] The "ruins of my own homeland and the miseries of neighboring provinces" drove him to explore "in writing" the means of repairing the damage. His work, he explained, was "born of the dissatisfactions, the disobedience toward magistrates, the rebellions against kings" that had marked his era.[16] The religious conflicts of the day had conveyed the lesson

> that according to God and Nature, everything must be directed to its true purpose and applied to its true and natural usage; that that which is secular must be managed by secular men, and that matters concerning religion must be left to the true ministers of religion. . . . In short, everything must be reformed.[17]

The needs of the "natural" world must be considered separately from matters of religious conscience, and for Turquet de Mayerne this meant that the organization of both government and the social order should be viewed with one concern in mind: "the utility . . . common to all of society."[18] The imperative to social utility required, on the one hand, that the government be knowledgeable about the society it managed and, on the other hand, that the social hierarchy reflect the various ways of contributing to the common good. To enhance his ability to govern, the king should give supervisory powers to central bureaus specializing in justice, finance, the military, and police. Local agents, called rectors, would represent the separate bureaus in the provinces. The rectors of the bureau of police, in addition to establishing sub-bureaus for charity, commerce, and the management of the king's domains, would also record the vocational identities of local citizens. All young men, after having been schooled in "letters, piety, military discipline" and their "duties toward the public," would be required to note their professional intentions on a roster compiled by the rector. Those who failed to have their names

---

15. According to Roland Mousnier, Turquet de Mayerne, who was Protestant, wrote the treatise in 1591—seven years before the Edict of Nantes. See Mousnier, "L'Opposition Politique Bourgeoise à la fin du XVIᵉ siècle et au Début du XVIIᵉ siècle: L'Oeuvre de Louis Turquet de Mayerne," *Revue Historique* 213 (1955): 1–20.

16. Turquet de Mayerne, *La Monarchie,* 30–31.

17. Ibid., 34.

18. Ibid., 22.

inscribed in the register by age twenty-five "would not be included in the ranks of citizens."[19]

To be denied the rank of citizen would be a serious penalty indeed, because Turquet de Mayerne made citizenship the basic prerequisite to honor and prestige. He envisioned five classes of citizens: the rich (a distinct category because they could afford any expenditures the public required of them), men of letters, businesspeople and wholesale merchants, artisans, and laborers. Citizens of any class who behaved virtuously and excelled in their private vocations became eligible for public functions and noble status. Nobility stood as a reward "for good behavior by an individual in his own class and his private business, in which he has given evidence of prudence, magnanimity, justice, and loyalty, all the things that may induce magistrates and farsighted princes to raise a man to office and public honors."[20] Noble status, conferred automatically by the highest public offices and honors, mainly signaled one's entrance into public life. In fact, the distinction between noble and common "has meaning in public" only. The noble enjoyed a hereditary mark of honor, but in private life his identity still derived from the class to which he belonged.[21]

Both Montchrétien and Turquet de Mayerne addressed the challenge of re-creating civil order by activating governmental authority and implicitly redefining utility, service, and merit. To protect the interests of the entire body of the state, the king must establish an efficient and comprehensive political administration. He should broaden his perspective and acquire knowledge of each individual member of his realm. To make full use of his people's strengths, he had to "uncover a thousand sources . . . of utility." This implied looking beyond the nobility, honoring all vocations, and, especially for Turquet de Mayerne, recognizing that all subjects had a potential for utility in the royal service. Indeed, Turquet de Mayerne made it clear that "nobility" should be seen not as a qualifying mark of social status but only as a reward awaiting those who crossed the line from private life to public service.

To view these ideas from the most illuminating angle, one needs to set them against the traditional image of the political and social order as expressed by the old nobility. By suggesting that the word *noble* be used

---

19. Ibid., 22.
20. Ibid., 131.
21. Ibid., 120.

solely to designate those who had entered the circles of government, Turquet de Mayerne dissolved the link between one's socially defined moral status and one's suitability for governing, an idea that would have seemed strange to the traditional nobility. Nobles served the monarchy by serving the person of the king, and this made it impossible for them to disentangle the personal from the public aspects of royal service. To merit placement in the king's service one had to exhibit generosity, loyalty, and other qualities valued in personal relations, and the nobility knew that social conditioning formed and reinforced these characteristics. Nobles enjoyed their privileged rank in society not simply because their political leadership could be taken for granted but also because they were expected to approach social relations in a particular way—from a generous and selfless perspective. The dual aspect of noble status explains why Florentin de Thierriat advised the prince that he "must always have personal contact with the nobility" and that he should also "employ them in his service in preference to others."[22] To nobles who viewed government service as another form of private relationship, the idea that nobility should have no meaning in private society would have been difficult to understand.

For similar reasons, most nobles would have been unfamiliar with the concept of utility implicit in the works by Montchrétien and Turquet de Mayerne. They would have had no trouble recognizing the word *utility* itself. As Claude de Marois explained in 1645, society had long ago been divided into three estates to insure the common good, "as it is true that the noble man was separated from the common people for the public utility."[23] But the interests of the realm were embodied in the person of the king, who could not be expected to see a difference between personal and utilitarian considerations. Nobles thus accentuated the personal aspects of the service they rendered, even when they had public utility clearly in mind.

At the Estates General, for example, nobles had asked the king to establish *collèges militaires* in each province to improve the skills of young nobles in all areas essential to the military career.[24] They unani-

---

22. Florentin de Thierriat, *Trois Traictez* (Paris, 1606), 66. "Le Prince doit toujours approcher la Noblesse de sa personne & s'en servir plustost que des autres."

23. Claude de Marois, *Le Gentilhomme Parfaict ou tableau des excellences de la vraye noblesse: Avec l'institution des jeunes gentilshommes à la vertu* (Paris, 1631), 538–39.

24. Deputies from Orléans suggested that "for the instruction of the poor nobility, there be established an academy in the Capital city of each province, where, from the age of eight

mously called on the king to "give the nobility the means to serve Your Majesty" by resuscitating his "ordinance companies," a traditional unit of military service now fallen into disuse.[25] But nobles also took seriously the prospect of serving the king as domestic officers. Noble deputies from Île-de-France reminded Louis XIII that "to manage your household . . . is the most excellent and worthy occupation the nobility can hope for."[26] As noble representatives from Champagne put it, those with "a generous soul" clamored for such "honorary recompenses"; and to supply "enough offices for those who want to merit them," the king should "reestablish the *gentilshommes de la chambre* [gentlemen of the king's bedchamber] and reduce their number to the level of the time of Henri III . . . allowing a number of the nobility to participate in the honor of approaching your person, which is so dear to them."[27] Nobles from Guyenne requested the same, "so that lords and *gentilshommes* of dignified upbringing who are without offices . . . can be gratified by following the court and serving Your Majesty by rank and order."[28]

Turquet de Mayerne and Montchrétien, by contrast, offered a vision of utility rooted in private vocation rather than moral identity. The king who stepped back to enlarge his view of the realm would assess his subjects not from a personal perspective but from the point of view of the entire body of the state. Specialized bureaus, shop supervisors, and local rectors would all help the king evaluate citizens, pull them from the crowd, and assign each person to his proper function. To find candidates for government positions and honors, the king would look for men with evident skills, developed and perfected in private life. The king might still admire a generous soul, but demonstrated excellence in a particular field, rather than one's willingness to serve the person of the king, now became the real measure of utility. In fact, Turquet de Mayerne would have the king reduce the size of the court and change its character to reflect the

---

to sixteen, *gentilshommes* could be instructed free of charge in the knowledge of *bonnes lettres* as well as in the exercises worthy of their birth." See Charles Mayer, ed., *Des Etats-Généraux et autres Assemblées Nationales,* 18 vols. (Paris, 1788–89), 18:308.

25. Bibliothèque de l'Arsenal (hereafter BA), MS 4485, "Cahiers particuliers de la noblesse (des 3 Etats) de diverses provinces de ce royaume, pour estre représentez en l'Assemblée des Etats généraux tenus à Paris" ("Île de France"), fol. 6r.

26. BA, MS 4485, "Cahiers particuliers . . . Île de France," fol. 5v.

27. BA, MS 4485, "Cahiers particuliers . . . Champagne et Brie," fol. 164v. The king was asked to "reduce" the number of *gentilshommes de la chambre* to its traditional level because many such posts had recently been created and promptly sold, thus degrading the honor of the office.

28. BA, MS 4485, "Cahiers particuliers . . . Guyenne," fol. 92r.

new thinking. He conceded that the officers of the king's household should be maintained because they added luster to the monarchy, but "men of leisure" had to be "discharged" promptly. The nobles who "take so much pleasure in coming to see the king and pay their respects," unless they needed also to attend to some "special and urgent affair," must be "sent away immediately." In doing this the king would help nobles become accustomed to "stay in their homes," avoid "superfluous expenses," and practice "moderation."[29]

Montchrétien and Turquet de Mayerne had no direct influence on the practitioners of royal government, and they certainly did not provide a script to be used by the proponents of absolute monarchy. Although Louis XIII and Richelieu proved willing to battle their coreligionists to raise France's political stature in Europe, a sense of religious purpose still motivated their policies, and the pointedly secular tone of these two treatises undoubtedly would have offended them.[30] Moreover, Turquet de Mayerne stressed the consultative aspects of his bureaucratic scheme of government, and French kings in the seventeenth century willfully broke with the monarchy's consultative traditions.[31]

Nevertheless, the works by Montchrétien and Turquet de Mayerne are useful because they show, through their discussion of the social reconfiguration implied by the creation of a supervisory governmental authority, why the process of state formation involved more rethinking than "building." To keep in view the entire body of the state and maintain order *for* society, the monarchy had to have the authority and the critical distance to act *on* society. This meant that royal power, and all the mechanisms through which king and society interacted, had to be reconceptualized. To evoke the image of a sovereign power as vast as the realm itself, the king had to articulate his authority through a vocabulary that transcended the context of immediate social relationships. In other words, his powers had to be understood as more than merely personal.

An obscure manuscript from the middle of the seventeenth century offers a revealing glimpse of this process of rethinking and restating the nature of the prince's power. In this brief tract, titled simply "Offices,

29. Turquet de Mayerne, *La Monarchie*, 459–60.

30. William Church has stressed the religious underpinnings of Richelieu's application of reason of state. See *Richelieu and Reason of State*, 86–88, 126–34.

31. See James Russell Major, *Representative Government in Early Modern France* (New Haven, 1980); and idem, *From Renaissance Monarchy to Absolute Monarchy: French Kings, Nobles, and Estates* (Baltimore, 1994), esp. chaps. 7–9.

Jurisdictions, Charges,"[32] the anonymous author went beyond the predictable elaboration of royal prerogatives and responsibilities so typical
of the "Mirror of Princes" genre. He attempted to fuse the identities of
the king and the state that possessed some of the attributes of government itself. Perhaps reflecting the influence of the advancing mechanical
philosophy, the author envisioned this state as a great machine.

> The state is an immobile entity regulated through the command of the
> sovereign and the obedience of subjects. Counsel, strength, and repu-
> tation are the foundations of the state, the three principal points on
> which the entire machine of the state rests; the same three points are
> the essential qualities that form the prince.

The state's reputation depended entirely on the quality of the prince's
counsel and forces. The author deemed counsel especially important, and
he defined it as follows: "Counsel, in this connection, is the light of reason that discovers for the prince the instruments of domination. . . .
These Instruments provide the intelligence [*entendement*] necessary to
penetrate and know perfectly the nature of subjects." The king and/or
state needed to be supplied with knowledge of all things.

The author then listed a set of attributes to be included among the
prince's "instruments of domination":

Prudence in order to give [the people] appropriate laws.
Ordinances to regulate the military.
Art, for conducting war.
Industry to maintain peace.
Vigilance to watch over and attend to any and all unexpected events.
Form to extend and expand the principality.
Judgment for balancing the estates.
Dexterity for temporizing in times of difficulty.
Maturity for deliberating.
Promptitude in executing.
Confidence in things that have been resolved.
Force against adversities.
Moderation in prosperity.

---

32. Archives Nationales (hereafter AN), KK 1454, no. 3. "Offices, Jurisdictions,
Charges." The manuscript is undated but is included in a *liasse* of documents dating from
the 1640s and 1650s. It clearly dates from midcentury.

Such assured *Knowledge* of things divine that superstition will not
render him/it fearful and license does not lead to his/its fall.

The nature of these characteristics makes it unclear what the author actually meant by the word *state*. Did it represent the realm being governed
(form, industry), the instruments of government (ordinances, art, force),
or the full human potential of a capable king (vigilance, judgment, maturity)? The ambiguity may be deliberate, because it serves the central purpose of diverting attention from the king's mere humanity. A prince is a
man, but he also resembles a "machine," an "immobile entity" whose
various instruments of "intelligence" allow him to "know perfectly" the
nature of his subjects. Here the king is made to resemble Hobbes'
Leviathan, "an Artificiall Man."[33]

The idea that the king possessed a double identity, that he occupied a
public persona separate and distinct from his own person, had informed
political theory since the Middle Ages. But the theory of the king's "two
bodies" had originally been created to separate kingly office from individual kings and therefore to insure the integrity and continuity of sovereign authority.[34] The seventeenth century introduced a new understanding of the king's two bodies. For some at least, the need to create a good
political administration serving the common utility of all the realm meant
that royal government had to expand beyond its customary social moor-
ings and that, furthermore, the king's perspective on such notions as service, merit, utility, and nobility must change accordingly. Turquet de
Mayerne's devaluation of those who lived "to see the king" and be seen
by him was by no means incidental to his sweeping plan for reform. He
and others were now inclined to describe as suprapersonal not merely the
vessel in which sovereign authority was theoretically contained but the
operation of sovereign authority itself. In France the origins of an administrative state distinct both from the monarch and from the subjects he
governed can be traced to these early attempts to articulate the other-
than-personal operation of royal power.[35]

---

33. Thomas Hobbes, *Leviathan* (London and New York, 1973), 1.

34. The classic work on the dual identity of the king is of course Ernst Kantorovicz, *The
King's Two Bodies: A Study in Mediaeval Political Theology* (Princeton, 1957). For the
French applications of the theory see Ralph E. Giesey, *The Royal Funeral Ceremony in
Renaissance France* (Geneva, 1960); and Sarah Hanley, *The "Lit de Justice" of the Kings of
France: Constitutional Ideology in Legend, Ritual, and Discourse* (Princeton, 1983).

35. A concern to recast the nature of sovereignty by redefining the state as a mechani-
cally efficient instrument of power was common to many jurists and political theorists of

The changing conception of monarchical power in the seventeenth century is revealed perhaps most tellingly in Richelieu's *Political Testament*, a document maligned and too often dismissed as self-serving and misleading. The first minister composed his political reflections late in life, and they retrospectively impose philosophical coherence on a career marked by pragmatism, flexibility, and chance.[36] But the *Political Testament* deserves scrutiny because it reflects Richelieu's own understanding of monarchy and its role in society, an understanding that paralleled in interesting ways those of Montchrétien, Turquet de Mayerne, and the anonymous author of the previously cited tract "Offices, Jurisdictions, Charges." "The public interest ought to be the sole objective of the prince and his councillors," Richelieu solemnly declared. Those who pursue "the public interest" inevitably act in ways "most advantageous to the state," in contrast to those who would twist the policies of government "to make them privately more agreeable or advantageous."[37] Like Montchrétien, Richelieu indicated that the king who pursues the public interest must take a broad and dispassionate view of things; he "ought to make reason sovereign" and insure, for example, "that each public servant is charged only with those functions for which he is suited."[38]

Richelieu's ways of translating into action this widely expressed concern for public interest make him as fascinating as he is important to the historian of politics. As an officer of the church, and as an expert in canon law, Richelieu recognized as well as anyone the importance of the distinction between individuals and the authority vested in their offices. To understand the motives behind Richelieu's policies and administrative techniques, as well as the confusion and animosity to which they gave rise, one does well to keep in mind the cardinal's new application of the theory of office to the practice of kingship. By his lights the concept of royal office provided a whole new strategy for expressing the relationship

---

the day. As André Stegmann notes: "More than an image of the Prince, it was the animated machine of State that jurists [now] described." See Stegmann, "Les Juristes et le Prince (1610–1640)," in *L'Image du Souverain dans les Lettres Françaises des Guerres de Religion à la Révocation de l'Edit de Nantes,* Actes et Colloques, vol. 24 (Paris, 1985), 153–68.

36. Among the many recent biographical treatments of Richelieu, the cardinal's pragmatic tendencies are explored most perceptively in Joseph Bergin, *The Rise of Richelieu* (New Haven, 1991). Also see Michel Carmona's popular but thorough *Richelieu: L'Ambition et le Pouvoir* (Paris, 1983).

37. Richelieu, *Testament Politique,* ed. Louis André (Paris, 1947), 330–31.

38. Ibid., 325, 357.

between the king and his subjects, a strategy that better reflected the priorities of the public interest.[39]

Richelieu aimed to restore "the dignity of the royal majesty" by persuading Louis XIII to fulfill "the duties of his office."[40] Kings have to do "many more things as sovereigns than they would have to do as private individuals," and Louis XIII therefore needed to learn his role as a "public person."[41] To act on reason of state the king must consciously transcend the customary frame of reference provided by the context of personal relations. The prince needed to announce through all of his actions "that he rewards those who are most useful to the public."

> There is this difference between the *graces* that are given in recognition of services and those that have no foundation other than the pure favor of kings: that the latter must be greatly moderated while the others should have no bounds other than the very services rendered to the public.

Conduct must be judged only by its effects on the public good, and the assignment of both rewards and punishments should reflect that same consideration: "[Even if] conscience might allow that we leave a signal action uncompensated or a notable crime unchastized, reason of state cannot permit it. Punishment and reward look more to the future than to the past." Kings therefore should no longer permit themselves "to overlook a misdeed [only] because he who has committed it has performed a notable service at some earlier time."[42]

"Private consideration . . . should never influence public affairs,"[43] and Richelieu was prepared to defend venality of office precisely on those grounds. By the 1620s the financial necessity of venality had become clear to all, but Richelieu also saw other advantages to the practice. Although he conceded that "the suppression of venality and of hereditary office conforms to reason," he cited the dangers implicit in requiring the king to choose all his officers personally: "Would there not . . . be

---

39. For discussions of the experiences that shaped Richelieu's political outlook see Church, *Richelieu and Reason of State,* 81–101; and Orest Ranum, "Richelieu and the Great Nobility: Some Aspects of Early Modern Political Motives," *French Historical Studies* 3 (1963–64): 184–204.

40. Richelieu, *Testament Politique,* 94, 452.

41. Ibid., 451, 454.

42. Ibid., 345–46.

43. Ibid., 332–33.

inevitable abuses committed in the distribution of functions so dependent on the simple will of kings? They would depend consequently on the favor and the artifice of those who would find themselves in a powerful position near the kings." "It is impossible to know," he claimed, "that in such a case the artifices of court would not be worth more than reason, and favor more than merit."[44]

The novelty of Richelieu's perspective is shown neither by his insistence that the crown recognize merit and grant rewards according to reason nor even by his constant invocation of the public interest; on these matters he spoke a language shared by all. What commands attention is Richelieu's denigration of the "simple will of kings." Richelieu's strict dichotomy between favor and merit reflected the division of the king into two persons, private and public, and the cardinal seemed to envision the complete subordination of the king's private self. Not unlike the "immobile entity" described earlier in this chapter, the efficient king remained above all emotional entanglements: "If it is true that reason ought to be the torch that lights the conduct of both princes and their states, it is also true that there is nothing in nature less compatible with reason than emotion."[45] This meant that princes must set aside "distracting interests, pity and compassion, favoritism, and importunities of all kinds" to "ignore private consideration."[46] The king, that is, must always look beyond his own "simple will."

The new relevance of this principle helps explain the aggressive policy of Louis XIII and Richelieu toward the noble custom of dueling, a policy put to the test by a cause célèbre involving a prominent noble family.[47] After fighting a duel on the Place Royale in flagrant violation of the famous edict against dueling issued just months before (in February 1626), the comte de Bouteville was condemned to death by *parlement* and executed in June 1627. Many nobles considered the arrest of this nephew of the duc de Montmorency an assault on their values, and they besieged the king with pleas for clemency to the day of execution. The king's own cousin, the prince de Condé, begged the king to have mercy on Bouteville and his second, Des Chapelles, for they had simply fallen

---

44. Ibid., 233.
45. Ibid., 326.
46. Ibid., 332.
47. As Richard Herr pointed out years ago, however, Richelieu and Louis XIII were in fact personally ambivalent about noble dueling and were thus inconsistent in their struggle against the practice. See "Honor versus Absolutism: Richelieu's Fight against Dueling," *Journal of Modern History* 27 (1955): 281–85.

error to "the custom of our realm, which makes honor consist of perilous actions." Bouteville thought to impress the king, not disobey him; he had been moved only "by a desire for glory."[48]

But the government, Richelieu later explained, could not afford to be impressed by such selfless demonstrations. Empathy and compassion, "although tolerable in a private individual," were weaknesses in a king.[49] "The valor, and the misfortune, of these young *gentilshommes* touched the hearts of everyone" and inspired a "universal compassion" that the cardinal himself privately shared. But when he considered the amount of noble blood lost over the years by the dangerous custom of dueling, Richelieu found "the force to resist" his heart and "to strengthen the king's resolve to do for the utility of his state what was so counter to everyone's feelings and against my own sentiments."[50] Although displays of courage appealed to the sentiments of both the king and cardinal, reason of state demanded an objective judgment and a carefully measured punishment.[51]

At court Richelieu's emphasis on the office of king and the unerring rationality of royal policy found expression in two ways. In his own behavior toward the king and also in the printed propaganda he sponsored, Richelieu stressed the majesty and mystery of kingship and sought to erase from the popular imagination any distinction between the royal person and the policies that expressed the royal will.[52] At the same time,

---

48. Letter from Condé to Louis XIII, as cited in Jean-Marie Constant, *Les Conjurateurs: Le premier libéralisme politique sous Richelieu* (Paris, 1987), 47.

49. Richelieu, *Testament Politique,* 276.

50. Ibid., 102–3.

51. Dueling continued to thrive at least into the 1650s. As Avenel explains, the final decline of the duel in the second half of the seventeenth century owed less to "l'action du gouvernement" than to a "changement de moeurs." See his discussion in *La Noblesse Française sous Richelieu* (Paris, 1901), 261–81. Avenel's line of interpretation is elaborated effectively by François Billacois, *The Duel: Its Rise and Fall in Early-Modern France,* trans. and ed. Trista Selous (New Haven, 1990).

52. On Richelieu's clever manipulation of ceremonial and etiquette see Orest Ranum, "Courtesy, Absolutism, and the Rise of the French State," *Journal of Modern History* 52 (1980): 426–51. For his use of printed propaganda see Sawyer, *Printed Poison: Pamphlet Propaganda, Faction Politics, and the Public Sphere in Early Seventeenth-Century France* (Berkeley, 1990); Howard Solomon, *Public Welfare, Science, and Propaganda in Seventeenth-Century France: The Innovations of Théophraste Renaudot* (Princeton, 1972): Gustave Fagniez, "L'Opinion publique et la presse politique sous Louis XIII, 1624–1626," *Revue d'Histoire Diplomatique* 14 (1900): 352–401; and idem, "Fancan et Richelieu," pts. 1 and 2, *Revue Historique* 107 (1911): 59–78; 108 (1911): 75–87. On Richelieu's efforts to emphasize the king's unique mental capacities and the power of his divinely inspired will see

the cardinal aimed to establish a clear distinction between decision making and the formulation of royal policy, on the one hand, and the king's
customary familiarity with the nobility, on the other hand. Richelieu considered himself a friend of the old nobility, but he was much troubled by
their ancient habit—most pronounced among the great nobles—of associating the king's personal favor with the granting of honors, titles, and
positions of authority.[53] Consequently he made the king less accessible to
people who had always been accustomed to equate royal favor with
power. More often the great nobles were made responsible for keeping
order and forestalling rebellion in the provinces in their own estates or as
provincial governors. Their presence at court seemed to be less frequently
demanded. Although they maintained their honorific titles as *conseillers
du roi*, Richelieu saw that the king rarely invited them to his council. Just
as important symbolically, the king's customary hunting expeditions
became less inclusive, and nobles therefore lost one of their cherished
opportunities for social contact with the monarch.[54]

These modifications to royal and aristocratic custom provide no more
than a partial view of government under Louis XIII and Richelieu, and
the innovative character of the ministerial regime perhaps should not be
exaggerated. After all, in practice Richelieu managed to exert his own
authority and that of the king by carefully cultivating his own network of
clients, or *créatures,* whose personal loyalty he rewarded handsomely.[55]
Nobles and others clearly had opportunities to form satisfying and
rewarding personal bonds with the leading figures at court. Moreover,
relatively few nobles found Richelieu's regime so offensive that it moved

Church, *Richelieu and Reason of State,* 134–37, 242–44, 270–73, 380–82; and Nannerl
Keohane's discussion of Richelieu in *Philosophy and the State in France,* 174–76.

53. Richelieu considered the nobility "one of the principal nerves of the state" (*Testament Politique,* 218), and he repeatedly expressed sympathy for the concerns of nobles
throughout his career. He took special interest in the education of the nobility. In 1636 he
endowed twenty scholarships for poor nobles at a Parisian riding academy, and as Mark
Motley points out, Richelieu also had plans to establish a grand school for nobles who pursued military and ecclesiastical careers. He succeeded only in founding a small academy for
this purpose in the town of Richelieu. See Motley, *Becoming a French Aristocrat: The Education of the Court Nobility, 1580–1715* (Princeton, 1990), 131–32. Richelieu's natural
affinity for the corps of old nobility is explored in Ranum, "Richelieu and the Great Nobility."

54. These changes are discussed in Ranum, "Richelieu and the Great Nobility,"
200–201.

55. On Richelieu's administrative techniques see Orest Ranum, *Richelieu and the Councillors of Louis XIII: A Study of the Secretaries of State and Superintendents of Finance in
the Ministry of Richelieu, 1635–1642* (Oxford, 1963).

them to conspiracy and rebellion. Richelieu's fiercest and most unforgiving noble opponents were the *grands* who resented their exclusion from the royal council.[56] The various conspiracies of the king's brother Gaston d'Orléans, and the attempt by the cabal of "Importants" to secure control of the regent's council after the cardinal's death, suggest that Richelieu's enemies at court resisted the first minister's policies mainly to contest his growing power and to protect their own interests.

There are many indications, however, that Richelieu's own personal success and his apparent domination of Louis XIII also raised more nebulous concerns about the direction of political change in France.[57] The cardinal's aggressive anti-Habsburg foreign policy created general controversy. And his efforts to keep the king physically beyond the reach of the nobles who customarily attended court, to envelop the king within an aura of majesty, and to offer a complicated rationale for decisions of policy seem to have tainted many nobles' perceptions of the social and political developments of the times. Louis XIII, remote and mistrustful by nature, did little to counteract the widespread impression that Richelieu usurped and misused royal authority for personal gain.[58]

The impression of enforced royal isolation made it easy for nobles to blame all disappointments on the cardinal's duplicity. The often quoted sieur de Pontis, for example, expressed frustration but not surprise when the king, after a long delay, finally recognized Pontis's services with a promotion to a captaincy in the guards.

---

56. The opposition of the great nobles to the policies of Richelieu has been well documented. The most recent examination of great noble conspiracies is Jean-Marie Constant, *Les Conjurateurs.* Also see, for example, Georges Pagès, "Autour du grand orage: Richelieu et Marillac, deux politiques," *Revue Historique* 179 (1937): 63–97; Georges Dethan, *Gaston d'Orleans: Conspirateur et prince charmant* (Paris, 1959); and Michel Carmona's *Richelieu.* Arlette Jouanna, in *Le Devoir de Révolte: La noblesse française et la gestation de l'Etat moderne (1559–1661)* (Paris, 1989), examines the long tradition of noble revolt in the sixteenth and seventeenth centuries.

57. Joseph Bergin has revealed the degree to which Richelieu used his position to enrich himself, his family, and his clients. See *Cardinal Richelieu: Power and the Pursuit of Wealth* (New Haven, 1985).

58. A. Lloyd Moote argues persuasively, in his biography of the king, that the aggressive policies of the 1620s and 1630s reflected Louis XIII's own will and intentions. Nevertheless, Louis's habitual silence created the perception that the cardinal was responsible for all unpopular measures. As Moote notes, "Louis was normally reticent to say anything." See *Louis XIII, The Just* (Berkeley, 1989), 3. Also see Moote's chap. 8, "Partnership of King and Cardinal."

> It seems that after the long service I had tried to render to the king, I might have hoped to receive the same recompense earlier. . . . [Others] less faithful than I . . . were building considerable fortunes; and for me . . . the inviolable attachment I had displayed all my life . . . toward the service of the king, quite far from procuring me any advantage, was on the contrary an obstacle.

Pontis did not wish to appear ungrateful for that portion of the king's bounty that he had received: "I say this not to complain . . . but to deplore the condition of a prince who . . . had less power to reward those whom he considered his most faithful servants than his minister had to increase the fortunes of his own."[59] How could the king be expected to prevent these injustices? When Louis XIII wanted to talk privately with his faithful nobles, Pontis charged, he had to do it in secret, out of sight of the jealous cardinal.[60]

Pontis's words evoke the colorful images of a Dumas novel, but they nevertheless represent a real, and common, noble response to the changes introduced by Richelieu. The king's seclusion confused and angered many. Writing his memoirs in the 1630s, the marquis de Beauvais-Nangis warned his son of the obstacles now preventing ready access to the king. He remembered that troubles had begun to appear as early as 1618. Named to the Ordre du Saint Esprit in that year, he was required to go through the formality of having the king personally inscribe his name onto the rolls of the order. Unable to arrange a meeting with the king himself, he had to make three separate trips to court to remind the *greffier des ordres du roi* to see that the king finally listed him among the knights of the Saint Esprit. Beauvais-Nangis pointed to his experience as evidence of the king's increasing isolation. He informed his son that, although the king wanted to gratify his *gentilshommes,* others at court frequently avoided executing his wishes. Furthermore, in an unmasked allusion to the influence of Richelieu, he warned that "you will perhaps experience more problems than I, because these days the difficulties are much greater than when I was at court."[61]

Fontenay-Mareuil, in his memoirs, also presented the king's detachment as a sad break with tradition. He fondly remembered "the old cus-

59. Pontis, *Mémoires,* Collection des Mémoires Relatifs à l'Histoire de France, ed. M. Petitot, ser. 2, vol. 32 (Paris, 1824), 245–46.

60. Ibid., 297.

61. Nicolas de Brichanteau, marquis de Beauvais-Nangis, *Mémoires* (Paris, 1862), 123.

toms still in fashion under the ministry of Luynes [1617–21]," in particular, "the kings' former manner of living with their subjects, by which they appeared rather as their fathers than as their masters." Louis XIII might learn much from the examples of his own father, Henri IV, who, after taking Paris and bringing an end to the Wars of Religion, had dined with a *président* of *parlement*, had had lunch with princes, and had eaten with others "of all professions with whom he might have business, only to honor them with his visit, which has not been practiced since then."[62]

Observations concerning the king's dining habits, or his inattention to services performed in his name, may seem petty or trivial, but they provide important hints about the broader changes in political culture experienced in the age of the *ministériat*. As they worked to articulate the monarchy's mastery over society and to expand the government's coercive powers—by marshaling resources for foreign wars, by pacifying the Huguenots, by increasing the powers and visibility of the *intendants*—Louis XIII and Richelieu simultaneously created anxiety about the nobles' relationship to the king in whose service they saw themselves. More specifically, many worried that the monarch's shifting (or obstructed) perspective signaled the abandonment of long shared assumptions regarding the nature of royal service and of the qualities that merited royal recognition and reward.

These concerns were repeatedly and forcefully conveyed during the midcentury crisis known as the Fronde. The political history of the 1640s and the specific conflicts that led to the Fronde are treated extensively elsewhere and need not be discussed here.[63] Specialists of the period have recently made it clear, however, that the wise historian treads lightly over this terrain. The ever-shifting composition of factions fighting both for and against the government during the Fronde (1648–52) makes it impossible to define with any clarity conflicting ideologies or recogniz-

---

62. As cited in Avenel, *La Noblesse Française sous Richelieu*, 14–15.

63. For a revealing portrait of conditions on the eve of the Fronde see Orest Ranum, *The Fronde: A French Revolution, 1648–1652* (New York, 1993), chaps. 1–3. Other full narrative accounts are supplied in Hubert Méthivier, *La Fronde* (Paris, 1984); and Ernst Kossman, *La Fronde* (Leiden, 1954). On judicial politics and the coming of the Fronde see A. Lloyd Moote, "The French Crown versus Its Judicial and Financial Officials, 1615–1683," *Journal of Modern History* 34 (1962): 146–60; idem, *The Revolt of the Judges: The Parlement of Paris and the Fronde, 1643–1652* (Princeton, 1971); Sharon Kettering, "The Causes of the Judicial Frondes," *Canadian Journal of History* 17 (1982): 275–306; and idem, *Judicial Politics and Urban Revolt in Seventeenth-Century France: The Parlement of Aix, 1629–1659* (Princeton, 1978).

able group interests. The variety of the rhetorical attacks leveled against Mazarin, in particular, poses extraordinary interpretive difficulties.[64]

But in the avalanche of criticism that fell on Cardinal-Minister Mazarin in 1648 and subsequent years, one detects clearly enough a critique of ministerial government that drew from and elaborated a language of protest long current in noble circles. In addition to continued complaints about secrecy and inaccessibility—made more serious by the nine-year-old king's inability to act on his own behalf—critics especially decried the fiscal policies developed by Mazarin and the superintendent of finances Particelly d'Emery. Those policies had encouraged a spirit of greed and profiteering that now characterized government at every level.[65] France seemed locked in an endless war with Spain, and for that Mazarin could not be held solely responsible. But the royal council's unquenchable thirst for money to finance the war had provided still more evidence that the monarchy itself had gone adrift since the days of Henry IV.

The following discussion is based largely on the corpus of political pamphlets, the so-called *Mazarinades,* that proliferated throughout the midcentury crisis, from the first confrontation between crown and *parlement* in 1648 to the final capitulation of the princes in 1652. These pamphlets, most of them penned anonymously, need to be interpreted with circumspection. Because little is known about the motives of authors engaged in the conflict, or about the reactions of those who read the pamphlets, one cannot take for granted the representativeness or even the sincerity of the views expressed in any given piece. Moreover, like all subversive propaganda, these pamphlets did not reflect with perfect accuracy the reality they ostensibly condemned. It is now well known, for example, that many wealthy nobles invested heavily in the tax-farming leases that aroused so much controversy in the 1640s. The financiers so

---

64. Christian Jouhaud has shown, in his study of the *Mazarinades,* that "ideological" presuppositions cannot be deduced from pamphlets that were typically rooted in, and composed in response to, local events and conditions. He argues that these texts should be seen not as serious and detached reflections of political principle but as instruments of political "action" (Christian Jouhaud, *Mazarinades: La Fronde des mots* [Paris, 1985]). For one indication of the bewildering diversity of antiministerial rhetoric in these years see Jeffrey Merrick, "The Cardinal and the Queen: Sexual and Political Disorders in the Mazarinades," *French Historical Studies* 18 (1994): 667–99.

65. See Orest Ranum's informative discussion of the *partisans* and their increasingly negative image in these years, in *The Fronde,* 36–41. For details on the *partisans'* careers as well as their professional and social activities see Françoise Bayard's remarkable study of the financiers, *Le Monde des Financiers au XVIIe siècle* (Paris, 1988).

roundly denounced by spokesmen of the old nobility in 1648 and after were actually linked to many nobles through credit networks that had formed to meet, and profit from, the crown's growing need for cash.[66]

The negative characterizations of money and monied men found in these pamphlets, though they cannot always be taken literally, still carried meaning for a wide audience. Some aristocrats happily advanced interest-bearing loans to the king behind the scenes—after all, the nobility had always been bound reciprocally to the monarchy through the exchange of "service" and "reward"—but this is no reason to assume that they did not share the general disapproval of the government's priorities and of the cast of characters who seemed to be determining those priorities. Discussions about money, greed, and the highly visible financiers who had recently achieved prominence at court served a specific rhetorical function in the *Mazarinades*. By scrutinizing the suspect values and family heritage of Mazarin, Particelly d'Emery, and their minions, pamphleteers refocused attention on the culture of personal selflessness central to French traditions of royal service and invoked an alternative vision of royal government that noble readers would instantly have recognized and applauded.

One writer pointedly sought to remind the king that he could not expect anything good to come from "a person of [Mazarin's] birth and of his temperament. His origin is not . . . illustrious. . . . His nobility is no older than the honors he has received in Your realm, without having merited them."[67] Indeed, Mazarin had acquired his position "not by his gen-

---

66. Both Daniel Dessert and Françoise Bayard have shown the extent to which members of the high nobility infiltrated the system of state credit—and vice versa—in the seventeenth century. See Dessert, *Argent, Pouvoir et Société au Grand Siècle* (Paris, 1984); idem, *Fouquet* (Paris, 1987); Dessert and Jean-Louis Journet, "Le Lobby Colbert: Un royaume, ou une affaire de famille?" *Annales, E. S. C.* 30 (1975): 1303–36; and Bayard, *Le Monde des Financiers au XVIIe siècle,* esp. pt. 3. Officials in the financial administration had already become a major source of credit for the crown by the early years of the seventeenth century. For the details on this system of internal borrowing see, in addition to Bayard, James Collins, *Fiscal Limits of Absolutism: Direct Taxation in Early-Seventeenth Century France* (Berkeley, 1988). Other important studies of crown finance in the pivotal first half of the seventeenth century are Julian Dent, *Crisis in Finance: Crown, Financiers, and Society in Seventeenth-Century France* (New York, 1973); Daniel Hickey, *The Coming of French Absolutism: The Struggle for Tax Reform in the Province of Dauphiné, 1540–1640* (Toronto, 1986); and Richard Bonney, *The King's Debts: Finance and Politics in France, 1589–1661* (Oxford, 1981).
67. *Le Tableau des tyrans favoris, et la description des malversations qu'ils commettent dans les Etats qu'ils gouvernent* (Paris, 1649), 11–12.

erosity . . . or by the choice of the king but by the intrigue of Cardinal Richelieu," and his underhanded methods could easily be explained by reference to his family background.[68]

The author of the *Genealogy and Lineage of Jules Mazarin* observed that Mazarin's thirst for private gain only renewed the failings of his own father's career and character. His father, a merchant in Sicily, had gone "bankrupt for an immense sum of money." Anxious to cheat his creditors, "he fled and took refuge in Rome."[69] There his wife gave birth to two sons—one the nefarious cardinal. Given Mazarin's vile origins, no one should be surprised that avarice determined every decision he made. Committed, like his father, to establishing his own fortune above all else, he seized every opportunity to embezzle money from the king's coffers. After becoming councillor of state, the cardinal had become "so rich and so opulent, that he is thought to have more gold and more silver than any lord in Europe."[70]

The most telling symptom of Mazarin's depravity, according to the pamphleteers, was his inability to recognize and reward true merit. Everyone knew that, under him, "demerits and crimes are rewarded and fidelities are punished."[71] One writer repeated to Mazarin the common complaint

that you have not obliged a single man graciously and in good faith; and they say that it is because of your preoccupation with your own advancement . . . that the gifts that are dependent on the liberality of the king . . . [and] of which you are the dispenser by unjust and violent usurpation are not distributed to anyone gratuitously, and that you have made of them an infamous commerce.[72]

68. *L'Ambitieux* (n.p., 1649), 4.

69. *Généalogie et Extraction de la vie de Jules Mazarin* (n.p., 1649), 1. At least two other titles from the period of the Fronde explicitly set out to attack Mazarin's family past: *La Vie, moeurs, et généalogie de Jules Mazarin, où se voient les banqueroutes de son père* (n.p., n.d.), a second edition of *Généalogie et Extraction;* and *Généalogie du Cardinal Mazarin* (n.p., n.d.).

70. *Généalogie et Extraction,* 2. Daniel Dessert's evidence proves, incidentally, that this was no idle charge. At his death, Mazarin's fortune totaled approximately thirty-five million livres—possibly the largest personal fortune accumulated in the history of the old regime. See Dessert, *Argent,* 292.

71. *Requête de la noblesse pour l'Assemblée des Etats-Généraux* (n.p., 1651), 5.

72. *Le Politique étranger* (Paris, 1649), 4.

Even the wicked and domineering Séjanus had allowed Emperor Tiberius "to reward those who merited it for good services rendered to his sacred person or to the state. Was Mazarin not ready to do the same?"[73]

According to some, Mazarin's cynical and selfish manner had infected the entire government—after all, Particelly d'Emery and that whole cabal of financiers had come from the same vile stock as Mazarin[74]—and writers declared that the atmosphere of profiteering and avarice harmed the nobility, and the king, in insidious ways. Money was admittedly "très necéssaire" to the functioning of the government, but it should be used principally to "maintain friends by paying them their *gages* or pensions, to nurture contacts in foreign lands, and to offer recompense to those who by their wisdom or valor oblige the state and the country."[75] Unfortunately, at the center of government itself the accumulation of wealth now took precedence over generosity, loyalty, and the recognition of true merit.

One publisher, evidently noting the continuity between the nobility's dissatisfaction with Mazarin and earlier arguments against venality of office, recycled a pamphlet first written in 1614. The "French Diogenes," in search of the "man of merit," attributed a host of social problems to the growing influence of money and of men who valued money for its own sake.

> O avarice, what a mortal wound you have inflicted on the state! Just as ancient Rome was lost the moment money was traded for functions, what should we be in fear of today? Alas! Our misfortune might be acceptable if we could long survive this disorder: But either this evil will kill us or we must kill it; that is the truth.[76]

Any practice that effectively allows men to purchase the king's favor inevitably "alienates the natural obligation that the subject owes to his prince, in that he estimates that his fortune was established only by the depth of his pocketbook."[77]

---

73. *L'Ambitieux*, 6.

74. Predictably, other pamphlets detailed the family backgrounds and corrupt *moeurs* of prominent financiers. See, for example, *Avertissement . . . Particelly* (n.p., 1649); and *Catalogue des Partisans, Ensemble Leurs Généalogies et extraction, vie, moeurs, et fortunes* (Paris, 1649).

75. *Plainte de la noblesse française faite contre les Partisans & Mange-Peuples* (n.p., 1651), 4.

76. *Le Diogène français* (n.p., 1652), 12.

77. Ibid., 14.

Nobles were willing to conduct business with tax-farmers and to benefit from their money-lending expertise, but none doubted for a moment the difference in moral quality separating the authentic noble from the ambitious financier. With the foreigner Mazarin and the financier Particelly d'Emery having guided the crown to the brink of financial disaster, the figure of the anonymous *partisan* thus conveniently came to symbolize the displacement of nobles and of noble values at court. One group of assembled nobles complained in 1651, for example, that the nobility now had to endure the insolence of *partisans* and "the avarice of Ministers of whom the *partisans* are tributaries, [while] our prerogatives and immunities are abolished by the jealousy of those who have neither the birth nor the virtue required to merit them."[78] Another writer, intending to evoke both pity and outrage, reported that faithful nobles now stood by helplessly as creditors claimed their lands and their châteaus fell into ruin without their having "the means to repair them": "That is why the nobility often says these days 'Where were these men on those memorable days when I spilled so much blood for your conservation? Must I be forgotten after so many services while these financiers enjoy the repose that I have merited?'"[79]

Besides the impoverishment of the nobility, many expressed concern that the spreading stain of avarice would even corrupt the nobility's natural gift for selfless behavior and sentiment. Guez de Balzac had already complained in the 1630s that

> this wretched self-interest . . . is now the god of the court, the object and desire of the courtier. . . .From the soul of the tax-farmers and tax-collectors, [it] has passed even into [the soul] of *gentilshommes* and Princes; it enters into professions that would seem to be the most removed from it.[80]

A frondeur commented on this same condition in 1652.

> It is a misfortune that in this corps [of nobility], formerly as generous as it was illustrious, it is [now] necessary to arouse its interest; but if [the nobility] looks on the state of the court today, it will see that it is an inn where everyone is treated according to his money and that there

---

78. *Journal de l'Assemblée de la Noblesse tenue à Paris l'année 1651* (Paris, 1651), 144.
79. *La Liberté de France et l'anéantissement des ministres étrangers* (n.p., 1649), 4.
80. As cited in Avenel, *La Noblesse Française sous Richelieu*, 291.

is a sordid traffic in all the things it used to purchase with its services; that there one must be dependent on petty men who treat the greatest people of condition like their valets.[81]

To bring an end to this persistent malaise, the king needed to seize the reins of government himself and exclude from influence base and self-interested men. In anticipation of an Estates General that never took place, nobles in 1651 composed remonstrances in which they asked the king to assert his own authority.

Sire, do not allow that your subjects should see during your reign the reestablishment of these First Ministers and these *Traitants*. . . . What is a First Minister other than a precious favorite to whom the prince confides the entire administration of his state and the disposition of his gifts? Such a great power is a violent temptation for the ambitious.[82]

Other writers, who posed as disinterested observers but may well have been in Mazarin's pay, tried to persuade noble readers that the importance to the king's service of trust, intimacy, and the generous qualities had not diminished. The author of *The Right Conduct of the Generous Courtier* (1649) urged disgruntled nobles to return to court immediately and offer themselves to the king's service; he assured them that the growing complexity of public affairs only underscored the king's need for generous servitors: "The more a Sovereign has servants and subjects, the more he has enemies to combat and ambushes to avoid. . . . their power creates as many persecutors as slaves."[83] Hence the king was in constant need of trustworthy confidants and generous friends: "A wise man once said that it is neither finances nor armies nor soldiers nor victories that conserve powerful monarchies but true friends. . . . The perfect friend is the generous courtier who suffers nothing base or degrading to touch the person of the king."[84] Nobles should not be discouraged by the current atmosphere at court, since "the generous courtier is a very necessary friend for a Prince, and the virtuous Prince who will recognize his merit and esteem him will keep him near his person, like the richest pearl dec-

81. *Les Justes Raisons et Sentiments des Princes, des Grands, De Tous les Ordres & de tous les Corps de l'Etat, pour la dernière exclusion du Cardinal Mazarin* (Paris, 1652), 5.
82. *Très-humbles Remonstrances Faites au Roy* (Paris, 1651), 19, 22.
83. *La véritable conduite du courtisan généreux* (Paris, 1649), 13.
84. Ibid., 13.

orating his crown." In managing the affairs of his realm, the king required "the judicious counsels and the sincere friendship of the wise courtier, as it belongs only to prudent and generous souls to counsel kings well."[85] The author instructed his noble readers to take heart, for despite the new demands involved in the governing of the realm, kings would still find the intangible personal qualities of reliable men to be of the greatest use.

Kings and States: Political Change as Cultural Dissonance

Anxiety over the fate of personal royal government does not by itself explain the contentious character of the nobility in the first half of the seventeenth century. The great nobles' repeated challenges to the authority of the king's ministers in these years can also be attributed to personal ambition, jealousy, family rivalries, loyalty to princely patrons, and other factors. The diversity of the nobility, and the range of motivations that inspired nobles to action or inaction, make it impossible to identify a single, coherent noble voice in this period. During the Fronde, in particular, the failure of Condé, Conti, Turenne, or any other natural leader of the nobility to articulate clear political goals, other than the ouster of Mazarin, insured that noble dissatisfaction remained unfocused and opposition to the government diffuse.[86] Few nobles outside of the princes' own armies identified with the *grands,* who behaved unpredictably and pursued interests that clearly set them apart from the corps of middling noblesse.

Nevertheless, public criticism of the crown's style of governing in the first half of the century clearly revolved around a dominant theme. In their belated response to the systematic sale of offices, in their denunciation of the ministerial "usurpers" Richelieu and Mazarin, and in their rejection of the values projected through the growing visibility and status of financiers, dissatisfied nobles and their various spokesmen repeatedly lamented the decline of traditional notions of royal service.

Nobles expected their king to observe and reward his servants person-

---

85. Ibid., 14.

86. As Orest Ranum notes, "there was a Fronde of the royal officials (particularly the judges), a Fronde of the princes (supported by their clients), and even a Fronde of the Jansenist priests of Paris; but there was never a *noble* Fronde. No collective entity with that name played a part in the Parisian Fronde or in the various provincial Frondes" (*The Fronde,* 13).

ally whenever possible, to value generosity and selfless sentiment above all else, and therefore to regard elevated birth as a positive sign of individual quality. They now confronted policies and circumstances that denied them free access to the king, facilitated the rise of men of "base" origins, and questioned the nobility's inherited role as natural partner in royal power. One might say that nobles had actually begun to experience a process that Montchrétien and Turquet de Mayerne had outlined only in the abstract. From the perspective of much of the nobility, the theory and practice of reason of state threatened to displace the person of the king from his role as supreme arbiter of merit and utility. But because no alternative point of focus had yet been provided, the king's displacement caused a kind of epistemological confusion. Nobles, instead of spontaneously adjusting their expectations and their own self-perception, responded by requesting restoration of familiar conditions. In 1649 an assembly of about two hundred nobles in Paris drafted a petition to send to the king and queen mother. In it they expressed concern that recent innovations might permanently "upset [the] just distribution of honors and titles" and thus affect the nobility so adversely that "it will become less united and less strong for the defense of the well-being and dignity of this state."[87]

The resistance of many nobles to reason of state in the first half of the seventeenth century stemmed not from opposition to the theory's implied objectives—in all public pronouncements nobles and their spokesmen supported the idea of strong monarchy and habitually voiced concern for the "public interest"[88]—but from bewilderment over its practical meaning. The disjuncture between the noble outlook and that of the ministerial government is reflected in a debate from 1649 concerning the employment of foreigners in the royal service. A frondeur pamphleteer began by recapitulating most of the familiar criticisms of Mazarin, to

---

87. AN K 118ª, no. 24, "Requête faite au Roy par le Corps de la Noblesse," 1649, 4.

88. Evidence of the nobility's support for the strengthening of monarchy is abundant. Concern for the "public good" framed many of the cahiers from the Estates General of 1614, a fact noted by Arlette Jouanna in *L'Idée de Race en France au XVIᵉ siècle et au début du XVIIᵉ siècle (1498–1614),* 3 vols. (Paris, 1976), 3:1287. For examples of noble proposals clearly designed to strengthen the monarch's hand see Charles J. Mayer, ed., *Recueil des Cahiers Généraux des Trois Ordres aux Etats-Généraux,* 4 vols. (Paris, 1789), 4:192, 199, 245. As Jeffrey Sawyer notes in his study of the pamphlet war between Marie de Medicis and the Prince de Condé between 1614 and 1617, both sides now consistently invoked the "public good," the "public interest," and the "good of the state" to justify their respective positions. See Sawyer, *Printed Poison,* 43–45.

demonstrate "that foreigners should never be admitted into the management of public affairs."[89] His argument centered on the assumption that foreign mercenaries, driven by their own selfish ambitions, could not possess the "passion" and willingness to sacrifice that were so essential to good service.

> A foreigner can never manage the state with all the passion that one finds in a natural subject. His greatest concern is to elevate his house, to accumulate treasure, and to make his retreat when there is nothing left in the realm to take. . . . Foreigners never work for things regarding the public good; they are passionate only for their private affairs.[90]

In a manuscript titled "Discourse on Employing Foreigners in the Offices and Dignities of This Realm," one of Mazarin's defenders responded that the advancement of the public good required hard work and ability more than anything else.

> They will respond again that, foreigners not being touched by this natural affection that all men have for their country, it is conceivable that, putting the public interests aside, they will only seek their own advancement—or even that they will conspire with their compatriots to achieve the ruin and subversion of the state.[91]

But if a foreigner had given proof of his integrity and industry, "it is not to be doubted that he will acquit himself of his duty admirably and will prefer the service of the prince and the public utility to his own interests."[92]

Still, this author did not base his argument in defense of employing foreigners on the assumption that they could work with a passion comparable to natives. For him, proof of passion and affection gave way to other considerations. He declared absurd his opponents' suggestion that the exclusion of foreigners from the king's service should be adopted as one of the realm's fundamental laws. If ever that came to pass, such a law

---

89. *Advis sur l'Estat, touchant les affaires présentes et le gouvernement étranger* (Paris, n.d.), 3.

90. Ibid., 7–8.

91. AN K 118ᵃ, no. 1, "Discours sur l'Employ des Etrangers Aux Charges et Dignités de ce Royaume" (1649), fol. 4v.

92. Ibid., fol. 19r.

would need changing, "since laws are introduced only for the common utility, and these must give way to other, more useful laws when the public utility requires [us] to change, revoke, or at least prevent the execution [of older laws that] deny the public some manifest advantage." The public simply could not afford to disqualify from service men with so many "recommendable qualities." The example of the Lacedaemonians, who refused all relations with foreigners, "must not induce us to refuse them employment in public offices if they are capable of exercising them more usefully." The most worthy man must be chosen to fill the position of first minister, regardless of nationality, and "according to this maxim . . . : that the public utility is preferable to the interests of individuals."[93]

What makes this exchange of opinion so revealing is that the authors never directly engaged the issue that divided them. Few nobles would have disputed that public utility was preferable to the interests of individuals. The key question remained, Who, or what, defined the public utility? The nobility's experience in the decades following the death of Henry IV had been shaped by one constant feature: their lack of connection with a strong king who demonstrably acted on his own behalf. In light of so much disconcerting evidence—the isolation of Louis XIII, the hostility toward dueling, the disrespect shown to nobles of long lineage, the marginalization of noble members of the regency council after 1644, the simultaneous secrecy and visibility of manifestly "selfish" financiers, Mazarin's inability to oblige noble servants of the crown with gifts and favors, the sequestering of Louis XIV at Saint-Germain-en-Laye in 1649—many nobles seem to have reached the troubling conclusion that their traditional notions of utility, service, and merit, all rooted in the personal modality, had been supplanted by new and alien ones. In 1645 the noble panegyrist Ceriziers made a passing remark that seems emblematic of the nobility's frustration with the monarchy's methods of governing under the two cardinal-ministers. He praised the comte d'Harcourt for his personal openness, a fundamental quality that had become all too rare.

He is not one of these inaccessible Princes whom one can scarcely approach. . . . In any case, we have no need of these invisible Majesties

---

93. Ibid., fols. 20–21. Ironically, the nobility won at least a Pyrrhic victory in this instance. As a political ploy, the king declared in 1651 that neither foreigners nor cardinals would ever again be invited to sit in the king's council. After the crown's final triumph, Mazarin was of course reinstated as first minister, a position he retained until his death.

among us, who only allow themselves to be seen amid thunder and lightning. One only loves what one knows: and how can one know a man who is always hidden away, either in his chambers or in his very demeanor?[94]

Nobles became less contentious under the personal rule of Louis XIV. Their change in behavior was once attributed to the Sun King's determination to tame the nobility through stern discipline and the force of his own will. But like other recent studies that have stressed the conciliatory spirit of monarchical politics after the Fronde, chapter 4 seeks to throw light on Louis XIV's constructive engagement with his nobility. Like Richelieu, Mazarin, and Louis XIII, the Sun King wanted to expand the apparatus of government and make loyalty to the monarchy unconditional for all subjects, including the nobles. But in contrast to his troubled predecessors, Louis XIV conveyed to the nobility, by his own conduct and by his methods of exercising power, that he did not intend simply to substitute a new and unfamiliar vision of utility for an older, outmoded one. Rather, he worked to enlarge the traditional concept of utility, making the definition implied by service to the state consistent and compatible with the definition implied by personal service. Louis XIV reestablished harmony between crown and nobility in the later seventeenth century in part because of his ability to resolve the cultural dissonance created by the implementation of reason of state.

---

94. [René] de Ceriziers, *Le Héros Français, ou l'idée du grand capitaine* (Paris, 1645), 196–97.

4

Through the Eyes of the King: Merit, Service, and the State in the Age of Louis XIV

Several material and psychological factors contributed to the nobility's unrest in the first half of the seventeenth century. The relative docility of the nobility under the personal rule of Louis XIV (1661–1715) can therefore be explained in many ways. Besides the obvious—that the long and costly war with Spain had ended in 1659 and the hated figure Mazarin had finally departed the scene—the advent of Louis XIV pleased the nobility in other ways, as recent research has shown. The king arbitrated disputes of rank and status between individuals and between corporate bodies throughout the realm; the crown had greater success in controlling troublesome popular uprisings in the provinces; the king insured that no individual or faction monopolized the distribution of patronage—a frequent complaint of nobles since the days of Henri III.[1] Furthermore, it seems likely that greater numbers of nobles benefited from crown fiscal policy in the years following the Fronde.[2] The image of the iron-willed king who lured his nobles to court and dazzled them with frivolous spectacles, thereby fulfilling their desire for social status while stripping them of political autonomy, can no longer bear the weight of historical evidence; specialists now agree that traditional elites acted deferentially toward Louis XIV primarily because they had good reason for it.

---

1. For references to the major works that have argued these points, see the introduction.

2. As Daniel Dessert has shown, the crown's chief financial officials concluded in the 1650s and 1660s that the war against Spain, as well as other royal expenses, had to be funded not through tax increases but through "extraordinary" means—the marketing of new offices, the creation of indirect taxes, farming out the various rights over the royal domain, and so on. This opened new opportunities for *traitants* and all who invested in their operations, including many well-placed nobles. For discussion of this new direction in the system of crown finance see Dessert *Argent, Pouvoir et Société au Grand Siècle* (Paris, 1984), esp. 158–66. For analysis of the various ways in which nobles could benefit from the crown's growing reliance on indirect revenues, see ibid., 342–62.

Old nobles drew many material advantages from the new regime of Louis XIV, and these tangible benefits no doubt help to explain changes in aristocratic attitudes and behavior. But there are several reasons why Louis XIV's success in establishing harmony between crown and nobility after 1661 should be viewed first from a cultural perspective. As earlier chapters have shown, to perceive how nobles interpreted changes in their relationship to the king, one must focus attention on the expectations and assumptions in terms of which that relationship was conceived and expressed. The nobility's conflicts with Richelieu and Mazarin can be, and often have been, described as a raw struggle for power. Through the language nobles used to articulate their anxieties, however, we have seen that their criticisms invariably addressed the values and mechanisms that mediated their relations with the monarchy. Old nobles did not see changes in crown policy simply as a threat to their naked interests; rather, they perceived a threat to the culture of power in which their interests, their self-perception, and their view of the world were entangled and embedded. Thus, to understand the improved relations between crown and nobility under Louis XIV, one must consider not only the degree to which Louis protected noble interests but also the evolving language through which the king's intentions, and his power, were conveyed.

My aim in this chapter is to expose the cultural basis for the new modus vivendi linking king to nobility in the later seventeenth century. The nature of this tacit understanding between king and nobility is revealed through close analysis of the terms in which Louis XIV and his deputies framed and communicated the king's ambitions. The discourse of royal service under Louis XIV retained the familiar emphasis on the qualities of heart and birth so important to the identity of the nobility in the seventeenth century. But by elaborating and extending the traditional idiom through which merit was expressed, and by subtly changing the nature of the gaze that approved and affirmed merit, Louis XIV also signaled his recognition of a new set of qualities and attitudes. The Sun King's hybrid culture of royal service contained and suppressed many tensions and contradictions—tensions that would persist down to the Revolution—but for all nobles attuned to the world of the royal court, the new regime eased the cultural adjustment necessitated by state centralization.

By bringing to light this particular dimension of the language of absolutism under Louis XIV, I hope to contribute to the analysis of political culture in the later seventeenth century. But I hope to do more. In my remaining chapters I will suggest that the epistemological assumptions underlying the traditional personal modality of service are actually woven through several related developments central to the history of the eighteenth century: the growth of the administrative state, the appearance of new professional sensibilities, and the gradual emergence of a distinct and autonomous public. Louis XIV sought to make the monarchy absolute by systematizing the personal modality of service; ironically, he succeeded so well that he laid the foundation for the development of an impersonal service culture that presupposed the centrality of an abstract polity.

Restoring Personal Monarchy

On 10 March 1661, just one day after the death of Mazarin, Louis dramatically announced the beginning of his personal rule. He summoned his councillors to tell them that he would now be managing his affairs independently. Making it clear that they would henceforth play only an advisory role, he ordered his secretaries of state "not to sign anything, not even a passport . . . without my command; to render account to me personally each day, and to favor no one."[3] The reign of first ministers now came to an abrupt end: "A king, no matter how able and informed his ministers are, is not at all responsible for a work, unless he himself appears in it."[4] With a vengeance, Louis XIV set out to "appear" in all the details of government from the very beginning. Immediately after taking control, as he later explained, "I began to cast my eyes on all the diverse parts of the state, and not indifferent eyes, but a master's eyes." Finding that "disorder reigned everywhere," the king anxiously set about reforming his realm and improving the performance of those who served him.[5]

Louis moved energetically to address the disorders he had detected. By

---

3. Louis XIV's address to the council, 10 March 1661. As cited in John B. Wolf, *Louis XIV* (New York, 1968), 133.

4. Louis XIV, *Mémoires, suivi de Réflexions sur le métier du roi, Instructions au duc d'Anjou, Projet de harangue,* ed. Jean Longnon, rev. ed., 2 vols. in 1 (Paris, 1978), 42. Jean Longnon's two-volume 1923 edition of the king's memoirs (of which the 1978 edition is a condensed version) was also consulted for this study. To avoid confusion and unnecessary repetition, the dates of the respective editions have been placed in parentheses each time they are cited.

5. Ibid., 34.

the sixth year of his personal rule, important reforms had been implemented in a number of areas: finance, justice, the army, the church, even the nobility. It is instructive, however, that the king focused first on the court itself, as indicated in the personal memoir he wrote and dictated for his son in the late 1660s.[6] "My court was in general still far removed from the sentiments in which I hope you will find it," he wrote. Disgruntled courtiers had been in the habit of negotiating with Mazarin for royal favors, and no one seemed satisfied with the situation. In general, royal *graces* "no longer obliged anyone."[7] Louis thus saw as his first challenge the need to establish that the dispensation of *graces* depended directly and exclusively on the royal person. He would award his bounty "freely and without constraint to whomever it pleased me and whenever it pleased me." Also, he wished to make it clear that in "favoring and elevating merit," he would be "governed by reason" rather than caprice.[8] With his every move Louis XIV reasserted the principle of personal proximity between monarch and noble and expressed his determination to be his own judge in all matters. Bussy-Rabutin, a noted writer, courtier, and noble army officer, indicated in his own memoirs that the king's ascent to power had indeed lifted the nobility's spirits. The Sun King, he explained, had put a stop to the incessant scheming, the uncertainties, the "weaknesses" that had marred the ministerial rule of Mazarin. After Louis's assertion of personal control, nobles saw only "the dignity and manner of behavior suitable to a great prince."[9]

In the eyes of the nobility, accessibility had always been one of the special features of a great prince, and Louis XIV made it the hallmark of his reign.[10] For example, in stark contrast to Richelieu's policy of distancing

---

6. For an account of earlier debates concerning the authenticity and authorship of the king's memoirs see Paul Sonnino, "The Dating and Authorship of Louis XIV's *Mémoires,*" *French Historical Studies* 3 (1964): 303–37. For most of the memoirs, it is impossible to determine the degree to which the text may reflect Louis's own words. Several authors contributed to the composition, including Colbert and the king's secretaries Périgny and Pellisson. Nevertheless, it is now agreed that the memoirs represent accurately the king's philosophy and experiences in the first ten years of the reign, and evidence of the king's close collaboration in the composition of the memoirs is abundant. To Sonnino it is clear that "Louis's control . . . extended to every step in the composition of the *Mémoires*" (336).

7. Louis XIV, *Mémoires* (1978), 34.

8. Ibid., 40.

9. Roger de Rabutin, comte de Bussy, *Mémoires,* ed. Ludovic Lalanne, 2 vols. (Paris, 1857), 2:108.

10. A medal struck in 1661 celebrated "the accessibility of the king." In the same year, Le Brun painted the famous portrait *Le Roy Gouverne par Lui Même* (The king governs for himself). Clearly, Louis XIV quite deliberately cultivated his image as an accessible and per-

the nobles from the court and king, Louis XIV's Versailles—the center of courtly activity after 1682—seemed designed to satisfy his nobility's craving for royal attention. Far from being lured to court, nobles likely would have come even without an invitation, since Versailles permitted personal contact between the monarch and more nobles than had ever congregated at court at one time.

Royal attention, once a matter of chance, now became regular and predictable. The king put himself on display from the moment he rose from bed each morning. The *lever,* as described in Spanheim's famous account (1690), proceeded in several stages, each one exposing the king to greater numbers of courtiers. At the *petit lever* appeared the *gens de la chambre,* those with the privilege of the so-called *première entrée*—the *premier gentilhomme,* the grand master of the wardrobe, the *premier valet de chambre,* and the *lecteurs du roi.* Then began the *seconde entrée,* as princes, lords "of the first rank," and officers of the household (the captain of the king's *garde du corps,* the *premier maître d'hôtel*) rushed in to greet the king as he began to dress. After these encounters, and just before the final *entrée libre* (which theoretically allowed entry to any courtier who wished to appear), the king might honor a few of those in attendance, "according to the consideration they enjoyed at court," by inviting them into his chambers ahead of all those still waiting in the wings. Around midnight, the ceremonies of the *grand* and *petit coucher* reversed the proceedings of the *lever du roi,* though with fewer courtiers in attendance.[11] According to the memoirs, the king listened most attentively to the personal requests of his courtiers during these moments of ceremonial intimacy.[12]

Other opportunities for personal contact with the king came when he dined. His meals were social events. Louis usually took his midday meal in the presence of family, advisors, and a few privileged friends only (*au petit couvert*), but especially at supper the king had his meal in the view of the whole court (*au grand couvert*). On rare occasions the king would even dine *au public,* as the halls of Versailles opened to anyone who was

sonally active king. On artistic representations of Louis see Peter Burke, *The Fabrication of Louis XIV* (New Haven and London, 1992); Ekkehard Mai, *Le portrait du roi: Staatsporträt und Kunsttheorie in der Epoche Ludwigs XIV* (Bonn, 1975); and Charles Maumené and Louis d'Harcourt, *Iconographie des Rois de France* (Paris, 1932), 2:3–284.

11. Ezechiel Spanheim, *Relation de la Cour de France en 1690,* ed. Charles Schefer (Paris, 1882), 145–48.

12. See W. H. Lewis, *The Splendid Century: Life in the France of Louis XIV* (New York, 1957), 46.

clean and properly dressed. The courtier, if he wished, could stand and observe the whole meal, but the commoner had to file through in line, passing before the royal dinner table only briefly.[13] Apart from mealtime, courtiers might also catch up with the king each day as he went to and from mass or as he walked in the gardens. The lucky few might even receive invitations to accompany him on his afternoon stroll—a special sign of distinction. At least once a week, Louis also hunted and thus gave his nobles a chance to engage in their favorite pastime in the king's presence.

Beyond arranging for routine personal interaction—through the performance of court ritual, through festivals, and through more informal types of entertainment at Versailles and the other royal châteaus[14]— Louis XIV also appealed to his nobles' thirst for honor by regulating rank at court. Confusion over rank had of course been characteristic of the first half of the seventeenth century. With the creation and sale of new offices and with the general inflation of honors that took place after 1600 in France (as elsewhere in Europe),[15] social and political frictions reached unprecedented levels as older and more firmly established elites contested the legitimacy of the honors and distinctions acquired by parvenus. The confusion even touched the king's council, where, according to the account of one observer in 1658, everyone remained standing throughout the deliberations "because of the dispute over Ranks."[16]

Louis XIV, however, claimed to have taken his greatest satisfaction in "keeping my people in good order."[17] At court, he established rank and dignity within a strict and ordered hierarchy where, as Norbert Elias has

---

13. Ibid., 50.

14. For full descriptions of the "Plaisirs de l'île enchantée" of 1664 and the entertainments held at the king's *appartements* at Versailles see François Bluche, *Louis XIV*, trans. Mark Greengrass (New York, 1990), 180–81, 377.

15. On the inflation of honors in England, for example, see Lawrence Stone, *The Crisis of the Aristocracy, 1558–1641* (Oxford, 1965), chap. 3. In his famous essay "The General Crisis of the Seventeenth Century," H. R. Trevor-Roper attributed the general unrest of the middle part of the century to a "country" backlash against "court" extravagance, that is, the cost of supporting an expanding bureaucracy and a larger number of crown pensioners. Trevor-Roper may have misinterpreted the effects of the court's expansion, but the phenomenon was certainly characteristic of the period. See Trevor Aston, ed., *Crisis in Europe, 1550–1660* (New York, 1965). For details on English bureaucratic expansion see G. E. Aylmer, *The King's Servants: The Civil Service of Charles I, 1625–1642* (New York and London, 1961).

16. Archives Nationales (hereafter AN), K 118[B], no. 88[2], "Estat des Conseils du Roy, avec la liste des personnes qui les composent."

17. Louis XIV, *Mémoires* (1923), 1:242.

shown, every individual behaved in accordance with the rank assigned him or her by past or present royalty and operated within a system of relations encompassing everyone from the king to the lowliest domestic servant.[18] Rank determined who could dine with the king at mealtime, who could hand him his shirt in the morning or his candle at bedtime. The right to enter the inner courtyard of a royal château on horseback, to remain seated in the presence of the queen, or to serve the king his plate at dinner were also concessions to rank.[19]

The king occasionally relaxed his rules of etiquette and decorum. Whenever Louis XIV traveled to Marly, for example, every woman of quality in attendance was invited to take a *taboret* at the king's meal.[20] At the gambling tables, the common courtier sat and rubbed elbows with the king, the queen, and the rest of the titled nobility. The king also remained accessible to those nobles without title or domestic office. He frequently accorded a kind of unofficial rank and distinction to lesser nobles by granting them his personal favors and attentions, such as private conferences and walks in the gardens. Nevertheless, rank was invari-

---

18. In *The Court Society,* trans. Edmund Jephcott (New York, 1983), Norbert Elias argued that Louis XIV and subsequent French kings asserted their power—both within the social field of the court and in the "wider dominion" of the country—by affirming and subtly manipulating the status hierarchy on which all members of the elite depended for their sense of self-worth. Elias's important thesis had the great advantage of recognizing and emphasizing the ways in which king and nobility were bound by ties of interdependence in the "social figuration" of the court. Unfortunately, though, Elias's myopic focus on status consciousness and competition marred his representation of both absolutism and the early-modern aristocracy. Since he assumed that a principle of competition suffused all of French society in the medieval and early-modern periods, he viewed both the king's management of court society and his increased control over the realm in the later seventeenth century as resulting from his great "victory" in history's "race" for status. This led Elias to make the improbable claim that "the king's rule over the country" in the later seventeenth and eighteenth centuries "was nothing other than an extension of and addition to the prince's rule over his household" (42). Elias's focus on competition similarly limited his understanding of the aristocracy. As indicated in the earlier chapters of this work, status consciousness was only one of a large constellation of values, beliefs, and assumptions important to the traditional nobility; consequently, the monarchy's efforts to reintegrate the nobility into a new kind of state and society necessarily involved more than appeals to vanity. For an appreciative reconsideration of Elias's thesis see Roger Chartier, *Cultural History: Between Practices and Representations,* trans. Lydia G. Cochrane (Ithaca, N.Y., 1988), chap. 3.

19. A concise guide to the system of rank at Versailles is Henri Brocher, *A La Cour de Louis XIV: Le Rang et l'Etiquette sous l'Ancien Régime* (Paris, 1934), esp. chaps. 1 and 2. See also Jean-François Solnon, *La Cour de France* (Paris, 1987); and Emmanuel Le Roy Ladurie, "Rangs et Hiérarchie dans la vie de cour," in *The Political Culture of the Old Regime,* ed. Keith M. Baker (New York, 1987), 61–75.

20. Brocher, *A la Cour de Louis XIV,* 30.

ably recognized in all public ceremonies, and no one breached protocol during the daily rites accompanying the king's schedule. Louis saw the desire for distinguished rank as "almost the first motive of all human actions, but especially of the most noble and most grand."[21] Consequently, while he multiplied the honors of the realm—occasionally naming lifetime dukes (*ducs à brevet*), creating a new chivalric order and new military offices, granting rights to wear distinctive dress—at the same time he aimed to insure that his courtiers would enjoy their distinctions on a predictable and regular basis. By systematizing rank and giving it a clearly defined value, Louis XIV governed his court strictly, but well within the tradition of personal rule. What gave rank its supreme importance, after all, was that it emanated directly from the king's person. For this reason, rank found its greatest expression through periods of ceremonial familiarity with the monarch. The king's active presence animated the entire structure of protocol and decorum, and it could be upset only if the king himself intervened.

Administration and the Personal Modality

In contrast to the earlier years of the century, when nobles had been frustrated by inaccessible and "invisible" majesties who too often abstained from social communication with the nobility, Louis XIV created a vibrant court where mutual visibility between monarch and courtier determined the very rhythms of life. But Louis did not limit his close personal attention to affairs of the court. Rather, he took one of the ideals central to the personal modality of service—that the king should be visible and observe everyone and everything—and made it the underlying principle of his reign. To govern more effectively, Louis assumed he must involve himself personally in all matters affecting the realm. He aspired "to have eyes opened over all the land" and even "to perceive in [my] subjects what they hide from me with the greatest care."[22] He wanted his people to believe of the king "that nothing escapes his view."[23]

In some respects, Louis XIV's attachment to the ideal of royal omniscience is not at all surprising. The notion lay implicit in the theory of absolute monarchy. Bishop Bossuet, for example, noted typically that "the prince must know all that takes place both inside and outside his

21. Louis XIV, *Mémoires* (1978), 105.
22. Ibid., 42.
23. Louis XIV, *Mémoires* (1923), 2:121.

realm."[24] One might also assume that the king's fondness for visual metaphors reflected the ocularcentrism that seems to have characterized the entire early-modern period.[25] But the ideal of royal omniscience becomes remarkable indeed when one recognizes that it did more than provide the king a useful or clever metaphor. For Louis, the work of the government and his own effort to deepen and enhance his perception of the realm comprised one and the same reality.

Kings, he wrote, must be "informed of everything."[26] Louis therefore intended to absorb gradually all the details of government, to become "instructed little by little, without tiring, of a thousand things that are not without use in general resolutions, and which we [kings] should know and do ourselves, if it is possible for a single man to know and to do everything."[27] With this end in mind, he informed his deputies that all information must be regularly exposed to his view.

> I commanded the four secretaries of state not to sign anything at all without speaking to me; to the *surintendant* [of finances] I said the same and told him that he should do nothing concerning the finances without its being registered in a book that would always remain with me, together with a much abbreviated extract where I could see at all moments and at a glance the state of the revenues and expenses made or to be made.[28]

The king and his ministers even conceived of statistical information as knowledge that the king himself could digest and exploit. In 1663, Controller General Colbert issued a circular entitled "Instruction for the Provincial Intendants." In it he ordered the collection of all information that might be relevant to the governing of the realm, "the king desiring to

---

24. See *Politique tirée des propres paroles de l'Ecriture Sainte*, in *Oeuvres de Bossuet*, 4 vols. (Paris, 1841–47), 1:352.

25. See Martin Jay, *Downcast Eyes: The Denigration of Vision in Twentieth-Century French Thought* (Berkeley, 1993), chap. 1. Analyzing changing attitudes toward the faculty of sight in modern French thought, Jay notes that "the dawn of the modern era was accompanied by the vigorous privileging of vision" (69). The positive reevaluation of human curiosity in the sixteenth century, as well as "the legitimation of probing vision" (65), prepared the way both for the scientific revolution and for a more general ocularcentric culture that marked French thought from the seventeenth century to the early nineteenth.

26. Louis XIV, *Mémoires* (1978), 49.

27. Ibid., 44.

28. Ibid., 43.

be clearly informed of the state of the provinces within his kingdom."[29] In the effort to translate the realm to paper, Colbert first requested of the *intendants,* not coincidentally, that they find detailed maps of their *généralité* or province or else provide the royal geographer with the information needed to draw up new ones.[30] Next they would compile information under four broad categories of governance: ecclesiastical, military, judicial, and financial. The data to be collected by the *intendants* resembled in many ways the data listed on any modern census—population counts, local economic profiles, details on tax revenues, and reports on the condition of forests, waterways, and bridges. But the *intendants* should also describe the quality and character of the leading figures in each province. Although the king already knew the particular "talents" of his governors and lieutenant generals, for example, *intendants* still were asked to record their family alliances and the extent of their influence in the province, report on their conduct, discover whether they protected the weak, and investigate any well-founded complaints against them. For the rest of the nobility, the king wanted to know how many lived in each *bailliage* and *sénéchaussée,* their family connections, their personal merits or services, and the revenues of their lands and properties. The personnel of the sovereign courts, too, should be investigated for their marriage alliances, their morals, their capacities, and the degree of their influence.[31] In the end, the king would have before his eyes an invasive analysis of both the quantitative and the qualitative resources of every province.

Later, in 1686, the marquis de Vauban—the first great social statistician in France's history—actually proposed that the king satisfy his thirst for knowledge about his realm by having detailed and statistically sound censuses of each province drawn up annually.

> Would it not be a great satisfaction to the king to know at a designated point every year the number of his subjects, in total and by region, with all the faculties, wealth & poverty of each place; [the number] of his nobility and of ecclesiastics of all kinds, of men of the robe, of

---

29. As cited in James E. King, *Science and Rationalism in the Government of Louis XIV, 1661–1683* (Baltimore, 1949), 130; the inquest is described fully on 130–35. The inquiry was not completed before Colbert's death in 1683, but much information was collected and forwarded to the controller general and presumably then put to use (King, 135). For the government's extensive use of data and statistics under Colbert, see King, 116–46.
30. Ibid., 130–31.
31. Ibid., 132, 136.

Catholics, and of those of the other religion, all separated according to the place of their residence? . . . . [Would it not be] a useful and necessary pleasure for him to be able, in his own office, to review in an hour's time the present and past condition of a great realm of which he is the head and to be able to know himself with certitude in what consists his grandeur, his wealth, and his strengths?[32]

Vauban assured that this knowledge could be easily represented in a table. At his very fingertips the king would have a "perfect knowledge of the number of families, of their quality," and of the "profession of subjects of every condition." To provide the king such valuable information, it would only be necessary to follow "a kind of formula done in ordered tables . . . where the name, surname, & quality of everyone can be distinguished in a succinct manner that explains in few words and without confusion."[33] The entire French population would then, in effect, be displayed before the king's eyes: "I see nothing more necessary to a prince who loves his people than to know precisely the state in which they find themselves . . . because men are indeed the possessors of land, but the true advantage of kings consists in possessing men."[34]

Louis XIV never adopted Vauban's plan, possibly for lack of money. But he attempted to make the realm immediately accessible to him in other ways. Like Xenophon's King Cyrus, whose personal agents had served as "the king's eyes and his ears," Louis XIV relied heavily on his servants to facilitate the flow of information to the king and his council.[35]

Neither we nor the ministers we employ can deliberate on anything with certainty if we do not have a very precise knowledge of all that happens around us; and just as reason itself, which rules over all the human faculties, cannot regulate its operations except according to the report of the senses, sovereigns can only act in their councils on the news that their agents send to them unceasingly from outside.[36]

32. Sebastien Le Prestre, maréchal de Vauban, *Méthode Générale et facile pour faire le dénombrement des peuples* (Paris, 1686), 14.

33. See Vauban, *Méthode Générale,* 1; and idem, "Pensées et mémoires politiques inédits de Vauban, recueillis par A. de Rochas d'Aiglun," *Journal des Economistes* 18 (1882): 191.

34. Vauban, "Pensées," 191.

35. James Tatum, ed., *The School of Cyrus: William Barker's 1567 Translation of Xenophon's Cyropaedeia,* vol. 37 of *The Renaissance Imagination* (New York and London, 1987), 188.

36. Louis XIV, *Mémoires* (1923), 2:95.

At court the king could observe and discern most everything himself. But where he could not be present, his agents had to do his observing for him.[37] Consequently, he demanded consistent application from his ministers and secretaries; they, in turn, expected the same of their subordinates, who were constantly reminded of the king's all-embracing vision. Colbert instructed one *intendant* to exercise "still more application" in collecting information relating to his *généralité*. He should "examine with the greatest care the state of the produce of the land," for example.[38] Colbert informed another *intendant* that "the most important application that His Majesty desires of you" was to insure the liquidation of community debts in his *généralité*: "He does not doubt that you are working with all the care and application necessary in such a great work, so desired by His Majesty."[39] Louvois, after becoming minister of war in 1667, released the old *commissaires des guerres*, who had too often neglected "the principal part" of their functions—"the reviews of the troops." He replaced them with appointed commissioners who, afraid of being recalled "for the least negligence," proved "much more exact in their duties."[40] Through their exactitude, the commissioners, like the minister to whom they reported, served as a valuable conduit to the king.

Despite the efficient service of intermediaries, however, many obstacles prevented the king from forming a full and clear picture of his realm and of the needs of his service. As the king said in his memoirs (quoted earlier in this chapter), when he first "cast . . . eyes on all the diverse parts of the state," he had been discouraged to find that "disorder reigned" in all his affairs. The king regarded the confusion of ranks at court as one symptom of a larger problem also manifested, for example, in the disordered state of the crown finances, the order of nobility (who

37. James E. King noted long ago that Louis himself, "had it been possible, would have personally discovered and administered every need of his kingdom," so much was he committed to the principle of personal oversight. Given the limits of mortality, the next best solution was to extend "the threads of the royal sense into the remotest parish" by instilling in the entire hierarchy of administration the same spirit of personal observation. A random sampling of the administrative correspondence of Colbert or Louvois demonstrates that in the reign of Louis XIV, it was accepted that "from the King downward, the best test in all matters was personal inspection." See King, *Science and Rationalism*, 128.

38. AN, G⁷ 1, 1680, letter from Colbert, June 1680.

39. AN, G⁷ 1, 1680, letter from Colbert, 29 February 1680. That the invocation of the king's name became a standard administrative technique under Louis XIV is also noted by William Beik. See *Absolutism and Society in Seventeenth-Century France: State Power and Provincial Aristocracy in Languedoc* (Cambridge, 1985), 304–5.

40. Bibliothèque Nationale (hereafter BN), MS fr. 14189, "Mémoire sur le Ministère du Marquis de Louvois," 53.

belonged and who did not?), and the army, where disputes over command and an apparent lack of discipline threatened to paralyze the troops. If one keeps in mind Louis's impression of endemic "confusion" and his inclination to impose a visible regularity on all phenomena, the work of his reign appears in a new light. The various reforms carried out in the first decade of his personal rule and renewed at several intervals thereafter all contributed to the objective of reducing the realm to a harmonious and measurable order, thereby making it easily decipherable and accessible to the king "at all moments and at a glance." Soon after 1661, the king and his closest advisors began to compose a well-ordered social tableau, one that would indeed allow Louis XIV "to have eyes opened over all the land."

The motive implicit in this grand enterprise underscores a point that many historians of absolutism now stress: royal centralization did not necessarily offend traditional elites. On the contrary, the king's goal of gathering useful social knowledge in his own hands, like his renewed attention to court life, seemed entirely consonant with the nobility's customary emphasis on the sovereign's discerning gaze. As noted in chapter 1, for example, nobles assumed that grand actions were of "little merit if they are not considered by the Prince,"[41] and for decades they had searched for a method to make their generosity known to the king. Many nobles published their family histories, but all recognized the need for more direct means to convey merit to the royal person. In 1614, noble deputies from Orléans had made the unlikely suggestion that the nobility of each province should send one *gentilhomme* to reside with the king at court. His only responsibility would be to provide the king information about all noble families living in his locality.[42] At the meeting of the Estates General, representatives of the second estate apparently thought it more practical for Louis XIII simply to establish "public registers that would contain the exact names and surnames of nobles, their coats of arms, and their memorable actions."[43]

These appeals went unanswered, however, until the 1660s. After taking over the government in 1661 Louis XIV had noticed that his nobility found itself mixed up with "an infinite number of usurpers, either without a title or with a title acquired by money and without service," and he

---

41. *La véritable conduite du courtisan généreux* (Paris, 1649), 4.
42. See chap. 1.
43. Louis-Pierre d'Hozier and A. M. d'Hozier de Sérigny, *Armorial Général ou Registres de la Noblesse de France*, 10 vols. (Paris, 1738–68), 1: "Au Roi."

considered this one of the principal "disorders" afflicting the realm.[44] Responding to the problem in 1664, Louis and Colbert decided that "to fix the quality and condition of all the king's subjects, it seems necessary to compose a Catalog of all those who will be judged truly noble."[45] With this end in mind, the crown carried out a series of general *recherches de la noblesse* between 1666–74 and 1696–1716.[46] In each province, every family of dubious status had to submit proof to the local *intendant* that its "nobility" had been formally recognized in 1560 or before.[47] Families whose pretensions had begun only after that date would be declared roturier and placed back on the tax rolls. Furthermore, in 1669 the crown announced that comprehensive catalogs of the names and coats of arms of local noble families would be compiled and registered for each *bailliage,* with copies to be sent to the royal library in Paris.[48] (In 1696, coats of arms were again collected and placed in a newly created *dépôt général.*)[49]

The office of the controller general had clear financial motives for establishing the *recherches.* Once deprived of their legal claim to nobility, those with sufficient financial resources could be expected eventually to buy their way back into the noblesse, especially if they had grown accustomed to the status and privileges that went with membership in the second estate. The crown could exploit the situation in a number of ways. A

---

44. Louis XIV, *Mémoires* (1978), 36.

45. Bibliothèque de l'Arsenal (hereafter BA), MS 6829, "Extrait des Mémoires sur les ordonnances en général fait par ordre de M. Colbert," fol. 419.

46. Monique Cubells discusses the general patterns of usurpation and the success of Louis XIV's *recherches* in restricting the practice in the late seventeenth and eighteenth centuries. See her useful article, "A propos des usurpations de noblesse en Provence, sous l'Ancien Régime," *Provence Historique* 20 (1970): 226–301.

47. Naturally, those ennobled by letter or office after that date had only to show their official *titres de noblesse.*

48. François Isambert et al., *Recueil général des anciennes loix françaises depuis l'an 426 jusqu'à la révolution de 1789,* 29 vols. (Paris, 1822–33), 18:204.

49. AN, M 608, no. 14. "Ordonnance du Roi concernant les Armoiries," 29 July 1760, 3; AN, O¹ 976, no. 9, "Edit . . . Grande Maîtrise," November 1696. Actually, the ordinance of 1696 announced that the *dépôt général* was to be administered by a *grande maîtrise générale* in Paris, aided by local *maîtrises particulières* throughout the provinces. The king was using the proposed regulation of coats of arms partly as a pretext for selling new offices. Unfortunately for the crown, the offices apparently were not sufficiently valuable to attract buyers, and the old office of *juge d'armes,* first established in 1615, had to be reestablished in 1701. (The project for a *dépôt* was eventually discontinued and was not taken up again until 1760.) Not surprisingly, however, the crown was able to squeeze some profit out of the operation by charging registration fees for all those who wanted their arms collected in the *dépôt.*

declaration of 13 January 1667, for example, revoked all letters of nobility issued since 1614 and thereby placed back on the taille rolls all those who had been ennobled by letter since that year—excepting those who had purchased letters of confirmation after the announcement of the general *recherche* in 1664.[50] By giving social status a solid legal basis, the crown cleverly increased the financial value of the "quality" it ostensibly purified.[51] In 1696, the year that marked the beginning of the second general *recherche,* Louis XIV put five hundred letters of nobility up for sale, and this can hardly be seen as a coincidence. Nobles were not blind to the crown's financial motives, and they complained frequently that the fiscal officials who oversaw the investigations treated them disrespectfully. They also protested the length and inefficiency of the verification procedure.[52]

Nevertheless, nobles knew that the investigations of 1666 spoke to a long-standing request.[53] In assembling a complete record of his nobility, Louis XIV protected the status of genuine noble families while also making lists of their qualities and services to consult as needed. In the catalog of nobles of the province of Champagne, published in 1673, the *intendant* Caumartin explained that the king had wanted such catalogs to be compiled and registered "in order to have recourse to [them] in the future."[54] As Caumartin described them, the catalogs would effectively serve the purpose of the "book of honor" that Blaise de Monluc had first proposed a century before, making a record of the services, merits, and qualities of each noble family immediately accessible to the king: "You

50. François Caumartin, *Recherche de la noblesse de Champagne* (Châlons, 1673), procès-verbal, 2.

51. David D. Bien details the crown's inventive exploitation of the marketability of "noble" status and other officially sanctioned privileges in his essay "Offices, Corps, and a System of State Credit: The Uses of Privilege under the Ancien Régime," in *The Political Culture of the Old Regime,* ed. Keith M. Baker (New York, 1987), 89–114.

52. The fiercely independent Breton nobility, in particular, resented the crown's investigation into the status of its members. For examples of Breton hostility see Jean Meyer, *La Noblesse Bretonne au XVIIIe siècle,* (Paris, 1972), chap. 2. Meyer notes, however, that even the nobles of Brittany eventually came to regard the findings of the *recherches de la noblesse* as an important safeguard of their own privileges and status. In the eighteenth century, Meyer writes, "the reformation [of the nobility], once spurned, became in the eyes of the Breton nobility an essential reference point, [it acquired] a quasi-sacred character" (47).

53. Gayle K. Brunelle has also emphasized the noble agitation that lay behind the *recherches* of the later seventeenth century. See her insightful article "Dangerous Liaisons: Mésalliance and Early Modern French Noblewomen," *French Historical Studies* 19 (1995): 75–103, esp. 77–78.

54. Caumartin, *Recherche,* procès-verbal, 1.

[the king] wanted to know the origin of Houses, their antiquity, their alliances, the dignities that they have possessed, the luster they have acquired, the services they have rendered, so that, under a reign as equitable as this one, merit would have its price."[55]

Caumartin readily acknowledged that not all the noble families of Champagne could boast truly ancient lineage. Some had only the minimum age required to enjoy the status of nobility. But if everyone were equal in dignity, it would be difficult to find candidates for the lesser posts of the realm, as everyone would have pretensions to the highest offices and distinctions. A certain inequality of family rank was desirable, because "it furnishes subjects for all sorts of positions." Now, with classified rosters at hand, the king would be able to match candidates perfectly with the needs of his service.

> It is by this knowledge that you [the king] dispose of posts and make the choice of people who should fill them. You know that one can expect more from those who are from a more illustrious family, because they have more motives and more reasons to serve well. For beyond the sentiments of strength and valor, which are communicated with the blood, the virtue of great men is revived in the person of their descendants; the passion to acquire glory, the natural desire to conserve [the glory] that has been acquired, the example of their ancestors, the shame of betraying their blood and rendering themselves unworthy of their own name, [all these] excite them unceasingly, and render them capable of the greatest things. . . . All these reasons, Sire, persuaded me that it would be both agreeable to Your Majesty and useful to the public to put into a collection all the houses of *Gentils-hommes* of Champagne and to have their genealogies printed.[56]

In various ways, the *recherches* did indeed signal a renewed recognition for the qualities attached to birth. Louis XIV rigorously defended the privileges of birth in public ceremonies and courtly protocol. Perhaps more important, in the same year that saw the beginning of the first general *recherche,* the king expanded and refined the court's school for pages. The two royal *écuries* had required genealogical proofs of old military nobility for admission since 1643, but enforcement had previously been lax. Now, Louis pledged to make sure that all future pages would

---

55. Ibid., epistle to the King.
56. Ibid., epistle to the King.

have the "qualités requises." Furthermore, in addition to increasing the numbers of pages by half, the king raised the level of instruction offered the pages so that they could "with time, by learning all sorts of [military] exercises there, add to the advantage of their birth the satisfaction of being useful to me."[57] Later, in 1682, Louis XIV and Louvois also established nine special companies of *cadets gentilshommes*—training corps where young nobles would learn their profession while serving a kind of apprenticeship in frontier city garrisons. The cadet companies produced thousands of noble officers for the king's armies in the 1680s and 1690s.[58] Finally, at the urging of Madame de Maintenon, Louis XIV founded in 1686 the Maison Royale de Saint Louis at Saint-Cyr, a school to educate daughters of the nobility. Only girls with four generations of nobility on the paternal side became eligible for admission.[59]

The general *recherches* thus served other than financial purposes. The verification of birth on a grand scale would guarantee that merit could indeed have its price. Nobles had long assumed that genealogy, functioning as a different form of heraldry, could be used by the king to identify better the men of courage, generosity, and valor. In setting strict admissions standards for the corps of pages and cadets on the basis of noble birth, Louis XIV used genealogical history the way nobles had intended for kings to use it all along. Nobles could now hope that their more firmly established merit would be rewarded by public offices and positions as well as lasting public recognition of their honor. Although it is unlikely that Louis XIV or his successors ever actually placed nobles in positions of influence after careful consideration of their genealogical histories, the *Armorial Général* still insisted in 1738 that the first *recherche* had been designed to insure that "the prince can know those of his subjects on whose attachment and services he can rightfully and most particularly depend."[60]

In analyzing other areas of governmental activity in the 1660s and

57. AN, O^1 974, no. 3, "Création du Seul Gouverneur des Pages," 9 February 1666.

58. André Corvisier, *Louvois* (Paris, 1983), 339–40. At any given time, the nine companies would have employed 4,275 men—475 men each. Two thousand were promoted to the active troops in 1683–84 alone.

59. For discussion of Saint-Cyr see Carolyn C. Lougee, *"Le Paradis des Femmes"*: *Women, Salons, and Social Stratification in Seventeenth-Century France* (Princeton, 1976), pt. 4.

60. Hozier and Hozier de Sérigny, *Armorial Général*, 1:viii. Ironically, the qualities thought to be reflected in high birth were overshadowed in the end by the very mechanism of the investigation. The desire to bring the nobility before the king "at a glance" compelled

1670s, one confronts the same irony brought to light by the preceding discussion of the *recherches*. Louis XIV, Colbert, Louvois, and the various councillors and committees they employed now took up a variety of tasks—the compilation of lists and statistics, the definition of rules and regulations, the extension or clarification of jurisdictions—that would seem to be impersonal almost by definition. Yet behind all of this work lay an intent to bring into sharper focus objects arrayed within the sovereign's field of vision, to extend the sovereign's eyes "over all the land."

Consider, for example, the reforming impulse that directed the monarchy's approach to law. Already in 1661 Colbert had begun to compile tables of royal ordinances dating back to the thirteenth century. "By these tables it is clear," he observed, that "no king has worked . . . to incorporate into a body all the ordinances of the realm."[61] Because of entrenched local customs and the patchwork of privileges that made up a central component of French jurisprudence, Louis XIV would never manage to issue a uniform statement of French law on the model of Justinian's code. But thanks to Colbert and the reforming Council of Justice that he established in 1665, the king did manage to issue two comprehensive ordinances—in April 1667 and August 1670—that established uniform procedures for civil and criminal cases. Order and clarity began to take the place of diversity and obscurity.[62]

Later, Louis XIV sponsored the production of Jean Domat's five-volume compendium of French law titled *The Civil Laws in Their Natural Order*, first published in 1689. In the preface to his first volume, the jurist drew attention to the general need for clarity of perception.

No one can fail to notice the value of order in all things; just as the proper arrangement of the parts that make a whole is necessary to bring into view things that are objects of the senses only, so order is all

---

the crown to abbreviate and eventually to do without biographical data. In the provincial *nobiliaires* collected during the investigations of 1696–1717, for example, "services" and "memorable actions" gave way to brief genealogical descriptions as it became clear that the *recherches* served mainly to clarify a family's tax status. See, for example, the *nobiliaires* covering the provinces of Bretagne, Limousin, and Picardie, all compiled during the second *recherche* between 1697 and 1716. AN, MM 689–91, 693–94, and 695–99[B], respectively.

61. As cited in King, *Science and Rationalism,* 266.

62. For a full discussion of the "reformation of justice" see Albert Hamscher, *The Parlement of Paris after the Fronde, 1653–1673* (Pittsburgh, 1976), 155–95. On the connection between the reformation of justice and the advance of governmental "rationalism" see King, *Science and Rationalism,* 264–74.

the more important if the infinite details that comprise a science are to be communicated to the mind.

Any body of knowledge contains a diversity of truths, and "the mind, needing to move from one to the others, must see them in their order."[63] Three of Domat's five volumes elucidated private law by comparing systematically the French and Roman legal traditions. In the end, however, Domat pointed with greatest pride to his other major accomplishment: a close and orderly examination of French constitutional principles. He aspired to "bring into view" a comprehensive and detailed statement of French public law, something never done before. In doing this, he remarked, he would give expression to "a new kind of science, [new] not because of the novelty of the material contained in it, but because of the system itself." The value of Domat's explicitly stated "system" would be not only "the order of its detail" but its all-encompassing scope. He proudly declared that his system contained "diverse matters that one does not commonly believe to be implicated in public law, but which must be included by virtue of their connection to the general order of a state."[64] Domat may well have overstated the novelty of his "science" of public law, but the methodology of this new science, with its intent to "bring into view" the entire body of law, "the detail of its definitions, its principles, its rules . . . [and] all that may be necessary to make it comprehensible,"[65] reflects the wider commitment to establish for the monarchy an orderly field of vision.

This same commitment is apparent in other reforms. In March 1667, for example, Louis XIV and Colbert turned their attention to policing the city of Paris—home to the principal residence of king and court until 1682.[66] Traditionally, the responsibility for keeping order in the city had been divided between the *parlement,* the office of the *prévôt des marchands* (mayor), and the *lieutenant civil* of the Châtelet (seat of the

---

63. Jean Domat, *Les lois civiles dans leur ordre naturel,* 5 vols. (Paris, 1695–97), 1: preface.

64. Ibid., 4: *avertissement.*

65. Ibid., 1: preface.

66. Michèle Fogel has argued that the ordinances of 1666–67 concerning the policing of Paris actually indicated "a new conception of space. . . . [urban] space becomes an object of reflection." Closer observation of the city was made possible by the drafting of a new map, completed in 1675, which permitted "the visualization of the territory and its subdivision according to geometric norms." See Fogel, *Les cérémonies de l'information dans la France du XVIe au milieu du XVIIIe siècle* (Paris, 1989), 118–19. For a thoughtful analysis of

bailliage court). Since each body necessarily attended first to its juridical duties, policing the streets remained a low priority.[67] To keep closer watch over potential troublemakers and "purge the city of whatever might cause disorders," the king created, in 1667, a *lieutenant de police* for the capital city.[68] Louis considered the lieutenant's task so important that he included him among the small group of councillors who periodically met with the king at the Louvre to discuss the "travail du roi." Nicolas de La Reynie, the first lieutenant (1667–97), wasted no time before setting to work. Soldiers had attracted attention for their habit of roaming the streets at night and carousing at every tavern that would take them in, and they were among La Reynie's first targets. In 1667, the office of the lieutenant prohibited

> all soldiers from wandering outside their quarter and their guards' troop past six o'clock from November until the last of March, and nine o'clock from the last of March until the first of November. . . . And so that the streets will be lighted beginning at dusk, we order that lanterns will be distributed in the quarters of the city and the faubourgs; even when the moon is bright, they will be lighted precisely at five o'clock in the evening. . . . And we expressly prohibit all pages, lackeys, and everyone else from breaking the said lanterns or tearing down the posts or lines [that hold them], on pain of being tried as enemies of the . . . public security.[69]

The realm's dark recesses would now be illuminated and closely observed. A later ordinance declared that the city's secret passages and escape routes must be located and sealed, "in order to remove from the

---

the theoretical underpinning of "policing" powers in the later seventeenth century, and of the relationship between state and society implied by this form of theorizing, see Daniel Gordon, *Citizens without Sovereignty: Equality and Sociability in French Thought, 1670–1789* (Princeton, 1994), 9–24.

67. For discussion of the jurisdictional confusion that lay behind the creation of the lieutenancy of police in 1667 see Alan Williams, *The Police of Paris, 1718–1789* (Baton Rouge and London, 1979), chap. 2. On the police lieutenant's relation to the royal council see, in addition to Williams, François Bluche, *Louis XIV*, 224–28. See also Joseph Klaits, *Printed Propaganda under Louis XIV: Absolute Monarchy and Public Opinion* (Princeton, 1976), chap. 2 and passim; Pierre Clément provides a still useful overview in *La Police sous Louis XIV* (Paris, 1866).

68. Isambert, *Recueil*, 18:100.

69. BN, MS fr. 21709, "De Par le Roy et Msr le prévost de Paris ou son Lieutenant de Police, 26 octobre 1667," fol. 18.

thieves of the night, or others with bad intentions, the means to commit crimes against individuals . . . and the ease of escape that is accorded them." Proprietors of homes and business establishments with doors opening onto the city's ramparts, for example, should keep their front doors closed "during the night" and wall up passageways "on the side of the said ramparts or moats, and this within three days of the publication of this ordinance [24 October 1671]." Finally, the city's inhabitants should report immediately any crimes they witnessed to the *commissaire de quartier,* so that the wrongdoers could be "found and recognized" more easily.[70]

The crown went to great lengths in its effort to "find" and "recognize" malefactors. When it became clear, for example, that soldiers from the regiment of French guards were also raising havoc on the streets, measures were taken to prevent their escaping detection. "Being obliged to search for the causes [of this problem], in order to apply an appropriate remedy," the king's council decided that soldiers could no longer mask their identities under any circumstances, since such anonymity permitted them to enter a public place "without being known, even by their officers."

> We have been informed that what gives the said soldiers the audacity to behave so badly is the expectation of not being recognized as soldiers, by means of changing their dress, and with this disguise [they are] able to hide their crimes more easily, which they commit with impunity.[71]

The police took the problem seriously. In 1698, for example, a French guardsman by the name of Fontenay was haled before the new lieutenant general of police, Voyer d'Argenson. A *commissaire de quartier* exposed Fontenay as one who "withdrew every night with Geneviève Touret, a woman of bad morals, into a room on the rue Montorgueil . . . in a disguised vestment, with his sword and with several other soldiers." The *commissaire* had caught Fontenay and company red-handed, barging in unexpectedly to find Fontenay

---

70. BN, MS fr. 21709, "Déclaration, 24 octobre 1671," fol. 20.
71. BN, MS fr. 21709, "Déclaration du Roy, 22 juillet 1692," fol. 8. A similar declaration, apparently not entirely effective, had been issued in December 1666.

dressed in a musk-colored *juste-au-corps,* [and he] remarked that there
were two [other] *juste-au-corps* hidden in the same room, one on the
canopy of the bed, the other under the covers, with two swords resting
on chairs . . . this room serving as a retreat for the soldiers to disguise
themselves, and with the help of their disguises mingle with the bourgeois and other inhabitants of this city . . . without being known even
by their officers.[72]

One is relieved to find that in this case the lieutenant indulged the
seemingly minor offense. He fined Geneviève Touret and the soldier
Fontenay ten livres apiece and ordered them not to consort with one
another unless they married, assuming that had been their intention.
Although he opted for leniency, d'Argenson nevertheless restated the
crown's "express inhibitions and prohibitions to all soldiers of His
Majesty's Guards Regiments to wander about at night." At all times they
should be wearing the clothes "suitable to their trade, profession, and
work . . . on pain of corporal punishment."[73] The police lieutenant's sensitivity to the crime of impersonation may appear disproportionate, but
the edict creating his office specified this responsibility: "to see that
everyone lives according to his condition and his duty."[74] To a king
determined that all should be openly visible to him, masking one's identity stood out as a serious offense indeed.

This theme of clarifying identities and duties appears also in Louis
XIV's reform of the army. In this special branch of royal service where
the nobility focused so much attention, the hierarchy of status and command remained unsettled, and this affected the noble officer perhaps
more than anyone. Rules of precedence determined not only the order of
march at times of military activity but also the order of appearance in
public ceremonies and the degree of honor accorded those belonging to
each company. Until the reforms of Louis XIV and the Le Telliers, no
uniform rule decided the order of precedence for officers of equal rank or
even for companies raised during the same levy. Just as confusing, the
responsibilities attached to each rank were not clearly defined, leaving
room for disputes, even at the highest levels, between officers of comparable distinction. A general, for example, might be called either *lieu-*

72. BN, MS fr. 21709, "De Par le Roy et Msr le Prévost de Paris ou Msr son Lieutenant-
Général de Police, 28 juin 1698," fol. 11.
73. Ibid.
74. Isambert, *Recueil,* 18:100.

tenant-général or *maréchal de camp,* and men bearing either title had the right to claim the honor to command the entire army. This situation not only undermined the performance of the military; it failed to satisfy the nobility's thirst for recognition.[75] Le Tellier, the secretary of state for war in the 1650s, had made some progress toward resolving these problems.[76] But the ranks were far from orderly when Louis XIV ascended the throne, and the king, who believed "I should not be assured of anything except from the assiduity of my own work," saw the disorder as another opportunity for personal intervention.[77] No one appreciated better the importance of rank, and Louis saw the imposition of order in the army as one of his great achievements.

> I also wanted to remove all the subjects of dispute that had so often caused disorder in my troops; and, without being taken aback by all the different pretensions that each corps defended so heatedly, and which no one had yet dared to decide, I regulated all their ranks, with as much equity as possible, and sustained this regulation so well by my authority that no one dared contradict it.[78]

In the first ten years of the reign, Louis, Le Tellier, and Louvois (the latter two worked as coministers of war until 1677) established a firm order of precedence for all the companies in the military. In May 1667, the twenty-four companies of the royal *maisons*—which had especially heavy concentrations of nobles—had their ranks clearly defined. Proximity to the king again assured highest place, and the new ordinance

---

75. On the confusion of ranks in the army in the early 1660s see Corvisier, *Louvois*, 97–108.

76. In his exhaustive studies of the Le Telliers, Louis André emphasized the diligent efforts of Michel Le Tellier to impose order on the troops in the period between the Fronde and 1661. A steady stream of ordinances and declarations in the 1650s testify to Le Tellier's patient work on the problems of discipline and hierarchy, but the thoroughgoing reforms of the 1660s and 1670s raise doubts about the efficacy of the elder Le Tellier's earlier attempts at reform. Louis XIV's personal involvement in issues of military administration seems to have provided the authority needed to effect lasting change. See André, *Michel Le Tellier et l'Organisation de l'Armée Monarchique* (Paris, 1906; reprint, Geneva, 1980), esp. 119–46, 167–88, 204–5, for an admiring account of Le Tellier's work. Le Tellier also receives much credit in André's *Michel Le Tellier et Louvois* (Paris, 1942; reprint, Geneva, 1974). For a short but thorough review of military change under Louis XIV see Ronald Martin, "The Army of Louis XIV," in Paul Sonnino, ed., *The Reign of Louis XIV* (Atlantic Highlands, N.J., 1990), 111–26.

77. Louis XIV, *Mémoires* (1923), 2:119.

78. Ibid., 1:241.

declared that the four companies of the king's *gardes du corps* would take precedence over all other regiments and companies of cavalry, both foreign and French.[79] Next in line came the company of His Majesty's gendarmes, the king's *chevaux-légers,* the Scotch gendarmes, the first and second companies of mounted musketeers, and the companies of English, Burgundian, and Flemish gendarmes. The troops of the other *maisons* came next. The gendarmes and *chevaux-légers* (the gendarmes always coming first) of the queen, the dauphin, and the ducs de Bourgogne, Anjou, Berry, and Orléans followed the king's own contingent.[80]

In 1670, another ordinance somewhat arbitrarily ranked all forty-four of the crown's infantry regiments. The measure affected some two-thirds of all French soldiers. As new regiments were created to fight Louis's great wars, they simply took precedence according to their date of creation (though two ordinances had to be issued to clear up confusion in December 1684 and July 1693).[81] Cavalry regiments, which since 1647 had taken precedence according to the date of their commanding officers' commissions, conformed to the same system as the infantry in May 1699. At the same time, Louis also provided regulations for determining the order within a given regiment or battalion. An ordinance of November 1671 declared that whenever a battalion was formed of companies from different regiments, all the companies of the highest ranking regiment would stand at the right and front of the formation, with the companies of the next ranking regiment moving to the left. The other troops would fall in behind, taking their places successively from right to left.[82] Precedence within the regiment, meanwhile, would generally be determined according to the date of the captain's commission.

The chain of command had also to be clarified. An ordinance of December 1670, for example, declared that majors, whose responsibilities as general overseers of a regiment had been increasing for years, would from now on enjoy the rank of captain, with the right to command over all captains whose commissions dated after their own. Their counterparts at the battalion level, the aide-majors, would enjoy the rank of lieutenant, commanding over other lieutenants with more recent com-

79. Foreign companies—such as the Swiss guards and Scotch gendarmes—were a permanent complement to French forces, most of them having originated in the fifteenth and sixteenth centuries.

80. Sr. de Briquet, ed., *Code Militaire, ou Compilation des Ordonnances des Roys de France Concernant les Gens de Guerre,* 3 vols. (Paris, 1728), 2:64–65.

81. Ibid., 1:426–33.

82. Ibid., *ordonnance* of 15 November 1671, 1:447.

missions.[83] According to the declaration of February 1679, the *cornettes*, subaltern officers whose role in the cavalry had likewise grown in importance, were to enjoy the same rank as "reformed" lieutenants and command the *maréchaux des logis*. Higher up, an ordinance of 1675 announced that any captain commanding ten or more companies should be considered a lieutenant colonel, an honor the other captains were forbidden to dispute.[84] Similar ordinances clarified and bolstered the positions of other officers, up and down the hierarchy, in the effort to bring systematic order to the military.

Writing in his memoirs, Louis XIV claimed that he had settled all disputes over precedence and rank "in such a way that, whichever troops might find themselves together, there would be no more place for doubting the rank or authority of him who should be commanding over them."[85] For Louis, the condition of the army had been analogous to the situation at court. With a newly clarified system of rank and hierarchy, both courtiers and career soldiers now knew exactly what honors and authority they could expect. They also now knew precisely what the king expected of them. In reinforcing hierarchy in the military, Louis knew that he increased not only the prestige of his officers but also their accountability.

In retrospect, the rationalizing measures just discussed supply clear evidence of the growing size and power of the French state in the second half of the seventeenth century. But although the later seventeenth century witnessed the steady development of administrative structures and routines, Louis XIV's own understanding of his actions suggests a new way of looking at the phenomenon. Clearly the monarchy's quest to gather information and extend royal authority to remote regions should not be ascribed to mercantilist ideas alone. Louis and Colbert did intend to

---

83. Ibid., *ordonnances* of 10 December 1670 and 25 July 1665, 1:504–5. The aide-major eventually came to enjoy the grade of captain.

84. Ibid., *ordonnance* of 25 October, 1675, 1:503.

85. Louis XIV, *Mémoires* (1923), 2:124. The military hierarchy was firmly in place by 1670. The listing here is taken from King, *Science and Rationalism,* 248. The right to command an army was reserved for a *maréchal de France,* followed by the lieutenant general (commanding a division), *maréchal de camp* (junior to the lieutenant general, but also in command of a division), brigadier (in command of a brigade), *maistre de camp* (of infantry or dragoons), lieutenant colonel (in command of a battalion), captain (in command of a company), lieutenant (second in command of a company), *sous-lieutenant* (third in command of a company), *cornette* (third or fourth in a cavalry company), and ensign (third or fourth in an infantry company).

exploit the realm's resources more efficiently than before, but the king's desire to bring a visible order to his realm did not spring from a specifically economic agenda.[86] The ordering of the army, the drafting of regional maps, the clarification of social status, the illumination of Paris, and the elaboration of a system of court etiquette were all reflections of the same unstated goal: to create an all-seeing monarchy in which the king theoretically could observe and evaluate the qualities, strengths, and weaknesses of his people and assess the needs of all the realm.

Convinced that a monarch could not claim responsibility for a work unless "he himself appears in it," Louis wanted to make it clear that he himself made every decision and stood behind every action of the monarchy. A long series of written ordinances spelled out the order of command in the army, but Louis knew that the newly regulated hierarchy was sustained "by my authority." At his insistence, estimates of revenues and expenses were inscribed in a small book "which would always remain with me." The king collected lists of noble families to "have recourse to them in the future," so that "merit would have its price." The jurist Domat worked to "bring into view" an entire system of law, while a corps of administrative assistants executed a variety of tasks "so desired by His Majesty."

Louis and his collaborators never saw the creation of an autonomous administrative state as an end in itself. This is why the popular analytic term *state building* distorts the actual experience of state formation in France. Louis's endeavor to stretch his eyes "over all the land" should instead be read as an inversion of the Hobbesian metaphor that likened the abstract power of the commonwealth to that of "an Artificiall Man." The small but growing body of provincial agents, the social statistics collected by *intendants* and ministers, the increasingly efficient lines of communication between Versailles and distant points in the realm, the rules regulating court life—for Louis, all these were mere artificial extensions of his own very *real* presence. It is in this sense that the descriptive term *absolutism* so often applied to the rule of Louis XIV still retains meaning. To Louis XIV, in contrast to Louis XIII and Richelieu, absolute power

---

86. On the links between mercantilist philosophy and state formation in France see Charles W. Cole, *Colbert and a Century of French Mercantilism,* 2 vols. (New York, 1939); idem., *French Mercantilist Doctrines before Colbert* (New York, 1931); and Lionel Rothkrug, *Opposition to Louis XIV: The Political and Social Origins of the French Enlightenment* (Princeton, 1965). For a comparative perspective on European *cameralism* see Marc Raeff, *The Well-Ordered Police State: Social and Institutional Change through Law in the Germanies and Russia, 1600–1800* (New Haven, 1983).

implied the establishment of his own full and uninterrupted presence throughout the kingdom.

In aggressively asserting his own presence, Louis XIV counteracted a troubling impression created and reinforced through several decades of ministerial rule—that the construction of an activist, supervisory royal government necessarily implied the physical withdrawal of the king. By dispelling that assumption, Louis not only made the growth of state power more intelligible to the old nobility; he also established an important line of continuity between the traditional culture of personal service and the expectations of service implied by the concept of reason of state. That the personal modality provided the conceptual and linguistic framework for the articulation of a new culture of service in absolutist France is nowhere better illustrated than in Louis XIV's methods of promoting good service, at court and beyond.

Reinventing the Sovereign's Gaze

Louis XIV's close attention to court life and his regularly scheduled accessibility certainly indicate his sensitivity to the attitudes of his nobility. But Louis's regime also spoke to the nobility's needs in other ways. The reform and expansion of the court's school for pages, for example, revived the nobility's diminishing enthusiasm for the unique form of instruction offered there. The school for pages, located in the *grande écurie,* was an important and long-established institution at court, a place where the sons of prominent noble families came to serve as page boys while learning horsemanship and military exercises in preparation for careers in the army. In the first half of the seventeenth century, however, the appeal of service in the king's stables had waned, and Louis XIV believed he knew why.

> I introduced . . . in my household a change that interested all the nobility of the realm. This was in regard to my *grande écurie,* in which I increased by more than half the number of pages and took care that they were better chosen and better instructed than they had ever been up to that point.
>
> I knew that what had previously discouraged men of quality from claiming these places was the ease with which all sorts of persons could gain entry there simply by recommendation, the limited opportunities the [pages] ordinarily had to approach my person, and past

negligence in seeing that they were perfected in their exercises. Thus, to remedy everything, I resolved to . . . name all the pages myself, to let them share with those of the *petite écurie* in all the domestic services they rendered me, and to choose for their instruction the best masters in my State.[87]

Louis had recognized, moreover, that in establishing direct relations with the men who served him, a monarch provided a powerful incentive to perform well.

[I] had often remarked, with pleasure, the almost infinite difference between the rest of the troops and those of my household, [in that] the honor of belonging to me more particularly, the more exact discipline, the more certain expectation of recompenses . . . rendered them absolutely incapable of a bad action.[88]

Louis therefore emphasized at every opportunity his own role in evaluating his servants. According to the hypercritical duc de Saint-Simon, for example, Louis reviewed his troops so often that "he became known to his enemies as 'the king of reviews.'"[89] The king boasted in his memoirs of having personally chosen the officers for his army, distributing "even the least important posts myself, in both the infantry and cavalry, something my predecessors had never done."[90] He preferred to confer appointments on those nobles whose abilities he knew firsthand, and he especially considered the troops of the royal *maisons* as officer training grounds: "I took care to exercise the troops of my household [myself], and it was from among them that I chose almost all the officers of the newly formed companies I raised, so they would bring the same discipline to their new posts that they had already grown accustomed to."[91] After creating two hundred new companies of infantry in 1666, for example, he appointed a number of young nobles as colonels, assuming that they would bring "more application" to their new positions, given their pen-

87. Louis XIV, *Mémoires* (1923), 1:170.
88. Louis XIV, *Mémoires* (1978), 142.
89. Louis de Rouvroy, duc de Saint-Simon, *Louis XIV et sa Cour: Portraits, Jugemens et Anecdotes extraits des Mémoires Authentiques du duc de Saint-Simon* (Paris, 1863), 36.
90. Louis XIV, *Mémoires* (1923), 2:119.
91. Ibid., 1:237.

chant for emulation and their "desire to please me."[92] Whenever military offices fell vacant, he remembered, "I took a good number of young *gentilshommes* whom I wanted to form with my own hand, so to speak, in the maxims of their profession."[93]

For all anyone knows, Louis may have been an incompetent teacher—his generals are said to have been wary of the king's sense of expertise in all things military[94]—but nobles undoubtedly thrived on the personal attention he accorded them in any case. Louis noted, for example, that the troops who served him at court had been so taken by his personal involvement that their satisfaction seemed to attract the attention of nobles from all over the realm.

> The particular care I had for those troops who served near my person made it so that most young French *gentilshommes* wanted passionately to learn their profession [*métier*] next to me, and even several reformed officers had a passion to reenter a service where one performed so near to my eyes.[95]

The peace of the Pyrénées brought a temporary reduction in the size of the army in 1661–62, but Louis, appreciating that nobles valued opportunities to be "so near" the king's eyes, nevertheless thought it wise to retain as many officers as possible "near my person." He created new positions in the royal *maisons,* including a new light cavalry company, to accommodate officers who otherwise would have been left unoccupied.

The term *professionalization* may apply better to analysis of the nineteenth century, a time when people throughout Europe segregated themselves by skill and function and developed performance standards and admission criteria that constituted their fields as discrete disciplines. The process of professionalization nevertheless had roots in the ancien régime, and in France its origins can be traced to Louis XIV's realization that an awareness of the king's presence would inevitably impel royal ser-

---

92. Ibid., 1:117.
93. Ibid., 2:118.
94. See Lewis, *The Splendid Century,* 31–32.
95. Louis XIV, *Mémoires* (1923), 1:242–43 n. 3: "Le soin particulier que je prenais des troupes qui servaient auprès de ma personne faisait que la plupart des jeunes gentilshommes français souhaitaient passionemment d'y venir apprendre leur métier, et que même plusieurs officiers réformés avaient passion de rentrer dans un service où l'on etait exposé de si près à mes yeux."

vants to work harder and with greater application to their tasks.[96] Louis
had made clear to his courtiers that he himself would dispense all royal
graces, that he would give his gifts to whomever it pleased him to favor,
and that he would do it always according to "reason." He intended to
teach others these same lessons. He would be "more esteemed," but also
"better obeyed," once his people recognized that the king "discerns
everything, that he weighs everything, and that sooner or later he pun-
ishes or rewards everything."[97] Behind the reorientation in the meaning
of discipline in the later seventeenth and eighteenth centuries—a process
that substituted consciousness of professional duty for general moral pre-
cepts—lay Louis XIV's self-conscious assertion of the sovereign presence.[98]

The key was to insure that all earned rewards proportionate to their
merits, for otherwise a king risked demoralizing even those with "the
best intentions in the world, since nothing excites them [to do well]."[99]
Once given the king's personal assurances that every merit would receive
due recognition, "all push themselves incessantly to do their duty." They
become convinced that their own worldly success is to be found "in the
practice of honorable things, the merit of glorious actions, and observation of the laws of the profession they have embraced."[100] All seemed to
depend, though, on the king's personal vigilance.

> The ambition to please him pushes [those who work for him] to exam-
> ine themselves continually. They permit themselves no relaxation,

---

96. That the king himself saw a connection between the assertion of his own presence
and increased discipline is indicated by royal iconography. On one of the four columns
placed along the perimeter of the Place des Victoires in 1686 stood a bas-relief celebrating
"Le Rétablissment de la discipline militaire." To represent this achievement, the artist
showed Louis XIV observing his soldiers. See Charles Maumené and Louis d'Harcourt,
Iconographie, 2:237–38.

97. Louis XIV, *Mémoires* (1923), 2:121.

98. On earlier meanings of military discipline see chap. 1, "Royal Service and the Personal Modality." In 1694 the *Dictionnaire de l'Académie Française,* 1st ed. (Paris, 1694),
still did not link *discipline* explicitly to professional practice, but Furetière noted in the *Dictionnaire universel* (The Hague and Rotterdam, 1690) that *discipline* sometimes signified "a
manner of life regulated by the laws of profession." This meaning had grown more specific
by 1771. The *Dictionnaire de Trévoux* (Paris, 1771) recorded that *discipline* implied "a regulated manner of life, a manner of conduct by which one conforms to certain laws, certain
rules." The intended laws and rules come through in the definition of *discipliner* (to discipline): "to impose good order, the rules of a profession; to form and regulate."

99. Louis XIV, *Mémoires* (1923), 1:152.

100. Ibid., 2:121.

because they know that nothing bad will be hidden from him; they are resourceful because they are convinced that no merit will fail to receive [from] the prince the approval that is due. . . . they are persuaded that the favor, influence, and elevation to which they aspire, are given in proportion to the zeal and fidelity that everyone demonstrates.[101]

Louis indeed sought to create the impression that he observed everyone's performance at all times and that nothing escaped his view. To pursue the elusive goal of royal omnipresence, however, he had to overcome the spatial and temporal boundaries imposed by the laws of physics. He made his presence, and his absences, always conspicuous at the one location where this was possible: the court. But elsewhere he made his presence known using other techniques. Well-timed personal appearances, demonstrations of his own knowledgeability, and the regular use of representatives all combined to convey the idea that the king himself watched over everything. The surprise inspection, carried out either by the king or his agents, became a distinctive feature of government under Louis XIV.

I reviewed the troops very often, both the new troops, to see whether [the companies] were full, and the old troops, to recognize whether they had been weakened [in number] by the new levies. . . . I ordered that I should be sent monthly salary rolls of all the corps I paid, however distant they might be; and in order to know that I was faithfully served in this, I deliberately sent *gentilshommes* from all parts in order to surprise and unexpectedly review the troops, which kept the captains . . . in a continual obligation to do their duty.[102]

In this way the king would keep all of his servants perpetually alert. Louis remembered, with some amusement, that he also occasionally surprised his ministers by discussing their work with them individually, even entering into the smallest details. And he did this "when they least expected it, so that they would be aware that I could also question them on other matters and at all hours."[103]

The assumption that periodic demonstrations of royal attention sufficed to stimulate dutiful service also lay behind a written proposal

---

101. Ibid., 1:152.
102. Ibid., 1:237–40.
103. Louis XIV, *Mémoires* (1978), 44.

sent to the king in 1677. The petitioner wanted to found a new noble riding academy in the city of Paris.[104] The plan called for the nobles to be separated into three squadrons (beginners, intermediate, and advanced). They learned their craft by competing against each other for prizes, six of which would be distributed every six months "to those who will have best performed their duty." Each Saturday the director would "correct the mistakes of those who will have been lacking in their duty during the week," and every month the *grand écuyer* (Keeper of the Stables) would receive from the director "an account of the advancement of the young *gentilshommes* in their exercises, to assure His Majesty of their progress." As reward for their efforts, the squadrons would spend part of their time serving with the Parisian guards regiment, with each in its turn having the chance to exercise "in the presence of the king, the queen, and the dauphin, so they will be able actually to serve His Majesty while learning their exercises and render themselves capable of filling the positions that it will please His Majesty to give them on leaving the academy."[105]

In this proposal, the noble students appeared before the king's personal gaze only occasionally, but the sponsor did not expect this to diminish the impact of the royal presence, which was integrated into the institution itself. After all, weekly corrections and semiannual prize competitions assured attention to duty, and the king and the *grand écuyer* regularly monitored the students' progress. Despite the king's prolonged physical absences, the establishment of routine communicated the sovereign gaze continuously, and its beneficial effects therefore went uninterrupted.

Officers, soldiers, and aspiring *militaires* still craved the approving gaze of the sovereign—a contemporary manual on the "art of the soldier" emphasized that "he who has the boldness and audacity to confront his enemy despite all obstacles" inevitably "wins the esteem of his prince"[106]—but mediation did not necessarily attenuate the power of

---

104. AN, O^1 915, no. 32, "Règlement pour l'établissement d'une Académie dans . . . Paris," 28 January 1677. Few records survive from the dozens of noble riding academies founded in the seventeenth and early eighteenth centuries. It is impossible to know whether the proposal discussed here led to the opening of a new academy in 1677 or if the Parisian academy founded later in 1690 followed an earlier model. In any case, this document provides one of the few detailed indications of the thinking that lay behind these institutions.

105. Ibid.

106. BN, MS fr. 2396, Pillon de Cleranueau, "L'Art du Soldat," [seventeenth century], fol. 196.

royal judgment. Further evidence of this assumption is found in a 1668 treatise on the subject of the army officer's duties. The author, captain Lamont, published his work soon after the completion of Louis XIV's first and most successful war, the War of Devolution fought to advance Queen Marie-Therèse's right of succession in the Low Countries. Lamont expressed delight in his first pages that Louis XIV had led his army into battle himself. The event had provided nobles and other men of service "an occasion to perform well."[107] No officer could fail to be inspired on noting that "amid the greatest dangers . . . [the prince] is going to judge for himself the merit of each man and weigh equitably the valor of each service." In fact, the king's personal attention imposed still greater obligations on his men: "And if this generous monarch shall regard with his own eyes, and with so much discernment, the talent of each person, would it not be an affront [to the king] . . . not to know the functions of one's office?" After the example of the king himself, "all must apply themselves to their duties and try to merit the posts that they have been honored to receive."[108]

Lamont clearly expected that officers engaged in battle, moved by a desire to please the king in his very presence, would show the same "application" and "continual obligation" to duty that Louis demanded of his servants at court. Further along in his discussion of the officer's duties, however, Lamont also suggested ways in which the king's imagined presence could have similar effects. In the effort to improve the quality of service, for example, colonels must frequently inspect all the companies of their regiment "and praise those who have done well, promising to make their service known to His Majesty." When "someone has performed a glorious or important work," the commanding officer must "inform the general of the army and His Majesty himself if at all possible."[109]

Lamont thought it important to encourage officers to apply themselves "to the study of the responsibilities attached to their positions." These responsibilities had been outlined with greater clarity in the king's recent ordinances, and Lamont included in his treatise a summary of all ordinances issued by the king since he reached his majority in 1651. But Lamont also proposed establishing a school for each regiment, where

---

107. Mr. de Lamont, *La Fonction de tous les officiers, depuis celle du sergent jusques à celle du colonel* (Paris, 1668), 1.
108. Ibid., 2–3.
109. Ibid., 125, 123.

new and prospective officers could learn the principles of their craft under the direction of a professor of mathematics. To enter the ranks of officers and to become eligible for promotion, the trainees would have to pass a regimental exam, the procedures of which Lamont described in detail. The examiner (the math professor) and the examinee took their position at the center of a large circle. Staff officers, persons of quality, and invited guests, all seated by rank, were arranged along the circumference of the circle. Presiding over the whole exam, and sitting in a visible location in the front row, would be the commander of the regiment or fortress, who "assumes the character of the king, so to speak, and represents his person." All those completing the exam successfully would be granted official "Letters of the Corps, to be presented to the king." The document, which certified one's competence and entitled the bearer to a higher rank, effectively proved that one had satisfied the king in absentia.[110]

Because of the repeated emphasis on the "discipline" prompted by royal observation, the language of Louis XIV's memoirs and other contemporary texts invites greater discussion of Michel Foucault's analysis of the classical age (ca.1650–ca.1800) and of the disciplinary techniques he thought characteristic of the period. As is well known, for Foucault the later seventeenth and eighteenth centuries witnessed the creation of a "disciplinary society" in which the inescapable gaze of multiple authorities imposed fixed norms on all behavior and forced individuals to internalize discipline. This "new modality of power," which found its ultimate expression in the "panopticism" of Jeremy Bentham, depended on the principle of "generalized surveillance":[111] "The exercise of discipline presupposes a mechanism that coerces by means of observation, an apparatus in which . . . the means of coercion make those on whom they are applied clearly visible."[112] The disciplining gaze could be found in many contexts—Foucault focused on the army, the school, and the prison—but he contended that it did not emanate from an institution or from any specific location. Rather, it came from "a whole set of instruments, techniques, procedures, levels of application," which included, for example, "hierarchical" observation and the development of the examination.[113]

---

110. Ibid., 163–65.
111. Michel Foucault, *Discipline and Punish: The Birth of the Prison*, trans. Alan Sheridan (New York, 1979), 209.
112. Ibid., 171.
113. Ibid., 215.

Generalized surveillance exercised through its anonymity an "uninterrupted, constant coercion," a "subtle coercion." "Supervising the
processes of the activity rather than the result," the gaze measured and
constrained the very movements of the body, their "economy,"
"efficiency," and "internal organization."[114]

The search for historical origins seemed to imply to Foucault a search
for the justification of relationships of power, and he therefore mistrusted
the conventional methodologies of historians.[115] Intent on studying on its
own terms the technology of power—that is, the details of its operations—he eschewed the evolutionary model of historical process and
instead took for granted the existence of "thresholds" in time, "great dis-
continuities" that segmented the past.[116] Foucault indicated that the rup-
ture dividing the Renaissance and classical worlds occurred sometime in
the second half of the seventeenth century. In 1666 Louis XIV struck a
medal commemorating a recent review of the troops. Foucault saw this
medal as "evidence of the moment" when "the unavoidable visibility of
the subjects" replaced the "visibility of the monarch," the latter a
"scarcely sustainable" ideal belonging to an earlier system of power.
Louis XIV crossed the threshold to the classical age, suggested Foucault,
for with Louis emerged the "rituals proper to disciplinary power": "We
are entering the age of the infinite examination and of compulsory
objectification."[117]

A different form of power did indeed take shape in the later seventeenth and eighteenth centuries, and Foucault correctly emphasized that
belief in a panoptic gaze animated the entire system. Nevertheless, by sev-

---

114. Ibid., 137.

115. The mistrust was mutual. Foucault's often abstruse language and his refusal to pursue the kinds of objectives recognized by scholars trained as historians have led most historians simply to ignore or dismiss his work. As Allan Megill has pointed out, however, historians' interest in Foucault's methodology increased after publication of *Surveiller et punir*
in 1975. That book—the first of Foucault's to be perceived as "recognizably like social history"—has inspired cultural historians attuned to issues of power relations and eager to
link the histories of social, linguistic, and institutional change. See Allan Megill, "The
Reception of Foucault by Historians," *Journal of the History of Ideas* 48 (1987): 117–41.
On Foucault's relationship to history and historians see also Lynn Hunt, "French History
in the Last Twenty Years: The Rise and Fall of the *Annales* Paradigm," *Journal of Contemporary History* 21 (1986): 209–24; and Patricia O'Brien, "Foucault's History of Culture," in *The New Cultural History*, ed. Lynn Hunt (Berkeley, 1989), 25–46.

116. Foucault's most explicit explanation of his own historical method appeared in his
preface to *The Order of Things: An Archaeology of the Human Sciences*, Vintage Books ed.
(New York, 1973), xv–xxiv.

117. Foucault, *Discipline and Punish*, 189.

ering panopticism from its social and historical roots, Foucault exaggerated the historical specificity of what he described and masked the assumptions that underlay the exercise of the power of the gaze in classical France. Foucault's rigid periodization distorted his images of both before and after. The problem appears in his characterization of the relationship of service that typified the Middle Ages and Renaissance. He referred to "vassalage" as a "distant relation of submission" in which "ritual marks of allegiance" were the signs that served a meaningful function.[118] He contrasted this with the classical period, when "observation" disciplined and "coerced" the subject to induce desired effects. This dichotomy is problematic, however, because it overlooks a notion that Foucault himself would surely have accepted: all cultures have standards of behavior, and furthermore, any standard of behavior necessarily implies the existence of a judge and appropriate means of judging. Contrary to what one might infer from Foucault's presentation, and as we have already seen, the early seventeenth century's culture of merit also presupposed the observation of "visible" men whose qualities either met or failed to meet prevailing standards. Moreover, one can hardly consider vassalage a distant relation, especially in its early-modern mutations; the "means of observation" intrinsic to this personalized culture implied propinquity.

If one keeps firmly in mind this historical background, the disciplinary gaze developed in the later seventeenth and eighteenth centuries looks substantially different from that described by Foucault. Louis XIV certainly employed new techniques of observation, and through these techniques he intended to encourage continuous and zealous attachment to his service. But royal surveillance in the later seventeenth century was far from anonymous, for all recognized intuitively its links to the past and to the person of the king. Louis XIV's routinized gaze assumed its exemplary form, after all, at the site where kings and their vassals/nobles had traditionally congregated—the court. In striving to appear in all the government's work, in acting with "assiduity" to keep his people "in good order," in trying to "discern everything," "weigh everything," and "punish or reward everything," Louis XIV simply systematized the personal modality and reinforced his full personal responsibility for the relationship between the king and those who served him.

As noted earlier in this chapter, Louis XIV used intermediaries and the

---

118. Ibid., 137.

clear prospect of surprise inspection to spread his eyes "over all the land." Louis's articulation of rules and regulations, which the modern eye perceives as mere administrative technique, likewise instilled an awareness of the king's presence. By imposing clarity, defining hierarchy, and specifying the responsibilities inherent in rank, Louis extended his discriminating gaze metaphorically. Undoubtedly, the king expected to benefit from increased discipline. One contemporary manuscript, for example, described the connection between clarification of the terminology of command in the army and the exact observation of duty. In a chapter titled "The Operation of the Definitions," one finds the following:

> It is necessary that all those in charge of exercises [*évolutions*] take care to utter the commands that correspond with what they want done, and according to the order here described, without adding or subtracting anything. . . . It is essential that each individual soldier, and all of them together, be obedient, following . . . the wish of those who command them; that there be a great silence, that they think of nothing else except promptly to execute their duty.[119]

The same spirit is reflected in a 1685 military treatise by Gatien de Courtilz de Sandras, a panegyrist, political observer, and propagandist employed by Louis XIV. The author boasted that no previous treatise had "supplied the detail that I supply here."[120] Drawing from the king's printed ordinances, he laid out the newly clarified officer hierarchy and discussed the duties attached to each rank. He stressed the exact service now required in the army and made it a special point to spell out the implications of this for the nobility: "the more a man is raised above others, the less he is able to hide his flaws."[121]

In embedding his vision and presence in an expansive regulatory matrix, Louis XIV sought to impose rigorous demands on his servants. Nevertheless, it would be misleading to describe the sovereign's gaze, wherever it appeared, as "coercive" in the sense implied by Foucault. Seventeenth-century nobles craved—even demanded—royal attention,

---

119. BN, MS fr. 24264. "Motions et Evolutions Militaires," [seventeenth century], fol. 29.

120. Gatien de Courtilz, sieur de Sandras, *La conduite de Mars, Necessaire à tous ceux qui font profession des armes* (The Hague, 1685), preface.

121. Ibid., 26.

and Louis XIV no doubt considered the routinization of his presence an emphatic response to noble requests. Moreover, the omnipresent royal gaze, rooted in the ancient ideal of mutuality, actually "coerced" the monarch and his servants reciprocally. Royal surveillance, as Louis XIV understood it and used it, did not slyly supervise the "processes of the activity" only; it focused on results. Louis balanced his demands for more "applied" service with the promise that he would bestow "favor," "influence," and "elevation . . . in proportion to the zeal and fidelity that everyone demonstrates." At court and elsewhere the king assured his servants that "no merit will fail to receive [from] the prince the approval that is due." At the same time that he used administrative methods to insure more disciplined service in the army, for example, Louis also activated automatic mechanisms of compensation. Thanks to Louvois's efficiency, Louis XIV paid his troops regularly and reliably—the first time a French king had done so. Perhaps the clearest indication of Louis's intent to make the principle of reciprocity nearly self-regulating was the construction of the Hôtel des Invalides. At this grand institution, dedicated in 1674, wounded and impoverished soldiers would benefit from royal *graces* for the duration of their lives.[122]

Foucault broke new ground by approaching the past (and present) from a novel angle. His relentless search for contemporaneous connections and correspondences, by revealing in fine detail coherent and pervasive modalities of power, brought to light the unarticulated motives and values that help to constitute authority and structure its use. But, perhaps ironically, Foucault himself did not escape the power of the norm. Although he conspicuously ignored the history of events, his periodization paralleled that of the conventional narrative in France's history of power. The label *classical age,* for example, did not disguise very well the age of absolutism long studied by political historians, and in locating the birth of modernity somewhere in the early nineteenth century, Foucault failed to deflect attention from the seismic shift of the French Revolution. Foucault also worked from an assumption implicit in the most traditional histories of the European state. In Foucault's mind the disci-

---

122. On troop salaries see Corvisier, *Louvois,* 108–14. For the numbers of soldiers who benefited from the founding of the Invalides, as well as the professional experiences and social backgrounds of those admitted, see Corvisier *L'armée française de la fin du XVIIe siècle au ministère de Choiseul: Le soldat,* 2 vols. (Paris, 1964), 2:791–820.

plinary gaze, like the ideal rational state described by Max Weber,[123] represented a type of power easily distinguished from that which preceded it. With a few minor adjustments, Foucault's historical framework could be easily superimposed on previous models he thought to abandon—those employing dichotomies between progressive and backward, modern and traditional, new and old.

Foucault's work can be used to illuminate the history of European state formation because it shows clearly that specific modes of "seeing" and judging are invariably integrated into systems of power. The French experience in the age of Louis XIV indicates clearly, though, that the development of both the disciplinary gaze and the structures of the administrative state involved not the negation or supersession of tradition but its transformation. This transformation, moreover, can be tied quite specifically to a historical "event" or process: Louis XIV's translation of the personal modality of service to a changing context in which the king sought to embrace personally his entire realm. Louis did not intend to create an anonymous, abstract, and therefore subtly coercive royal power. Rather, to exercise his authority more efficiently, he hyperpersonalized the established culture of service. The effects of Louis XIV's work may not be sufficient to explain all the phenomena that Foucault described, but changes in the modality through which merit was judged, expressed, represented, and rewarded certainly need to be considered in terms of their relation to the sovereign's personal gaze. To trace the line of continuity linking the traditional personal modality to the disciplining gaze of modern institutions, we now need to examine one other phe-

---

123. For Weber's well-known typology of authority see *The Theory of Social and Economic Organization*, trans. A. M. Henderson and Talcott Parsons (New York, 1964), 324-423. Weber's typology, which distinguishes between "charismatic," "traditional," and "rational" modes of domination, is certainly useful in comparative analysis of state power. Nevertheless, it seems inappropriate and misleading to differentiate between types (or emergent types) of authority when studying the history of the early-modern French state. Weber's useful term *routinization* captures well the gradual transformation of the modality of royal service in the seventeenth and eighteenth centuries—as I hope to make clearer in subsequent chapters in this book—but it should not be used to evoke the drift of "charismatic" authority in a "traditional" or "rational" direction. The characteristics that Weber ascribed to his three types of authority always overlapped in early-modern France; the categories themselves therefore have limited utility. For a critique of Weber, written from the perspective of a seventeenth-century specialist, see Sharon Kettering, *Patrons, Brokers, and Clients in Seventeenth-Century France* (Oxford, 1986), 224–31.

nomenon Foucault considered central to the construction of the disciplinary society: normalization.

Normalizing Merit: Birth, Talent, and Application in the Service of the King

In 1665 Pierre Le Moyne wrote a lengthy political treatise (*The Art of Governing*) that celebrated the reign of Louis XIV. In it he praised Louis's "continual application" to the business of governing. All the best features of the regime, it seemed, stemmed from the king's decision to forgo the use of a first minister.

> Since Your Majesty decided to rule on your own, rather than through others, how many examples have you given of that sparkling and subtle intensity that discovers by its light all things obscure, that sorts out things that are entangled? . . . There is no more confusion, no clouds blocking your perception of the truth.[124]

After noting Louis's wisdom and his keen eyesight, a combination quite rare in a young man, Le Moyne added a verse comparing the king to the sun.[125]

> I cast my eye on all things, but a luminous eye,
> Which never mistakes appearances for the truth.
> With my gaze I create a light
> That pierces the fog surrounding the darkest objects:
> Equally present, far or near,
> No obstacle hinders me, I penetrate secrets.[126]

Le Moyne's piece is worth noting for several reasons. When considered in conjunction with the king's own memoirs and other texts from the first decade of Louis's reign, it underscores Louis's intent to establish his image as a personally active and ever-watchful king. Le Moyne cited the king's "liveliness" and his "assiduous work;" he praised him for being "always vigilant, always open." Indeed, even the analogy of the sun did not adequately express Louis's application, for "the Rising" and

---

124. Pierre Le Moyne, *L'Art de Régner* (Paris, 1665), epistle to the King.
125. Ibid. Le Moyne noted that "l'âge des bons yeux ne soit guere l'âge du bon sens."
126. Ibid.

"the Setting" of the sun implied a merely cyclical activity. Le Moyne improved on that image. "There, without relaxation, without diversion, at night and in daylight, I am in action."[127]

Le Moyne's adulatory treatise is also revealing, however, because it underscores the greatest challenge facing Louis XIV. Precisely because of his commitment to the old ideal of personal government, the king endeavored to be "equally present, far or near." This meant that, in addition to insuring his regular visibility at court, Louis had also to emphasize the power, the extent, and the *reality* of his metaphorical presence and thus communicate to his people that "no obstacle" impeded his perception. For the king and his contemporaries, the sovereign's gaze delimited the size and scope of the monarchy itself. The efforts of the king and his deputies to expand and improve the efficiency of royal administration, I have argued, need to be understood in light of that assumption. But new ways of projecting the sovereign gaze also necessarily implied new ways of perceiving and representing merit. The reconceptualization of the king's vision and presence paralleled the evolving definition of royal service in the later seventeenth and eighteenth centuries.

Through his own expansive presence, Louis XIV insinuated into the service culture new criteria for judging utility. In aggressively asserting the personal nature of his power, Louis continued to emphasize that the king's own sensibilities established the ultimate measure of merit. But in making his field of vision coextensive with the realm itself, the king also subsumed within his gaze the diverse interests of the state. These needs, too, helped form the standard for defining utility. An intelligent king, wrote Louis XIV, learns to utilize his people. He "finds the means of profiting from whatever they have that is good. . . . he knows how to render them useful in his affairs."[128] This implied, first of all, the need to identify specific abilities before making assignments. To help him in the delicate affairs of his government, the king noted in his memoirs, "I wanted to choose men of diverse professions and of diverse talents, according to the diversity of matters that ordinarily fall under the administration of a state."[129] But the king also had to take account of the diversity of abilities and duties beyond his council chambers and the walls of Versailles. Louis remarked that "each profession contributes, in its way,

---

127. Ibid.
128. Louis XIV, *Mémoires* (1923), 2:42.
129. Ibid., 2:286.

to the support of the monarchy (farmers, artisans, merchants, financiers, judges)."[130] Thus, as the king cast his eyes "on all the diverse parts of the state," he analyzed "everything that is executed for [my] service."[131]

The foregoing discussion of Louis XIV's reforms already indicated that the word *talent* assumed a more prominent place in the lexicon of royal service in the later seventeenth century than it had before, and this reflected an important change. Merit, as traditionally understood, could actually be manifested in an infinite variety of contexts. Virtue vaguely signified a "habit of the soul, which inspires it to do good things."[132] Talent, however, suggested a quite specific capacity or set of capacities. Furetière defined talent as a "gift of nature, disposition, natural aptitude for certain things." Moreover, talent demanded to be put to use: "It is said figuratively, 'Make the most of talent' as a way of saying, 'usefully employ one's mind, one's skill.'"[133]

Louis XIV indeed showed a determination to employ his subjects' diverse skills with unprecedented efficiency. An edict of 1669, for example, described the attachment that subjects feel to their sovereign and their native country as "the most indissoluble of civil society" and stated that the "obligation of service that everyone owes them [is] recognized universally as the first and most indispensable duty of men." The king therefore prohibited all French subjects from emigrating to foreign countries and "working there at all the exercises of which they are capable."[134]

The king's desire to strengthen his subjects' commitment to the duties attached to their condition and rank had been implicit in his reordering of the military hierarchy, his close attention to noble service at court, and even his more rigorous policing of Paris. But the king also encouraged "observation of the laws of the profession [one has] embraced" by establishing new institutions to cultivate, enhance, and reward the varied talents of those who served him. For example, in addition to reforming the court's school for pages, sponsoring a dozen or more noble riding academies, and creating companies of *cadets gentilshommes,* the crown also moved to improve the performance of the military by establishing separate schools for artillery and navigation.[135] Louis also opened new

130. Ibid., 1:250.
131. Ibid., 2:121.
132. *Dictionnaire de l'Académie Française,* 1st ed. (Paris, 1694).
133. Furetière, *Dictionnaire universel.*
134. Isambert, *Recueil,* 18:366.
135. Of the nineteen royal riding academies whose letters of creation survive, eleven were founded during Louis XIV's reign, seven between 1663 and 1698. See AN, O¹ 915,

avenues of advancement for talented roturiers. In 1693 he founded a "new purely military order"—the Order of Saint Louis—and declared that "virtue, merit, and services rendered with distinction in our armies will be the only grounds for entry."[136] The king of course knew that his officer corps was overwhelmingly noble, but he nonetheless wanted all soldiers to believe that one could acquire new distinctions by signaling one's professional abilities.[137]

Determined to find the best "in everything that is executed for [my] service," Louis did not focus solely on military matters. To supplement the Académie Française, established by Richelieu in 1635 to clarify and purify the French language, the crown also founded new academies of dance (1661), inscriptions (1663), sciences (1666), music (1669), and architecture (1671). Provincial elites, who "saw themselves in the mirror of Paris," established analogs to the Parisian academy of science in subsequent years.[138] In 1666 Colbert persuaded the king to establish an Académie de France in Rome, a school of the fine arts.[139]

At the same time, the crown focused much attention on the judi-

---

no. 1. Louis XIII initiated the trend by founding an academy at Aix in 1611. Louis XIV sponsored establishments at Toulouse (1663), Angers (1670), Besançon (1674), Strasbourg (1681), Lille (1687), Riom (1689), Paris (1690), Bordeaux (1698), Blois (1698), Montpellier (1708), and Lyon (1715). Soon after Louis's death, others were founded in Grenoble (1716), Rouen (1719), Caen (1719), and Rennes (1739). Letters of creation also survive for the establishments at Montauban, Saumur, and Sedan, but these are undated. The listing here would seem to be a partial one, since there is reason to suppose that another academy was about to be established in Paris, for example, in 1677.

136. Archives de la Guerre (hereafter AG), Y^a 208, dossier 1, "Edit de l'institution de l'Ordre de Saint Louis," April 1693.

137. André Corvisier has studied the 276 generals who served in Louis XIV's armies. Of the 178 whose social origins can be determined with some precision, 114 (or 63 percent) boasted noble lineages dating to the fifteenth century or earlier; 56 (or 31 percent) belonged to families ennobled in the sixteenth and seventeenth centuries; only 8 came from "bourgeois" or not-yet-ennobled *robin* families. The social composition of the colonels and brigadiers—from whose ranks almost all generals came—and of the *maréchaux de France* mirrored that of the generals. Corvisier observed that some commoners did indeed ascend to the top of the military hierarchy under Louis XIV. But "if there existed roturier officers in the seventeenth century, it seems that they were confined to the inferior grades, with a few exceptions." See Corvisier "Les généraux de Louis XIV et leur origine sociale," *XVIIe Siècle* 42–43 (1959): 23–53.

138. Daniel Roche, *Le siècle des lumières en province: Académies et académiciens provinciaux, 1680–1789*, 2 vols. (Paris and The Hague, 1978), 1:19. See also David Lux, *Patronage and Royal Science in Seventeenth-Century France* (Ithaca, N.Y., 1989).

139. For the monarchy's systematic use of cultural establishments under Louis XIV, see Natalie Heinrich, "Arts et sciences à l'age classique: Professions et institutions culturelles," *Actes de la Recherche en sciences sociales* 67/68 (1987): 47–78.

ciary.[140] Royal edicts and declarations of 1665, 1669, and 1672 clarified the age requirements of potential judges and clerks.[141] The king also spelled out for future jurists the educational standards they should meet. In 1679, and again in 1682 and 1683, the king declared that "no one [shall] be received as an *Avocat,* an indispensable condition for being provided with an office in the judicature, until after having completed three years of studies [in civil and canon law], during which [he will have] done the acts, sustained the theses, and taken the degrees of licensed bachelor."[142] To help improve the training of his judicial officers, the king also reestablished civil law in the curriculum of the University of Paris and instituted a program devoted specifically to French law.[143] Although these new rules were enforced unevenly and inconsistently— for financial and political reasons the crown frequently sold dispensations from age and training requirements—they provide further indication of the monarchy's aspiration to exploit talent fully and efficiently.

In generalizing the royal gaze, then, Louis XIV would do more than make his servants more disciplined. One might say that Louis's disembodied gaze gained strength in proportion to its distance from the king's person, for the monarchy now also intended to differentiate various kinds of talent and thus harness its subjects' resources to a diversity of tasks. To put it a slightly different way, one could say that the differentiation of skills in the seventeenth century's culture of royal service increased in direct proportion to the growing awareness of the dichotomy between government and society. Antoine de Montchrétien had advised kings, a half-century earlier, to keep in mind "the entire body of the state." In assessing the value of "each individual member" of the realm, he noted, kings would inevitably "uncover a thousand sources

---

140. See Hamscher, *The Parlement of Paris,* 25–27, 155–95.

141. The details of these provisions were periodically restated. Typical expectations were laid out in an "Edit" of November 1683 and in "Déclaration du Roy: Portant Dispense d'Aage, de service & de parenté à ceux qui voudront estre admis aux offices de Judicature," 9 February 1683. See AN Z[1A] 572. They required minimum ages of twenty-eight years for presidents in the *parlements, chambres des comptes,* and *cours des aides;* twenty-six years for *maîtres des requêtes ordinaire de l'Hôtel;* twenty-five years for presidents and lieutenant generals in *bailliage, sénéchaussée,* and *présidial* courts, as well as for all *avocats* and *procureurs;* and twenty-three years for all other offices—*huissier* and *trésorier,* for example.

142. AN Z[1A] 572, "Edit," November 1683.

143. Hamscher, *The Parlement of Paris,* 192.

of profit" overflowing with utility.[144] Louis XIV's approach to government sounded echoes of Montchrétien and Turquet de Mayerne, for he self-consciously personified royal government and thus viewed the needs of his service through a kaleidoscopic lens.

The monarchy's wish to control and exploit a variety of equally valuable talents is reflected in a two-volume work published by Charles Perrault, a prominent member of the Académie Française and a close collaborator of Colbert. Perrault presented to the public in 1697 a collective portrait of "illustrious men" who had earned distinction in the preceding century. Perrault chose to categorize his book by talent and profession, and he himself called attention to the originality of this approach: "Up to now, collections of eulogies of illustrious men were only of a single type of man," most often of great warriors who had distinguished themselves throughout the centuries. Although a few authors in the past had separately treated men of letters, painters, or sculptors, noted Perrault, "I have taken pleasure here in assembling extraordinary men in all sorts of professions."[145] He would even sing the praises of a number of artisans, since "the genius and extraordinary capacities of workers" should not be neglected either.[146] Moreover, whereas past works detailing the exploits of knights had made no distinction between, say, Spanish, Italian, and French heroes, Perrault intended his work to be a strictly national collection, "having in view only the honor of France."[147] Nature, Perrault explained, from time to time shows its power by endowing those she favors with a "wealth of talents." And despite the unpredictability of nature, everyone knew that her largesse normally comes "when the heavens have resolved to give to the earth some great prince." Then, at the same time, she causes to be born "a group of men of an extraordinary merit in order to receive him and to be either the instruments of his grand actions, the builders of his magnificence, or the trumpets of his glory."[148]

After expressing hope that his readers did not see in this collection of men "of such different professions" a "disagreeable assortment," he proceeded to eulogize many of the "instruments" and "builders" who toiled under France's seventeenth-century kings. Perrault applauded the appli-

---

144. Antoine de Montchrétien, *Traicté de l'Oeconomie Politique, dedié en 1615 au Roy et a la Reyne Mere du Roy*, ed. Th. Funck-Brentano (Paris, 1889), 18, 35.

145. Charles Perrault, *Les Hommes Illustres qui ont paru en France pendant ce siècle*, 2 vols. (Paris, 1697), preface.

146. Ibid., 2: *avertissement*.

147. Ibid., 1: preface.

148. Ibid., 1: preface.

cation of soldiers, jurists, artisans, and men of letters to their work. Blaise
François, comte de Pagan, for example, had been such a skilled soldier
that he earned the praise of Louis XIV himself. After suffering an inca-
pacitating wound, which had rendered him unable to serve "by his arm
and his courage," he devoted himself to the study of mathematics and
fortifications, "in order to become useful by his mind and his industry
and in that way be able to fight for his prince and for his country."[149]
Auguste De Thou, having found in his various robe functions "the
opportunity to show the talents that he had received from nature," also
cultivated those talents "by continual study."[150] In his youth the noted
engraver Robert Nanteuil had felt such a "strong inclination for drawing" and had "applied himself" so well in his training that after finishing
his schooling he left his native Reims for Paris, where he knew "these talents" would be of "great utility."[151] La Fontaine had similarly worked to
cultivate "the marvelous talent given him by nature."[152]

Colbert himself occupied a central place in Perrault's collective eulogy,
for two reasons. First, he had possessed great talents in his own right.
Perhaps his finest achievement had been to clear up the "impenetrable
obscurity" of the crown's finances: "He applied himself to this with so
much care and success that these same finances have become . . . what is
clearest and best regulated in the realm."[153] But Colbert also deserved
praise for his determination to cultivate the diverse talents of others—all
for the advancement of the king's glory. "There was not a single savant
of distinguished merit, whether in eloquence, in poetry, or in mathematics, however far from France," whose services Colbert failed to solicit.[154]
Among the foreign luminaries attracted to Paris in the course of Colbert's
life were the physicist Christian Huygens, the architect and sculptor Gio-
vanni Bernini, and the cartographer and astronomer Jean-Dominique
Cassini. The last was called on to direct the newly constructed Observatory—a structure that stands as the perfect metaphor for Louis XIV's
entire reign.[155]

The perspective of Perrault's *Illustrious Men* indeed contrasted

149. Ibid., 1:28.
150. Ibid., 1:41.
151. Ibid., 1:97.
152. Ibid., 1:83.
153. Ibid., 1:37.
154. Ibid., 1:37.
155. On the history of the Observatory and its place in the history of French science see
Charles Wolf, *Histoire de l'Observatoire de Paris: De sa fondation à 1793* (Paris, 1902).

sharply with earlier collective eulogies. In 1617, two-thirds of Claude Malingre's *Chronological History of Several Great Captains, Princes, Lords, Magistrates, Officers of the Crown, and Other Illustrious Men* praised great warriors in traditional fashion.[156] The "valor and magnanimity" of Charles de Bourbon had led Francis I to make him *connétable de France* in 1516. The comte de Laval, meanwhile, had had to travel far to express his valor: "after having acted valiantly in France in the service of the late king [Henry IV], seeing that there was no more opportunity in the realm to exercise his courage and valor, [he] went away to Hungary to make proof of his virtue and generosity, [although] not without permission and leave from His Majesty."[157] Laval no doubt would have thought twice before asking Louis XIV's permission to fight in someone else's army.

Louis XIV's intent to "penetrate" all the "secrets" of his realm fueled his desire to cultivate and make use of a variety of discrete talents. But the increasing attention to talent reflected more than the monarchy's growing breadth of vision. Because it implied both specificity and self-motivation, the norm of talent became generally enforceable and enabled the expression of merit in the king's actual absence/metaphorical presence. The centrality of the term *talent* in the expanding lexicon of royal service reflected two simultaneous and overlapping developments: on the one hand, the creation of a well-defined space of mediation between the sovereign's personal gaze and the services he judged; on the other hand, the normalization of merit made necessary by this physical and theoretical distancing of the king from his servants, the servants from the served.

The need to normalize merit to make it visible for an omnipresent but ever-absent king also helps explain the phenomenon of numeration. The process became routine only in the eighteenth century, as I shall note in chapter 5, but already by the later seventeenth century it had become common to explain and justify promotions and the conferral of royal *graces* by pointing to numbers—of services performed, battles attended, wounds suffered. The king ennobled one of his *garde du corps* in 1676, for example, after noting that, "having served in that capacity for eleven

---

156. Claude Malingre, *Histoire Chronologique de Plusieurs Grands Capitaines, Princes, Seigneurs, Magistrats, Officiers de la Couronne, & autres hommes illustres* (Paris, 1617). One hundred seventy-one pages extoll the virtues of *militaires*, from kings and princes down to simple knights; twenty-three pages are given to ecclesiastics; thirteen to chancellors and Keepers of the Seal; thirty-seven to jurists; and thirteen to physicians and poets.

157. Ibid., 13 and 125.

years," he had suffered six musket wounds and had had one horse killed under him in a recent battle.[158] The valor of deserving officers and soldiers also found numerical expression. A letter written on behalf of a soldier named Marieux, captain of a company of grenadiers, noted that he had been "wounded at Barcelona by four rifle shots and one pistol shot. The Maréchal de Berwick has said that he distinguished himself there."[159]

Perhaps the clearest example of the monarchy's increased reliance on numerical symbols of merit came in 1675. In that year the war minister Louvois, who already shared Louis XIV's power of promotion, established his famous "order of the table," a schedule of advancement that ranked all the officers of each grade according to the dates of their commissions. Promotions to the rank of general officer now followed the order prescribed by seniority. The table measured and rewarded the merits of active officers, in one way at least, by using numbers of years of service as a visible substitute for loyalty and bravery.[160] Nobles, in particular, had some difficulty adjusting to the institutionalization of the seniority principle. Some complained that with royal *graces* in the hands of Louvois, "recompenses are not always distributed according to merit." But Colbert, in his posthumously published *Political Testament*, explained the practical need for such standardizing measures. The king himself, despite his best efforts, could not actually keep constant watch over everything and everyone: "How could he know all his officers and the merit of each one, he who has so many different armies that perform so far from his eyes?"[161]

Like the spreading ideal of "discipline," then, the new norm of talent and the phenomenon of numeration should not be read teleologically as markers of modernization, rationalization, or bureaucratization; rather, the monarchy's demand for more specific signs of merit required alternative methods of seeing and being seen by the king. The direction of the shift becomes especially clear when one considers the reshaping of the nexus of royal "gaze" and noble "merit" at court. In an earlier time, the noble had aspired to "feed his spectators' eyes with all those things that

158. AN, O¹ 20, January 1676, fol. 31r.
159. AG, "Travail du Roi, 1706–1739," 29 December 1714.
160. See Corvisier, *Louvois*, 185.
161. Colbert, *Testament Politique de messire Jean-Baptiste Colbert* (The Hague, 1693), 464.

. . . may give him added grace."[162] Nobles still had opportunities to appear before the king's eyes in the later seventeenth century—Louis XIV had taken measures to guarantee it. But even when enjoying the king's presence, nobles found themselves arranged quasi-numerically by rank and lineage, and Louis XIV's determination to see everyone regularly meant that individuals felt the direct royal gaze only intermittently. Nobles learned to rest content in the knowledge that the king could see "at a glance" all the personal qualities of "grace" signified by their rank and birth. But any noble who wished to impress the king further when his turn for royal attention finally came had to express generosity, fidelity, and affection through continuous and demonstrable attachment to the service of the king. Saint-Simon wrote of Louis XIV that "no one escaped him": "He looked right and left when rising in the morning, when retiring, at his meals, at his *appartements,* in the gardens." But if many nobles now performed their duties with greater efficiency and exactitude, their motivation lay in the anticipation, rather than the fact, of royal recognition. By favoring courtiers with his gaze at long but regular intervals, Louis kept everyone "assiduous and anxious to please him."[163]

One might say that Louis XIV exerted both an imaginary presence and an imaginary absence at court. As a consequence, the sovereign's gaze no longer merely affirmed the qualities characteristic of aristocratic bearing; it also promoted assiduity. Louis XIV's systematic ordering of his court signaled in one way the creation of a space that diffused the sovereign's gaze and, at the same time, deflected the gaze of his servants. For while the monarch scanned the horizon for concrete and normative expressions of merit, the king's servants increasingly focused their attention on the tasks and duties that gave rise to such expressions. The counting of wounds and services, the tabling of seniority, and the constant invocation of talent—like genealogical records and hierarchies of honor—all indicated the need to evince specific and verifiable signs of one's attachment to the king's service. So, too, did the praise now commonly accorded the quality of "application," a concept that actually joined the new ideals of talent and discipline. The dictionaries of Furetière and the Académie Française wasted few words on their definitions of *application;* perhaps reflecting the novelty of the word's use in the later seventeenth century,

---

162. Baldesar Castiglione, *The Book of the Courtier,* trans. Charles Singleton (Garden City, N.Y., 1959), 99.

163. Saint-Simon, *Louis XIV et sa Cour,* 66–69.

the Académie Française noted merely that it has "les significations de son verbe [*appliquer*]." Nevertheless, an eighteenth-century dictionary, the *Dictionnaire de Trévoux*, later conveyed well the new significance of the word: "*Application . . .* signifies attentiveness in considering an object to which one attaches oneself. 'He works with extreme application.'"[164]

Ironically, then, at the same time that Louis XIV captivated his courtiers through elaborate court ritual and the force of his own commanding presence, he also instructed his nobles to avert their eyes from the person of the king to fix on the work he demanded of them. Certainly this shift in focus is what many observers now prescribed. In 1688 La Bruyère criticized the misguided courtier who believed he could please the prince by "arranging to be seen, positioning himself before [his] eyes, showing [him] his face." The true *honnête homme* takes satisfaction "in the application he brings to his duty"; rather than appear importunate, he "presents himself" to the prince only when duty requires.[165] Antoine de Courtin urged the noble readers of his treatise that they should "never use this name of *qualité* as a cover for idleness." On the contrary, the man of quality should feel an obligation "to work with more application" and "want to use [his] talents well."[166]

In his *Instructions for a Young Lord* (1702), Trotti de la Chétardie addressed even more directly the distinction between traditional expressions of merit and the new requirements of royal service. The author assured his noble readers that "actions of generosity" would still acquire for them "friends, servants," and "creatures."[167] To attract the attention of the king and his ministers, however, one would need more than a generous heart. To achieve fortune and glory at court, he wrote,

> it is necessary, according to the different posts to which one is called, to do one's duty with extreme application, so that Your Master or those whom he selects to make the choice of persons can find in you something worthy of their *graces;* because whatever inclination they might have for you, there is no sense in hoping for [*graces*], unless you

164. *Dictionnaire de Trévoux.*
165. Jean de La Bruyère, *Les caractères; ou les moeurs de ce siècle,* ed. Robert Garapon (Paris, 1962), 100.
166. Antoine de Courtin, *Traité de la paresse, ou l'Art de bien employer le temps en toutes sortes de conditions* (Paris, 1673), 116.
167. Trotti de la Chétardie, *Instructions pour un jeune seigneur, ou l'idée d'un galant homme,* 2 vols. (Paris, 1702), 1:112–17.

give them a legitimate pretext for preferring you to an infinity of other persons who might have claim to them.[168]

"Be punctual and exact," he said, since "exactitude is the mark of an ordered mind." Even if one aspired to military glory, he exhorted, "it is not enough to have valor; one must also have an extreme application."[169] As Chétardie explained it, the intangible moral qualities were still useful, even essential, but they had to be expressed as "legitimate pretexts"—application, exactitude, order—to draw the attention of the king "or those whom he selects to make the choice of persons."

The new imperatives of zeal and specificity also shaped opinion concerning career training and education. One author of a pedagogical treatise praised the techniques of an instructor identified only as "Monsieur de Morbidi." He concentrated on the education of nobles, and his greatest strength lay in his single-minded approach: "He regards as useless and dangerous all occupations . . . not intended directly to cultivate our faculties, to perfect our talents, and to render us more capable of fulfilling the duties of our profession."[170] In a similar vein, Nicolas Remond des Cours stressed that each person must engage only in the kinds of service appropriate to him.

It is an action with dangerous consequences, to choose too hastily a profession [état] for all the course of one's life. You should not make that decision until after having examined your inclinations, your strengths, your talents, and then having considered whether you are capable of fulfilling all the duties attached to the profession you wish to embrace, and whether you will be able to take the work and pain involved.[171]

Remond des Cours did not deny that hereditary habit usually offered a reliable guide in choosing a career path. Indeed, "if after having examined everything, you do not at all find that God is calling you to another condition, you should remain in the one into which you were born."[172]

168. Ibid., 1:95.
169. Ibid., 2:70, 133.
170. *Lettre de M. le Marquis du P., à un gentilhomme de ses amis sur les études et sur la méthode de M. de Morbidi* (Paris, 1707), 30.
171. Remond des Cours, *La véritable politique des personnes de qualité* (Paris, 1692), 61.
172. Ibid., 61–64.

But, as La Bruyère had also noted, everyone had to "labor in order to make [oneself] worthy of filling some office," and the imperative to fill a position for which one was suited now required thoughtful self-examination before setting off on a career course.[173] Remond des Cours made clear the expectation that everyone should "work according to his resources and according to the talents he has received," to be "useful to the public."[174]

Writers of biographies, panegyrics, and family histories in the later seventeenth century captured well the change in values. Although the accounts themselves cannot be accepted uncritically, the logic governing the writers' choice of language is most revealing. By the end of the century, "exactitude," "precision," and "diligent attention to the smallest necessities of the state" counted among the prize characteristics of all royal servants.[175] Colbert, "the most applied and the most laborious minister who ever was, and especially the most attentive at following the intentions of his master," stood out in Perrault's mind as the prototypical servant of talent and energy.[176] The great minister's biographer similarly lauded his "astonishing exactitude" and called the controller general "indefatigable in work."[177] Louvois shared in the ethic of self-discipline. The king saw in his war minister much that would inspire confidence: "indefatigable labor, an unequaled activity in the execution of [the king's] orders." He demonstrated "diligence" and "incredible application"; and like the king himself, he had shown a determination to see and make sense of everything. "Nothing escaped him," and his excellent memory stored everything "with admirable order."[178]

If one believes the biographers, the new devotion to work and order was not confined to the ministers. People of various backgrounds, not least some old nobles, had it equally. Courville, colonel of an infantry regiment during the War of the League of Augsburg, had "distinguished himself on all occasions with much valor and exactitude." Known as a "man of application," Courville stood out from the crowd of "unapplied" people who entertained only "vague designs."[179] The biographer

---

173. La Bruyère, *Les caractères*, 98.
174. Remond des Cours, *La véritable politique*, 29–30.
175. La Bruyère, *Les caractères*, 288.
176. Perrault, *Les Hommes Illustres*, 1:38.
177. *La Vie de Jean-Baptiste Colbert* (Cologne, 1695), 2.
178. BN, MS fr. 14189, "Mémoire sur le Ministère du Marquis de Louvois," 67–68, 37, 42–43.
179. [H. F. La Rivière], *Abrégé de la vie de M. de Courville, Colonel du Régiment d'Infanterie du Maine, & Brigadier des Armées du Roy* (Paris, 1719), 14–16.

of another warrior, the duc de Bouillon, described how the duc "entered into detail in the smallest things in order to know them in depth." He was "active and vigilant," was "laborious to the last point," and never recoiled from "any labor of the mind or body." He acquired the admiration of his troops, readers are told, "by his courage and by his great talents for war."[180]

Du Prat wrote to praise another career soldier, the maréchal de Gassion, not only for his "fine birth," but also for his "powerful mind" and "generous work." He, too, seemed "indefatigable, vigilant, marvelously active." He "lost not a moment of time" in taking advantage of the enemy.

> The dying words of the Emperor Severus to the Captain of the Praetorian Guards were the words of the maréchal de Gassion for all his life: 'Let us work.' . . . Not all who are generous are able to work as he did. . . . I would be surprised to find another man who takes his pleasure . . . in perpetual work, and who rests only when nothing is left to do.[181]

Gatien de Courtilz de Sandras predictably praised the maréchal de Fabert for his "intrepid courage," but he also praised his "indefatigable application" and the "judgment and penetration" of his mind. Trained first in the regiment of French guards, he fulfilled his duties as a soldier "with the greatest exactitude." He had such a violent desire "to excel in his profession that he attached himself to it entirely, searching with extreme care for every opportunity to learn it." The diversity of his abilities so impressed his peers that "no one ever knew for certain what the greatest of his talents were."[182]

Perhaps the best example of the evolving lexicon of merit comes from another work by Du Prat, a genealogical history of the family of Voyer d'Argenson, the lieutenant of police for Paris. The marquis came from a quite ancient noble family, but his merits were remarkable in other ways: "What judgment, as penetrating as it is profound! What vigor! What broad and sublime genius! What a prodigious and faithful memory! What accurate discernment! What sharp precision! . . . all these rare

---

180. Jacques de Langlade, baron de Saumières, *Mémoires de la vie de Frédéric-Maurice de La Tour d'Auvergne, duc de Bouillon, avec quelques particularités de la vie et des moeurs de Henri de La Tour d'Auvergne, vicomte de Turenne* (Paris, 1692), 11–14, 26.

181. Du Prat, *Le Portrait du maréchal de Gassion* (Paris, 1694), 17, 50, 47.

182. Gatien de Courtilz de Sandras, *Histoire du maréchal de Fabert* (Amsterdam, 1697), 1, 5, 13.

talents crowned by unparalleled rectitude in public affairs."[183] The description of d'Argenson's merits demonstrates unusually well the connection between the crown's quest for perfect knowledge and the spread of a new ideal of service in the later seventeenth century. Du Prat drew special attention to the marquis's uncanny ability to root out the truth. He brought an "indefatigable application" to the administration of the police—one of Louis XIV's new tools of order—and the job demanded a great deal:

> to know intimately the city of Paris, the marvel of the universe, to know in depth the morals of each part of this infinite people; to banish those whose conduct renders them suspect, to foresee and forestall the dangerous effects [of their conduct]; . . . to examine with unrelaxing assiduity the life of all foreigners, to have them followed in their every step; to be informed of their habits; to penetrate secrets; to render a faithful account of them to the ministers and to His Majesty.[184]

Tellingly symbolic of d'Argenson's achievements was "the cleaning and illumination of the streets" of the city, which helped to preserve order while contributing to the health and welfare of the inhabitants.[185] The marquis indeed stood out as a model royal servant. In applying himself to the task of observing the city of Paris, he resembled Louis XIV in miniature.

According to the analysis of Foucault, normalization made generalized surveillance possible and served as one of its key instruments of coercion. Through the disciplining impulse, argued Foucault, "the Normal [was] established as a principle of coercion," and together with this "power of the Norm" came a new system of signification. "The marks that once indicated status, privilege, affiliation were increasingly replaced . . . by a whole range of degrees of normality indicating membership of a homogeneous social body" and assisting "in classification, hierarchization, and the distribution of rank."[186] The new identifying marks, indicating "degrees of normality," were established in part through the examination that sorted people by ability. Foucault described the examination as

---

183. BA, MS 4161, Du Prat, "Généalogie de M. le marquis d'Argenson," fol. 53r.
184. Ibid., fol. 49v.
185. Ibid., fol. 51r.
186. Foucault, *Discipline and Punish*, 184.

"the fixing . . . of individual differences, as the pinning down of each individual in his own particularity." And the "modality of power" in which the examination played such an important role contrasted with an earlier modality where ceremonies manifested marks of "status, birth, privilege, function."[187]

The evidence suggests that Foucault at least partially misconstrued the purposes and effects of normalization in ancien régime France. In exercising the "power of the Norm," Louis XIV had no intention of devaluing status, birth, affiliation, and their symbols. On the contrary, these indicators of social heterogeneity, displayed most prominently at court, were the first things to be "fixed," "classified," and thus "normalized" by the king. In sharpening distinctions of rank and clarifying the criteria for determining social status, Louis XIV did not undermine but rather visibly reaffirmed the importance of birth, hereditary status, and the qualities they represented.

Furthermore, one must not infer, with Foucault, that normalization implied the simple replacement of one concept of merit with another. To be sure, nobility had to adjust to new expectations under Louis XIV. Early seventeenth-century nobles had hoped to merit royal offices and favors, and they planned to do it by showing "as much testimony of our fidelity in the exercise of justice as in [the king's] armies."[188] In the later seventeenth century, by contrast, the king expected each person to find the specific role reserved for him by inclination and talent and then to exercise it with hard work and demonstrable efficiency. But the special qualities of the nobility continued to be recognized nonetheless; the king signaled the nobility's preeminence by giving them automatic preferment in the army and in various educational institutions, and also by guaranteeing their status at court. Through the routinization of the king's gaze, the regulation of reciprocity, and the normalization of merit, Louis XIV actually reintegrated traditional noble values into a hybrid culture of royal service.

Louis XIV's rigorous normalization of merit meant that all crown servants had to exhibit the qualities of a disciplined and "ordered mind"— application, exactitude, precision, diligence. Moreover, the new requirements of service implied in one sense the existence of a "homogeneous social body," since people of both noble and common condition could aspire to meet them. At the same time, though, Louis conveyed to the

187. Ibid., 192.
188. See chapter 1.

nobility, through the mechanisms he used to govern, that the king still valued the merits reflected in birth and expressed through the personal idiom. The space he opened between the person of the sovereign and the people who served him created room for regulation and the structures of a centralizing administrative state. But by suffusing that space with his own metaphorical presence Louis XIV made the new culture of royal service—as reflected in the methods of seeing, recognizing, representing, expressing, and rewarding merit—compatible with the traditional personal modality. Nobles, and others, simply learned that they could and should express generous and affectionate devotion to the king through discipline, application, and the cultivation of specific talents.

Interpreting French Absolutism: Louis XIV, the Nobility, and the Context of the *Longue Durée*

Governmental centralization affected virtually all European monarchs and all nobilities in the early-modern period, and despite the well-known particularities of each national case, a general picture of the Europewide phenomenon emerged long ago. According to the conventional view, far-sighted leaders, such as Louis XIV, Russia's Peter the Great, and the Hohenzollerns in Prussia, worked hard to build more rational and efficient governments. They succeeded in part by subduing the traditional nobility, limiting its claims to hereditary privilege and authority, forcing all aristocrats to serve the interests of the monarchy, and making merit a new determinant of social status.

This line of analysis reflected the assumption that the traditional values of the nobility were intrinsically incompatible with the formation of rational administration, an idea that appeared in even the most nuanced studies of early-modern state formation. In his classic study of the Prussian state, for example, Hans Rosenberg indicated that "a policy of domesticating the nobility," as well as the "drive for the raising of professional standards," led Prussian kings to increase the number of commoners in state service and deny nobles automatic access to positions of power.[189] In the bureaucratic state created principally by Frederick William I (1713–40), Rosenberg found an amalgamation of a "new merit system" and the traditional spoils system characterized by aristocratic

---

189. Hans Rosenberg, *Bureaucracy, Aristocracy and Autocracy: The Prussian Experience, 1660–1815* (Cambridge, Mass., 1958), 67.

patronage, social heredity, and amateurism.[190] As Rosenberg saw it, professionalism gradually replaced amateurism as the nobles began to see themselves as a bureaucratic, rather than simply aristocratic, elite.

Evidence internal to Rosenberg's own argument shows, though, that what he called the "new merit system" in absolutist Prussia integrated more traditional assumptions than might be supposed. In the military, and even in the civil administration, "the richest rewards and the highest responsibilities were from the beginning a noble preserve."[191] Moreover, Prussian kings did not assign nobles to high positions merely to purchase their acceptance of monarchical strength. Frederick II preferred to employ the sons of established functionaries because of their "inbred qualities" and "natural fitness" for service. He even exempted many noble-born servants from the supposedly universal civil service exams instituted in 1770.[192]

The impression that tradition may have served as the very basis for the innovations of centralizing rulers is reinforced when one considers the Russian case. As Brenda Meehan-Waters has pointed out, the Muscovite nobility had become a service class long before the reign of Peter the Great. Already in the later sixteenth century the czars had composed a formal system of precedence—the *mestnichestvo*—which ranked aristocratic families according to their status and their service traditions. The Boyar grandees, the Muscovite nobles, and even members of the more distant provincial nobility all made precedence claims on the basis of the *mestnichestvo* system.[193] In the later seventeenth century, however, the elaboration of essentially bureaucratic forms of service permitted members of common families to claim honor based on their own records of service to the autocrat. Because the *mestnichestvo* could not accommodate the rapidly multiplying variations on the traditional link between service and status, Czar Fedor simply abandoned the system in 1682; he even destroyed the books in which the rankings of aristocratic families had been recorded.

Peter the Great did not formally adjust the traditional status hierarchy until he instituted the famous Table of Ranks in 1722. Another formal and manifestly visible expression of a system of social precedence, the

---

190. Ibid., 75.
191. Ibid., 69.
192. Ibid., 81, 163.
193. Brenda Meehan-Waters, *Autocracy and Aristocracy: The Russian Service Elite of 1730* (New Brunswick, N.J., 1982), 7.

Table of Ranks built on the precedent of the *mestnichestvo*. But Peter's table made it possible for ill-bred men to acquire noble status by advancing through fourteen ranks included in three parallel hierarchies—one for military service, one for civil administration, and one for the court. Each rank corresponded to a set of offices in an administrative hierarchy; promotion often led to a higher rank, and the higher ranks signified hereditary nobility.

Because it theoretically facilitated social mobility, the Table of Ranks is customarily seen as a sign that "merit" meant more to Peter than mere hereditary distinction.[194] In examining the composition of Russia's service elite in 1730, however, Meehan-Waters found that more than two-thirds of the members of the *Generalitet* (comprising the top four ranks in the table) actually came from families of the upper nobility. Although Peter did want to reward the merit of lower-born and foreign servants, his efforts to make the native nobility "westernized, educated, and militarily proficient" indicate that he intended to infuse new skills, not new blood, into the service hierarchy.[195] Moreover, the individual experiences of the service elite show that the compartmentalization of state service scarcely affected them. They led armies, headed administrative jurisdictions, and governed provinces—all in the course of the same career: "Their expertise was leadership; and their qualifications were distinguished birth, distinguished service, and a new blend of personal and professional qualities." Although Russian nobles had been integrated into an expanding state apparatus, notes Meehan-Waters, "they perceived themselves as faithful servants of a monarch to whom they felt personal ties of loyalty, duty, and even affection."[196] In Prussia and Russia, as in France, the rise of the administrative state did not spur the invention of meritocracy; rather, it implied the refashioning of a traditional notion of merit closely linked to assumptions about birth and upbringing.

Despite its surface similarities to the eastern model of state formation, however, the French case best exemplifies the subtlety and complexity of the process that transformed the meaning of merit. Dramatic political change came to the east later, and more rapidly, than in France. In many

194. See, for example, Evgenii Anisimov's discussion of the Table of Ranks in *The Reforms of Peter the Great: Progress through Coercion in Russia*, trans. John T. Alexander (Armonk, N.Y., and London, 1993), 188–90.

195. Meehan-Waters, *Autocracy and Aristocracy*, 20.

196. Ibid., 64, 69.

ways the Romanovs and Hohenzollerns followed in the footsteps of their French, Spanish, and English predecessors, and their work therefore reflected a highly self-conscious awareness of "the state." Determined to create efficient administrative structures corresponding to the societies they ruled, Prussian and Russian monarchs actually saw themselves as agents of a historic political transformation.

French kings articulated the abstract power of the state in a very different context. The administrative structures of the French monarchy began their evolution in the fifteenth century, if not earlier. All the features that forecast the emergence of French absolutism—the standing army, a sprawling and multilayered system of crown finance, the habit of dividing administrative work among a handful of *secrétaires d'état*, a centralizing court—appeared at a time when a distinctively personal culture of service still mediated the relations between the king and the people who served him. In this premodern political matrix, kings, like the princes and lesser lords that surrounded them, necessarily and especially valued fidelity, generosity, courage, and the capacity for affectionate service—qualities thought to be embodied by the nobility.

Unlike the east, then, where ambitious rulers attempted to place fully articulated states on top of societies ill-prepared to receive them, the French state evolved slowly from *within* a society characterized by a well-developed culture of personal government. Evidence presented in earlier chapters suggests that the chronic tension between the monarchy and the nobility, apparent by the early decades of the seventeenth century, can be seen as resulting from the gradual disaggregation of state and society and the articulation of a transcendent supervisory power operating above the context of personal relations. It is against the background of this long-term process that one can fully appreciate the dimensions of Louis XIV's achievement.

Taking account of his nobility's apprehensions, Louis XIV recognized that the expansion of the monarchy's powers had to proceed on the basis of the cherished traditions of personal rule. By extending the sovereign's gaze and elaborating its functions, Louis simultaneously allayed the anxieties of his nobility and increased his control over the realm. The two-sidedness of the king's increased visibility introduced into French government a subtle but important irony. By regularizing his own physical presence at court, the king appealed to traditional sensibilities and gave his nobles and court officers multiple opportunities to appear before the king's eyes. But even as he regularized his real presence, he diminished its significance. Louis's very appreciation for the importance and potential of the sovereign gaze led him to go beyond it. In emphasizing order, clarity, and thoroughness in everything they did, in creating a metaphorical royal presence, Louis and his collaborators aimed to establish a panoptic monarchy; they would reconstitute society by making it visible before the monarch.

Two salient features of modern political culture—a reified administrative state and a regulated society subject to state surveillance—made their appearance in the age of Louis XIV. The point to emphasize, though, is that the king conceived both elements of this dyad in terms of the traditional culture of royal service. The gaze that Louis used to perceive and regulate civil society, though increasingly embedded in institutions, descended directly from the sovereign's gaze so dear to the nobility and so central to the personal modality of service. Louis manifested this link through his routinized presence at court. Moreover, the king's artificially extended vision, which made it theoretically possible for him to see the kingdom "at a glance," performed the customary functions of the sovereign's personal gaze: seeing, recognizing, and rewarding merit.

Yet Louis's regime also pointed royal service in a new direction. The king's metaphorical gaze, projected by a variety of royal agents and institutions, touched an array of people in many different professions. The normative merits of talent and discipline were not limited to those of aristocratic birth, and in any case, the noble class could not be expected to develop the wide diversity of talents necessary to the functioning of a complex state apparatus. Thus, an implicit equalizing tendency underlay the expansion of the king's metaphorical gaze. Through his own commanding presence, at once real and imaginary, Louis XIV actually forged a synthesis between the personal modality of service that had formerly given coherence to the relations between king and nobility and an emerging public modality in which the state's well-being stood as the final measure of utility. In building on and transforming the established service culture in this way, Louis XIV provided a bridge between tradition and modernity.

Despite its outward coherence, however, Louis's regime sublimated a number of contradictions—all of which stemmed from the simultaneously personal and impersonal character of the regime. This basic duality reflected what Michèle Fogel has called "the double necessity of presence and absence."[197] Louis differed from his predecessors by striving for ubiquity; yet he also broke with precedent by remaining fixed at court.

---

197. Fogel, *Les cérémonies*, 243.

Apparently viewing royal itinerary as a tacit acknowledgment of his inability to be everywhere at once, Louis wanted his subjects to dissociate the royal presence from the king's actual physical presence.[198] Thus, the king restricted the range of his own movement and intentionally projected his presence in abstract ways. Fogel has already pointed out the monarchy's increasingly frequent use of a new royal ceremony, the *Te Deum*, invented by Henry III in the 1580s. The *Te Deum*, which combined the vocal expression of thanks to God with a celebration of some action by the king or royal family (a battle won, a marriage or birth, the king's travels), differed from all other royal ceremonies in one important respect: it did not require the king's presence. Parisians sang the *Te Deum* forty times between 1620 and 1661; during his personal rule (1661–1715), Louis XIV had them observe the ceremony on eighty-nine occasions.[199]

At court Louis found inventive ways to project his presence. According to Saint-Simon, the king's determination "to know all that happened around him" meant that "spies and informers were everywhere." They lurked in the hallways and passageways inside the palace and in the courtyards and gardens outside. After watching the comings and goings of the courtiers and eavesdropping on their conversations, the informants reported their "discoveries" to the king.[200] Meanwhile, Louis made his continuous presence known to his councillors by arranging the seating in his privy council so that the king's own chair dominated the proceedings—even when empty.[201] Later, the king also placed in the throne room of Versailles the famous royal portrait painted by Rigaud in 1701.[202]

Visual images of the king proliferated.[203] Louis XIV, according to two specialists of royal iconography, enjoys the distinction of being the most

198. On the tradition of royal itinerary and its demise under Louis XIV see Ralph E. Giesey, "The King Imagined." In *The Political Culture of the Old Regime,* ed. Keith M. Baker (New York, 1987), 41–60.

199. Fogel, *Les cérémonies,* 189–245. See also Roger Chartier, *The Cultural Origins of the French Revolution,* trans. Lydia G. Cochrane (Durham, N.C., 1991), 126–32.

200. Saint-Simon, *Louis XIV et sa Cour,* 71, 75.

201. Michel Antoine, *Le Conseil du Roi sous le Règne de Louis XV* (Geneva, 1970), 63.

202. Burke, *Fabrication,* 9.

203. Louis Marin has argued that the use of official images of the king under Louis XIV signified a shift in the theory of representation. The "king's portrait," taking on the symbolic qualities of the eucharist, no longer served merely as a mimetic device; it became the true sign of sovereignty. "The king is himself figured in his visible portrait," writes Marin, "whose incessant epiphany, in all places and at all times, celebrates the multiple presence." The new objective was to produce "a rare portrait, and a multitude of copies." See Marin, *Portrait of the King,* trans. Martha M. Houle, Theory and History of Literature, vol. 57 (Minneapolis, 1988), 209–10.

"represented" of all French kings.[204] Some of the most famous artistic renderings of the king remained at Versailles—the historical tableaux and tapestries of Le Brun, the military scenes of Van der Meulen, the original Rigaud portrait. But Louis's image gradually infiltrated other parts of the kingdom. The king ordered copies of the Rigaud painting, for example, and by 1702 the artist's shop had become a "veritable portrait factory" devoted mainly to reproductions of the great portrait. The copies were "immediately dispersed throughout France and Europe."[205] The king's image also appeared through other media, some less grand than others. In the course of Louis's reign, the Académie des Inscriptions struck hundreds of medals to celebrate important themes and events. In 1702 the academy reproduced some of the images from these medals in a volume of 286 engravings. Titled *Médailles sur les principaux événements de Louis XIV* (Medals of the principal events in the reign of Louis XIV), the work appeared in an expensive folio edition and a cheaper quarto one.[206] The king, who ordered his *intendants* to keep copies of the book on their desks, personally helped revise the volume for a later, expanded edition.[207]

Beginning especially in the 1680s, representations of the king in sculpture also filled the public spaces of provincial cities. Encouraged by the example of the duc de La Feuillade, who commissioned in 1679 a colossal equestrian statue of the king for the new Place des Victoires in Paris, some twenty provincial cities commissioned equestrian statues, marble busts, and bronze bas-reliefs for the glorification of the king; Louis XIV defrayed some of the expenses for these projects. In 1696 the town councillors of Marseilles wished to emulate their counterparts in other cities; unable to bear the costs of an equestrian statue, however, they settled instead for a portrait of the king. Others had more luck—even the Québecois acquired a bronze bust of the king in 1686.[208]

In myriad ways, then, Louis underlined the personal nature of his authority and associated the monarchy's power with his own seemingly inescapable presence. Ironically, though, by the last years of his reign Louis's hyperpersonal governing style had become a source of irritation

---

204. Maumené and Harcourt, *Iconographie*, 3: "Nul souverain, sauf peut-être Napoléon, n'a été autant 'portraituré.'"
205. Ibid., 91–93.
206. Burke, *Fabrication*, 118–19.
207. The second edition appeared in 1723, however, eight years after Louis's death.
208. Maumené and Harcourt, *Iconographie*, 228–56.

to many. On the one hand, the aging king's partial withdrawal from court activity—Louis performed the ceremony of the *coucher* for the last time in 1702, for example—exposed the excessive formality of courtly protocol and led critics, such as La Bruyère and Saint-Simon, to mock the artificiality of courtiers and their world.[209] On the other hand, Louis's sometimes overbearing presence prompted others to criticize him for being too conspicuous. The would-be reformer Fénelon advised the duke of Burgundy in 1699 that he should avoid close involvement in the monarchy's work once he became king: "A king's skill . . . does not consist in doing everything by himself: it is wild vanity to hope to do all things or to try to persuade the world that one is capable of it." The wise king stays above "detail"; he governs "by choosing and guiding those who govern under him."[210]

If Louis's reign inspired conflicting attitudes toward the image of the king—the monarch was expected to be always visible yet never visible—much the same can be said about the regime's impact on the nobility. The fixing of social categories had made nobles more secure in their status and better able to define and therefore protect their hereditary honors and privileges. But Louis's genealogical investigations and his continued meddling in the corps of nobility also objectified noble status—thus completing a process begun at least a century earlier. The new tendency to focus on nobility as a signifier, rather than a quality signified, is reflected in the legal treatises of the period. La Roque's *Treatise on Nobility, and on All Its Different Types* (1678), Alexandre Belleguise's *Treatise on Nobility and Its Origin* (1700), and many similar discourses devoted disproportionate attention to assessing the legal impact of the *recherches de la noblesse,* defining the different legal categories of nobility, and outlining the various legitimate means of acquiring it.[211]

Thus, precisely because of the normalization of noble status, the concept of nobility became at least partially disengaged from the personal modality that had traditionally shaped its meaning. Together with the rise of a state-centered view of utility, this phenomenon opened to ques-

---

209. Saint-Simon declared that some court ceremonies had become so exaggerated under Louis that they were "partly burdensome and partly ridiculous" (*Louis XIV et sa Cour*, 61). La Bruyère took aim at the "ridiculous vanity" of courtiers whose sole "profession is to be seen and then seen again" (*Les caractères*, 224, 226).

210. François de Salignac de La Mothe-Fénelon, *Les aventures de Télémaque, fils d'Ulysse,* ed. Charles Le Brun (Philadelphia, 1834), 365.

211. Gilles André de La Roque, *Traité de la Noblesse, et de Toutes ses Différentes Espèces* (Paris, 1678); Alexandre Belleguise, *Traité de la Noblesse et de son origine, suivant*

tion two assumptions that old nobles had always taken for granted: that
merit reflected hereditary qualities and that these qualities found expression in noble status. The new confusion surrounding noble identity is
apparent in the work of Vauban. The master of the science of
fortifications turned his attention to the social and political order late in
his life, and he noted the discrepancies between the reality and the ideals
of the French nobility.[212] He lamented that standards of ennoblement,
once based on the generous sacrifices of men faithful to the king, had
become a travesty.

> Our kings, whom one might call the creators of the French nobility
> . . . established it only to encourage with marks of honor and distinc-
> tion those among their subjects who were the most brave and valiant
> in the conservation of their person and their state. . . . They shared
> with them their bounty and their government; they entrusted to them
> the protection of their person and the defense of the realm and contin-
> ued to honor them to the point of qualifying them as their friends and
> cousins, contracting alliances with them, making them their compan-
> ions in arms, and considering them the true supports of the state.[213]

Now, claimed Vauban, one could acquire the status of nobility so easily that some nobles, far from ever having "put their lives in danger or

---

*les préjugez rendus par les commissaires députez pour la vérification des Titres de Noblesse:
Avec la Déclaration de Sa Majesté, Arrests & Règlements du Conseil sur le fait de ladite
vérification* (Paris, 1700). The process of legal objectification began a century before, as
Ellery Schalk and others have shown, but the shift to a strictly legalistic view of nobility
only became obvious in the late seventeenth century. Monique Cubells, for example, suggests that between the "recherches" of 1666 and 1696, the criteria used by the crown to
define nobility changed noticeably, marking the movement away from a "positive" view of
nobility, which emphasized the role nobles played in society, toward a strictly juridical
view. The investigations of 1666, she says, "had accorded great importance to real, tangible social qualities, those which gave their possessors an effective social role," such as the
possession of *seigneuries* and the exercise of certain professions. By 1696, however, crown
officials accorded much more importance to "the simple possession of titles [*qualificatifs*],
which had become the only continuous sign of nobility" recognized by law. "It seems,"
writes Cubells, "that there was an orientation, at the end of the seventeenth century and the
beginning of the eighteenth, toward a more juridical and more formal conception of nobility." See Cubells, "A propos des usurpations de noblesse en Provence," 281.
    212. On Vauban's career as a writer and critic see F. J. Hebbert and G. A. Rothrock,
Soldier of France: Sebastien le Prestre de Vauban, 1633–1707, American University Studies, ser. 9, History, vol. 51 (New York, 1989), chap. 6.
    213. Vauban, *Oisivetés,* 2 vols., ed. Antoine-Marie Augoyat (Paris, 1842–45), 1:149.

exposed themselves to some peril, which is the only legitimate means of arriving at nobility," had "never even risked a cold for the service of the state."[214] Many had simply purchased legal titles. Thinking to sort out the mess, Vauban compiled another of his tables. This one ranked twenty degrees of old nobility in chronological order (e. g., those occupying rank five, with proofs dating back 180 to 200 years, would be termed "established nobility"; those occupying rank thirteen, with proofs dating back at least 450 years, would be termed "very fine nobility"). The novelty of Vauban's ranking lay in its openness. Roturier soldiers would be free to move through the ranks of this table of nobility as they moved from grade to grade in the ranks of the army. In that way, "roturiers could equal the condition of the oldest houses by their merit."[215] Good performance in a specific military function would entitle an individual born roturier to the same rank of nobility held by someone noble by birth.

Vauban's remarks are revealing because they point up both the long-term problems and the possibilities that Louis XIV's regime created for the nobility. On the one hand, the crown's success in defining explicitly the legal definition of nobility meant that the gradations of rank and *ancienneté* became clearer than ever before; it also meant that the corps of noblesse would be constantly replenished, for the monarchy's standards of ennoblement could be met by many individuals in the upper reaches of the third estate. On the other hand, as Vauban emphasized, the fixing of classes essentially separated noble status from the qualities it was meant to signify. As a result, the nobility encompassed not only generous and valorous servants of the monarchy but also people who had "never even risked a cold" on the path to social eminence.

The aspect of Vauban's proposal that most fascinates, however, is his attempt to lead nobility back to its origins in merit. On this point, too, Vauban's thinking demonstrates Louis XIV's dual impact on the noblesse. Vauban spoke nostalgically of a time when only the "most brave and valiant" servants of the king earned ennoblement, royal bounty, government positions, and the right to be considered "friends," "cousins," and "companions" of monarchs. To signal the superiority of those who had earned noble status in the traditional way, Vauban devised a social hierarchy that ranked noble families according to their age. But in offering an alternative means of acquiring the well-established

---

214. Ibid., 1:150–51.
215. Ibid., 1:139, 147.

degrees of social distinction—that is, in acknowledging that through single-minded attention to the duties of one's function, one could work for the "conservation of [the king's] person and [his state]"—Vauban also removed the concept of merit from its context in direct personal relations and dislodged its traditional aristocratic axis. To reconcile two different perspectives on merit, two principles of social distinction, Vauban actually composed overlapping social hierarchies and based them on an ambiguous notion of royal service—a notion that implicitly combined personal and institutional norms.

Vauban's brief proposal brings to light the delicate equilibrium at the heart of the new culture of royal service. Louis XIV had succeeded in personifying the state, and he had imposed his presence on the consciousness of all servants of the crown. But the all-embracing process of normalization actually incorporated contradictory principles—the assumption of both royal presence and royal absence. The implications of this contradiction are evident in Vauban's plan, for his reconstituted nobility—deriving its status from birth, on the one hand, and functional competence, on the other hand—would actually find itself suspended between the personal and the emerging public modalities of royal service. As I intend to show by examining the experience of the army, this underlying tension in the service culture of absolutism became ever more apparent in the course of the eighteenth century, as nobles, monarchs, and administrators groped for answers to two perplexing but generally unstated questions: What is merit? How and by whom is it judged?

5

Extending the Sovereign's Gaze in the Eighteenth Century: Merit, Nobility, and the Army

The administrative state's emergence as an independent category of ontology and its permanent inscription within the modality of royal service at the turn of the seventeenth century both stabilized and complicated the relationship between the monarchy and the old nobility. The structures of royal government had acquired the character of permanence by the end of Louis XIV's reign, and nobles signaled their awareness of this phenomenon in a variety of ways.[1] Clearly, the integration of the aristocracy into the crown's financial operations—a process detailed by Daniel Dessert—rested on and reaffirmed the basic premise of structural stability.[2] Similarly, the new tendency among some nobles to set "nobility" in opposition to "monarchy," that is, to define the aristocracy as the main bulwark against an intimidating despotism, reflected both a growing awareness of the monarchy's pervasive presence and an acceptance of its self-sustaining power.[3] This same awareness, one could argue, lay behind the attempt by Boulainvilliers and others to ground the nobility's

---

1. On the fundamental consistency in crown government from 1661 to 1715 see Michel Antoine's illuminating study of royal councils, *Le Conseil du Roi sous le Règne de Louis XV* (Geneva, 1970), esp. 43–175.
2. See Dessert, *Argent, Pouvoir et Société au Grand Siècle* (Paris, 1984); idem, *Fouquet* (Paris, 1987).
3. On the emergence of this new aristocratic self-image see especially Denis Richet, "Autour des origines lointaines de la Révolution française: Elites et Despotisme," *Annales, E. S. C.* 24 (1969): 1–23. On the general ferment in aristocratic thinking in this period see Lionel Rothkrug, *Opposition to Louis XIV: The Political and Social Origins of the French Enlightenment* (Princeton, 1965); Joseph Klaits, "Men of Letters and Political Reform in France at the End of the Reign of Louis XIV: The Founding of the Académie Politique," *Journal of Modern History* 43 (1971): 577–97; and Thomas Kaiser, "The Abbé de Saint-Pierre, Public Opinion, and the Reconstitution of the French Monarchy," *Journal of Modern History* 55 (1983): 618–43. The most thoughtful analysis of aristocratic attitudes in this

social position in a mythic past. In invoking the Frankish origins of the aristocracy, Boulainvilliers intended to give the corps of nobility a permanent and unchallengeable status in the social and political order—a permanence of status that corresponded to the newly established fixity of royal government.[4]

Even the short-lived experiment in aristocratic government under the regency only served to underscore the nobility's reconciliation to the practices of a powerful and centralized monarchy. Despite superficial and temporary changes to the organization and composition of the royal councils between 1715 and 1718, the *polysynodie* and its less than competent leaders from the high aristocracy scarcely disrupted the governmental routines bequeathed by Louis XIV.[5] In contrast to earlier periods of royal minority—1648, 1614, 1560—on this occasion the authority of central government did not dissipate in the absence of an active and vigilant king, and when Louis XV assumed control of the regime in 1723 he ruled through the same set of governing structures designed and elaborated by Louis XIV and his deputies.[6]

By the beginning of the eighteenth century, then, the old nobility had begun to assimilate through experience the independent reality of the centralizing administrative state. In this chapter and in chapter 6, how-

---

period is Harold A. Ellis, *Boulainvilliers and the French Monarchy: Aristocratic Politics in Early-Eighteenth Century France* (Ithaca, N.Y., 1988)—valuable both because it takes the ideas seriously and because it emphasizes the degree to which even critics of the *grand monarque* "belonged to the world of Louis XIV's absolutism" (61).

    4. Ellis notes that Boulainvilliers sought a "premonarchical" past where royal "grandeur" posed no threat to noble "glory." Thus for Boulainvilliers, the representatives who formerly gathered on the Champ de Mars constituted a primordial "nation" whose principal constituents were the Frankish nobles themselves. Kings were officers elected by this "nation." See *Boulainvilliers and the French Monarchy*, 30, 80.

    5. On the formation of the *polysynodie* see Henri Leclercq, *Histoire de la Régence pendant la minorité de Louis XV*, 3 vols. (Paris, 1921), 1: 140–56. The new regime, writes Leclercq, made no attempt to alter "the relations established between local authorities and the central government." The *polysynodie* was "in no position to realize the plan of decentralization foreseen by [the duc de Bourgogne]" (145).

    6. On the slow but steady growth of administrative personnel in the provinces see Charles Godard, *Les pouvoirs des intendants sous Louis XV* (Paris, 1901); Julien Riccomard, "Les Subdélégués des intendants jusqu'à leur élection en titre d'office," *Revue d'Histoire Moderne* 12 (1937): 338–407; idem, "Les subdélégués des intendants aux XVIIᵉ et XVIIIᵉ siècles," *L'Information Historique* 24 (1962): 139–48; Henri Fréville, "Notes sur les subdélégués généraux et subdélégués de l'intendance de Bretagne au XVIIIᵉ siècle," *Revue d'Histoire Moderne* 12 (1937): 408–38. On the social origins of the *intendants* see Vivian R. Gruder, *The Royal Provincial Intendants: A Governing Elite in Eighteenth-Century France* (Ithaca, N.Y., 1968).

ever, I want to focus attention on the ongoing cultural adjustment implied by this gradual reification of the state apparatus. Because Louis XIV viewed absolutism through the lens of the personal idiom, he had acted on his centralizing aspirations by hyperpersonalizing royal government. In doing so he not only made state power intelligible to those attuned to the language and values of the personal modality of service; he also insured that the sovereign's personal presence would remain integral to state structures to the end of the ancien régime. The abstract state would never fully displace the image of the personal sovereign in the years before the Revolution, and this meant that the inheritors of Louis XIV's legacy struggled to reconcile the traditional principles of personal government with the deliberately suprapersonal means now used to communicate and project the sovereign's power.

Evidence of an unresolved tension in contemporary perceptions of the monarch's power had already appeared in the waning years of Louis XIV's reign. Vauban, with his dual understanding of utility, merit, and social status, provides one example of this tension. Fénelon and *The Adventures of Telemachus* (1699) provide another. In that important text, curious for its combination of reactionary and forward-looking ideas, Fénelon observed that "people speak incessantly of virtue and merit without knowing precisely what they are." These were merely "fine words," "vague terms" to which men never tired of referring.[7] Ironically, though, Fénelon's own reflections on the meaning of merit betrayed the kind of ambiguity that would come to characterize much of eighteenth-century discourse. He sounded quite traditional when he stressed the king's personal responsibility for finding and rewarding merit: "It is necessary to study men in order to know them, and to know them one must see them and have relations with them. . . . A king who is inaccessible to men is also inaccessible to the truth."[8] Yet Fénelon also noted that to recognize "those who are reasonable and virtuous" one must have in mind stable images of "reason" and "virtue." Therefore he insisted on the adoption of "constant principles" and a "fixed standard" for judging merit, a development that would effectively efface the identity of the king, who "arranges, orders, and prepares things from afar": "While doing nothing, [he] does everything." Fénelon averred that "the essential purpose of *the government* [emphasis mine] is to discern well the differ-

---

7. François de Salignac de La Mothe-Fénelon, *Les aventures de Télémaque, fils d'Ulysse,* ed. Charles Le Brun (Philadelphia, 1834), 389.

8. Ibid., 388–90.

ent characters of mind in order to choose and employ [men] according to their talents."[9]

Although it occupies a small place in a lengthy work on the nature of kingship, Fénelon's discussion of merit actually points to the basic paradox underlying French absolutism in the eighteenth century. Despite the common and persistent emphasis on the personal authority and gaze of the sovereign, the routine operation of royal power necessarily implied the transference of the sovereign's gaze from the person of the king to the agents, institutions, and procedures that represented him. As Fénelon's words suggest, and as I already noted in chapter 4, the metaphorical and suprapersonal sovereign gaze judged and measured merit in ways that distinguished it from the gaze of the traditional personal modality. The sovereign's metaphorical gaze, surveying a space of royal service coextensive with the monarchy's powers of administration, used the universally applicable standards of talent, discipline, and application to encourage and assess merit. The new gaze and its homogenizing character indeed permitted the king to arrange, order, and prepare things from afar, as Fénelon had suggested, but the normalizing process to which it gave rise continued to integrate the basic assumption of the sovereign's personal presence. As a consequence, the eighteenth century's definition of the ideally meritorious royal servant continued to incorporate the signs of birth, all the qualities associated with nobility, and the underlying premise of personal familiarity with the monarch.

To understand the importance of this paradox for the political culture of the eighteenth century, we need to examine at close range the shifting perceptions of birth, merit, nobility, and the gaze in the aftermath of the changes wrought by Louis XIV. The army provides an ideal site for such an examination. Because of the traditional importance of the military vocation to the old nobility, and because of the army's role as the principal arm of monarchical power, kings, nobles, and administrators gave the army their sustained attention from the later seventeenth century to the Revolution. Evidence of this attention is found in a rich array of documents, including educational treatises, administrative memoranda, performance reports sent to the *secrétaire d'état de la guerre*, proposals for reform, minutes of committee meetings, statements of policy, and diagnoses of problems large and small. In these documents, one finds varied

---

9. Ibid., 367, 388.

and often probing discussions of the very principles of the ancien régime's social, political, and service hierarchy.

All historians of early-modern institutions recognize that such documents measure ideals and wishful thinking more than actual behavior. The shifting intentions and aspirations of the monarchy and its servants in the eighteenth century form a uniquely valuable subject, however, for they illustrate well both the diffusion of the sovereign's powers of judgment and the intended impact of that diffusion. In listening to noble officers and other agents of the monarchy articulate and attempt to apply a new ideal of the *militaire,* one perceives the connection between the refashioning of professional identity and service and the operation of a royal gaze that gradually became merely metaphorical after 1700.

My analysis of the evolution of military service in these last chapters is intended to show that the experience of monarchy and old nobility in the eighteenth century needs to be understood in light of the contradiction implicit within absolutism's culture of service, a contradiction elaborated to the breaking point by the kings, nobles, and administrators who succeeded Louis XIV. As the king's personal and transitory gaze increasingly gave way to the permanent gaze of the government or state—that is, as the personal modality of service completed its metamorphosis and became a public modality of service—the monarchy and its servitors found themselves making an increasingly troublesome epistemological adjustment, an adjustment reflected in the language used to describe, assess, reward, and convey merit. I argue that the monarch and the old nobility, principal interlocutors in this discourse of renegotiation, participated unwittingly in a process that would finally exclude them. Efforts to clarify the meaning of merit and to fix the procedures necessary for knowing and judging it eventually produced, by the last decades of the eighteenth century, a hesitant, highly ambiguous, but increasingly self-conscious critique of the very principles of personal government and hereditary distinction.

Observing Merit in the Army

Young nobles and officers serving in the king's armies in the later seventeenth and early eighteenth centuries would have had good reason to question the source of the gaze for which they were asked to perform. In schools, barracks, garrisons, and battle, they learned that the power of the gaze was no longer a direct function of proximity to the king or court;

the monarchy's normalizing gaze exerted its pressures in a variety of impersonal ways. The young noble learned, in the words of La Bruyère, that he earned recognition not by "positioning himself before [the king's] eyes" but rather by his "application" to duty.[10] Application had to be enforced continuously.

The instructional techniques embraced by various military training institutions from the later seventeenth century to the 1770s indeed suggest an ever-rising emphasis on surveillance. In 1691, for example, Louis XIV consolidated six Parisian riding academies and left only two of the schools remaining in operation. The king, or Louvois, also devised a common curriculum and schedule for the two schools to follow.[11] A 1691 *règlement* prescribed the subjects to be studied and specified the amount of time to be devoted to each; at the same time, it stressed that the students, most of whom were noble, should rarely be left to themselves: "No *gentilhomme* will ever be present without the director of the academy, who will stand guard." At nine o'clock the students reported to the chapel to say their evening prayers. There, "so as to avoid confusion, a place on the bench will have been marked for each *gentilhomme*." The nobles should not even be permitted to socialize except under the watchful eye of the instructors: "After prayers, all will retire to their own rooms, without going to any other room for any reason at all; and this will be observed inviolably, regarded as an order from which absolutely no dispensation is allowed."[12]

Documents detailing the daily regimen of pages at the court's *école des pages* in 1722 show the same concern for keeping watch over the students.[13] Depending on the day of the week, the pages spent their afternoons studying mathematics, writing, dancing, drafting, or performing military exercises. Administrators observed all the afternoon activities with close attention: "Sometimes the governor himself will be there; but

---

10. Jean de La Bruyère, *Les caractères; ou les moeurs de ce siècle,* ed. Robert Garapon (Paris, 1962), 100.

11. Archives Nationales (hereafter AN), O¹ 915, no. 39, "Règlement," 1 and 10 January 1691.

12. Ibid.

13. On the history of the school for pages see Gaston Carné, *Les pages des écuries du roi: L'Ecole des pages* (Nantes, 1886); H. Lemoine, "Les écuries du roi sous l'Ancien Régime," *Revue de l'Histoire de Versailles* 35 (1933): 150–83; and François Bluche, *Les pages de la grande écurie,* 3 vols. (Paris, 1966).

the subgovernor . . . must always be present, in order to see that both the masters and the pages remain assiduous."[14]

When not actively engaged in teaching, the staff had the responsibility of keeping an eye on the pages at all times. At lunchtime, the governor, the two subgovernors (who served alternately by week), the tutor, and the almoner gathered to eat with the pages, "who form four tables of ten or eleven each. The pages must never be absent from the meals without the permission of the governor, who must know where they are if they go elsewhere." In the evenings, the pages had to be in bed by no later than ten o'clock, when the subgovernor made a first round of the sleeping quarters. A half hour later, the governor would make his rounds "to see that everyone is in bed, after which no one is permitted to go out, and the servant boys or valets who sleep in their rooms [with them] must report all that goes on [after that time]." To insure that the overseers would be in a position to regulate all the day's activities, "the doors of the rooms must not open in the morning until the hour when the pages scheduled to ride that day leave to go to the stables."[15]

Charles de Lorraine, who oversaw the operation of the school for pages in his capacity as *grand écuyer,* urged even more stringent discipline in a memorandum he sent to the governor of the *école* in 1741. "Their assiduity in their exercises being an essential part" of the education of the pages, he wrote, "we have determined it necessary to renew certain points of our old *règlements.*"[16] Specifically, he stressed that the pages should not miss any of their studies or exercises, leave them before they were completed, or emerge from their rooms in the morning before the appointed time. Tardiness, too, now had to be punished. A separately issued *règlement* instructed governors to "be exact in examining all the pages' exercises, to distinguish at which ones they excel, and to report the exactitude of the masters."[17]

The directors of the *école des pages* apparently did begin to watch their charges more closely. The pages, free in the 1720s to leave the school during hours of recreation, had a separate space designated inside

---

14. AN, O¹ 970, no. 105, "Mémoire en forme de règlement sur Mssrs les Pages de la Grande Ecurie," January 1722, article 12.

15. Ibid., articles 15 and 16. See also AN, O¹ 970, no. 103, "Journée des Pages de la grande écurie," [1722].

16. AN, O¹ 970, no. 109, "Memorandum du Grand Ecuyer," 1741.

17. AN, O¹ 970, no. 108, "Règlement nécessaire," 1741.

for their recreation by the 1740s, and a tutor (*répétiteur*) supervised them constantly. During recreation now, the pages could neither "leave the enclosure nor return to the building, either individually or in groups, without the express permission of the tutors."[18] The *grand écuyer* further instructed that "the *répétiteur* will compile a report of all disorders that are committed and will submit it to me each morning, and the professors will compile similar reports weekly. I will send a report to the parents every month and to the minister [of war] every three months."[19]

The pages' supervisors tried to exact the students' silent obedience to the rules. All the hours of study "must be spent in silence." The pages could not utter even a word to any of their neighbors. And if the rule was violated, "the *répétiteur* will immediately take note of all that is said." When moving from one class to another the pages must "enter the designated room in an orderly manner, always in silence." Once installed in the *salle d'étude,* the pages again had to "observe the greatest possible silence . . . carefully avoiding giving their comrades any excuse for disorder."[20] On days of military exercises, usually Friday and Saturday, the pages gathered in their divisions "at the precise hour fixed for the exercise." Joking and playing were forbidden, and "if the lesson is individually administered, the rest of the division must remain in silence and be attentive to the demonstration in order to profit from it." The masters should "take care to note in their books the conduct and progress of each student, so as to mention it in their weekly report."[21] Finally, to allow surveillance even throughout the night, the *grand écuyer* now ordered that "the pages will not close the doors of their rooms during the night under any pretext."[22] Each new measure indicated a concern to increase the students' visibility.

Evidence of this kind of thinking appears in many places. In the five artillery schools reorganized in 1720, for example, the regent ordered that discipline should be "observed severely." Precision being so important to artillery service, "where the smallest mistake can have the greatest consequences," the commanders should discipline their officer-stu-

---

18. AN, O¹ 970, no. 131, "Règlement pour la salle d'exercises, Recréation," undated. This and the following documents concerning the pages are undated, but they are thematically consistent with Charles de Lorraine's 1741 memorandum and are grouped in a series of documents from the 1740s and 1750s. They clearly date from about midcentury.
19. AN, O¹ 970, no. 130, "Règlements pour la salle d'études," undated.
20. Ibid.
21. AN, O¹ 970, no. 131, "Règlement pour la salle d'exercises, Recréation," undated.
22. AN, O¹ 970, no. 132, "Règlement pour Messieurs les Pages," undated.

dents "without interruption."[23] Instructors must "report to the director and to the inspector of their department on the application and the progress of each officer and [on] whether some are neglecting their studies, so that, on the basis of these reports, some will be rewarded and others punished."[24] The companies of *cadets gentilshommes,* which the crown reestablished in 1726 after a long hiatus, also attracted attention. The cadet companies provided young officers an apprenticeship in active regiments, and the cadets were expected to absorb many of the principles of their profession simply through contact with more experienced officers.[25] To encourage the cadets to work harder, though, one observer suggested that they should be lodged in adjoining rooms, "so the officers can look after the conduct of the *gentilshommes* more easily." Also, to impress on the cadets that no "disordered conduct" would be tolerated, the writer advised that officers see that "they make their beds, that their rooms are clean, and that they themselves are clean."[26] Another hopeful reformer clearly got carried away. He fantasized that instead of having one observer for every fifty cadets, that ratio might be inverted. In that case, "the cadets, being an insignificant number compared to those who are watching their conduct . . . , will not dare to be disorderly or remain idle, having as witness of their every move not only their governors and corps commanders but all officers, even soldiers [if necessary]."[27]

Several imperatives lay behind the emerging ideal of generalized surveillance. Two explicitly stated objectives appeared in virtually every institutional innovation and reform proposal throughout the century; educators wanted to encourage application, on the one hand, and to identify and cultivate distinct talents and abilities, on the other hand. One critic observed in 1736, for example, that the war minister needed to develop a new plan for educating officers. The war of the Polish succession had demonstrated that French generals were "not applied" and that

---

23. "Instruction" sent by the regent to the director and inspector general of the artillery schools at Metz, Strasbourg, La Fère, Grenoble, and Perpignan, 23 June 1720, in Sr. de Briquet, ed., *Code Militaire, ou Compilation des Ordonnances des Roys de France Concernant les Gens de Guerre,* 3 vols. (Paris, 1728), 2:46.

24. Ibid.

25. "Ordonnance pour l'établissement de 6 Compagnies de Cadets de 100 Gentils-hommes chacune," 16 December 1726, in Briquet, *Code Militaire,* 2:254.

26. Archives de la Guerre (hereafter AG), MR 1781, no. 62, "Mémoire concernant la discipline qui doit être observée dans les compagnies de Gentilshommes," undated (but included in a *liasse* marked 1682–1733; it clearly dates between 1727 and 1733).

27. AG, MR 1781, no. 19, "Projet pour un nouvel établissement de Cadets gentils-hommes," [1742], 9, 7.

other officers similarly lacked "application and obedience."[28] The solution seemed clear: all officers must be "persuaded of the need to instruct themselves" and nurture their abilities: "Now is the time to remedy [these problems]; those who have talents for war have just discovered them in the . . . campaigns recently completed."[29] Another observer, writing in the same year, sounded equally hopeful: "The French nobility has all the talents necessary to form great men; we have only to cultivate them and prevent their being corrupted."[30]

The growing attention to the specificity of talents and inclinations is shown best by the Ecole Royale Militaire, an institution founded in 1751 to provide five hundred young *gentilshommes* rigorous military training. Those involved in the planning of the Ecole Militaire, as well as those who sought to improve it in later years, all agreed on the need to both develop and differentiate abilities. One observer, who applauded the new plan to establish a school for the nobility, remarked in 1750 that nobles needed an institution

> where care is taken, at an early stage, to study their natural dispositions that will lead them toward a profession in life; . . . where, constantly in the presence of the most skilled masters, watched by respectable men made responsible for their education, and sometimes even honored by the sovereign's own observation, everything combines to inspire a vivid emulation, capable of pressuring even the most incorrigible personality.[31]

Preliminary versions of the edict establishing the Ecole Militaire stressed these very advantages. "This education . . . , while cultivating and multiplying talents, will also put us in a better position to judge them closer to their source."[32] Boys would come to reside at the school between the ages of eight and eleven.[33] Entering with at least a basic level

---

28. AG, MR 1702, no. 58, "Mémoire," 1736, 6.

29. Ibid., 1.

30. AG, MR 1702, no. 43, M. de la Garrigue, "Mémoire sur la nécessité d'appliquer les officiers à s'instruire et étudier l'art militaire," 1736, 38.

31. AN, K 149, no. 1, "Mémoire sur l'utilité de l'établissment d'un collège académique pour la jeune noblesse de France," 11 January 1750.

32. AN, K 149, no. 26, "Projet d'édit," undated, fol. 3v.

33. For the organization of the Ecole Militaire see L. Hennet, *Les compagnies de cadets gentilshommes et les écoles militaires* (Paris, 1889); Robert Laulan, "Pourquoi et comment on entrait à l'Ecole royale et militaire de Paris," *Revue d'Histoire Moderne et Con-*

of literacy, the students would go on to study history, geography, drafting, fortifications, tactics, military exercises, and, especially, mathematics. At age sixteen they would be placed at the base of the hierarchy of commissioned officers in active regiments—as *cornettes* in the cavalry or sublieutenants in the infantry. A few would be directed to the artillery. The crown thought to create a "new race" of warriors, "whom we will employ more confidently, [because] we will know and penetrate their morals, tastes, and characters." To supplement the "natural valor of the nation," these students learned to join "talents and knowledge[, which are] as useful in war as courage itself."[34] After having "perfected" their educations, and being made "ready to serve the state usefully, our will is that they should be employed in our troops, or in other areas [*parties*] of war, according to the talents and aptitudes we will have recognized in them."[35] One other benefit deserved mention. By taking care to educate nobles in this way, the crown set a useful new example that would "inspire envy [among others] for a similar education."[36]

Despite the high expectations, or perhaps because of them, the Ecole Militaire received only mixed reviews. Some thought the curriculum overburdened the student, who wasted time on subjects less than "absolutely necessary for the function to which he is destined."[37] Others held the opposite view and asserted that the course of instruction was too narrow.[38] All who recommended changes in curricular content or instructional technique shared a basic assumption, however: there could never be too much surveillance or too close attention to the distinct qual-

---

temporaine 4 (1957): 141–50; David D. Bien, "The Army in the French Enlightenment: Reform, Reaction, and Revolution," *Past and Present* 85 (1979): 68–98; and Marcel Marion, *Dictionnaire des Institutions de la France aux XVIIe et XVIIIe siècles* (1923; reprint, Paris, 1984), 196.

34. AN, K 149, no. 26, "Projet d'édit," undated, fols. 3v and 1v.

35. AN, K 149, no. 11, "Projet d'édit," 12 May 1750, fols. 17 v–18r.

36. AN, K 149, no. 26, "Projet d'édit," undated, fol. 3v. The actual edict of creation suggests that the crown hoped to help improve domestic education in noble families by providing fathers a new model to imitate. See Marion, *Dictionnaire*, 196: "We hope that the utility of this establishment, which seems to have only part of the nobility as its object, will be communicated to the entire corps, and that the plan that will be followed in the education of the five hundred *gentilshommes* will serve as a model for fathers who are in a position to educate their children similarly; in this way [perhaps] the old prejudice that held that valor alone was sufficient to form the man of war will imperceptibly give way to a taste for the military studies we have introduced."

37. AN, K 149, no. 24. "Plan d'éducation," [before 1763], fol. 8.

38. For more on the pedagogy of the Ecole Militaire and the debates swirling around it see Bien, "The Army in the French Enlightenment," 84–86.

ities of the students. One critic complained, for example, that the students lacked "vigor" and "precision" in handling arms and performing their military exercises.[39] He advised breaking the students into smaller groups, increasing the number of officers to train and exercise them (taking some from among the students themselves), and choosing one man to keep close watch over the entire program of instruction. He expressed confidence that "the machine would function more smoothly under the hand of a single leader."[40] Another observer recommended that the Ecole Militaire establish

> a kind of novitiate that brings out and develops the dispositions of each student, and [it] should insure that the masters only direct [the students] toward the things best suited for them. From there they will go on to the [regular school], where, according to the knowledge and individual dispositions of each student, each will apply himself in the subjects to which he is suited.

Each student then had the opportunity to "perfect his talents" for the good of society.[41]

To understand the obsession with detecting talents and reinforcing them through surveillance and discipline, one needs to consider the course of long-term changes specific not to France but rather to the military profession.[42] The size of France's army had grown steadily since the 1660s.[43] But more important, all continental armies had reorganized

39. AN, K 149, no. 21. "Réflexions d'un militaire sur l'état militaire de l'Hôtel de l'Ecole Militaire," [after 6 May 1755], fols. 1–2.

40. Ibid., fol. 4.

41. AN, K 149, no. 24. "Plan d'éducation," [before 1763], fol. 1r.

42. The background for the changes in tactics and organization marking the rise of the "modern" army in Europe can be found in Michael Roberts, *The Military Revolution, 1550–1660* (Belfast, 1956). The eighteenth-century army in France has been covered best by André Corvisier. See his *L'armée française de la fin du XVIIe siècle au ministère de Choiseul: Le soldat*, 2 vols. (Paris, 1964). Especially useful for our purposes is Corvisier's article "La Noblesse Militaire: Aspects militaires de la noblesse française du 15e au 18e siècles," *Histoire Sociale/Social History* 22 (1978): 336–55. For the broader European perspective, see his *Armies and Societies in Europe, 1494–1789*, trans. Abigail T. Siddall (Bloomington, Ind., 1979).

43. On this point see John Lynn, "The Growth of the French Army during the Seventeenth Century," *Armed Forces and Society* 6 (1980): 568–85.

their fighting units as the result of a shift in tactics.[44] Since the Thirty Years' War, an emphasis on speed and maneuverability had led military leaders increasingly to employ linear formations on the field of battle. These formations, in turn, required greater numbers of officers to perform more finely articulated functions precisely and efficiently. Thus, by the later seventeenth century the military art required two qualities of all officers and soldiers. Each had to be conscious always of his own individual duties, and this meant that he must possess, develop, and practice the skills needed to execute those duties. At the same time, each individual had to perform in coordination with others, and this meant that both duty and function had to become a matter of reflex.

Future officers had to become habituated to routine, and this is one reason why those who observed and trained them emphasized disciplined regularity. Louis XIV himself had recognized the importance of instilling good habits.

> Habit is the surest and simplest means we can use to make all things easy. Even the most difficult labor is nothing to those who have been subjected to it over a long period, and the most terrible dangers have so little effect on those who have become accustomed to them that they often face them without any reflection. . . . In truth, with habit you can make brave those who are not [brave] by nature, and you will find that with care you can make all sorts of men into good soldiers.[45]

In the eighteenth-century army, officers and soldiers learned through repetitive exercises to handle their arms, march in step, execute maneuvers, give and receive orders, and confront the enemy unflinchingly. Men had to march, for example, "in such perfect accord that the battalions can maintain themselves in the best order." Through regular practice "the habit becomes like a second nature to them."[46] In infantry, the practice of *évolutions*—a set of elaborate drills typically described as "one of

---

44. See John Lynn, "Tactical Evolution in the French Army, 1560–1660," *French Historical Studies* 14 (1985): 176–91. An illuminating survey of tactical and technological changes and their implications for the performance of the eighteenth-century soldier is John Childs, *Armies and Warfare in Europe: 1648–1789* (Manchester, 1982), esp. 105–20.

45. Louis XIV, *Mémoires, suivi de Réflexions sur le métier du roi, Instructions au duc d'Anjou, Projet de harangue,* ed. Jean Longnon, 2 vols. (Paris, 1923), 2:112–14.

46. AN, M 653, no. 4, "Du Pas Militaire," [eighteenth century].

the principal parts of military discipline"—conditioned soldiers to move as a unit rather than as a collection of individuals.[47]

> It is only by long usage that [soldiers] contract the habit of maintaining themselves in their files and ranks in such a solid manner that they can execute with precision the orders that are given them. Even more, without constant practice they can never acquire this precious exactitude that is the strength of the infantry.[48]

The habit of mechanical efficiency would allow soldiers to perform their duties almost unconsciously: "The less the troops are given the chance to reflect the better."[49] Ideally, maneuvers should be so simple and orderly that they required "no intelligence, no presence of mind to execute [them]." To succeed in this, wrote one reformer, officers should arrange their troops

> in an order that never varies, in such a way that whatever the movement being performed, the soldier never finds himself out of place; he sees the same person at the head of the file, the same man to his right and to his left; he obeys the same officers and the same sergeants, who are always positioned in the same place. In this way, nothing depends on the soldier as an individual, since he only forms part of a corps that moves in its totality.[50]

To "maintain themselves in the best order," officers and soldiers had to be uniformly efficient in executing their assigned tasks. But despite the emphasis on uniform discipline, none could forget that the army's success depended on the performance of discrete parts that acted in unison. As the renowned Italian general Montecuccoli had remarked in the middle seventeenth century, "order is the arrangement of things in their place

---

47. AN, M 655, no. 1. Among the many contemporary documents at the Archives Nationales devoted to the art of *évolutions,* this quote comes from a collection titled "Affaires Militaires," [eighteenth century].

48. Ibid.

49. AN, M 644, no. 7. "Méthode pour mener un Bataillon à la charge et le rallier en bon ordre," 1746.

50. AN, M 639, no. 3, "Réflexions sur les évolutions de l'infanterie," 1755. The final sentence reads: "Par cette voye, rien ne coule plus sur le soldat en particulier, puisqu'il ne fait que partie d'un corps qui se meut dans sa totalité."

... [and] it is from order that success in war ordinarily comes. Disorder, however, always has the opposite effect—confusion and failure."[51]

Military service came increasingly to be described through mechanical metaphors in the eighteenth century. This change reflected not only a desire to project an image of efficiency but also increased awareness that the military enterprise involved bringing together disparate components in a common cause. "The general order that must be observed in the operations of war" demanded that the "degrees of capacity" of everyone in the officer corps be determined. "Each *militaire* has his talent," this observer wrote. To make good use of them, one had to "consider the scope of particular functions and determine the knowledge and talents demanded by each post, in order to choose and employ people usefully in the positions that suit them."[52] The leaders of the military must be "exact in the choice of the parts that compose [the] machine."[53] Discriminating commanders needed to insure that "everyone finds his place."[54] To coordinate men performing diverse functions and to exact precision and maximum effort from them all, commanders had also to impress on the men the general need for subordination. The ideal of subordination became so important that the chevalier de Rochelambert called it the very "strength of the state."[55] More than blind obedience to superiors, however, the word *subordination* implied constant application to a well-defined role. As one of the planners of the Ecole Militaire stated it, the "spirit of subordination . . . has to do with knowledge of one's duties."[56]

---

51. Bibliothèque Nationale (hereafter BN), MS fr. 12365, Raimondo Montecuccoli, "Principes de l'art militaire," 1712, 4. Montecuccoli, who first put his thoughts on paper in the 1640s, was a precocious strategist and tactician; his biographer calls him a "chief founder of the modern Austrian army." Montecuccoli's memoirs, including the "Principes," were widely studied in the eighteenth century. Published first in Italian in 1704, they appeared in a French edition in 1712, and eight more printings appeared in French to 1760. For a close look at this scientific tactician see Thomas M. Barker, *The Military Intellectual and Battle: Raimondo Montecuccoli and the Thirty Years War* (Albany, N.Y., 1975).

52. AG, MR 1702, no. 61, Le comte de Bombelles, "Mémoire sur l'état militaire," [1738], 2.

53. AG, MR 1703, no. 32, M^r. le Chevalier de Montaut, "Réflexions sur la manière de former de bons soldats d'Infanterie, avec un essay sur la conduite politique d'un Lieutenant-Colonel envers son Regiment," [1747–48], 2.

54. AN, M 650, no. 5, "Differentes pensées sur les devoirs de l'homme de guerre," undated, 17.

55. AG, MR 1709, no. 20, Chevalier de la Rochelambert, "Meditation Militaire," 1760, 5.

56. AN, K 149, no. 26. "Projet d'édit," undated, fol. 3r.

Clearly, then, military institutions placed a premium on surveillance because all took for granted the need to reinforce both particularity and uniformity. As one career officer wrote, commanders had to take on the responsibility of sorting out "characters and abilities," for then everyone serves "in his proper sphere; everyone happily does his duty; everyone loves his work, because it is always in proportion to talents and capacities, [and this] is the surest means of making the best use of officers."[57] But at the same time, in having their talent, application, and skills judged continuously, all officers would learn to perform with "more exactitude" and "more wisdom," since they knew that opportunities for advancement and rewards depended on "a perfect attachment to their duties."[58] In Foucauldian terms, one might say that the army, in using close observation as a means both to judge and to stimulate good behavior, sought to produce the "docile bodies" whose strength and abilities it needed to manipulate.[59]

But the tilt toward intensive monitoring of performance in army institutions must also be seen in the context of a broader cultural change in which the military only happened to play an important part. In paying precise attention to the development and performance of their subordinates, in attempting to observe and discipline them without interruption, in faithfully noting talents, application, zeal—the "legitimate pretexts" for promotion and reward in the king's service—French army officers and educators elaborated the new modality of service that had taken shape in Louis XIV's (omni)presence. The evolution in methods for defining, determining, and evaluating merit in the eighteenth-century army reflected the ongoing reconceptualization of the sovereign's gaze—and vice versa.

The marquis de Feuquières had already recognized this connection in the first decade of the century. In discussing the ethos of military service in his memoirs, he emphasized that "young men of quality who are destined for war must try to attract the king's eye by their application to their profession."[60] And this meant that they must become accustomed

57. BN, nouvelles acquisitions française 384, Langeron, "Traité sur les devoirs d'un colonel," 1751, 4–5.

58. AG, MR 1702, no. 43, M. de la Garrigue, "Mémoire sur la nécessité d'appliquer les officiers à s'instruire et étudier l'art militaire," 1736, 62.

59. For more on Foucault's "docile bodies" see *Discipline and Punish: The Birth of the Prison*, trans. Alan Sheridan (New York, 1979), 135–69 and passim.

60. BN, nouvelles acquisitions française 9521. Antoine de Pas, Mis de Feuquières, "Mémoires sur la guerre," [eighteenth century], 8. The manuscript is undated, but

to having their merits judged in a different light. "The prince," he wrote, "must examine continually the officers whose good qualities for war might put them in a position to command at some point. Having recognized their talents for war in an unprejudiced way, he must place them as soon as possible." But the king's responsibility did not end there. He must continue to observe them and "discover their ability," "perceive their manner of thinking and the extent of their capacity for war," so as to promote them "as he senses that their capacity is increasing." Feuquières pointed out the benefits of this unremitting attention; "this method of cultivating talents and inspiring emulation in young men will make them more applied."[61]

Feuquières's remarks are interesting in part because they express two incompatible ideals. On the one hand, he stressed that young nobles destined for the army must be examined continually to insure that their talents were judged in an unprejudiced way and that each officer was placed in a position appropriate to his ability and capacity. On the other hand, Feuquières preserved for his noble readers the image of the ever-present prince who personally sees all. In truth, as Colbert had earlier observed, the king himself could not verify the specific merits of men who generally performed "so far from his eyes." From the beginning, the normalization of merit had implied the simultaneous mediation of the sovereign's gaze through agents who represented him metaphorically. Thus, the common impulse to make military merits visible, specific, and tangible also indicated that army officers themselves now served deliberately as instruments of the sovereign's gaze.

Officers became increasingly conscious of their new role. An army lieutenant named Lamée observed, in a 1741 essay on "the military art," that "it is up to the colonel to open the door to honors for those officers who . . . perform well in their profession." Perhaps more to the point, "it is up to them to fill the great void that separates them from the prince." However much the king and his ministers hoped "to recognize and encourage merit," Lamée lamented, "they cannot perceive it at such a great distance. It is up to colonels to bring it closer and find occasion to

---

Feuquières lived from 1666 to 1709, and the manuscript seems to be from the first years of the eighteenth century. Feuquières' memoirs were later published in several editions, the first being *Mémoires sur la guerre, où l'on a rassemblé les maximes les plus nécessaires dans les opérations de l'art militaire* (Amsterdam, 1730).

61. Ibid., 9.

show it to [the king and his ministers]."[62] The author of a 1718 military memoir made a similar point. He noted the growing importance of regimental commanders, who, as general overseers, often had the responsibility of representing their corps before an official: "They are sometimes called on to represent [the interests of the regiment] to a general, to a minister, to an *intendant*, . . . so that it often depends on their intelligence and ability to make the most of their regiment." Consequently, the office of major required "vigor, activity, exactitude," "integrity and precision in detail." The office, though "difficult to fill with distinction," could be considered ideal "for those who wish to make themselves known."[63]

Colonels, majors, and other officers should earn distinction by observing, using, and making known the merits of others; this idea found expression both in prescriptive literature and in practice. In 1737, for example, the crown issued an "instruction" reminding superior officers that they should "examine the talents of [subordinate] officers, their application, and how they use their authority."[64] The officers probably had no need for an official reminder, for they heard this advice at every turn. Ideal officers "would always be inspectors," because of the need to match abilities with functions:[65] "To command men well, it is first necessary to know them, to have seen them in different situations, to have studied their every move: [the officer should] know how their souls work, distinguish their talents, cultivate them, and then use them."[66] This officer, writing in the 1740s, suggested that discipline would be improved if the army were reorganized on the model of the Roman Legions, with one man (a general) selecting the candidates for promotion to important offices in every legion.

> It is obvious that such an officer at the head of a corps would know all the subjects perfectly. . . . The court would be well informed of all that

---

62. AG, MR 1703, no. 9, M. Lamée, "Essai sur l'art militaire," 27 December 1741, 27.

63. BN, MS fr. 12387. "Mémoires sur le service journalier de l'infanterie," 1718, 2:1–2.

64. BA, MS 4817, "Instruction dressé par ordre du roy, pour les officiers généraux que sa Majesté a jugé à propos d'entretenir sur ses frontières sous les ordres de ceux qui en auront le commandement en chef," 1737, in a collection titled "Recueil de pièces curieuses," 376.

65. AG, MR 1709, no. 20, Chevalier de la Rochelambert, "Meditation Militaire," 1760, 7.

66. AG, MR 1705, no. 36, "Mémoire de la Discipline de l'Infanterie," [1741–48], 7. The passage reads: "Pour bien commander aux hommes, il faut auparavant les connaître, les avoir vus dans les situations différentes, savoir à leur moindre mouvement: connaître le Tac de leurs âmes, distinguer leurs talents, les faire naître, et les Employer."

happens in the infantry service, of which colonels and other officers are devoted to their profession, and of the different talents of each—the talent of this general being to cultivate and employ [the talents of others].[67]

Most aspired only to increase the efficiency of the existing system. To achieve this, each colonel had to know "all the details of his regiment" personally.[68] He should "see and examine [the troops] everyday" to encourage discipline and exactitude. He must verify all things "with his own eyes," ready to detect small abuses invisible to him from a distance.[69] The conscientious colonel observed his regiment to "sort out the different characters and talents, so as to put each one in its place when naming people to positions."[70] Moreover, to maintain objectivity in this and other matters, he should avoid "familiarity" and "close friendship" with the officers below him and should resist showing "predilection for anyone."[71]

The lieutenant colonels should behave much like the colonel. "No one is in a better position to know the characters, talents, virtues, and vices of everyone in the regiment," since the lieutenant colonels generally were men of long experience. With "a little application," they could note differences "not only between the excellent and the good but also between the mediocre and the bad."[72] Up and down the officer hierarchy, everyone was observant in a good regiment. Majors and aide-majors watched the conduct of the sergeants to "study their morals and their capacities." Everyone had similarly to observe and evaluate the common soldiers to "see what they are lacking."[73]

To insure both the encouragement and the detection of merit, the chevalier de Rochelambert proposed in 1760 a new method of record keeping. He would assign a respected lieutenant general or maréchal de camp to every brigade. There they would remain at all times, in war and peace: "They will have before their eyes constantly all the subjects who serve with application and affection. They will identify, at the same time,

---

67. Ibid., 24–25.
68. BN, MS fr. 12387, "Mémoires sur le service journalier de l'infanterie," 1718, 2:217–18.
69. Ibid., 237.
70. Ibid., 210.
71. Ibid., 212.
72. Ibid., 147–48.
73. Ibid., 3–5.

those who practice the profession because they have nothing better to do." They will keep "favorable and unfavorable notes" of everyone's conduct, and the notes, when joined to those from other brigades, would "constitute a table [of merits] for the minister of war. This table would insure that mediocre subjects shall never usurp *graces,* posts, or gifts destined for true merit."[74]

That the rise of this mentality paralleled the gradual relocation of the sovereign's gaze in a sprawling administrative matrix is indicated by a brief military memoir from 1736. After noting typically that lieutenant colonels "must be determined to know the talents of the officers, overlook no opportunity to cultivate them, [and] encourage them to increase their application," the author invoked the memory not of an assiduous king but of an administrator famous for his efficiency.[75] In contrast to Louis Guyon, who had urged princes in 1617 to emulate Julius Caesar and know all their soldiers "by their names," this writer held up as a model the great war minister Louvois. He was reputed to have known "all the officers in the army, either himself or according to the precise account he had given to him by the commanders of the [various] corps." He had even been suspected of keeping "spies in each regiment, who informed him of the application, morals, talents, and faults of each officer." In imitation of Louvois, then, the current war minister, d'Angervilliers, should "establish suitable arrangements for knowing the capacity of each of the officers in every regiment."[76]

Perhaps the most telling sign of the diffusion of the sovereign gaze is the methodology used to "fill the great void" separating the king from the meritorious services he needed to reward. Feuquières had noted that nobles had to "attract the king's eye" by their professional application and talents, and we have seen that directors of training institutions and superior officers were expected to record the "assiduity," "conduct," and "progress" of those they supervised. One should not be surprised to find that this emphasis on specificity and careful discrimination appeared also in assessments of performance in battle. The maréchal de Broglie remarked in 1760 that the honor of the French military required that "the king be informed of action[s] of fidelity and disinterest." When the

74. AG, MR 1709, no. 20, Chevalier de la Rochelambert, "Meditation Militaire" (1760), 13.
75. AG, MR 1702, no. 43, M. de la Garrigue, "Mémoire sur la nécessité d'appliquer les officiers à s'instruire et étudier l'art militaire," 1736, 9–10.
76. Ibid., 3.

king accorded *graces* for such actions he reminded his troops that "honor and fidelity are, by their essence, the first virtues of the military profession and that [these qualities] attract the sovereign's attention and his recompense." Even those whose "rank and birth have placed them far from his person" needed to have this assumption reinforced.[77]

To articulate the connection between service and reward "at such a great distance," however, the mediators of the king's eyes had to make valor and courage subject to objective analysis. Thus, continuing a trend already apparent in the second half of Louis XIV's reign, eighteenth-century army officers found ways to express tangibly the generous sacrifices of their men. In 1712, for example, his commanding officer requested a gratification of six hundred livres for "sieur de la Giboudière, engineer . . . , who lost a leg [*a perdu une cuisse*]" at the siege of Douai. (The "arm and shoulder broken at the same siege" by a sieur de Millot, however, merited only four hundred livres.)[78] According to a report from the marquis de Broglie in 1714, meanwhile, a grenadier named Feuillera had "performed actions of great valor" at the siege of Barcelona and "would not retreat from battle until he had received a musket wound."[79] He clearly deserved a royal pension.

Officers invariably quantified appendages lost, length of service, and courageous actions performed. In 1740, the war minister received a list of grenadiers to evaluate for promotion to the rank of brigadier. One, a chevalier de Caligny, had joined the infantry in 1691 and was present at the bombardment of Brussels and three other sieges before being named engineer. There followed "thirty-eight years of service" as an engineer and attendance at "five sieges, one defense of a fortress, [and] several campaigns." At the close of this summation of his accomplishments, the recommending officer listed "two wounds." Another man, named Gittard, seemed even more deserving. He could boast "fifty years of service, three sieges, two defenses of fortresses, several expeditions, [and] two serious wounds."[80]

77. AG, Y^a 516, dossier 1, no. 1, letter from Broglie, 27 September 1760.

78. AG, Travail du Roi, 1706–39. The "Etat de gratifications," undated except for the year 1712, lists the rewards given "au s. de la Giboudière ingenieur à Hesdin qui a perdu une cuisse au mesme siege [de Douay]" and "au s. de Millot ingenieur à Arras qui a eu le bras et l'espaule cassez au mesme siege."

79. AG, Travail du Roi (1706–39), "Estat des Officiers d'infanterie qui se sont trouviez [sic] au siege de Barcelone, et qui M. le Mis de Broglie dis [sic] meriter des pensions tant par la manière dont ils y ont servy que pour leur anciens services precedents," 14 December 1714.

80. AG, Y^a 70, dossier 1, "Promotions," "Etat des Ingénieurs que l'on propose pour être Brigadiers d'Infanterie en 1740."

The new pattern of representation is shown also by the formalization of criteria for winning the Cross of Saint Louis. A typical proposal submitted in 1731 suggested that the king promote one hundred men to the Order of Saint Louis every other year. Candidates would be selected after the war minister first drew up a great list, "naming only those who will have supplied verifiable certificates of the sieges, battles, combats, and other actions of war at which they have been present, together with the wounds they have received." After perusing the list, the king would then choose his new chevaliers "from among those in each regiment who will have more actions and wounds to their credit."[81]

In an edict of 1779, the crown actually clarified the steps necessary to verify a courageous action.

> The action of bravery for which the Cross [of Saint Louis] will be awarded will be stated in a procès-verbal, drawn up on the spot or on the day that the said action will be said to have taken place, by the staff officers who will be present . . . or by notables of any profession or condition, who will certify it by an act drawn up in a formal manner.[82]

The procès-verbal would be passed on from the officers of the regiment to the general of the army, "who will address it to the secretary of state for war, to be presented to His Majesty, who will award or refuse the Cross according to circumstances."[83]

Normalization affected both sides of the service-reward exchange. Just as officers translated merit for the king by objectifying it and conveying it through well-established channels, the king and minister of war devised standard signs of recognition. By the 1740s, at least, the court had developed protocols for administrative correspondence, and these protocols applied both to the brevets announcing promotions and to the letters awarding royal gratifications. A model letter "to accord the rank of Major" pointed to familiar criteria of distinction.

---

81. AG, Y^a 208, "Mémoire sur la manière de faire les promotions de chevaliers de St. Louis," July 1731.

82. AG, Y^a 208, "Edit du Roi," January 1779.

83. "Ordonnance," 1 June 1781, in Thiroux de Mondésir, ed., *Ordonnances Militaires*, 33 vols. (n.p., n.d.), 4: fol. 237.

The King . . . desiring to recognize the good and faithful services rendered to him by [M.]——, *Capitaine* in the infantry regiment of ——, where he gave proofs of his valor, courage, experience in war, vigilance . . . , good conduct, and his fidelity and affection for his service, His Majesty has given to him the rank of Major.[84]

Thanks to the normalizing process, in the eighteenth century the king rarely had the occasion, or the need, to see actions of valor performed "near our person." The form letter may be seen as an unconscious acknowledgment that, at the same time, the king no longer needed to praise such actions "with his own mouth."

Professional and Noble: The Meanings of Military Merit

Attempts to reshape the culture of military service in the eighteenth century indicated a growing emphasis on preparing and impelling army officers to play highly specified roles assiduously and efficiently. In the process of internalizing discipline and developing a healthy sense of subordination, young officers may well have continued to regard themselves as objects of the king's gaze; at the Ecole Militaire, according to one planner, they might still dream of being honored by the "sovereign's own" observation. But it is important to emphasize, again, that in learning to encourage, check, and record the progress and performance of their subordinates, the officers themselves embodied and exerted the power of the gaze.

The immanence of the sovereign's judging powers altered traditional conceptual horizons. Especially in the case of nobles, who comprised the vast majority of the French officer corps throughout the eighteenth century,[85] the new service expectations implied a subtle adjustment of attitudes, an adjustment already detectable early in the century. In a 1718

---

84. AG, Y^a 516, no. 3. Most of the protocols, contained in a series of unnumbered booklets, date from the 1770s and 1780s; the one quoted here is undated.

85. David D. Bien has shown, through careful analysis of available personnel records, that commoners made up no more than about 5 percent of the regular officer corps throughout the century; this figure excludes the small minority of *officiers de fortune*, who, in any case, never rose above the rank of captain of grenadiers. See Bien, "La réaction aristocratique avant 1789: L'exemple de l'armée," *Annales, E. S. C.* 29 (1974): 23–48, 505–34; see esp. 23–35. For a revealing case study on the nobility's enduring attachment to the profession of arms see Philippe Béchu, "Noblesse d'épée et tradition militaire au 18e siècle," *Histoire, Economie, et Société* 2 (1983): 507–48.

treatise on infantry service, for example, a career army officer described the qualities most important to a colonel (the commander of a regiment). He began by affirming that such a lofty position should only be occupied by those of "illustrious birth." "Great names" easily attracted others to serve under them, and this counted as a real advantage at a time when colonels and captains still recruited their own soldiers. More important, though, *gentilshommes* could always be expected to have some of the prize attributes of leadership: "a magnanimous heart, a noble bearing, an extreme courtesy . . . , an air of command, sentiments of honor." Because these *gentilshommes* were endowed with a "sincere love of virtue," their motives were always "filled with justice . . . [and] valor."[86]

But in addition to these moral attributes, the colonel's responsibilities demanded other qualities. The ideal colonel also possessed "vigilance, a superior mind, acumen, foresight, and regularity down to the last detail."[87] Contrary to the assumptions of the typical soldier—who believed that to achieve distinction in the military, "it is enough to be brave and to have a mind for grand projects"—even the highest military officers should pay attention to "minute detail." "An officer's honor consists not only in bravely facing the most dreadful dangers but even more in excelling in his post, in filling it well even in its smallest functions."

As this last comment suggests, the change in outlook implied by the expanding definition of the ideal *militaire* can be captured by noting the semantic drift of traditional concepts. For example, in the early seventeenth century's culture of royal service, the "execrable" word *ambition* had been used to evoke the self-interested motives thought to prevent commoners from obtaining honorable reputation and royal recognition. By the early eighteenth century, however, the term also conveyed the energy that one devoted to one's profession. Set in another context, ambition had become praiseworthy. In 1720 the regent, Philippe d'Orléans, seemed prepared to abandon the older connotation altogether. In a memo sent to the directors of newly founded artillery schools, he urged army officers to embrace ambition wholeheartedly.

Those who have ambition (and everyone should have this) are not satisfied by what they see and hear in the schools; they study by them-

86. BN, MS fr. 12387. "Mémoires sur le service journalier de l'infanterie," 1718, 2:208–10.
87. Ibid., 210.

selves, [and] they take private lessons; it often happens that, by their own meditations and their application, they surpass the instructions that have been given them . . . [and] they become men of the first merit in their profession; this should be the officer's sole objective.[88]

This same assumption shaped the perspective of the marquis de Monteynard, who served as minister of war between 1771 and 1774. In an essay on the "qualities of a Major," he described the ideal officer candidate as being "ardent for work," "studious," and "filled with ambition." Similarly, one writer in the 1750s urged reform of the system of promotion, which "must provide a vehicle for men who nurture their ambition."[89]

Unlike ambition, the word *émulation* had always connoted a positive quality. In 1694 the Académie Française had called emulation a "kind of jealousy that inspires one to equal or surpass someone else in some praiseworthy endeavor." The quality had been counted among the specific virtues of nobility. In fact, Furetière had defined emulation as a "noble jealousy between people of learning or of virtue that makes them compete to acquire the most glory. Emulation is often the cause of grand actions."[90] The seventeenth-century noble had learned to emulate a broadly useful model of virtue, some of the exemplars of which could be found in his own family history. Pierre Hutin, genealogist of the La Rochefoucauld family, typically boasted that everyone in that lineage had "had the same emulation to surpass everyone else, so much are excellence, courage, and virtue hereditary in this illustrious house."[91]

In the eighteenth century the word *émulation* still implied a kind of competition between individuals striving to meet mutually recognized goals, but the concept's frame of reference had changed significantly. The army lieutenant Lamée remarked in 1741 that "emulation is the desire to achieve what someone else has achieved, in using the same methods." But now one commonly used as a model a person "whose talents, or merit, have elevated and sustained him in the rank that he occupies." "Emula-

---

88. "Instruction," 23 June 1720, in Briquet, *Code Militaire*, 2:47.

89. AG, MR 1786, no. 60, [Marquis de Monteynard], "Reflexions sur les qualités d'un Major et sur les moyens d'etablir une bonne discipline dans les troupes," [1771–1774], unpaginated; AG, MR 1705, no. 37, "Introduction au Code Louis XV," [after 1753], 30.

90. *Dictionnaire de l'Académie Française*, 1st ed. (Paris, 1694); Antoine Furetière, *Dictionnaire universel* (The Hague and Rotterdam, 1690).

91. Pierre Hutin, *Généalogie de la très-grande, très-ancien* [sic], *et très-illustre maison de La Rochefoucauld* (n.p., 1654), 7.

tion," he continued, "is shown only by our exactitude in filling with distinction the grade where fate has placed us. . . . It is in this manner that
we can obtain a higher grade."[92]

The evolution in the meaning of emulation reflected not only the rising
emphasis on discipline but also a narrowing of the standard the *militaire*
aspired to meet and a sensitivity to the new judge(s) in whose eyes his
merits were measured. The young noble in 1650 hoped to live up to the
name of his "illustrious house" and, more specifically, to reenact the
examples of generosity set by his predecessors; he knew that his fellow
nobles, his posterity, and ideally the monarch himself would take note of
his failure or success. By contrast, the noble army officer in 1750 set his
sights on the next highest rank in the hierarchy, and he intended to
acquire it by performing with "exactitude" the duties attached to his present grade. Two forms of pressure reinforced this method of emulation:
the discriminating gaze of one's superiors and the success of peers who
rose by their own exactitude and talent. Students at the Ecole Militaire,
placed "constantly in the presence of the most skilled masters, watched
by respectable men made responsible for their education, and sometimes
even honored by the sovereign's own observation," competed with their
fellow students in an atmosphere where "everything combines to inspire
a vivid emulation." The abbé de Saint-Pierre, in an educational treatise of
1740, asserted that "this precious emulation" could never be fostered in
the context of "domestic education." "The child needs every day to be
surrounded by peers with whom he can compare and measure himself."
The more peers the student has, "the more he exerts himself to acquire
the talents and virtues that earn him praise."[93]

The expanded meanings of ambition and emulation signal a shift away
from a merit validated through personal relations and toward a merit
specific to profession and defined within the parameters of rank and
function. The direction of this change seems clear in retrospect, but one
needs to recognize that those who effected this transformation lived
through a process of which they were not fully conscious. As leading
members of the officers corps that often acted as the arbiter of merit,
eighteenth-century nobles helped articulate and probably aspired to meet
the new demands of discipline and expertise. Yet despite the growing tendency to verify merit through standards of measurement embedded in the

---

92. AG, MR 1703, no. 9, M. Lamée, "Essai sur l'art militaire," 27 December 1741, 27.
93. Abbé Castel de Saint-Pierre, *Avantajes de l'Educaison des Colèges sur l'educaison
domestique* (Amsterdam and Paris, 1740), 7–8.

very organization of service—and scarcely visible to the sovereign—most still took for granted the inherently personal nature of royal service, and the meaning of merit in the military continued to reflect that basic assumption.

As the focus on talent and discipline intensified, so did the monarchy's attention to family background. The new ideals of military training and performance showed up most prominently at institutions designed specifically for nobles—most notably the school for pages and the Ecole Militaire. At the same time that the army sought to instill and cultivate the well-defined merits of talent and discipline, it recognized the intangible qualities of birth by giving general, and eventually exclusive, preference to the nobility. For example, the documents detailing the operation of the *école des pages,* cited earlier in this chapter, provide evidence of a general reform of the school undertaken in the 1720s, a reform that began when the authorities toughened admissions standards in 1721. Instead of the usual four generations (or one hundred years) of nobility, the king's *écuries* now required families of prospective pages to prove "old and military nobility" dating to at least 1550.[94] Several years later, when the war minister reestablished the corps of *cadets gentilshommes* in 1726, he intended to exclude from it everyone but those who could prove four generations of nobility. The only exceptions were the commoners whose fathers currently served at the rank of captain or higher or had died while serving in one of those grades. When the cadets were disbanded in 1733, officials explained the action by citing the infiltration of roturiers who had fooled administrators with fraudulent proofs of old nobility.[95] The directors of the Ecole Militaire, no doubt having learned from the carelessness that had undermined the *cadets gentilshommes,* enforced their own admissions standards with unprecedented rigor. Without exception, families had to present to the royal genealogist original documents proving four degrees of nobility on the paternal side. When choosing from this restricted applicant pool, the directors gave preference to the poor and to those whose fathers had died while serving in the military.

---

94. AN, O¹ 970, no. 2, "Mémoire de ce qui est nécessaire pour entrer Page du Roi dans sa Grande Ecurie," May 1721.

95. One observer, who wanted to revive the cadet companies in 1742, complained that within a year of their creation in 1726 the corps of cadets had been "filled with provincial commoners, to the prejudice of the *gentilshommes* for whom it had been established." See AG, MR 1781, no. 19, "Projet pour un nouvel établissement de Cadets gentilshommes," [1742], 5.

The assumption that one should simultaneously emphasize noble birth and professional excellence found expression at many points throughout the century. In 1758 Minister of War Belle-Isle reminded army inspectors that no one should be admitted to any position in the officer corps if he could not produce a certificate of nobility; in 1759 he extended this provision to officers in the traditionally more inclusive *milice*.[96] After 1777, one had to prove three hundred years of nobility to become a lieutenant in the regiment of French guards. According to André Corvisier, by the 1770s even the artillery school at Mézières, and the smaller artillery schools scattered throughout cities of the north and east, accepted only the sons of aristocrats and knights of the Order of Saint Louis.[97] The most famous measure taken to insure noble privilege in the army, the Ségur ruling of 1781, applied the principle of exclusion still more rigorously. Although sons of men who had earned the Cross of Saint Louis became eligible automatically, all other candidates for the office of sub-lieutenant and above now had to submit original documents proving at least four generations of nobility on the paternal side.[98] Then, in 1788, even sons of the holders of the Cross of Saint Louis were disallowed, unless their fathers currently served at the rank of captain or higher.[99]

Meanwhile, the court of Louis XV showed a similar scrupulousness in recognizing the qualities of distinguished birth. Beginning early in his reign, Louis XV honored particularly distinguished nobles—those whose lineage stretched back some three hundred years—by granting them the right to enter the king's carriage. In 1732, the year the royal genealogist began keeping exact registers of those entitled to the "honors of the court," Louis also extended to old nobles the privilege of "presenting" their wives to the king and queen.[100] In 1759 Louis XV reacted to a dispute over precedence by further formalizing the already encrusted system of courtly protocol. In a *règlement* of 31 December, the king announced that to enjoy official "honors of the court" visitors now had to prove that their noble lineage dated to 1400 or earlier. The regulations specified that

---

96. Corvisier discusses these measures in *Armies and Societies in Europe,*167–70.
97. Ibid., 168.
98. For analysis of the Ségur law see Bien, "La réaction aristocratique avant 1789."
99. Ibid., 524–25.
100. Even those who failed to qualify officially for the right of "presentation" could still hope to enjoy this right *par grace*. For examples see Jean-François Solnon, *La cour de France* (Paris, 1987), 476–79.

applicants had to present three original documents attesting the nobility of each degree in the lineage.[101] Thus, when not busy verifying the credentials of candidates for various military honors, the royal genealogist kept himself occupied by reviewing the records of the countless *gentilshommes* who laid claim to the honors of the court.[102]

These various manifestations of the monarchy's own genealogical consciousness help to illuminate the connections between noble identity and the development of military professionalism in the eighteenth century. As army officers became habituated to the practice of judging and translating the personal merit of others, they remained acutely aware of family status and genealogy. Noble officers in the eighteenth-century army learned to implement and uphold professional standards, but it is important to remember that the self-aware professional unconsciously integrated three criteria of excellence: talent, discipline, and birth. Royal recognition of noble birth, like the king's presence itself, had become a permanent but generally implicit feature in the structures of royal service.

In paying close attention to genealogy, the monarchy made noble privilege an unremarkable and generally unquestioned feature of the military and of the wider society. For the nobility, though, this process had both positive and insidious consequences. On the one hand, the nobility never had reason to doubt its own relevance. For example, precisely because the intrinsic value of aristocratic birth could be taken for granted in the eighteenth century, many self-respecting nobles appropriated prevailing Enlightenment ideas without evincing a trace of irony. As David Bien has demonstrated, many nobles were able to adapt their own assumptions about child development to the pervasive environmentalist assumptions of Lockean pedagogy and "sensationalist" psychology. Army nobles, in particular, seem to have had little trouble modulating between this dis-

---

101. The regulations of the honors of the court, as well as the names and genealogical proofs of all the nobles who officially enjoyed them, are listed in François Bluche, *Les Honneurs de la cour*, 2 vols. (Paris, 1957).

102. The honors of the court fell under the jurisdiction of the royal genealogist, or *généalogiste des ordres du roy;* this officer is not to be confused with the *juge d'armes*, who checked the credentials of royal pages. Originally created in 1595 to verify the nobility of candidates for the Order of Saint-Esprit, the office of royal genealogist assumed ever greater importance in the eighteenth century. After 1781, for example, all officer candidates needed a certificate of nobility signed by the royal genealogist. In the course of Louis XV's reign (1715–74), these officials extended the honors of the court to 942 families. See François Bluche, *Les Honneurs de la cour;* and idem, *Les pages de la grande écurie.*

course of the Enlightenment and a more traditional discourse of aristo-cratic privilege.[103]

But on the other hand, the value of distinguished birth was also now "taken for granted" in the other sense implied by that phrase. Nobles rarely bothered to explain or justify their status explicitly, either to them-selves or to others.[104] The decline of noble self-consciousness is shown, ironically, by the changing tone of genealogical histories. Seventeenth-century genealogists had often explored at length the cultural and social implications of family background; they deliberately connected the fam-ily's living heirs to the traditions associated with the house. This eager-ness to address the importance of family background and generous incli-nations is conspicuously absent from eighteenth-century texts. The genre itself grew tiresome—one author conceded in 1779 that "the public has little interest in the history of an individual house, no matter how illus-trious it is"[105]—and this reflected its predictability. Although they kept alive the tradition of compiling detailed family histories, for the most part eighteenth-century nobles (or those who wrote their histories) seemed content to elaborate the structural patterns inherited from the previous century.[106]

Many were openly derivative. The author of a manuscript history of the Loynes family, himself a member of the house, acknowledged that he based his work on earlier histories by Anselme, Blanchard, Chevillard the

103. See Bien, "The Army in the French Enlightenment." For a discussion of environ-mentalist assumptions and their influence on educational theory before the Revolution, see R. R. Palmer, *The Improvement of Humanity: Education and the French Revolution* (Princeton, 1985), 3–78.

104. A speech by Chancellor D'Aguesseau in the first half of the century, remarkable for its traditional tone, constitutes a striking exception to the old nobility's unself-conscious acceptance of its privileges. In an address to the *parlement* of Paris, he singled out for praise the magistrates of ancient lineage. The merits of their "generous blood" stood in contrast to those of the "new people" who crowded the "sanctuary of justice." What would the esteemed magistrates of past centuries say, he asked rhetorically, if they could witness such a "sad spectacle?" "They would say," according to the chancellor, " 'Let us dismiss those of inferior birth who have been deprived of the advantage of a patrician education. They were not able to study the images of their ancestors early in life and increase their virtue in the shadow of domestic examples. In their childhood they saw nothing to excite that noble emulation that has shaped so many great men.'" Cited in Marcel Marion, *Dictionnaire*, 372.

105. Gabriel Brizard, *Histoire généalogique de la maison de Beaumont* (Paris, 1779), *avertissement*.

106. For figures on the production of family histories and genealogies in the eighteenth century see chap. 2, table 2.2.

elder, and "several others."[107] The genealogist Dubuisson noted as a mark of pride that "the house of Béthune, of Flanders, is one of those whose histories was written by the savant André Duchesne in the last century; there are few houses whose *ancienneté*, brilliance, and splendid alliances *were so easily proven*" (emphasis mine).[108] Dubuisson's history of the house of Béthune merely restated well-established verities. Such examples could be multiplied endlessly. Short histories of individual families, such as the *Genealogy of the House of Roquelaure* (1762), are often found to be embellished excerpts from one of the great composite collections—*père* Anselme's *Histoire Généalogique et Chronologique des grands officiers de la couronne* (1674) and Louis-Pierre d'Hozier and A. M. d'Hozier de Sérigny's *Armorial Général* (1738–68)—whose authors, in turn, had borrowed much of their scant narrative detail from early seventeenth-century predecessors.[109]

What do these changes in the style of genealogical presentation tell us about noble self-perception? Obviously, one cannot infer that eighteenth-century nobles no longer identified with the values of generosity, fidelity, and so on simply because family histories often neglected to emphasize those qualities. In any case, when discussing earlier generations of a family, authors not infrequently included anecdotes revealing generous sacrifice and familiarity with kings; sometimes they recycled stories from seventeenth-century histories.[110] Some accounts of eighteenth-century figures even displayed evidence of personal recognition by the king and other testimony of their subjects' valor, fidelity, and courage.[111]

107. BN, MS fr. 33167, "Généalogie de la famille de Loynes," [1748], 2.

108. Dubuisson, *Mémoire historique et généalogique sur la maison de Béthune* (Paris, 1739), 1.

109. *Généalogie de la Maison de Roquelaure* (Paris, 1762); Anselme, *Histoire généalogique et chronologique des grands officiers de la couronne* (Paris, 1674); Hozier and Hozier de Sérigny, *Armorial Général* (Paris, 1738–68).

110. Augustin Calmet, author of the genealogical history of the Chatelet family, detailed the services rendered to French kings by Jean du Chatelet in the late sixteenth century. He cited a 1588 letter from Henry III "in which he remarked [to Chatelet], in very flattering terms, on the great confidence he had in his fidelity and in his valor." See Calmet, *Histoire généalogique de la maison du Chatelet, branche puînée de la maison de Lorraine* (Nancy, 1741), 89.

111. For example, the chevalier de Chamborant de Drou, writing the history of his own family in 1783, cited a letter from Choiseul in which the war minister made clear the king's satisfaction with the performance of André-Claude, marquis de Chamborant, who had served as a *maistre de camp* in the Seven Years' War: "Monsieur, I have just informed the king of your services, and of the distinction with which you acquitted yourself in the affair of the first of this month [July 1762], and in order to signal his own satisfaction His Majesty wishes to name you Brigadier." See Chevalier Chamborant de Drou, *Inventaire des Titres*

Nevertheless, the increasingly formulaic structure and tone of noble family histories seems symptomatic of a broad change in attitude regarding the value and function of noble birth, a change that can be traced to the last decades of the seventeenth century.[112] Louis XIV had succeeded in establishing the legal foundations of noble status. The official *recherches de la noblesse* had required legal titles to prove a family's nobility, and since that time the monarchy had served as the official monitor of social status. The crown's permanent intervention into the definition of nobility shaped noble consciousness in two ways. First, the legal verification of social status freed nobles from the implicit duty to test their own behavior against the evanescent ideals of nobility. At the same time that nobles in the military were learning to become always more sensitive to their professional development and performance, they and other nobles seem to have become less sensitive to the content of their characters *as nobles.* Yet in freeing nobles from this form of self-examination, the monarchy encouraged them to focus their attention on the superficial signs of noble birth. No longer compelled to affirm or rearticulate the personal qualities implied by their legal status, old nobles developed a new tendency to distinguish themselves—from commoners, from the new nobles who continued to crowd the corps, and from each other—by degree of *ancienneté.*

Eighteenth-century genealogies often served this express purpose. In a typical preface, the historian of the ducs de Croy stated bluntly that "the goal of this work is to publicize [*faire connaitre*] the proofs that establish the filiation of this house" whose history stretched back to a "distant

---

Originaux généalogiques conservés jusqu'a ce jour, des branches existantes de la maison de Chamborant (Paris, 1783), 218. In a manuscript history of the house of Croismare, Louis Eugene de Croismare is praised for having been granted "the *cordon rouge,* which he had the honor of receiving from the king's own hands at Compiègne . . . ; the same day he had the honor of dining with His Majesty." See BN, MS fr. 32375. "Généalogie de la maison de Croismare avec des alliances," 1765, 22.

112. My interpretation differs from that of Ellery Schalk, who argued that nobility itself, having become purely a sign of legal status, was "relatively unimportant" in the eighteenth century. See Schalk, *From Valor to Pedigree: Ideas of Nobility in France in the Sixteenth and Seventeenth Centuries* (Princeton, 1986), 212. My view is closer to that of Monique Cubells. who contends, in her study of eighteenth-century *parlementaires* in Aix-en-Provence, that nobility still had specific meaning in this society—implying a certain moral code, the possession of specific privileges, certain kinds of professional activity, and so on—even if that meaning had become crystallized in a "system defined by the law." See Cubells, *La Provence des Lumières: Les parlementaires d'Aix au XVIIIᵉ siècle* (Paris, 1984), 26. The legal fixing of noble status resulted not in the declining importance of nobility but in a lessened need to articulate its importance.

epoch."[113] The chronicler of the family of La Rocheaymon, writing in 1776 on behalf of the cardinal de la Rocheaymon, archbishop and duke of Reims, admitted that "the reader will find [in this account] none of those bold actions that have elevated many men of quality to the highest positions in the realm." The cardinal wanted only to preserve in the "public opinion" one of the "advantages" that distinguished his house—the privilege of having an origin so ancient that "the passing of time" made it most uncommon.[114]

Of course seventeenth-century family historians had also discussed the genealogical record and often in prodigious detail. The difference one notes in the eighteenth century is the almost obsessive focus on the proofs of legal certification. One is not surprised to find, for example, that statements issued by the commissioners who investigated noble status in the later seventeenth century, as well as other official attestations of social status, frequently enter into the narrative of the eighteenth-century histories. The chronicler of the family of René Després, sieur de Rochefort, cited many such documents and then boasted that his history "leaves no room for doubting the nobility of his house."[115] The genealogist of the family of Sainte-Marie in Normandy proudly quoted a certificate granted by the *intendant* Chamillard in 1671, for in it he declared that "the said S[eigneur] D'Apres is recognized as being among the number of old nobles in the province of Normandy."[116]

The family historian of the house of Courvol, who may have been a member of the clan, appropriately titled his work the *Genealogy of the house of Courvol, in Nivernois, established on the basis of original titles and on the judgments of the intendants, rendered at the time of the investigations of the nobility of the realm in 1666 and afterward.* He urged the heirs of the widely dispersed Courvol name to define the family identity in the strictest terms.

I exhort those in this house, in order to avoid . . . different spellings and pronunciations, which can become quite troublesome with the passing of time and the multiplicity of variations, to fix on that of

113. *Chronologie historique des ducs de Croy* (Grenoble, 1790), 5,

114. *Généalogie historique et critique de la maison de La Rocheaymon* (Paris, 1776), ii.

115. BN, MS fr. 33206, "Estat de la Genealogie de Rene Després Escuyer Sr de Rochefort," 1708, fol 4r.

116. BN, MS fr. 32394, "Généalogie de la famille de Sainte-Marie," [eighteenth century], 77.

Courvol, under which their [legal] proofs were established in 1667, and also to conserve their titles with great care.

He went on to recommend that the head of each branch of the family "keep a register of the births, baptisms, marriages, and deaths of their children, [also] describing there the coats of arms of their wives, in order to have recourse to it when they need to prove their nobility for the Order of Malta or for some other order or noble chapter."[117] Indeed, the need to prove one's lineage to the royal genealogist and other officials provided one of the most powerful incentives to produce, or reproduce, a family genealogy in the eighteenth century. Evidence of this can often be found on the title pages of noble family histories stored at the Bibliothèque Nationale. Many published histories, as well as those in manuscript, bear the signature of the royal genealogist or *juge d'armes* asked to certify their authenticity—d'Hozier, Clérambault, Chérin.

To trace the evolution of the meaning of merit within the military, then, one needs to keep in mind the context that framed the evolutionary process. In the course of the eighteenth century the monarchy elaborated two distinct sets of standards for measuring merit. On the one hand, a range of experts—from general inspectors to directors of training institutions to experienced officers—noted the signs of talent, application, exactitude, and personal sacrifice that became apparent in the process of practicing or performing service in the army. On the other hand, the crown became ever more fastidious in using the criterion of noble birth to screen candidates for various positions and honors. The experts responsible for judging talent and application certainly acknowledged the standard of distinguished birth—after all, the vast majority of the experts were themselves noble—but the upholding of this standard also reflected and reinforced the monarchy's ancient habit of identifying the crown's most valued servants as the personal associates of kings. The royal court had been the center of gravity within the traditional personal modality of service, and the signs of noble birth were therefore recorded and recognized most meticulously by the king and his agents at court.

The eighteenth-century army officer expected to be judged, then, from two perspectives. The meaning of military merit was still anchored in the two modalities of royal service—personal and public—fused within

---

117. BN, MS Dossiers Bleus 219, fol. 69, "Généalogie de la maison de Courvol, en Nivernois, dressée sur ses titres originaux, et sur des jugements des intendans, rendus lors de la recherche de la noblesse du royaume en 1666 & depuis," 1753, 7.

Louis XIV's reinvented sovereign gaze. I intend to show in chapter 6, however, that by the second half of the eighteenth century, the progressive routinization of the sovereign's metaphorical gaze and the diminishing relevance of the personal gaze of the king created a more explicit awareness of the distinctness of merit's two modalities. As nobles increasingly invoked by reflex their proofs of distinguished birth, as courtiers with little military experience continued to acquire commissions through royal or ministerial favor, and as army professionals continued to stress the cultivation of talent and discipline, it became possible to regard birth and merit as opposing principles. Nobles and others slowly came to this realization in the course of the Seven Years' War and the decades following, when the monarchy sought to establish a firm basis for efficacious army reform.

6

Military Reform in the Later Eighteenth Century: Birth, Merit, and the Gaze of Absolute Monarchy

A long series of military disappointments from the 1740s to the 1760s, including the particularly demoralizing loss to the overmatched Frederick the Great in the Seven Years' War, led the French army into decades of self-analysis.[1] As is well known, the top-heavy officer corps bore the brunt of criticism for France's humiliations. According to the critics, officers generally entered the army with insufficient prior training, they regularly abandoned their regiments at the first opportunity, and they sought military status not out of a desire to serve but rather for its prestige value.[2] This general inattention to duty had cost the army dearly in battles with Prussia and its allies.[3] The midcentury crisis increased reformers' determination to attack the army's problems at their source. Above all, they sought to expose and eliminate the defective procedures used in appointing, promoting, and rewarding officers. In addressing these concerns, reform-minded thinkers brought new intensity to a theme that had run through military discourse since the age of Louis XIV: to make the army a more efficient institution, the king, the war minister, and the generals had to take greater care in cultivating and rewarding true merit.

Casting a shadow over all proposals for reform in this period was the

---

1. On the army's growing frustrations, see E. G. Léonard, *L'armée et ses problèmes au XVIIIe siècle* (Paris, 1958).

2. David D. Bien evokes well this critical atmosphere in "The Army in the French Enlightenment: Reform, Reaction, and Revolution," *Past and Present* 85 (1979): 68–98, esp. 68–74.

3. That was the common impression in any case. For examples of the officers' preoccupation with status and petty rivalries see Lee Kennett, *The French Armies in the Seven Years' War: A Study in Military Organization and Administration* (Durham, N.C., 1967), 61–71.

resented but resilient system of venality of office. Officially venality only affected two grades in the military hierarchy—those of captain and colonel. But in practice, the sale of offices at these two grades shaped the entire appointment process and effectively screened from consideration many deserving candidates for offices at every rank.[4] Only the comfortably well-off or well-connected noble could afford the purchase price of a company—between five thousand and fifteen thousand livres throughout most of the century. Even fewer could afford the twenty-five thousand to seventy-five thousand livres needed to acquire a regiment of infantry; cavalry regiments were more expensive still. Consequently, many capable and experienced lower officers had to wait patiently for promotion to one of the nonvenal offices—lieutenant, second captain, major, or lieutenant colonel—whose order of ascent roughly paralleled the upward course taken by venal officers. Here another complication emerged, however, for promotion to one of these grades often demanded more than patience and hard work. To recoup their own investments, captains and colonels frequently offered promotions to the "non-venal" grades in exchange for unofficial financial considerations.[5] Moreover, even if the meritorious but penurious noble somehow overcame all obstacles and rose to the top ranks of brigadier and general, he would almost certainly be unable to sustain the normal expenditures incurred by high-ranking officers in the king's armies—expenses for food, travel, equipment, recruitment of soldiers, entertainment, and so on.

War Minister Choiseul shifted all responsibility for recruitment to the crown in 1762–63, and in 1776 his successor Saint-Germain began the gradual elimination of venality of office in the army. Despite these measures, however, criticisms of the army in the last decades of the ancien régime continued to reflect the widespread perception that the system of appointments and promotions unfairly privileged wealthy men with undue influence at court. Signs of concern and resentment appear in the ubiquitous condemnations of luxury, the unflattering characterizations of the court and courtiers, complaints about overcrowding in the upper

---

4. The discussion that follows is based largely on Samuel Scott's excellent survey of conditions among the officer corps on the eve of the Revolution. See *The Response of the Royal Army to the French Revolution: The Role and Development of the Line Army, 1787–93* (Oxford, 1978), chap. 1. Also helpful is André Corvisier, *L'armée française de la fin du XVIIᵉ siècle au ministère de Choiseul: Le soldat*, 2 vols. (Paris, 1964), 1:129–31.

5. For examples, see Scott, *Response*, 21; Corvisier, *L'armée*, 1:130; and idem, "La Noblesse Militaire: Aspects militaires de la noblesse française du 15ᵉ au 18ᵉ siècles," *Histoire Sociale/Social History* 22 (1978): 348.

tiers of the hierarchy, the juxtaposition of (good) martial and (bad) mercantile values in discourses on army and society, and the growing emphasis on the importance of seniority and educational credentials. Between 1750 and 1789 many officers and military theorists set out to reform the army in hopes of insuring that merit always rose, unimpeded, to its deserved rank in the king's service.

To this point in this study I have intended to show that the construction of absolute monarchy in the later seventeenth and eighteenth centuries proceeded on the basis of traditional cultural assumptions important to both the monarchy and the old nobility. These assumptions were integrated into the structures of the centralizing administrative state through the mechanism of a reinvented sovereign gaze. In analyzing the hybrid modality of royal service articulated by Louis XIV and his contemporaries and elaborated by their successors—a complex cultural construct that melded two distinct conceptions of utility within an expansive but ambiguous definition of royal service—I have attempted to demonstrate why it is important to study the growth in governmental power in the early-modern period through the evolving images of the meritorious individual and the sovereign's judging gaze.

In this final chapter I want to extend my argument and suggest that the French Revolution, like all great political events including the rise of monarchical absolutism, involved a transformation internal to a prevailing culture of power. All students of the eighteenth century can agree that in 1789 the principles of absolute monarchy and a social hierarchy based on privilege and the rights of birth gave way to a more democratic "public sphere," more open and "rational" governmental processes, and the ideal of "careers open to talents." But these new values were not simply constructed *outside of* and against the absolutist political order. By examining reformist perspectives articulated by or on behalf of a particular segment of the old nobility in the last decades of the ancien régime, I intend to show that the inclusive ideals associated with 1789—far from being imposed on the powers that be or appropriated by them at some site beyond traditional thinking—actually emerged from a dialectical process operating *within* absolutism's culture of royal service. This dialectic shaped and ultimately lent revolutionary force to the eighteenth century's understanding of merit and utility.

In the decades before the Revolution, earnest military reformers worked with ever greater urgency to complete the normalizing process first given direction by Louis XIV, a synthesizing process that valorized the qualities of talent, discipline, *and* birth. Paradoxically, their aggressive assault on what seemed the principal obstacles to normalization—money and favor—diverted their attention from the rhetorical contradiction that they themselves now pressed. They intended to improve the operation and efficiency of the sovereign's gaze, especially as it affected the nobility in the context of royal service. But because their attack on corruption involved an extensive critique of court favoritism and high aristocratic snobbery, their own arguments left unprotected and undefended the features of merit long considered specific to the nobility and cherished by the personal gaze of the sovereign. Not having come to terms explicitly with the transformed character of the sovereign gaze—personal in theory, the gaze eventually became wholly metaphorical and hence homogenizing—they embraced principles of merit that ultimately stood in direct contradiction to one another.

Army Reform and the Hierarchizing Gaze

In 1758 the marquis de Langeron, a *maréchal de camp* agitating for military reform, began his discussion of current conditions by making a point on which "everyone agrees," namely, "that the nobility must be preferred in the selection of officers." The nobility had long ago "earned the right to be charged with defending the state," and the army would achieve great victories in the future if it only exploited more efficiently the nobility's "love for glory and its valor."[6] The "rule" of preferring nobles should be violated only in the "rarest" circumstances. Indeed, Langeron insisted that, if left up to him, "I would announce that, in the future, only the nobility will have the right to enter my infantry." Even the foot soldiers would come from that "inexhaustible seedbed" of *militaires,* the country's "eight thousand families of *gentilshommes.*"[7]

Despite Langeron's prejudices in favor of the nobility, the theme of the infantry's social composition occupied only a secondary rank in his treatise. He wanted mainly to establish solid criteria for professional advancement, and he placed emphasis on a single idea: promotion must be the reward of talent, application, and experience. To illustrate his point, he compared two hypothetical routes to success. Consider the case

---

6. Bibliothèque Nationale (hereafter BN), nouvelles acquisitions françaises 366, Langeron, "Mémoire sur l'Infanterie Française, Autrichienne et Prussienne, par M. le Mis de Langeron, Mal de Camp," 1758, 18.

7. Ibid., 44, 37.

of an elder son from a prominent family: "bedecked with titles," he uses the "influence of his parents" to gain entry to the officer corps at a high rank. Having acquired a regiment "on leaving *collège*," he waited only a year or two for a "promotion accorded through favor." He might even achieve the rank of *maréchal de camp* before being "awakened to the need to instruct himself." The young leader who rose in this way would undoubtedly be "brave, generous, likable, even zealous for his profession," but "what could one expect from such a general officer" in the event of a prolonged war?[8]

To this unflattering image of the aspiring officer Langeron opposed another based on seriousness, hard work, and skill. The ideal officer candidate had enjoyed the diversions of youth only to interrupt briefly his periods of "serious study." He received a "military education," and by rising through the subaltern grades, he acquired the art of command by learning first to obey. His ambition served only "to augment his emulation." He "developed his talents" and looked constantly for occasions to acquire recognition. Passed over for promotions, he simply "redoubled his exactitude" and "fulfilled all his duties." When he finally arrived at the grade of colonel, it came as a "well-merited advancement" for having served the state with distinction.[9]

Langeron returned to the theme repeatedly. Each captain must come to regard the post of lieutenant colonel as a rank he could acquire "by his talents and his application."[10] The lieutenant colonel had to maintain the regiment's "emulation, discipline, [and] subordination by his own example"; he must possess "the talent necessary to instruct his men" well.[11] After having acquired "an exact knowledge of all the men who [currently] fill each post," the commander should "place each one according to his talents," beginning with the "colonels, lieutenant colonels, battalion commanders, captains, . . . majors."[12] One could take for granted the overall superiority of nobles, but the generals of the French army must choose for the office of colonel "those among the nobility who have the most talent."[13]

Projects for reform sounding this same theme—that the army's performance would inevitably improve if nobles only became more talented

---

8. Ibid., 23–24.
9. Ibid., 24–25.
10. Ibid., 32.
11. Ibid., 30–31.
12. Ibid., 42.
13. Ibid., 21.

and applied—flooded the office of the *secrétaire d'état de la guerre* from the 1750s to the 1780s. One anonymous author stressed that young officers must strive to improve themselves "through continual instruction and by their application." The need to "instruct young officers, to teach them little by little," was something even "heads of regiments must not neglect," for "an officer who thinks about his profession only while doing drills will never acquire the necessary talents."[14] Each regiment should have a school where young officers learned to execute everything "with the greatest order." Instructors should "habituate [the officers] to the work almost imperceptibly," slowly moving from simple to complex ideas.[15]

Another proponent of military education recalled that Louis XV, in establishing the Ecole Royale Militaire, had been motivated by more than his desire to assist the "indigent nobility": "He also had in view the glory of his armies, for [he knew that] nothing better encourages military discipline than to provide a uniform education and to study the talents of each person before appointing him to a position."[16] The writer spelled out the obvious course of action: "nothing would be wiser than to multiply these *écoles militaires* so that every aspiring hero can acquire the necessary principles." The king would need to establish between eight and twelve schools in or near garrisoned cities, with buildings "vast enough to contain all the *gentilshommes* from around the realm aged thirteen to seventeen." The nobility "could hope for nothing better," and "once having reached the age of eighteen, [each student will be placed] according to his talents and in the branch of service where he will have distinguished himself."[17]

The most striking feature of these reformist tracts is that, on the one hand, their authors stressed qualities and instructional techniques that by their very nature implied wide applicability—through habit, application, and a uniform education officers must develop more talent and skill—while, on the other hand, they employed ever more systematically a traditional language of social exclusion. As Langeron had noted, it seemed that the nobility's special qualifications for the king's service scarcely needed reiteration. The chevalier de Keralio, after noting sadly in 1780

14. Archives de la Guerre (hereafter AG), MR 1715, no. 5, "De l'instruction des officiers," [after 1776], 1.

15. Ibid., 2–3.

16. AG, MR 1709, no. 3, "Idées concernant l'art de la Guerre," [1760], 6.

17. Ibid., 7–9.

that the provincial *écoles militaires* established in 1776 turned out students for the most part "incapable," casually proposed two remedies: enforce the examination requirements and check the students' genealogical proofs more rigorously.[18] The infantry captain Blangermont, also writing in the years before the Ségur *règlement,* similarly urged stricter enforcement of genealogical restrictions in the recruitment of officers. He complained that "a simple certificate sufficed to prove one's extraction," and these documents were sometimes given to men scarcely qualified for the title of bourgeois. Indeed, Blangermont asserted that some certified "nobles" still practiced "the vile professions of the most common *roture.*" Blangermont suggested that every aspiring officer should have his genealogical proofs checked by three separate authorities—the war minister, the officers of the corps, and the royal genealogist. Then "one could be sure that he is worthy, by his birth, of the king's gifts."[19]

David Bien's research has shown that the army's ever increasing emphasis on genealogy was more a reflection of its close preoccupation with professional issues than a sign of general aristocratic reaction in the eighteenth century. The army's leaders intended to recruit officers primarily among the established, and preferably poor, nobility because they took for granted the spartan inclinations of most of the *noblesse ancienne;* restrictive policies on recruitment formed part of the army's program against luxury, money, caprice, social ambition, and other corruptive influences that now threatened to degrade the military.[20] It is important to recognize, however, that the army's reinforcement of the principle of exclusion also stemmed from and built on elemental social prejudices. Army reformers of the second half of the eighteenth century held fast to a long-accepted idea: nobles stood above other social types because of the moral milieu that produced and formed them.

In *La Noblesse Militaire* (1756), for example, the chevalier d'Arc justified his vision of an all-noble military by evoking a traditional cul-

18. AG, Y^a 147, dossier "1780," Letter addressed to War Minister Montbarey, 26 October 1780.

19. AG, MR 1781, no. 20, Blangermont, "Mémoire sur l'éducation des jeunes militaires et sur la composition des Officiers des Régiments d'Infanterie française," [1777–80], 9–11. The noble was "digne par sa naissance des bienfaits du Roy."

20. David D. Bien, "The Army in the French Enlightenment." Also see, idem, "La réaction aristocratique avant 1789: L'exemple de l'armée," *Annales, E. S. C.* 29 (1974): 23–48, 505–34; and idem, "Military Education in Eighteenth-Century France: Technical and Non-Technical Determinants," in *Science, Technology, and Warfare. Proceedings of the Third Military History Symposium, U.S. Air Force Academy, 8–9 May 1969,* ed. Monte D. Wright and Lawrence J. Paszek (Washington, 1971): 51–59.

tural opposition. Whereas businessmen were driven by self-interest, he noted, the man of honor strived to achieve the "consideration" of others—consideration earned only through the "continual sacrifice of self-interest."[21] If the king hoped to keep "generous souls" in his service, he therefore had to preserve the conditions that fostered this prejudice "that we know by the name of 'honor.'"[22] At the very least, the king should create special regiments of "volunteers" consisting "entirely of *gentils-hommes.*" The "volunteers" might then communicate the sentiments (*esprit*) of the nobility to the whole army.[23] The same assumptions found expression in later years. Captain Blangermont noted that "honor is the guide of the nobility or should be. Interest is the guide of the people: these two germs must never be allowed to divide the corps [of *militaires*]."[24] "Love for their king" and "a passion for service" had always been "characteristic marks" of the nobility, wrote another observer in 1784, and these features alone "should serve to qualify [nobles] as the only ones eligible for the honorable employ of officer."[25]

Many would-be reformers thus consciously affirmed the long-established connection between the monarchical form of government and the social preeminence of the nobility—a group identified chiefly by its attachment to honor and the generous virtues. In the eighteenth century this connection had been given an explicit theoretical rationale first by Montesquieu, who asserted that nobility "enters into the essence of monarchy," and then by the medieval historian La Curne de Sainte-Palaye, who joined the author of *De l'esprit des lois* in making honor the animating principle of monarchy.[26] What bears special emphasis here is that the reform plans articulated by Arc, Blangermont, and others implicitly corresponded to a vision of royal service in which a personally active monarch cherished and rewarded "sacrifice of self-interest" and the other

---

21. Philippe-Auguste de Sainte-Foix, chevalier d'Arc, *La Noblesse Militaire, ou le patriote français,* 3d ed. (n.p., 1756), 60.

22. Ibid., 56–59.

23. Ibid., 169.

24. AG, MR 1781, no. 20, Blangermont, "Mémoire sur l'éducation des jeunes militaires et sur la composition des Officiers des Régiments d'Infanterie française," [1777–80], 10.

25. BN, MS fr. 9174, "Idées sur quelques objets militaires, adressés aux jeunes officiers," 1784, in a collection titled "Mémoires . . . militaires," fol. 19v.

26. Charles-Louis de Secondat, baron de Montesquieu, *De l'esprit des lois,* 2 vols. (Paris, 1979), 1:139. On the linkage between honor, nobility, and monarchical government in the thinking of La Curne de Sainte-Palaye see Lionel Gossman, *Medievalism and the Ideologies of the Enlightenment: The World and Work of La Curne de Sainte-Palaye* (Baltimore, 1968), esp. 273–99.

merits of his generous servitors. "In the bottom of my heart," Arc revealingly intoned in the preface to his work, "I am unable to distinguish between the prince and the country."[27] Another onlooker praised the nobles' unwavering "love for their king."[28] The infantry captain Doizal similarly emphasized the nobility's natural attachment to the royal person. "It is in the king's interest," he wrote, "to raise and uphold the nobility. . . . it is the only corps interested in defending his crown, because it finds honor in obeying the king."[29]

Although this emphasis on the centrality of the king's person within the culture of royal service continued to make sense theoretically, changes in the operation of royal power since the last decades of the seventeenth century increasingly pointed to a disjuncture between theory and practice, a disjuncture with far-reaching social and cultural implications. Since 1715 the person of the king had gradually receded into the background of the monarchy's service relationships, and this subtle structural change—the result of a process that unfolded almost imperceptibly throughout the eighteenth century—ultimately strained the unique ties of reciprocity that traditionally linked king and nobility. Those who repeatedly invoked the honor of the nobility and stressed its special claim to the king's gifts unwittingly pushed the culture of royal service to the limits of its contradictions.

Army Reform and the Homogenizing Gaze

The fixity of crown institutions had altered the king's relationship to the governing process in countless subtle ways. In the course of his long reign, for example, Louis XV evinced a degree of detachment from the monarchy's structures that Louis XIV could never have imagined. As Michel Antoine's work has shown, the difference in sensibility cannot be attributed to royal lethargy. Louis XV did all the work required by duty and more.[30] He attended council meetings religiously and often surprised his councillors by leading their discussions in unexpected directions.

But Louis XV also found ways to disengage from the "governmental

---

27. Arc, *La Noblesse Militaire*, iv.
28. BN, MS fr. 9174, "Idées sur quelques objets militaires, adressés aux jeunes officiers," 1784, in a collection titled "Mémoires . . . militaires," fol. 19v.
29. BN, MS fr. 14868, M. Doizal, "Dissertation sur la subordination, avec des Refléxions sur l'exercice, et sur l'art militaire," 1752, 28.
30. Michel Antoine, *Louis XV* (Paris, 1989), esp. 443–56; idem, *Le Conseil du Roi sous le Règne de Louis XV* (Geneva, 1970), 610–11.

machine" described by Antoine.[31] At court, he came to regard the customary courtly protocol and all the "liturgy of the royal person" as the "monotonous duty of representation." He continued to observe all the courtly formalities, but he also used the role of sovereign as a "facade" behind which he obsessively guarded his privacy and cultivated intimate personal relations. He escaped Versailles at every opportunity, and contemporaries noted the often eerie emptiness of the royal palace.[32] In council, he lacked confidence in his own opinions and refrained from imposing his views. He most often deferred to his councillors, who, in turn, often met in the king's absence to form deliberative "committees."[33] As the *Conseil royal des finances* fell into desuetude from the 1730s, Louis surrendered control of finances to the controller general and the assembly of *intendants des finances*.[34] At the same time, though, Louis found a private retreat—an office, but also literally a hidden compartment[35]—where he put his thoughts to paper and reflected on the realm's affairs. As Antoine put it, "what he did not dare say aloud, he confided to paper."[36] He maintained a vast network of correspondents, and by 1746 there had developed a secret alternative organ of government. Known even at the time as the *secret du roi,* Louis XV used it to gather information and to launch secret policy initiatives.

Louis XV seemed determined to lead a private, even secret, existence in the shadow of the monarchy itself.[37] This tendency is explained in part by the king's personality; Louis appears to have been pathologically

31. Antoine, *Louis XV,* 444.
32. Antoine, *Le Conseil du Roi,* 600, 612. Jean-François Solnon notes, in *La cour de France* (Paris, 1987), that eyewitness accounts of court activity under Louis XV reveal little more than the scrupulous "preservation of acquired privileges, formalism, repetitive and stereotyped gestures" (427). On Louis's thirst for intimacy see Solnon, 428–32; on his frequent excursions from Versailles, and on the atmosphere this created there, see 438–39.
33. Antoine, *Le Conseil du Roi,* 612–13.
34. Ibid., 146–51, 174–75.
35. For details on Louis XV's "petits appartements" see Henry Racinais, *Un Versailles inconnu: Les petits appartements des roys Louis XV et Louis XVI au château de Versailles* (Paris, 1950).
36. Antoine, *Le Conseil du Roi,* 613.
37. This penchant for secrecy even showed through in the way Louis XV discharged what was arguably his most important duty as a "public" figure. Antoine reports that when Louis moved to take personal command of his army in May 1744 during the War of the Austrian Succession, he left Versailles under the cover of darkness—in secret, without fanfare, at three o'clock in the morning (*Louis XV,* 367–68).

timid.[38] Just as important, the systematic elaboration of personal government in the eighteenth century had made the prince's power so relentlessly impersonal that Louis XV understandably came to view the functioning of the monarchy and his own personal identity as being quite distinct. The burdensome weight of his public persona seems to have awakened Louis XV to "the charms of private life." It is well known that this new taste for domesticity, characteristic of the eighteenth century, also colored the attitudes and behavior of Louis XVI and Marie Antoinette.[39]

Louis XV's effort to establish distance between himself and the roles he played as sovereign—an effort that ultimately produced what Antoine calls a "double existence"—also paralleled another process of dissolution, however: the gradual separation of the sovereign gaze from the person of the king.[40] We have seen that, as a matter of practice, the process of expanding and routinizing the royal gaze had been under way since the later seventeenth century at least. By the middle of the eighteenth century, theory reflected the change in practice. Whether expressed by Enlightenment figures or simply by those familiar with the monarchy's aspirations and habits, the new expressions of the ideal of kingship maintained only a tenuous link between the image of the sovereign leader and the idea of the prince as a physical being. The French increasingly pictured the monarch as an omniscient manager of political society, a distant legislator, an all-seeing mechanic who controlled the diverse parts of a great machine.[41] Even the infantry captain Blangermont, one who urged renewed attention to noble honor in the military, recognized the difficulties inherent in addressing the sovereign personally: "It is not possible in an empire as great as yours for the sovereign, or his ministers, to perceive details that are, by their nature, distant from you; occupied with the movement of the great political machine, your attention has to be

---

38. Antoine, *Le Conseil du Roi*, 599.

39. For a discussion of how royal attraction to the "charms of private life" altered life at court in the decades before the Revolution see Solnon, *La cour de France*, 428–46.

40. Antoine, *Louis XV*, 438.

41. For examples of this thinking, and discussion of its broad ideological implications, see George Armstrong Kelly, *Mortal Politics in Eighteenth-Century France*, in *Historical Reflections/Réflexions Historiques* 13, no. 1 (spring 1986), esp. 24–34, 212–17. See also Joyce Duncan Falk, "The Concept of the Ideal Prince in the Literature of the French Enlightenment, 1700–1780" (Ph.D. diss., University of Southern California, 1969), esp. chap. 7.

fixed there." Blangermont nonetheless hopefully submitted his written reflections, while acknowledging that they dealt with matters far "beneath [the level] where you necessarily fix your gaze."[42]

One observer grounded the new image of sovereignty in the state of nature. He explained that "after having divided the labor necessary" to meet every need of their community, the first inhabitants of the earth "gave themselves a leader who would see that all the parts acted together in the order essential to the common good." The king, coordinating the community's various specialties, held in his hands the reins guiding all the orders of society. To "bring glory to the master," this writer continued, each person must work "to acquire distinction in the profession in which he finds himself." The king deserved to be revered in this way, for he insured everyone's happiness by "forcing them to work together for the greatness of the state": "That is how I envision France and every other purely monarchical government."[43]

Now even royal subjects demanded that the sovereign's vision extend beyond all physical and social boundaries. As one would-be military reformer remarked in 1749, "there is not a single person, to the lowest artisan or the crudest villager, who does not possess some precious innate talent." Ideally, the king should identify them all. "If the Prince and [his] minister could know the individual tastes and talents of all his subjects! What great progress would be made in all the professions of society!" The author of this proposal even suggested establishing a central bureau to examine "the inventions, productions, discoveries, projects, and plans of each and every individual" interested in making his talents known.[44]

The documents just quoted reflect, on the one hand, the eighteenth century's elaboration of a conceptual dyad present in French political culture since the age of Louis XIV; one finds both the panoptic monarch and the diversified society theoretically subject to his penetrating gaze. On the other hand, when juxtaposed to the reflections of rigidly aristocratic military reformers, such as Arc, Blangermont, or Doizal, these texts throw into sharp relief the basic tension ingrained in the service culture of absolutism: the king's gaze imagined (*pace* Ralph Giesey) actually exercised two kinds of normative power. In judging merit, the monarch

---

42. AG, MR 1781, no. 20, 1–2, "C'est sous ce point de vue que j'ose addresser mes Réflections à mes maîtres qui [sic] quoiqu'au dessous de celuy ou ils doivent fixer leurs regards n'en sont pas moins utiles au bien de l'état et à la bonne constitution militaire."

43. AG, MR 1705, no. 37, "Introduction au code Louis XV," [after 1753], 3–4.

44. AG, MR 1703, no. 40(?). "Réflexions politiques sur le militaire," 7.

and many of his governing institutions approved, promoted, and gave special recognition to the intangible qualities of heart and birth that justified and explained noble privilege. At the same time, though, an anonymous and impersonal gaze, coextensive with the kingdom itself and presupposing the operation of a public modality of service, indiscriminately encouraged the development of discrete talents and professional discipline. By the middle of the eighteenth century this gaze, linked only implicitly to its source in the sovereign power of the king, was identified variously with the government, the administration, the state, the monarchy, the nation.[45] The operation of this anonymous gaze reoriented the meaning of service and merit because it imposed on those it touched a set of impersonal obligations toward the person of the king.

This shift in sensibility found expression in the work of the educational theorist Vanière, who explained that "the interests of the prince are linked in an essential way to those of the state, [the interests] of the state [are linked] to those of individuals, and the interests of individuals are linked to the practice of duty." All must therefore devote themselves to "the cultivation of their talents."[46] A commentator on the army voiced the same sentiments in 1774. Everyone knew that soldiers had to aim for "precise observation in everything prescribed to them" and "perfect knowledge of everything relating to their respective grades." But the soldier need not feel singled out: "All conditions, all professions impose on those who exercise them the necessity of acquitting themselves of the duties inseparable from them." The obligation applied to everyone, without respect to age, sex, or social status, for "to embrace a profession and not fulfill its duties . . . is to evade one's vow to God and to society."[47]

Of course the assumption that one's birth helped to determine one's character and personal value still enjoyed wide currency. But that traditional idea now gave ground to the equally widespread assumption that an impersonal and anonymous entity stood as the focal point of royal service. The comte de Vauréal, for example, pointed out to readers of his

---

45. Michel Antoine notes that the words *king, council, government,* and *administration* came to be used interchangeably by politically engaged subjects over the course of the eighteenth century. He traces this process of depersonalizing the concept of the state to the period of the regency. See Antoine, "La Monarchie Absolue," in *The Political Culture of the Old Regime,* ed. Keith M. Baker (New York, 1987), 3–24.

46. M. Vanière, *Discours sur l'éducation* (Paris, 1760), 1, 3.

47. AG, MR 1713, no. 10, "Exposé" (1774), 5–8.

educational treatise that the services of "generous hearts" must be directed "to the *patrie*."[48] This growing tendency within the discourse of royal service to substitute an abstract and all-encompassing entity for the person of the king meant that discussions of merit no longer revolved around the moral qualities distinctive of the old nobility.

Abbé Coyer, writing in 1756, went so far as to link France's traditional reverence for all the martial virtues with the "barbarous times of feudal government" when it seemed that "the sword was the instrument most essential to the state."[49] Coyer still respected the nobility's traditional "generosity." He thought it admirable that every young noble wishes "to lay down his life in the service of the king . . . [and that] his brothers would hope to do the same." But the abbé pointedly observed that "the king does not need so many servants; the state needs them."[50] The crown, he argued, must therefore encourage young nobles and others "to cultivate all talents, to profit from all dispositions in whatever area they might be: theology, jurisprudence, politics, the sciences, the arts."[51]

The representation of an immanent sovereign gaze, one that captured the global interests of the kingdom, altered not only the image of the served within the modality of royal service but also the corresponding images of the servants and of the service they rendered. The connection is made clear both in the attempt by the profession-minded Coyer to focus his readers' attention on the state rather than the king and in the fantasy of the anonymous author who aspired to inform the distant king of "the tastes and talents of all his subjects." In the light of this diffuse but all-encompassing gaze, associated with the king but also with the government and nation, one manifested merit by skillfully and zealously executing one's function, a function valued for the place it occupied in some larger scheme.

This new conception of merit, already enunciated at midcentury in several treatises devoted specifically to the concept, eventually made its mark on the work of lexicologists.[52] Later editions of the *Dictionnaire de*

---

48. M. le comte de Vauréal, *Plan ou Essai d'Education Général et National.* (Bouillon, 1783), dedication.

49. Coyer, *La Noblesse Commerçante* (Paris and London, 1756), 11.

50. Ibid., 15.

51. Ibid., x–xi.

52. Le Maitre de Claville stressed, in his *Traité du vrai Mérite de l'Homme* (Paris, 1750), that the duty to "make oneself useful" applied not only to "great names" and "the most respected positions" but to workers "of all orders and all classes" whose individual efforts

l'Académie Française issued under the ancien régime failed to capture the change in mentality—talent does not appear as a criterion of merit until the edition of 1798—but in 1771 the *Dictionnaire de Trévoux* conveyed *merit*'s commonly accepted meaning.[53] Among their definitions of the word *merit* the editors noted the following:

> Once one supposes that man is subjected, by his nature and by his situation [*état*], to certain rules of conduct, [it is through] the observation of these rules that one realizes the perfection of human nature and of one's situation. . . . Consequently, we recognize that those who meet the challenge of their station [*répondent à leur destination*] and do what duty requires, and thus contribute to the well-being and the perfection of the system of humanity, are worthy of our approbation . . . and that they have some claim to the advantageous effects [of this approbation].[54]

All who applied themselves to the duties imposed by their situation, and who contributed to the perfection of society, earned personal merit and the recognition invariably attached to it.

The irony of this development—given the army's generally ardent attachment to the idea of aristocratic exclusiveness—is that the military itself had served as a principal laboratory for testing and extending the more inclusive conception of merit.[55] There the disciplinary gaze of the service hierarchy, stretching from the king to the lowest officer, had long

---

combined "to move the whole machine." This universal imperative "produces marvelous effects; it engages our attention . . . it forces us to master our vocation [*état*], [and] it inspires in us a burning desire to acquire merit, for it is through merit that one obtains [recompense]" (88). Diderot's 1745 translation and elaboration of a treatise by Shaftesbury similarly emphasized the bonds of civil society and the duties of the productive citizen. See Diderot, *Principes de la philosophie morale, ou Essai de M. S*** sur le mérite et la vertu,* in *Oeuvres complètes: Édition chronologique,* ed. Roger Lewinter (Paris, 1969), 1:9–266.

53. The editors of *Dictionnaire de l'Académie Française,* 5th ed. (Paris, 1798), included the following in their definition of *mériter:* "One says in an absolute sense, 'This man merits much,' as a way of saying that this man deserves recompense for his talents, his services."

54. *Dictionnaire de Trévoux* (Paris, 1771). The full definition in the original reads: "Il faut remarquer, dit Burlamaqui, que dès qu'on suppose que l'homme se trouve par sa nature & par son état, asujetti à suivre certains règles de conduite; l'observation de ces règles fait la perfection de la nature humaine & de son état. . . . En conséquence nous reconnaissons que ceux qui répondent à leur destination qui font ce qu'ils doivent, & contribuent ainsi au bien & à la perfection du système de l'humanité, sont dignes de notre approbation . . . & qu'ils ont quelque droit aux effets avantageux qui en sont les suites naturelles."

55. On this point see also David D. Bien, "The Army in the French Enlightenment."

since imposed a kind of equality on the individuals engaged by the institution. The unique requirements of the military operation inevitably reshaped the thinking of those who participated in it. One wrote, for example, that the French army appeared to be "a machine composed of homogeneous parts."[56] The infantry captain Laureau explained that "the army is a mechanism whose smallest and greatest parts are equally necessary to its movement. . . . Each has its particular kind of utility, but each in isolation would be powerless, or at least insufficient. . . . Consequently, they all have the same merit."[57] The author of a treatise that defined the "duties of the man of war" wrote in a similar tone. In his eyes "each function has its merit," since each required of him who exercised it some degree of ability and the discipline to use that ability effectively. One learned the military art "by degrees," after all, and soldiers and officers alike knew that by being "exact in the smallest post," they increased their chances of "obtaining the greatest post."[58]

The military theorist Louis de Boussanelle explicitly addressed the homogenizing effects of military service in a well-known treatise of 1770, *Le Bon Militaire* (The good soldier). In a revealing chapter, Boussanelle discussed the meaning of the word *subordination*. He refuted those who emphasized its connotation of servility and blind obedience and thereby made *subordination* a term of degradation. If the word implied inferiority, said Boussanelle, then the status of inferiority applied to all: "Everyone who is inferior is subordinate; everyone therefore is subordinate, because everyone is inferior before the eyes and power of the monarch." Since "everyone owes equally the most precise obedience from grade to grade in everything that concerns the service of the king," *subordination* placed everyone on an equally honorable plane.[59] The leader of a corps had always to remember that "he commands his companions and his equals," for "the profession of obedience is also [the profession] of honor and of equality."[60] He noted casually that the road to merit lay open

---

56. AG, MR 1703, no. 32, M[r] le Chevalier Montaut, "Réflexions sur la Manière de former des bons Soldats d'Infanterie avec un Essay sur la conduite politique d'un Lieutenant Colonel envers son Régiment," [1747–48], 1.

57. Archives Nationales (hereafter AN), M 640, no. 4, Laureau, "Observations pour servir à un plan de Constitution militaire, selon le génie des français," 1772, "Troupes de ligne."

58. AN, M 650, no. 5, "Differentes pensées sur les devoirs de l'homme de guerre," undated, 6–7.

59. Louis de Boussanelle, *Le Bon Militaire* (Paris, 1770), 55.

60. Ibid., 67.

"indistinctly to all men." The nature of the profession of honor and equality made it "possible for all to acquire it."[61]

The principle expressed by Boussanelle, that all men had an equal capacity to acquire merit, had its limits within the context of an increasingly aristocratic army. Nevertheless, the assumption of underlying homogeneity was so deeply ingrained in military practice that War Minister Saint-Germain purposefully integrated the theme into his reform of the Ecole Royale Militaire in 1776. In a *règlement* of 28 March Saint-Germain announced that the king now wished to "share the advantages of the [Ecole Militaire] with all the nobility, as well as the king's other subjects," and that he had therefore "decided to distribute the young *gentilshommes* throughout several provinces . . . in different *collèges*" administered by religious orders.[62] Each of the provincial *collèges* took in fifty to sixty *éleves du roi*, that is, *gentilshommes* admitted to the Ecole Militaire under the old entrance requirements.[63] After six years of training, and after having reached at least the age of fifteen, the *éleves du roi* did one of two things. Most entered the line regiments with the title *cadet gentilhomme* and the expectation of being named sublieutenant within a year's time.[64] Other students, more gifted, went on to Paris for further training. They shared the status of *cadet gentilhomme* and were generally named to sublieutenancies after spending two years in Paris.[65]

To prepare young *gentilshommes* for successful careers in the military thus remained the express purpose of the Ecole Militaire; none of the reformers of the Ecole Militaire thought to question the innate superiority of old nobility. Still, one is struck by the degree to which the reforms flattened out social difference. The sixty *éleves du roi* actually studied

---

61. Ibid., 50.

62. AG, Y[a] 145, 1776. "Règlement . . . les nouvelles Ecoles Royales Militaires," 28 March 1776.

63. In 1783 the crown announced that the schools would only accept children aged seven to ten; until this time, only children aged eight to eleven were eligible. See AG, Y[a] 157, dossier "1783," "Règlement," 26 July 1783.

64. The number of vacancies varied over time. At first, each regiment kept eight places for *cadets gentilshommes*; in 1784 the rank of cadet was abolished altogether; in 1788 the cadets reappeared, but only two were assigned to each regiment. See Bernard Deschard, *L'Armée et la Révolution: Du service du roi au service de la nation* (Paris, 1989), 49.

65. AG, Y[a] 149, dossier "1782," *cadets gentilshommes*. Some of the students sent to Paris stayed on for specialized training in artillery or engineering. Students who showed no inclination toward military service might go to La Flèche, where young nobles were also trained for ecclesiastical and legal careers; the choice had to be made by age thirteen, however.

side by side with an equal number of externs—children from common or noble families whose parents paid their expenses. The royal *règlement* announced that, in everything concerning their education, the *gentils-hommes* would be "mixed together . . . with the other boarders" who "will be subjected to the same discipline, the same rules, the same methods of instruction . . . , the same uniform; in short, [there will be] no difference between them."[66]

By uniting the *gentilshommes* "with children from the other classes of citizens" the crown intended to "mold their characters and reduce the pride that the nobility is too easily disposed to associate with its upbringing."[67] In place of the old curriculum, considered too narrowly military by some, the directors simply followed the example of the traditional *collège* and introduced a broad program of instruction for everyone to follow. Subjects included Latin, German, rhetoric, writing, mathematics, geography, music, drafting, fencing, and dancing. The students experienced a "general education that allows no distinctions," and emulation became an "objective common to everyone."[68]

Noble army officers of the eighteenth century found it natural, then, to perform before an impartial gaze that looked past broad social differences to individuate and reinforce ever more specific expressions of utility: skills, talents, and inclinations. At the various provincial *écoles militaires*, the young *gentilshommes* even learned to expect regular visits from an itinerant inspector who noted the students' progress and conduct on forms resembling the modern report card.[69] Some of the army's leaders accepted the self-enforcing norms of talent and discipline so fully, so unquestioningly, that they became responsible for what may be described as the supremely ironic cultural event of the pre-Revolutionary decades; they finalized the long-term transformation of the meaning of merit by systematically attacking the principle of privilege. Despite the wide con-

---

66. AG, Y^a 145, 1776, "Règlement . . . nouvelles écoles."

67. Ibid.

68. AG, Y^a 145, 1776, memoir titled "La Flèche."

69. The war ministry received frank and often pessimistic evaluations of the students. After observing and testing a *gentilhomme* named Blotteau at Tyron in 1788, for example, the subinspector Reynaud remarked disparagingly that "this student is of uncommon mediocrity and has a rough exterior—no talent has developed in him with age. His only quality is his good memory." The chevalier Keralio offered only discouraging words after completing his evaluation at Effiat in 1777: "I consider it an absolute impossibility to assemble the fifty cadets, if this [promotion] is to be the recompense of good conduct and of talents." See AG, Y^a 158, evaluation forms of 27 July 1788 and 4 October 1777, respectively.

sensus in favor of a thoroughly aristocratic military, the dominant rhetoric of army reform—as developed by noble officers and other army leaders—obliquely undermined the special status of the nobility itself.

The tension within the military nobility's reformist language was already apparent in Langeron's treatise of 1758. There the marquis had boldly asserted that nobles should invariably receive preferential treatment; this appeared to him a principle on which "everyone agrees." Yet Langeron sharply criticized candidates who relied on favor to earn promotion, the young dandies who emerged from *collège* "bedecked with titles" and promptly bought commissions in the officer corps, the men who—despite their natural dignity and generosity—performed their functions miserably for lack of talent, application, and experience. This critical refrain gradually rose to a crescendo between the Seven Years' War and the last years of the ancien régime.

In an odd twist, many well-established nobles who were firmly committed to the idea of an all-noble officer corps found themselves attacking those signs of distinction and privilege most apt to be associated with nobility in the popular imagination. Reformers assailed everything symbolizing arbitrary disruption of the normal routines of service, promotion, and reward. Inspectors at the Ecole Militaire echoed Langeron in complaining of parents who routinely used connections to obtain appointments for young cadets who had not finished the required training regimen.[70] Another officer, meanwhile, pinpointed a source of festering and widespread resentment: "it seems the intention will always be to give preference to the men of the court."[71]

According to one reformer, looking back in retrospect in 1788, the sad turning point came in 1759 when the crown had clarified the criteria needed to qualify for honors of the court. Everyone knew that this event had touched off a "genealogical fever among the nobility." Even worse, though, status-conscious nobles "aspire to the highest military offices on the false pretense that, having gained entry at court, they are a privileged

---

70. See, for example, AG, Yᵃ 148, dossier "1787," "Eleves de l'Ecole Militaire"; and Yᵃ 157, dossier "1783," Reynaud, "Resultat des Observations du Chevalier de Reynaud après l'Inspection des 12 Ecoles Royales Militaires réparties dans les différentes provinces du Royaume à l'Epoque du Ier Octobre 1783." Reynaud noted that parents use their connections to have colonels "call up the young men as soon as they reach the age of fifteen, without anyone having certified that these students are sufficiently well instructed to become officers."

71. AG, MR 1762, no. 129, "Mémoire sur la maniere d'employer les officiers generaux," undated, 3.

class that must not be allowed to languish in the subaltern grades."[72] Several critics charged, with some justification, that new offices—such as that of second colonel—had been created solely to enable the army "to accord the nobility a greater number of posts."[73] Since then, wrote another officer, "promotions have multiplied" because "a *gentilhomme* is ashamed to remain a [mere] captain."[74]

Reformers objected less to the simple existence of privilege within the *gentilhommerie* than to the very nature of the privileged path to success. The chevalier de Keralio typically asserted that men attuned to the lavish and theatrical world of the court invariably lacked true military principles. He declared the *maison militaire* the "breeding ground of the worst general officers ever to exist."[75] If the army failed to act with discipline, Keralio noted, the responsibility lay not with the subaltern officers but rather with "the heads of the corps who will always be detestable so long as they are chosen from among the *militaires* of the court, the so-called *gens de qualité*."[76] This conviction led Keralio to announce, on the eve of the Revolution, that "if the court continues to dominate the army, there will be no hope."[77]

To perceive the potentially destabilizing effect of the critical dynamic that propelled the discourse of army reform in the decades before the Revolution, let us consider a brief but revealing reform project submitted to the war ministry by the marquis de Rochambeau at the height of the Seven Years' War. The future commander of French forces in Revolutionary America considered a relatively mundane matter in 1761; he wanted to improve discipline and increase emulation in the officers of the French infantry. Despite its brevity and its relatively narrow scope, Rochambeau's *mémoire* deserves scrutiny because it makes explicit the cultural tension underlying the theory and practice of military service in

---

72. AG, MR 1939, no. 44, Grimoard, "Mémoire historique du comte de Grimoard sur la présentation à la Cour et sur les inconveniens que les règlemens du mois de mai 1781 et du mois de janvier 1786, les preuves de noblesse exigées pour l'admission au service, produisent dans le royaume en general et dans le militaire en particulier," 1788, 6, 12.

73. AG, MR 1715, no. 13, "Mémoire sur les promotions," 1 January 1778, 3.

74. AG, MR 1791, no. 22, Baron Félix de Wimpffen, "Mémoire sur l'Encouragement Militaire, adressé au Comité Superieur de Messieurs les Inspecteurs," 1783, 14.

75. AG, MR 1791, no. 46, [Keralio], "Mémoire sur l'armée de France," [after 1763], 8.

76. Ibid.

77. AG, MR 1716, no. 35, Chevalier de Keralio, "L'Armée de France," [1787], non-paginated.

the eighteenth century. The marquis, himself an old noble, expressed the same spirit of resentment toward the court, favoritism, and undeserved privilege that one encounters in most of the writings of military reformers after 1750. But in articulating that resentment, Rochambeau made use of a telling set of juxtapositions.

Rochambeau introduced his plan by pointing out that the French army could never achieve a "perfect formation," given "the rights of the court nobility in France." The court's influence on appointment and promotion decisions meant that the only solution to the army's growing morale problem was to make the lower grades more attractive to the *gentilhommerie* while reserving some positions for distribution "without regard to the rights of birth."[78] At the time of his writing, the French infantry contained eighty-four regiments—twelve regiments with four battalions, one with three, fifty-two with two, and nineteen with one.[79] In Rochambeau's new infantry, twelve newly constituted regiments would have four battalions each; all other regiments would have two.

The interest of this plan lies in its guidelines for regulating promotions. According to Rochambeau, the "general officers" chosen for the twelve larger regiments would be selected "solely on the basis of merit." As positions of command became vacant in the other regiments, the war minister would alternate the criteria of selection. On the first occasion he would choose "by merit" from among the ranking lieutenant colonels and majors. For "the turn of birth, or the court," he could choose any of the aide-majors or captains—provided they had served as commissioned officers for five years. Rochambeau imposed these alternating criteria for appointment and promotion even down to the lowest grades. Each battalion comprised ten companies, and the captains "must be named on an alternating cycle." At the level of captain a third criterion, seniority, entered the rotation along with merit and distinguished birth, but the arrangement was unique to that rank.[80] Each of the eight fusilier companies in every battalion had eight corporals, "four chosen by merit, four *gentilshommes*." In addition, the companies included three sergeants, one quartermaster, and four "volunteers." Rochambeau specified that the "lower-officer *gentilshommes* and the volunteers should not be accepted unless they have certificates of nobility signed by the four prin-

---

78. AG, MR 1709, no. 21, Rochambeau, "Mémoire sur l'infanterie," 1761, 1.
79. See Lee Kennett, *The French Armies,* 29.
80. AG, MR 1709, no. 21, Rochambeau, "Mémoire sur l'infanterie," 1761, 3.

cipal *gentilshommmes* in the province." The other lower officers presumably would need no such proofs.[81]

One must be careful not to infer too much from this brief, and quite possibly incomplete, reform project. Rochambeau's disdain for the nobles who spent most of their time at court is an important marker, for it shows that he contrasted merit not with nobility per se but with court privilege and the foppish high aristocracy. By opening new avenues of promotion, Rochambeau intended, in part, to make the lower grades more attractive to less well connected *gentilshommes;* he undoubtedly supposed that serious nobles without court connections would be the principal beneficiaries of his plan. One should not conclude, then, that the marquis wished to end social discrimination in the military's recruitment and promotion policies.

Still, Rochambeau's stark language points to a revealing conceptual dichotomy. He juxtaposed a process of selection by merit with another process that recognized rights of birth, *gentilshommes,* distinguished birth, and certificates of nobility. In so doing, he left readers to understand that if one judged "solely on the basis of merit," the signs of social status would not enter one's calculations. For the historian, the significance of this conceptual polarization becomes more apparent when Rochambeau's thinking is contrasted to noble discourse of the early seventeenth century. Given his own manner of framing the issue of military reform, Rochambeau would have had much greater difficulty than his seventeenth-century counterparts in explaining—to himself or anyone else—why birth and merit could be considered synonymous or even correlative. Although noble superiority was a point on which "everyone agree[d]" (at least within the circle of the army's leadership), reformers were more in the habit of stressing the importance of talent, application, and discipline—and of decrying the corrupting influence of venality and cronyism—than in articulating the rationale for giving preference to nobles when recruiting officers. The Rochambeau document therefore exemplifies a peculiar inconsistency in military discourse in the second half of the eighteenth century. The target that focused reformers' resentment and inspired their attacks on the status quo—the role of money and favoritism—also made it possible for them to overlook or repress the homogenizing implications of their own rhetoric.

---

81. Ibid., 5.

Army Reform and the Public Gaze

In light of Rochambeau's disassociation of the concept of merit from the most prominent indicators of noble privilege, and given the army's general assault on court influence and the frequent placement of unmeritorious nobles in the officer corps, the modern reader is naturally inclined to see the army's ever more stringent policies of social exclusion—which culminated in the Ségur ruling of 1781—as a sign of hypocrisy, defensiveness, or both.[82] I argue, though, that the royal army, and the old nobility of France more generally, had *genuinely* come to embrace a contradictory position in the last decades of the ancien régime. In the movement for military reform after 1750, one sees army leaders enforcing and advancing the norms implied by the public modality of royal service. Rochambeau and his contemporaries, including Arc, Blangermont, and the rest, understood well that they earned and demonstrated merit not by positioning themselves before the prince's eye but through application to duty. This conviction shone through even in Rochambeau's effort to define with precision those offices open to "birth, or the court." He explained that by marking clearly their upward path through the hierarchy, he intended to give court nobles a new "object" to animate them. They, too, could "render themselves capable" through "émulation."[83]

The language of military reform shows that army professionals had been so thoroughly normalized to accept the primacy of talent, skill, and efficiency that they themselves had come to regard the exercise of personal influence at court—in the form of favoritism, venality, exceptional promotion decisions made by the king or ministers, the granting of offices as gifts—as disruptive, irregular, and anomalous. The conceptual and institutional apparatus of the traditional personal modality of service, in which the public modality was still so deeply enmeshed, now stood out as largely superfluous in the eyes of army reformers. The enduring normative power of the personal modality complicated their perspective, however, because military nobles readily accepted two other assumptions traditionally inscribed within the culture of royal service— namely, that the king exercised a personal surveillance over the domain

---

82. David D. Bien has already shown that those who drafted the Ségur ordinance were driven by complex motives. See both "The Army in the French Enlightenment" and "La réaction aristocratique avant 1789."

83. AG, MR 1709, no. 21, Rochambeau, "Mémoire sur l'infanterie," 1761, 1.

of royal service and that his gaze affirmed the old nobility's superior moral status in the social and political order.

This balancing of personal and public modalities was not new; it had been an implicit condition of royal service since the age of Louis XIV. The synthesis of the personal and public perspectives began to unravel after midcentury only because the gradual effacement of the king and the routinization of the metaphorical and abstract royal presence finally imposed on the sovereign's gaze an unsustainably ambiguous status. In their protracted discussions about merit—how to instill it, how to find it, how to recognize and promote it, how to insure that it received its just rewards—army reformers tried explicitly to define the meaning of the sovereign gaze; they thereby brought the personal and public modalities of royal service into open contradiction and placed the nobility itself in a vulnerable position.

A proposal sent to the minister of war two years before the Revolution provides a clear indication of the stresses and strain now placed on the image of the gaze. The author of the plan compared basic mechanisms for selecting and promoting superior officers—advancement by seniority, nomination of the prince, and strict peer review (*scrutin*).[84] This reformer unhesitatingly expressed his preference: nomination by the prince. "There must never be an intermediary between [merit, talent,] and recompense," he wrote. In reserving for himself the right to make all nominations, "the prince always occupies the road to justice" [le prince est donc toujours dans la voie de la justice].[85] He expressed his assumptions about the king's role in rewarding merit by employing a revealing metaphor: "An army may be compared to a circle of which the prince occupies the center. Each corps and each individual in these corps, placed along the points of the circumference, are connected to him by rays of hope for advancement." After lamenting the rise of an esprit de corps that he considered divisive, he added that "the army must not be composed of several families; it must be but one family, with one mind. . . . all eyes are fixed on the prince, and his eyes must be fixed on everyone, watching over everything."[86]

For this observer, then, the king's vision still animated the military

---

84. AG, MR 1717, no. 4, "Vue sur le Choix des Officiers Supérieurs des Régiments," [1787], 1.

85. Ibid., 14.

86. Ibid., 6, 8.

machine. Nevertheless, it would be hard to overemphasize the difference in perspective separating this *militaire* from the maréchal de Schomberg in the early seventeenth century or even from captain Lamont in the later seventeenth.[87] In fact, he went on to complain in his treatise that "the military profession is the only one in our society in which candidates are not required to prove their knowledge of the art before being admitted." He then proposed that any candidate for promotion above the rank of sublieutenant be required to prove his professional virtuosity by writing a long essay, or presenting an oral report, on some specific aspect of the service. Only after reviewing this chef d'oeuvre would his superior officers pass along his nomination, with a letter of recommendation, to a board of examiners composed of general officers. They would then test the candidate to insure his "military capacity," "expansiveness of mind," "sound judgment," and "morality." The weight of "public opinion," brought to bear at some unspecified point after completion of the examination, would increase the examiners' rigor and make indulgence impossible.[88] Finally, after the approval of the general officers, the candidate would be made eligible for royal nomination. In theory, promotions would be made by "nomination of the prince," but in fact the nominations came only "after three *scrutins*." In this plan the prince functions merely as the abstract overseer of professional norms, norms actually applied by experts who, the author elsewhere acknowledged, "act as intermediaries" between the prince and the candidates for promotion.[89] The king himself, "watching over everything" at a distance, exercises little more than an imaginary presence.

The army's awareness of the king's merely figurative involvement in the monitoring and judging of its service explains one of the impulses driving military reform after the Seven Years' War: the desire to substitute fixed standards of judgment for the personal discernment of the sovereign. One anonymous critic contrasted the situation of the French king with that of the "king of Prussia, who, seeing his troops for himself, is in the best position to distinguish merit and make choices while keeping in view [the value of] experience." Because the French king lacked a mechanism for making informed decisions, this writer suggested, he should

---

87. See chap. 1, p. 39 and chap. 4, p. 157.
88. AG, MR 1717, no. 4, "Vue sur le Choix des Officiers Supérieurs des Régiments," [1787], 10.
89. Ibid., 12.

award at least half of all offices in the superior grades strictly on the basis of seniority.[90]

The baron de Bohan made a serious attempt to articulate the principle of self-regulation in his *Critical Examination of the French Military* (1781). Bohan recommended that the king abolish the office of *secrétaire d'état de la guerre* and replace it with a board of experts that would carry the title *Conseil de Guerre*. Bohan made clear the purpose of the change: to give experienced and knowledgeable officers responsibility for making all nominations to vacant offices. Bohan anticipated the objection that "this form is essentially contrary to the constitution of a monarchy, where the king must be the sole dispenser of offices and *graces*, especially in his military." But he dismissed the validity of that argument. He pointed out that the king already had "a minister in charge of his department of war," and that ministers, acting on the king's behalf, frequently passed over the most deserving candidates. "I am merely offering to put in place of this minister," he wrote, "a council whose members may be nominated by the king." The council members had "a greater likelihood of being well-informed and [thus] of proceeding with greater justice."[91]

Although it may be coincidental, Louis XVI did indeed establish a reforming commission called the *Conseil de la Guerre* in October 1787, and the king tellingly surrendered much of his decision-making power to that council.[92] In the *règlement* that established the new system, Louis made it clear that, although he convened the council to address the immediate need for reform, the board would be constituted "in a permanent manner." In the future the board would "regenerate itself" by choosing appropriate nominees "in the event of a vacancy." Moreover, in setting forth the agenda of the council, the king emphasized that the new institution had as its primary goal the eradication of arbitrariness. The board would bring an end to "the continual fluctuation of principles" and thus would bring improvements to the military that would

90. AG, MR 1791, no. 3. "Mémoire sur la nouvelle constitution," [1761–71], 16, 18.

91. Bohan, *Examen critique du militaire français,* 2 vols. (Geneva, 1781), 1:189 n. 1.

92. Albert Latreille provides the most thorough discussion of the *Conseil de la Guerre*'s reforms. See *L'Armée et la nation à la fin de l'ancien régime: Les derniers ministres de la guerre de la monarchie* (Paris, 1914), 236–303. For concise accounts see Deschard, *L'Armée et la Revolution,* 18–21; Samuel Scott, *Response,* 31–32; and Pierre Chalmin "La Désintégration de l'armée royale en France à la fin du XVIIIᵉ siècle," *Revue Historique de l'Armée* 1 (1964): 75–90.

rival in scope and importance the reforms that everyone now anticipated in the system of crown finance.[93]

Louis vested in the *Conseil de la Guerre* all the consultative and legislative powers formerly conferred on the minister of war, who became, in effect, the council's executive officer. Composed of nine general officers, with the highly regarded tactical theorist Guibert serving as rapporteur, the council solicited ideas and suggestions and deliberated for several months before arriving at a general plan of reorganization. The council's conclusions were published in an omnibus military ordinance on 17 March 1788.

The reforms of the council, it has been noted, created command structures and principles of troop movement that would survive the ancien régime and serve well the armies of the Revolutionary republic.[94] To grasp the broad cultural changes crystallized in the council's deliberations and findings, however, one needs to leave aside the technical aspects of reform, important though these were, and focus on the attitudes expressed in the key ordinance on appointments, promotion, and hierarchy that Guibert himself considered "the basis of the new military constitution."[95] Each measure adopted by the council reflected its desire to define and fix the operation and effects of the gaze that judged military merit.

As Keralio had earlier observed, the old habit of giving regiments "to the men of quality, *militaires de cour,* and all the grades of superior officer to their protégés," meant that undeserving and ineffective dilettantes populated the officer corps.[96] The *Conseil de la Guerre* therefore tried to correct the procedures of appointment and promotion by reducing the size of the court, on the one hand, and by restricting the channels through which the court and courtiers gained access to regiments of the

93. AG, Yᵃ 499, "Règlement portant établissement d'un Conseil d'Administration du Département de la Guerre, sous le titre de Conseil de la Guerre," 9 October 1787, 2–3.

94. See, for example, Deschard, *L'Armée et la Révolution,* 18; and Léonard, *L'armée et ses problèmes,* 287–88. On the transition from royal army to revolutionary army see, in addition to Deschard, Samuel Scott, *Response;* and John Lynn, *Bayonets of the Republic: Motivation and Tactics in the Army of Revolutionary France, 1791–94* (Urbana and Chicago, 1984).

95. Guibert, *Mémoire adressé au public et à l'armée, sur les operations du Conseil de la Guerre* (n.p., n.d.), 60.

96. AG, MR 1716, no. 35, Chevalier de Keralio, "L'Armée de France," [1787], nonpaginated.

line, on the other hand. Guibert himself hoped to do away with the companies of *chevaux-légers, gendarmes de la garde,* and Swiss guards. He also approved the "impossible" idea of abolishing the *gardes du corps du Roi,* "the corps that absorbs the most pensions and *graces* of every type."[97]

Although the king did not go quite so far as Guibert would have liked, financial imperatives and the advice of the *Conseil de la Guerre* succeeded in persuading Louis XVI to reduce the size of his *maison militaire.* By an ordinance of 2 March 1788, the king disbanded the *corps de la gendarmerie* and sharply reduced the personnel serving in the other corps. The *gardes du corps du roi* and *troupes à cheval,* for example, were merged into a single unit, and the officers were forced to share privileges and prerogatives formerly belonging to each corps individually. The remaining officers of the two corps had to find solace in the prospect of enjoying closer proximity to the king. The ordinance emphasized that "by uniting them in a single quarter, closer to his person," the king "placed them more constantly before his eyes and made it easier [for the officers] to perfect themselves in all the parts of discipline, service, and instruction."[98]

The reduction of the *maison militaire du roi* carried important symbolic value, but the *Conseil de la Guerre* placed much greater emphasis on the need to regularize appointment procedures. By right and custom, the king, the war minister, and the princes and other grandees made military appointments at their discretion. Thus, to reduce further "the ill effects of influence and favor on the choice" of officer candidates, Guibert and his partners on the council tried to insure that appointment and promotion would no longer depend on access to the courtly circles of power.[99]

Deliberations from the very first sessions of the *Conseil de la Guerre* in October of 1787 captured the essence of the new system. In a wide-ranging memorandum, Guibert observed that the king had to name a number of new lieutenant generals each year to replace retirees, and he fixed on this perennial need as an opportunity to introduce a new method of selection. "To this effect," he wrote, "the *Conseil de la Guerre* might present

97. AG, MR 1790, no. 37, [Guibert], "Maison du Roi," 19.

98. AG, *Ordonnances Militaires,* 1787–88, "Ordonnance," 2 March 1788, fol. 64v.

99. AG, MR 1790, no. 24, [Guibert], "Rapport fait au Conseil Concernant l'Universalité des Emplois d'officiers Généraux, officiers Supérieurs, officiers inférieurs, officiers dit de remplacement, de Réforme, attachés, ou à la suite," 1.

to the king each year at the end of December a list [of candidates] chosen by vote [*au scrutin*]." To provide the king options, the council would propose twice as many candidates as vacancies. In addition, "The list would be accompanied by notes on their services, on the length of their record, on their talents, in short, on all the motives that led the *Conseil de la Guerre* to select them." The king might solicit another list of equal length from the generals "he deems it appropriate to consult." The king, after "weighing and comparing" the two lists in consultation with his *secrétaire d'état* "and with his *Conseil de la Guerre,*" would then announce the promotions.[100] Guibert and company specified in later meetings that princes and other members of the general staff, who had the customary right to name their lieutenant colonels and majors, should also be required to choose candidates from a list provided by the council.

This basic idea, that candidates to all positions must have their merit authenticated by impartial professionals, underlay the provisions regulating appointment and promotion in the 1788 ordinance. The organization of the new infantry was designed to insure that the army's commanders could see and verify the merit of prospective candidates. The monarchy now grouped all infantry regiments into twenty-one divisions, placed lieutenant generals in charge, and assigned an inspector to each division. The divisional inspectors and lieutenant generals were required to hold regular and uniform reviews and to keep detailed notes on the performance and service records of all officers beginning with the rank of sublieutenant.[101] Moreover, every officer in the infantry now had to carry a permanent record of his credentials. The king announced that "each officer will have in his letter of appointment [brevet] . . . proofs and authentic notes that can make known, at any time, the nature and type of his services." Any officer who made special requests or tried to obtain the king's *graces* would need to base his claims to favor on the proofs of service contained in the brevet.[102]

---

100. AG, MR 1790, no. 24, [Guibert], "Rapport fait au Conseil de la Guerre Concernant l'Universalité des Emplois Généraux, officiers supérieurs, officiers inférieurs, officiers dits de remplacement, de Réforme, attachée ou à la suite," 47–49.

101. AG, *Ordonnances Militaires,* 1787–88, "Ordonnance du Roi, Portant Règlement sur la Hiérarchie de tous les Emplois Militaires, ainsi que sur les Promotions & Nominations auxdits Emplois," 17 March 1788, fol. 222r.

102. AG, *Ordonnances Militaires,* 1787–88, "Ordonnance Portant Règlement sur la Hiérarchie," fol. 243v. The brevet would list nine sets of facts in the following order: the date the officer joined his regiment; the date he passed his qualifying examination; the number of campaigns in which he had participated and the grade occupied during each

The appointment process outlined in the ordinance placed a premium on impartiality. When making nominations at every level, commanders ideally gave preference to the senior person at the next lowest rank. Every candidate had to adduce impressive credentials, however, and commanders had the right to move down the seniority list if the first logical candidate proved unworthy. The process for selecting *capitaines commandants* epitomized the new regime. Twice each year the lieutenant general held a competitive exam (the *conseil de concours ou d'examen*) for lieutenants and captains. The lieutenant general, the divisional inspector, the brigade commander, and the superior officers of the regiment in question—including the two ranking captains—all appeared to test the competency of the candidates. The results of the exam were "discussed in depth and with the most severe impartiality." After careful consideration, the committee of examiners voted on its nominee. The lieutenant general drafted a letter of recommendation (*mémoire de proposition*) for the candidate and forwarded copies of the document, which carried the signatures of every member of the examining committee, to the *secrétaire d'état de la guerre* and to the colonel of the regiment.[103] If no irregularities arose, the favored nominee received his promotion.

The *Conseil de la Guerre* created similar procedures for appointment at all other grades. As previously noted, the divisional inspectors and lieutenant generals sent to the *secrétaire d'état de la guerre* accounts of the conduct of all officers beginning at the rank of sublieutenant, along with notes recording their assessment of the various reviews. This body of credentials, carefully compiled, produced candidates for the superior grades. After analyzing and discussing the inspectors' reports, the council drew up a list of nominees. This list, as Guibert had initially foreseen, contained details "on the type of services [rendered], on the distinctive-

---

campaign; the number of wounds received; the number of battles and other actions at which he had been present; all monetary *graces* obtained; the date of the officer's admission into the Order of Saint Louis (or the analogous Protestant Order of Merit, created in 1759); whether letters of command had ever been granted, and if so, the "action de guerre" invoked to justify it; and finally, for *officiers de fortune*, the length of their services as a soldier and as an officer.

103. AG, *Ordonnances Militaires*, 1787–88, "Ordonnance Portant Règlement sur la Hiérarchie," fol. 240v. The system used in the light horse units paralleled that of the regular infantry. The king announced that a captaincy in the *troupes à cheval* should be awarded to the lieutenant or second lieutenant who "showed the greatest aptitude, zeal, and intelligence in his profession [*métier*]." Thus, aspirants would earn their appointments through a competition convened by an assembly of general officers that would also include "the superior officers and the two ranking captains of the regiment" (ibid., fol. 230r).

ness of talents, on the length of their good record," and on the "condition of their regiments." Thus, only after having their records screened by superiors at two different levels did candidates have their names advanced for consideration by the king and *secrétaire d'état*. Candidates for positions of general officer—that is, above the rank of colonel—had fewer formal obstacles to clear. For each rank, the council specified only the number of years of service needed to become eligible for consideration. But the ordinance stressed the king's intent "to demand more talents of those to whom he accords [these grades]." Consequently, the council would again assist the king by providing lists of names.[104] At virtually every level of the army's hierarchy of officers, evaluative routines now enabled the king to assess merit fairly, objectively, and efficiently.

The reforms of the *Conseil de la Guerre* help one to interpret the breakdown of the social and political order at the end of the ancien régime, because they expose the fragile foundations of the culture of power in which the principles of royal authority and hereditary privilege were embedded. Guibert and his comrades did not speak for a monolithic army, of course, and the experience of the army provides only a limited and particular perspective on the broad social forces that transformed French society in the eighteenth century. But because of the institution's importance to both the monarchy and the old nobility, and because of the competing claims brought to bear in the pursuit of military efficiency throughout the eighteenth century, the movement for military reform in the decades before the Revolution casts a piercing light on the long-term shift in attitude that underlay the final assault on the absolutist order in 1789.

The work of the *Conseil de la Guerre* revealed the fundamental incoherence that now undermined the operation of the sovereign's gaze. Perhaps without realizing it, the officers of the council sounded a theme that had also run through the work of Louis XIV, Feuquières, the designers of the Ecole Militaire, and the anonymous officer who still maintained in 1787 that the prince "watches over everything." They sought to extend the sovereign gaze to make it always and everywhere efficacious, to encourage discipline, survey talent, and reward merit in such a way that all royal servants would willingly serve the prince zealously and usefully.

104. Ibid., fol. 239r–v. See also AG, *Ordonnances Militaires*, 1787–88, "Ordonnance Portant Règlement sur la constitution de l'Infanterie, & specialement sur la formation & la solde de l'Infanterie Française," 17 March 1788, fol. 212r.

It is important to point out, moreover, that some of the council's provisions maintained or even reinforced certain traditional features of the royal army, features that bespoke the importance of the sovereign's personal presence. The king still held in his gift half of all vacancies at the sublieutenant level, and he had the freedom to name to this office any *cadet gentilhomme* or noble courtier, provided the divisional inspector "judged him capable of performing the service [required]."[105] The king also retained the prerogative of honoring with promotion to the officer ranks commoners (the *officiers de fortune*) whose services he regarded as "distinguished and personal," even though all recognized that this placed the beneficiaries "above the rules and in a position of favor."[106]

Just as important, individuals and groups close to the king continued to enjoy privileged status. Officers from the corps of the *maison du roi* entered the troops of the line at a higher rank than that held in the *maison*—captains in the *gardes du corps,* for example, entered the regular cavalry at the rank of colonel—and more significant, the king still used irregular recruiting procedures to staff the *maison du roi*. According to a royal ordinance, for example, only those who enjoyed honors of the court—a distinction conferred at the king's discretion—could be considered for inclusion in the *gardes du corps*.[107] The council also made no attempt to separate the princes of the blood and the *fils* and *petits-fils de France* from the regiments they controlled by right. More generally, of course, the nobility received special attention. As the maréchal de Broglie had indicated in 1760, all nobles in theory enjoyed closeness to the king's person simply by virtue of their "rank and birth," and the *Conseil de la Guerre* happily preserved a norm held dear by noble reformers and firmly rooted in the monarchy's tradition of personal government;[108] for posi-

---

105. AG, *Ordonnances Militaires,* 1787–88, "Ordonnance Portant Règlement sur la Hiérarchie," fol. 225r. The ordinance further specified that "in order to attest this opinion in a positive manner, and provide an initial statement on the degree of zeal and application [found in] this *cadet gentilhomme* or officer, the inspector shall make note of it on his brevet."

106. AG, *Ordonnances Militaires,* 1787–88, "Ordonnance Portant Règlement sur la Hiérarchie," fol. 228r: "His Majesty wishing to insure that distinguished actions in war will always place above the rules and in a position of favor those who have made themselves known by them, he reserves the right to name to the office of second captain an *officier de fortune*." The ordinance further noted that the king would issue letters of dispensation only in recognition of actions "well proven, and which will have been shown to be *distinguished and personal.*"

107. AG, *Ordonnances Militaires,* 1787–88, "Ordonnance," 2 March 1788, fol. 68v.

108. AG, Yª 516, dossier 1, no. 1, letter from Broglie, 27 September 1760.

tions in the army's officer corps, only nobles of at least four generations need apply. The council continued to accept, then, that those who served in the royal household, came from the king's own family, or simply belonged to the corps of nobility deserved special consideration because of their presumed closeness to the king and because of the merits of which such closeness formed an expression.

The *Conseil de la Guerre* integrated into the reformed army a private, irregular, and frankly partial royal gaze—one that affirmed privilege and the existence of innate social distinctions—but these measures departed from the general thrust of the reforms, which aimed instead to establish over the military an impartial and regular gaze, one that uniformly applied the norms of talent, application, zeal, and experience. And unlike previous officers and administrators in the royal army, including especially those who had extended the principle of royal surveillance throughout the corps, the members of the *Conseil de la Guerre* consciously worked to wrest away from the king much of his power to judge; this power, though implemented by objective professionals, would work implicitly through the operation of fair and open evaluative routines. As a rule, appointments and promotions would now be based on examinations, "impartial" discussions, and the assessment of credentials whose authenticity could be openly and frequently verified. Thus, despite its token recognition of the king's centrality, the *Conseil de la Guerre* articulated in a very particular context a new conception of power, one that came to permeate French society in the last decades of the eighteenth century. The operation of this power rested on the assumption that, in the words of Foucault, things should be known and people seen "in a sort of immediate, collective, and anonymous gaze."[109]

But the *Conseil de la Guerre,* like Langeron, Keralio, Rochambeau, and all military reformers of the second half of the eighteenth century, really recognized the authority of two gazes—one the hierarchizing personal gaze of the king, the other the homogenizing, collective, and anonymous gaze associated only metaphorically with the person of the sovereign—and the council's work actually represents the culmination of a process initiated by Louis XIV himself. In seeking fully to routinize the gaze and thereby make its effects both equitable and automatic, the council transformed it into a transparent apparatus of normalization; this goal would certainly have suited Louis XIV, who aspired not only to have

---

109. Michel Foucault, *Power/Knowledge: Selected Interviews and Other Writings, 1972–1977,* ed. Colin Gordon (New York, 1980), 154.

"eyes opened over all the land" but also to inform royal servants everywhere that "reason" governed the monarchy's assessment of merit.

Nevertheless, the normalizing process finally painted the army and old nobility into a corner from which they would not be extricated before the Revolution. The *Conseil de la Guerre* gladly upheld the principle of noble privilege—after all, the belief in familial merit had formed an important element of the traditional personal modality, and the enforcement of genealogical criteria had always been central to the process of normalization. Yet the council also effectively assumed control over the operation of the sovereign's gaze and consciously subordinated the key epistemological assumption of the personal modality of service—the assumption that the king himself judges and rewards merit. This development, though it resulted from the logic internal to the normalizing process, simultaneously undermined the personal modality through which the nobility and its privileges had been absorbed into the emerging public modality of service. In part because of military reformers' own persistent and vocal attacks on the claims of birth, titles, court connections, and marks of *qualité* in the 1770s and 1780s, and also because of the army's consistent application of the principle of homogeneity, this displacement of the king had the effect of exposing the nobility's merits fully to the light of the public gaze, a gaze that failed to recognize the aristocracy's distinctive position.[110]

In March 1788—within days of the announcement of the latest military reforms—the new war minister Brienne sent a memo to the members of the *Conseil de la Guerre* informing them that "the entire third estate of the realm" stood in opposition to the newly restated genealogical restrictions on officer recruitment.[111] One wonders to what extent the third estate's reaction actually surprised Guibert, the rest of the council,

---

110. The nobility's mystique evaporated in the later eighteenth century not only because nobles spoke a language of merit shared by all literate members of society. As Sarah Maza has shown, individual noble families also exposed the seamy underside of the traditional community of honor by "washing their dirty linen in public" through a series of sensational lawsuits. The details of the cases became public through the published trial briefs (*mémoires judiciaires*) written and distributed by lawyers working on the cases. In presenting their tarnished reputations for judgment before a panel of legal experts—but also before an interested reading public—nobles appeared, as one author of a *mémoire judiciaire* put it, "before the first and most equitable of tribunals, before which all ranks, decorations, dignities and fame disappear." See Sarah Maza, *Private Lives and Public Affairs: The Causes Célèbres of Prerevolutionary France* (Berkeley, 1993), 141, 153.

111. AG, MR 1717, no. 17, [Brienne], "Projet de places pour la classe aisée de la Bourgeoisie sous le titre de gardes drapeaux, étendars et guidons," March 1788, nonpaginated.

and the army more generally. Commoners may have taken offense at the direction of military reform in the last years of the ancien régime, but thanks to the military nobility's contradictory normalizing efforts, they also found in those reforms all the rhetorical ammunition they needed to launch a critique of privilege, hereditary rights, arbitrariness, and the royal court.

Conclusion: From the Sovereign's Gaze to the Gaze of Sovereignty

I began this book by criticizing the long-established tendency to regard merit and meritocracy as direct products of the Enlightenment. I argued that this tendency had led many historians to misrepresent the history of aristocratic culture. For most, the nobility's aversion to meritocratic ideas helped explain its demise. For others, the nobility's surprising identification with merit during the Enlightenment signaled its acceptance of modernity and, implicitly, pointed to the injustice of the Revolution. Because both perspectives seemed flawed, I decided to write an account that would incorporate the prehistory of the relationship between the nobility and merit. The sources determined my general strategy at the outset, for seventeenth-century texts demonstrated clearly that the fragile but enduring partnership between monarchy and nobility was based on certain assumptions about merit: its content, its expression, its judgment.

In tracing the transformation of those assumptions, I have pursued three main arguments: (1) that the culture of royal service—understood as the values, assumptions, and habits mediating relations between the king and those who served him—conditioned the evolution of the "state," both as ontological category and as locus of power; (2) that the construction of absolute monarchy by Louis XIV and his successors proceeded on the basis of an implicit cultural understanding between monarch and old nobility; and (3) that although they permitted the expansion of the governing apparatus and the articulation of a new relationship between the monarchical state and the society it supervised and governed, the terms of this tacit understanding between king and nobility eventually proved untenable in light of the culture of power that kings and nobles had themselves collaborated to create.

To clarify this last piece of my argument, let me summarize the first two points. I maintain that in the early seventeenth century the old nobility commonly articulated its position in society, its behavioral ideals, and its relationship to the monarchy through the language of a personal modality of service. Through the lens of this modality, fashioned over the course of centuries, nobles saw the king as one who governed through personal relations. Like all individuals who required the good services and fidelity of others, the prince valued and rewarded generosity, courage, fidelity, and other honorable qualities prized in the context of personal relations and most often cultivated and sustained by family traditions. Moreover, since true merit could be tested and validated only through personal interaction, the judgment and affirmation of merit implied the actual presence of the judge or at least his own appreciation of the capacity for rendering personal service.

The personal modality of service provided kings and nobles a common language, and precisely for this reason it underlay both the monarchy's expansion and the nobility's reconciliation to that expansion in the later seventeenth century. Louis XIV hyperpersonalized the monarchy's structures and its service culture. Governing in a way that came naturally, he appealed to the nobles by focusing his subjects' attention on his pervasive presence and his own role in seeing and affirming all merit. But ironically, through his emphasis on regularity and routine, and by his determination to exercise the power of the sovereign's gaze continuously and in all places, the king articulated a new space of mediation between the person of the prince and those who served him, a space filled by the metaphorical presence of the sovereign. In this space, the structures of a centralized administrative state took shape, and the notion of merit expanded to include a new emphasis on talent and on disciplined application to the object of one's service. Both the king's new methods of encouraging, perceiving, and rewarding merit and the new language used to express it reflected the change. The new normalizing categories—talent, discipline, and application—encompassed a broad social field and held up a universal standard of merit. Yet, because the king, the nobility, and the mediators of the sovereign's gaze (many old nobles among them) articulated the emerging public modality of service within the framework of the traditional personal idiom, the concept of merit actually fused the valued moral attributes of high birth with the ideal of functional efficiency. In the later seventeenth century these two perspectives on merit were joined in a coherent mix through the monarchy's routinization of both a real and an imagined royal presence.

My examination of the techniques of cultivating, describing, recording, representing, and rewarding merit in the eighteenth-century army indicates that, in the years after Louis XIV, the culture of royal service reinforced the duality of the sovereign gaze. The king's metaphorical and institutional presence continued to promote application and exactitude while it also individuated talents and abilities. But the qualities of heart and birth also received recognition—from the king at court, from those who articulated the still-evolving ideal of the military professional, and from the army's leaders, who erected a series of genealogical barriers to recruitment and promotion. In the eighteenth century, normalization proceeded along two trajectories, one elaborating the homogenizing and widely accessible merit of the emerging public modality, the other elaborating the restrictive and aristocratic merit of the personal modality.

To make sense of the collapse of the ancien régime is, in part, to understand why the normalizing process became problematic for both the monarch and the nobility. As noted in the final chapters of this book, army reformers reflexively reinforced the special status of military nobles even as other voices intoned that merit belonged indistinctly to all men. But the roots of the army's crisis lay not so much in conflicting perspectives on merit—a conflict discernible since the later seventeenth century—as in the changing operation of the sovereign gaze. The king's routinized presence perpetuated both the linguistic and the institutional habits associated with personal service to the monarch—a fact attested by courtly protocol, the nobility's persistent genealogical fever, the accepted formulas for conveying and recognizing military merit, the standard invocations of the "honor" and "generosity" of the nobility, and the seemingly insoluble link between service at court and appointment to the officer corps. But as the norms for measuring each of the two sides of merit came finally to be fixed in institutions, monitored by the king's deputies and articulated at many points throughout the hierarchy, the person of the king virtually disappeared from the monarchy's relationships of service; he was replaced by an image of omnipresent sovereign power, a power that enclosed all the public space of the realm.

To understand why this specific contradiction undermined the status of monarchy and nobility, one needs to recast the familiar concept of the pre-Revolutionary "public sphere." Following Habermas, historians of the ancien régime have generally regarded the emerging public sphere of the eighteenth century as a forum for "the public use of reason by private individuals, first with respect to their private experiences, and then increasingly with respect to 'public' matters."[1] The public sphere, according to the prevailing view, constituted a space of open and rational discussion separate from and opposed to the absolutist state, a space where private persons whose perspectives had been shaped by a "public literary sphere" increasingly subjected the monarchy's activities to a "rational"—and ultimately corrosive—critique.[2]

This analytical model makes a good deal of sense. Thanks to the careful and imaginative research of recent social and cultural historians of France, we now understand better the processes whereby "private individuals" came together to comprise an "oppositional" public sphere in the political arena of the later eighteenth century. The rapid growth of commercial publishing; the creation of new venues for the reading and discussion of "Enlightened" (and other) works; the growing tendency (associated with the rising popularity of Rousseau) to universalize the meaning of subjective experience; the legal profession's withering attacks on ministerial "despotism" in the pamphlet wars of the later 1760s and early 1770s; the crown's own practice of justifying its policies and appealing for popular support through the medium of print—all of these phenomena and more contributed to the creation of a political culture in which an abstract "public opinion" finally stood as the ultimate source of legitimacy.[3]

---

1. Sarah Maza, "Women, the Bourgeoisie, and the Public Sphere: Response to Daniel Gordon and David Bell," *French Historical Studies* 17 (1992): 937. The starting point for an examination of the public sphere as a tool for historical analysis is Jürgen Habermas, *The Structural Transformation of the Public Sphere: An Inquiry into a Category of Bourgeois Society,* trans. Thomas Burger and Frederick Lawrence (Cambridge, Mass., 1989). Habermas's framework is clearly explained—and fruitfully applied to developments in eighteenth-century France—by Roger Chartier in *The Cultural Origins of the French Revolution* (Durham, N.C., 1991); see esp. 20–37. Habermas's vocabulary continues to be tested and refined by other eighteenth-century specialists. See, for example, Keith M. Baker, "Defining the Public Sphere in Eighteenth-Century France: Variations on a Theme by Habermas," in *Habermas and the Public Sphere,* ed. Craig Calhoun (Cambridge, Mass., 1992), 181–211.

2. Chartier, *Cultural Origins,* 20.

3. For publishing and reading, see especially the work of Roger Chartier and his collaborators: Roger Chartier and Henri-Jean Martin, eds., *Histoire de l'édition française,* vol. 2, *Le Livre triomphant, 1660–1830* (Paris, 1984); Chartier, ed., *Pratiques de la lecture* (Marseilles, 1985); Chartier, ed., *Lectures et lecteurs dans la France d'Ancien Régime* (Paris, 1987); and Chartier, *The Cultural Uses of Print in Early-Modern France,* trans. Lydia G. Cochrane (Princeton, 1987), esp. chaps. 6–8. For the contemporary emphasis on the connection between the private and the political, see Sarah Maza's important work of synthesis, *Private Lives and Public Affairs: The Causes Célèbres of Prerevolutionary France* (Berkeley, 1993); and Dena Goodman, "Public Sphere and Private Life: Toward a Synthe-

The criticism to be made of this important and illuminating literature on the eighteenth-century public sphere is that, in generally accepting Habermas's dichotomy between the state and the public sphere of private persons, recent work underestimates the extent to which the absolute monarchy was itself responsible for creating and gradually transforming an abstract public space.[4] The Habermasian dichotomy—like the dichotomy between "state" and "nobility" that once informed analysis of early-modern state formation—is dissolved if one focuses on the culture of power that framed the monarchy's operations. The public sphere of the second half of the eighteenth century may have been partly the product of social, economic, and cultural forces bearing little or no relation to the structure of monarchical power, but it is important to recognize that the "public sphere in the political realm" shared important features with absolutism's hybrid modality of royal service.[5]

To articulate their expansive public power, French kings since Louis XIV had mediated their presence through subtle administrative mechanisms and a metaphorical gaze, thus reconstituting the "public" as that which could be "seen" by the king. But in thus articulating the French kingdom's legal and administrative unity, the monarchy not only extended its power; it *changed* its power by enacting a new mode of royal surveillance. The creation of a space of mediation between the sovereign and his subjects, a space where the king's servants were uniformly encouraged to cultivate talent and show application, required and presupposed the operation of a collective and largely anonymous critical fac-

---

sis of Current Historiographical Approaches to the Old Regime," *History and Theory* 31 (1992): 1–20. On the emergence of "public opinion" as a constitutive element of French politics see Keith M. Baker, *Inventing the French Revolution* (Cambridge, 1990), 167–202; Mona Ozouf, "L'Opinion Publique," in *The Political Culture of the Old Regime*, ed. Keith M. Baker (Oxford, 1987), 419–34; and Jack Censer and Jeremy Popkin, eds., *Press and Politics in Pre-Revolutionary France* (Berkeley, 1987). On changing public attitudes about the nobility in the later eighteenth century see, in addition to Maza, *Private Lives*, Henri Carré's impressionistic *La Noblesse Française et l'Opinion Publique au XVIIIᵉ siècle* (Paris, 1920), esp. pt. 2, "L'évolution de l'opinion sur les nobles et l'évolution de la noblesse"; and André Decouflé, "L'Aristocratie Française devant l'Opinion Publique à la veille de la Révolution," in Decouflé, François Boulanger, and Bernard-André Pierrelle, *Etudes d'histoire économique et sociale du XVIIIᵉ siècle*, 1–52 (Paris, 1966).

4. This specific criticism has also served as a point of departure for the work of David Bell who uses the experience of an agency tied to the state—the Parisian order of barristers—to chart the long transition from a "politics of privilege" to a new "politics of public opinion." See *Lawyers and Citizens: The Making of a Political Elite in Old Regime France* (Oxford, 1994).

5. Chartier, *Cultural Origins*, 20.

ulty. Army officers, we have seen, learned of their collective responsibility always "to bring [merit] closer and find occasion to show it to [the king and his ministers]."[6] Strictly *within* the domain of royal authority, then, there developed in the eighteenth century the ideal of autosurveillance, a surveillance exercised over and *by* the servants of the king. Over time, the routinization of the sovereign's gaze and the king's own absence from the routines that governed the domain of royal service came to imply that the procedures for encouraging, identifying, and rewarding merit should be immediately and transparently equitable, rooted in that neutral space of mediation that communicated and represented the sovereign's public power.

Habermas and his followers have stressed that the construction of absolute monarchy helped produce the "public sphere in the political realm" because the crown's "secrecy," "despotism," and "arbitrariness" provided the public sphere its veritable raison d'être. That characterization of pre-Revolutionary political change tells only part of the story, however, for the developing absolute monarchy of the later seventeenth and eighteenth centuries also legitimized the assumption that the fair and efficient exercise of an expansive sovereign power implied the existence of an immanent gaze, a gaze activated, implemented, and regulated by theoretically impartial agents of the sovereign. If the "private persons" engaged in the "political public sphere" of the later eighteenth century are understood as having opposed not monarchical power per se but a closed, concealed, irregular public authority too often shaped by caprice, then the servants of the crown in the later eighteenth century should be seen as inhabiting a kind of parallel public sphere, for they themselves increasingly contested the king's personal control over the sovereign gaze. Indeed, Guibert later claimed, in the summer of 1789, that the *Conseil de la Guerre* had carried out its work in light of "the general will . . . to place everything under the safeguard of publicity."[7]

That a crisis involving the definition and locus of the sovereign gaze underlay the political turmoil of the 1780s is indicated by one of the key events of the French "pre-Revolution," the Assembly of Notables of February through May 1787. The notables had been convened to consider

6. AG, MR 1703, no. 9, M. Lamée, "Essai sur l'art militaire," 27 December 1741, 27.

7. Guibert, *Mémoire adressé au public et à l'armée, sur les operations de la Conseil de la Guerre* (n.p., n.d.), 29. Guibert noted, in this treatise written shortly after the outbreak of the Revolution, that the "esprit général du moment est avec raison de mettre tout sous la sauve-garde de la publicité."

the crown's proposed solutions to the ongoing financial crisis. In his opening address to the assembly, Controller General Calonne stressed repeatedly the king's own interest in the results of the gathering. In being charged with the task of providing the notables all the details of the present situation, Calonne felt "especially honored" because the king had come to regard the proposals as "entirely personal, due to the close attention he gave to each [idea] before adopting it." Calonne reported that he had "placed before [the king's] eyes all the accounts, so that he could consider from every point of view the true situation of his finances." The notables should be filled with confidence on hearing of "the application, assiduity, and constancy with which the king devoted himself to this long and arduous work."[8] Calonne then immediately reemphasized the king's personal control: "I placed before the king's eyes all the official accounts; he saw them and examined them; they remain in his hands."[9] The king's application, moreover, had led to an important and reassuring result: "His Majesty . . . is at this time better informed [of the financial situation] than anyone else in the realm could possibly be."[10]

Discussions of the significance of the Assembly of Notables generally focus on the notables' ultimate rejection of the crown's reform package on grounds that it failed to protect property rights and customary social distinctions. But the pivotal event at the assembly actually occurred before the formal rejection of the reforms. The notables, after breaking into committees to discuss the proposals presented by Calonne, had reached a nearly unanimous conclusion; they needed to see the accounts for themselves. The spokesman for the committee headed by the duc d'Orléans, for example, explained that serious deliberation could not proceed because the committee needed first "to have before its eyes the lists of receipts and expenses" as well as the details of "the economizing measures His Majesty has proposed."[11]

The king gave in to the notables' request and further promised "the annual publication of details of the public debt and of the funds assigned to it" as well as the yearly "publication of [lists of] gifts, *graces*, and pensions" accorded by the king.[12] At the final meeting of the assembly,

8. M. J. Mavidal, M. E. Laurent et al., eds., *Archives Parlementaires de 1787 à 1860, première série (1787 à 1799)*, 97 vols. to date (Paris, 1867–), 1:189.
    9. Ibid., 1:190.
    10. Ibid., 1:193.
    11. Ibid., 1:220.
    12. Ibid., 1:235.

Chancellor Lamoignon reminded the notables that the king had "revealed everything to you without disguise;" that he had "placed before your eyes the table of state revenues and expenses."[13] But the king had made these concessions to no avail. The assembly could not accept the proposed reforms because, as one spokesman ironically put it, the erosion of privilege actually threatened "the authority of the monarch and the existence of the monarchy."[14]

When the king tried to have *parlement* ratify the measures even without the notables' seal of approval, he encountered resistance from the judges, who likewise insisted on seeing the royal accounts for themselves. Louis XVI balked at this latest affront to his authority and reminded the *parlementaires* in a *lit-de-justice* of 6 August that, though he doubted "neither your wisdom nor your zeal . . . for [my] service," the judges had no need or right to see the royal accounts, which, in any case, would soon be published. Louis insisted that the king is by right "the sole administrator of his realm," and that *parlement* had no choice but to enact the royal legislation.[15] This test of wills sparked a series of confrontations between king and *parlement* that finally culminated in the announcement, in August 1788, that an Estates General would be convened in the following year. It seems no exaggeration to say that the notables and *parlementaires* foreshadowed the seizure of the king's sovereignty in 1789 by first challenging the legitimacy of his gaze in 1787.

The brief history of the Assembly of Notables hardly encapsulates the much longer history of the evolving conception of royal service that this book has addressed. The notables' failure to reach an understanding with the crown is relevant to the story, however, because it illuminates and in some respects replicates the experience of the royal army in the century between Louvois and Guibert. In both contexts, the king and the aristocracy carried on a conversation whose immediate implications seemed confined to the specific issues at hand: the desire to encourage merit in the army and the crown's quest for solvency at the Assembly of Notables. Also, these conversations had similar subtexts, for every exchange revealed assumptions regarding the very nature of the sovereign's gaze. More important, the forces set in motion by the Assembly of Notables show why even the most limited and circumscribed discussions about the

13. Ibid., 1:231.
14. Ibid., 1:220.
15. Ibid., 1:245.

operation and effects of the sovereign's gaze could lead, in the 1780s, to unintended and undesired consequences.

The culture of merit that had grown up within the structures of the absolute monarchy in the eighteenth century paralleled in striking ways the discussions about accountability, equity, fairness, and natural rights that now circulated outside the context of monarchical institutions. The army's discourse of merit and the wider discourse of political reform, though linked by a common vocabulary, differed in at least one important respect: in the former discourse, the ultimate legitimizing gaze was still to be found, theoretically, in the person of the king; in the latter, this gaze was located in a vaguely defined public space. But the ease with which the boundary separating these two discourses could be transgressed had already been demonstrated by Rousseau in his *Considerations on the Government of Poland* (1771). In a chapter devoted to military matters, Rousseau connected the display and recognition of military merit to the unrelenting pressure of an abstract public gaze. If the noble framers of Poland's new constitution hoped to inspire in the people a patriotic "effervescence," wrote the Genevan, they must insure that

> all citizens feel themselves incessantly to be under the gaze of the public [*sous les yeux du public*]; that no one advances or achieves success except through public favor; that no grade, no position shall be filled except through the will of the nation; that everyone from the last noble . . . to the king, if possible, relies so heavily on public esteem that nothing can be acquired or achieved without it.[16]

The army of the ancien régime, whose particular corporate identity was affirmed and protected by the king alone, certainly never imagined subjecting the merits of its officers to the critical gaze of an amorphous "public." But many years before publication of Rousseau's reflections on Poland, military experts had begun to articulate the power of a routine, anonymous, equalizing gaze that made meritorious service a civic duty. Even the army's staunchest supporters of hereditary privilege and aristocratic distinctiveness would have seen good intentions in Rousseau's novel plan.

By openly attacking the fiction that the king's eyes possessed special powers of discrimination, the Assembly of Notables merely went one

16. *Oeuvres complètes de J. J. Rousseau,* ed. V. D. Musset-Pathay, 22 vols. (Paris, 1823–24), 5:351.

step beyond the halting and contradictory reform measures that characterized the army down to the eve of the Revolution. The notables transmuted the sovereign's gaze into a free-floating "gaze of sovereignty" susceptible to control by others. In doing so, they forged a connection between the public modality of royal service that had evolved under the umbrella of absolutism and the "public opinion" that undergirded rational political discourse in the wider public sphere. Once appropriated by spokesmen of the "nation," the sovereign gaze applied the familiar principle of homogeneity openly and universally, thus obliterating the seemingly artificial restrictions placed on it by tradition and the personal modality of service.

The effects of exposing the privileged nobility to the gaze of a sovereign public, a gaze fully detached from the person of the king, are discernible in many pockets of public discourse in 1788–89—from Abbé Sieyès's denigration of noble "generosity" and his sarcastic refutation of noble "honor," to the complaints among *bas-officiers* that the *Conseil de la Guerre* had gone too far in protecting aristocratic interests, to the furor over the *parlement's* September 1788 declaration concerning representation at the coming Estates General.[17] But perhaps the most interesting change of direction took place outside the glare of the revolutionary spotlight, at an institution initially founded on behalf of the nobility. When the renamed Ecole Nationale Militaire was reestablished in the summer of 1789, reformers specified that all applicants to the six schools that comprised the institution would now receive equal consideration, irrespective of social background; the methods used to implement the principle of openness are telling.

Reformers prescribed that all examinations—those determining entry

---

17. In *Qu'est-ce que le tiers état?* Sieyès mocked the nobility's "generous" offer to assume its share of the tax burden, an offer that had recently been articulated by the princes in charge of the second Assembly of Notables of November 1788: "Yes, you will pay; not out of generosity, however, but out of justice; not because you consent to do so, but because you have to." In his *Essai sur les privilèges* the abbé took delight in exploding the obsolete notion that honor was incompatible with the pursuit of profit. Lost in "ecstasy" before the portraits of their ancestors in the privacy of their dusty châteaus, nobles had been deluded to think that they alone possessed honor. These references can be found, respectively, in Keith M. Baker, ed., *The Old Regime and the French Revolution* (Chicago, 1987), 169; and Sieyès, *Oeuvres de Sieyès*, 3 vols., Editions d'Histoire Sociale (Paris, 1989), 1:19. For the reaction of the army's lower officers to the reforms of Guibert, see Latreille, *L'Armée et la nation à la fin de l'ancien régime: Les derniers ministres de la guerre de la monarchie* (Paris, 1914), 297–301; and Pierre Chalmin, "La Désintégration de l'armée royale en France à la fin du XVIIIᵉ siècle," *Revue Historique de l'Armée* 1 (1964): 75–90.

into the *école* and those determining fitness for the officer corps—would now take place in public. Detailed grading sheets would be kept during the course of exams, and after the examination the rankings of students would immediately be made public, to enforce impartiality.[18] Another writer explained the thinking behind the reform. He highlighted the need "to establish a true public competition that inspires confidence, a competition capable of exciting emulation and assuring that talent is always given preference." The publicness of the exam defined the very essence of the institution. He contrasted desirable "publicity" with the "favor, considerations, and influence" that had often corrupted the judgment of examiners in the past. To avoid "any suspicion of partiality," in fact, this observer recommended that all examinations take place at one central site rather than in the provincial schools where secret irregularities might creep into the process.[19]

This preoccupation with openness and publicity at an institution designed to encourage and instill a set of specialized skills is intriguing. It encourages us to consider from a new vantage point the broad shift in mentality that underlay the assault on the old order in 1789. In its reshuffling of the social order, the Revolution clearly signified something other than the long-delayed victory of "meritocratic" values, for meritocratic ideas of one kind or another had been championed by members of the social elite throughout the history of the ancien régime. It would be more accurate to say that the Revolution coincided with the passing of one culture of merit and the open formalization of another. When the deputies to the National Assembly declared in the summer of 1789 that "all citizens, being equal in [the eyes of the law], are equally admissible to all public dignities, positions, and employments, according to their ability, and on the basis of no other distinction than that of their virtues and talents,"[20] they drew on and finalized a process initiated by the absolute monarchy and its servants; their unspoken point of reference was that immediate, collective, and anonymous gaze rooted in the former public modality of royal service.

The revolutionaries of 1789 found a new strategy for "assuring that

18. AG, Yª 157, dossier "1789," "Projet de Decret sur la formation des Maisons Nationales de concours Militaire et sur le mode d'admission au service en qualité d'officier," undated.
19. AG, Yª 157, dossier "1789," "Des Examens et des Emplacements des Ecoles Militaires," undated.
20. As cited in Baker, *The Old Regime*, 238.

talent is always given preference," a strategy that perhaps could never have occurred to the likes of Rochambeau, Rochelambert, Langeron, or Guibert. They disentangled the two modalities that had formerly structured royal service, jettisoned the apparatus of the personal modality, and thus escaped the contradictory effects that had characterized the operation of the panoptic gaze of absolute monarchy. Rejecting the authority of the king's personal gaze, they made it clear that henceforth merit would be judged in light of a gaze whose standards were theoretically enforceable and attainable by all who were eligible to inhabit the nation's public space.

Bibliography

Archival and Manuscript Sources

Archives Nationales (AN)

Series G^7 (Contrôle Générale des finances). 1.
Series K (Monuments Historiques). Ecole militaire, collège militaire de La Flèche, cérémonial. 118^A, 118^B, 148–49, 675, 675^2.
Series KK (Miscellaneous). Cérémonial. 1454.
Series M (Ordres Militaires . . . Mélanges). Affaires Militaires, Cérémonial. 608, 638–40, 644, 648, 650, 651, 653, 655.
Series MM (Registres et Rouleaux). Titres nobiliaires, recueils généalogiques. 689–91, 693–94, 695–99^B.
Series O^1 (Maison du Roi). Actes royaux, papiers du grand écuyer, école des pages. 13, 20, 915, 970, 974, 976.
Series Z^{1A} (Cour des Aides de Paris). Lettres patentes et provisions d'office. 537, 570, 572.

Archives de la Guerre (AG)

Ordonnances Militaires.
Series MR (Mémoires et Reconnaissances). 1701–3, 1705, 1707, 1709, 1713, 1715, 1716–17, 1762–63, 1781, 1786, 1790–91, 1939.
Series Y^a (Documents d'intérêt collectif ou général). Ecoles militaires, Pensions, Officers-Généraux, Règlements. 70, 145, 147–49, 157–58, 182, 208, 499, 516.
Travail du Roi. 1706–1739.

Bibliothèque de l'Arsenal (BA)

MS 4161. Du Prat. "Généalogie de M. le marquis d'Argenson."
MS 4485. "Cahiers particuliers de la noblesse (des 3 Etats) de diverses provinces

de ce royaume, pour estre représentez en l'Assemblée des Etats généraux tenus à Paris. 1615."

MS 4817. "Recueil de pièces curieuses."

MS 4905. "Manuscrit contenant l'Origine et les Armes de plusieurs familles."

MS 4920. Valles. "Généalogie des très illustres et très anciennes maisons de Montauban et d'Agoult, comtes de Sault." 1632.

MS 6829. "Extrait des Mémoires sur les ordonnances en général fait par ordre de M. Colbert."

Bibliothèque Nationale (BN)

MS fr. 2396. Pillon de Cleranueau. "L'Art du Soldat." [Seventeenth century].

MS fr. 9174. "Mémoires . . . militaires."

MS fr. 11465. "Généalogie de l'illustre maison de Bertrand, de Bricquebec et de La Bazinière." [Seventeenth century].

MS fr. 12365. Raimondo Montecuccoli. "Principes de l'art militaire." 1712.

MS fr. 12387. "Mémoires sur le service journalier de l'infanterie." 1718.

MS fr. 14189. "Mémoire sur le Ministère du Marquis de Louvois."

MS fr. 14868. Doizal, M. "Dissertation sur la subordination, avec des Réflexions sur l'exercice, et sur l'art militaire." 1752.

MS fr. 18670. Georges Viole. "Généalogie de l'ancienne maison des sieurs de Viole." 1660.

MS fr. 21709. Police. Discipline.

MS fr. 23042. [Lesdiguières]. "Discours de l'art militaire, faict par Msr le Connétable de Lesdiguières."

MS fr. 24264. "Motions et Evolutions Militaires." [Seventeenth century].

MS fr. 32375. "Généalogie de la maison de Croismare avec des alliances." 1765.

MS fr. 32394. "Généalogie de la famille de Sainte-Marie." [Eighteenth century].

MS fr. 32621. Pierre d'Hozier. "Généalogie de la maison d'Aumont." 1627.

MS fr. 32629. "Généalogie de la maison de Chabert, et ses alliances." [Seventeenth century].

MS fr. 32926. "Cahiers de la noblesse—1651."

MS fr. 33206. "Estat de la Genealogie de Rene Desprès Escuyer Sr de Rochefort." 1709.

MS Collection Duchesne 42. André Du Chesne. "Histoire de la maison de Vergy." [Seventeenth century].

MS Dossiers Bleus 219, fol. 69. "Généalogie de la maison de Courvol en Nivernois, dressée sur ses titres originaux, et sur des jugemens des intendants, rendus lors de la recherche de la noblesse du royaume en 1666 & depuis." 1753.

Nouvelles acquisitions françaises 366. Langeron. "Mémoires sur l'Infanterie Française, Autrichienne et Prussienne, par M. le Mis de Langeron, Mal de Camp." 1758.

Nouvelles acquisitions françaises 384. Langeron. "Traité sur les devoirs d'un colonel." 1751.

Nouvelles acquisitions françaises 9521. Antoine de Pas, Mis de Feuquières. "Mémoires sur la Guerre." [Eighteenth century].

Published Primary Sources

Advis, remonstrances, et requêtes aux estats généraux tenus à Paris, 1614: Par six Paysans. Paris, 1614.

Advis sur l'Estat, touchant les affaires présentes et le gouvernement étranger. Paris, n.d.

A. G. E. D. G., *L'idée du bon Magistrat.* N.p., 1645.

L'Ambitieux. N.p., 1649.

Anselme. *Histoire généalogique et chronologique des grands officiers de la couronne.* Paris, 1674.

Arc, Philippe-Auguste de Sainte-Foix, chevalier d'. *La Noblesse Militaire, ou le patriote français.* 3d ed. N.p., 1756.

Auger, M. l'abbé. *Projet d'éducation pour tout le royaume, précédé de quelques réflexions sur l'Assemblée Nationale.* Paris, 1789.

Avertissement . . . Particelly. N.p., 1649.

Avity, M. d'. *Panégyrique à Mgr Lesdiguières, maréchal de France et lieutenant général pour le roi en Dauphiné.* Lyon, 1611.

Bachot, E. *Tableau de Mr le Mal de Schomberg.* Paris, 1633.

Baïf, Jean Antoine de. *Les mimes, enseignements et proverbes.* Ed. Prosper Blanchemain. Paris, 1880.

Bartoli, Cosimo. *Conseils Militaires, fort utiles a tous Generaux, Colonels, Capitaines & Soldats, pour se sçavoir deuëment & avec honneur acquitter de leurs charges en la guerre.* Trans. Gabriel Chappuys. Paris, 1586.

[Baudier]. *Histoire du Maréchal de Toiras.* Paris, 1644.

Beauvais-Nangis, Nicolas de Brichanteau, marquis de. *Mémoires.* Paris, 1862.

Belleguise, Alexandre. *Traité de la Noblesse et de son origine, suivant les préjugez rendus par les commissaires députez pour la vérification des Titres de Noblesse: Avec la Déclaration de Sa Majesté, Arrests & Règlements du Conseil sur le fait de ladite vérification.* Paris, 1700. First edition published in 1688.

[Belloy]. *Mémoires, et recueil de l'origine, alliances et succession de la royale famille [sic] de Bourbon, branche de la maison de France; ensemble de l'histoire, gestes et services plus memorables faictz par les princes d'icelle aux rois et couronne de France.* La Rochelle, 1587.

Billon, Jean de. *Les principes de l'art militaire.* Rouen, 1626.

Blanchard, François. *Les Présidents au mortier du Parlement de Paris, leurs emplois, charges, qualitez, armes, blasons et généalogies, depuis l'an 1331 jusques à présent: Ensemble un catalogue de tous les conseillers selon l'ordre des temps et de leurs receptions, enrichy du blason de leurs armes et de plusieurs remarques concernans leurs familles.* Paris, 1647.

Blanchard, François, and Jean-Baptiste l'Hermite de Souliers. *Les Eloges de tous les premiers présidents du Parlement de Paris depuis qu'il a esté rendu sedentaire jusques à présent, ensemble leurs généalogies, épitaphes, armes et blasons. . . .* Paris, 1645.

Bohan, François-Philippe Loubat, baron de. *Examen critique du militaire français.* 2 vols. Geneva, 1781.

Bossuet. *Oeuvres de Bossuet.* 4 vols. Paris, 1841–47.

Boussanelle, Louis de. *Le Bon Militaire.* Paris, 1770.

Bretonneau, Guy. *Histoire généalogique de la maison des Briçonnets.* Paris, 1620.

Briquet, Sr. de, ed. *Code Militaire, ou Compilation des Ordonnances des Roys de France Concernant les Gens de Guerre.* 3 vols. Paris, 1728.

Brizard, Gabriel. *Histoire généalogique de la maison de Beaumont.* Paris, 1779.

Brosse, Jacques. *Tableau de l'homme juste, sur les vertus et à la mémoire de François de Montholon.* Paris, 1626.

Broue, Salomon de la. *Le Cavalerice François.* Paris, 1628.

Bussy, Roger de Rabutin, comte de. *Mémoires.* ed. Ludovic Lalanne. 2 vols. Paris, 1857.

Calmet, Augustin. *Histoire généalogique de la maison du Chatelet, branche puînée de la maison de Lorraine.* Nancy, 1741.

Castel de Saint-Pierre, Abbé. *Avantajes de l'Educaison des Colèges sur l'educaison domestique.* Amsterdam and Paris, 1740.

Castiglione, Baldesar. *The Book of the Courtier.* Trans. Charles Singleton. Garden City, N.Y., 1959.

Catalogue des Partisans, Ensemble Leurs Généalogies et extraction, vie, moeurs, et fortunes. Paris, 1649.

Catéchisme Royal. Paris, 1650.

Catilhon, Antoine Boniel de. *La vie de m. Claude Expilly.* Grenoble, 1660.

Caumartin, François. *Recherche de la noblesse de Champagne.* Châlons, 1673.

Ceriziers, [René] de. *Le Héros Français, ou l'idée du grand capitaine.* Paris, 1645.

Chamborant de Drou, chevalier. *Inventaire des Titres Originaux généalogiques conservés jusqu'a ce jour, des branches existantes de la maison de Chamborant.* Paris, 1783.

Chevalier, Guillaume. *Discours de la Vaillance.* Paris, 1598.

——. *Discours des Querelles et de l'Honneur.* Paris, 1598.

Cheverny, Philippes Hurault, comte de. *Les Mémoires d'Estat de m. Philippes Hurault, comte de Cheverny, Chancelier de France, Avec une Instruction à Msr son Fils, ensemble La Généalogie de la Maison des Huraults.* Paris, 1636.

Chifflet, [Jules]. *Histoire du bon chevalier, m. Jacques de Lalain, frère et compagnon de l'ordre de la Toison d'or, par Georges Chastellain.* N.p., 1634.

————. *Les Marques d'Honneur de la Maison de Tassis.* Antwerp, 1645.

Chronologie historique des ducs de Croy. Grenoble, 1790.

Claville, Le Maitre de. *Traité du vrai Mérite de l'Homme.* Paris, 1750.

Colbert, Jean-Baptiste. *Testament Politique de messire Jean-Baptiste Colbert.* The Hague, 1693.

Courtin, Antoine de. *Traité de la paresse, ou l'Art de bien employer le temps en toutes sortes de conditions.* Paris, 1673.

Coyer, Gabriel-François, abbé. *La Noblesse Commerçante.* Paris and London, 1756.

————. *Plan d'éducation publique.* Paris, 1770.

Dictionnaire de l'Académie Française. 1st, 4th, 5th eds. Paris, 1694, 1762, 1798.

Dictionnaire de Trévoux. Paris, 1771.

Diderot, Denis. *Principes de la philosophie morale, ou Essai de M. S*** sur le mérite et la vertu.* In *Oeuvres complètes: Édition chronologique,* ed. Roger Lewinter, 1:9–266. Paris, 1969.

Le Diogène français. N.p., 1652.

Discours de la vie, mort et derniers propos de feu Mgr de Mandelot. Lyon, 1588.

Domat, Jean. *Les lois civiles dans leur ordre naturel.* 5 vols. Paris, 1695–97.

Dubuisson. *Mémoire historique et généalogique sur la maison de Béthune.* Paris, 1739.

Du Chesne, André. *Histoire Généalogique de la maison de Béthune.* Paris, 1639.

————. *Histoire Généalogique de la maison de Vergy.* Paris, 1625.

Du Faur. *La Généalogie de la maison Du Faur, divisée en trois branches, ou trois chefs de famille.* Toulouse, 1649.

Du Paz, Augustin. *Généalogie de la maison de Molac.* Rennes, 1629.

Dupleix, Scipion. *Les Loix Militaires Touchant le Duel.* Paris, 1602.

Du Plessis. *Les vies de m. Jacques et Antoine de Chabannes, tous deux grands maîtres de France.* Paris, 1617.

Du Prat. *Le Portrait du maréchal de Gassion.* Paris, 1694.

Du Refuge, Eustache. *Traité de la Cour ou instruction des Courtisans.* Paris, 1658.

Feuquières, Antoine de Pas, marquis de. *Mémoires sur la guerre, où l'on a rassemblé les maximes les plus nécessaires dans les opérations de l'art militaire.* Amsterdam, 1730.

Flurance, David de Rivault de. *Les Etats, èsquels il est discouru du prince, du noble, et du tiers état.* Lyon, 1596.

Furetière, Antoine. *Dictionnaire universel.* The Hague and Rotterdam, 1690.

Généalogie de la Maison de Roquelaure. Paris, 1762.

Généalogie du Cardinal Mazarin. N.p., n.d.

La généalogie du premier président. Paris, 1652.

La généalogie du Prince, et comme tous ceux de cette maison ont été funestes au roi et au peuple. Paris, 1650.

Généalogie et Extraction de la vie de Jules Mazarin. N.p., 1649.

Généalogie historique et critique de la maison de La Rocheaymon. Paris, 1776.

Le Gentilhomme français, armé de toutes pièces pour le service du roy, adressé à Messieurs les Princes et autres Seigneurs de la Cour. N.p., 1649.

Grenaille, M. de. *L'Honneste Garçon, ou l'Art de bien Elever la Noblesse à la Vertu, aux Sciences, & à tous les exercices convenables à sa condition.* Paris, 1642.

Guibert, Hippolyte de. *Mémoire adressé au public et à l'armée sur les operations du Conseil de la Guerre.* N.p., n.d.

Guyon, Louis. *Diverses Leçons.* Lyon, 1617.

L'Hercule François. Harangue au Roy Pour la Noblesse de France en l'assemblée des Notables tenuë à Rouen. Par le Sieur D. B. N.p., n.d.

Histoire de Henry, duc de Rohan. Paris, 1666.

Hobbes, Thomas. *Leviathan.* London and New York, 1973.

Hozier, Louis-Pierre d', and A. M. d'Hozier de Sérigny. *Armorial Général ou Registres de la Noblesse de France.* 10 vols. Paris, 1738–68.

Hozier, Pierre d'. *Généalogie et alliances de la maison des sieurs de Larbour dite depuis de Combauld.* Paris, 1629.

Hutin, Pierre. *Généalogie de la très-grande, très-ancien [sic], et très-illustre maison de La Rochefoucauld.* N.p., 1654.

Isambert, François, et al. *Recueil général des anciennes loix françaises depuis l'an 426 jusqu'à la révolution de 1789.* 29 vols. Paris, 1822–33.

Journal de l'Assemblée de la Noblesse tenue à Paris l'année 1651. Paris, 1651.

Les Justes Raisons et Sentiments des Princes, des Grands, De Tous les Ordres & de tous les Corps de l'Etat, pour la dernière exclusion du Cardinal Mazarin. Paris, 1652.

La Béraudière, Marc de. *Le Combat de Seul a Seul en camp clos.* Paris, 1608.

La Bruyère, Jean de. *Les caractères; ou les moeurs de ce siècle.* Ed. Robert Garapon. Paris, 1962.

La Colombière, Marc Vulson de. *Généalogie de la maison de Rosmadec.* Paris, 1644.

―――. *Le Vray Théâtre d'Honneur et de Chevalerie ou le Miroir héroique de la Noblesse.* 2 vols. Paris, 1648.

La Coste, Henry de Montagu, sieur de. *La Descente généalogique depuis St. Louis de la maison royale de Bourbon; enrichie de l'histoire sommaire des faits, vies et morts de tous.* Paris, 1609.

L'Alouëte, François. *Des affaires d'estat, des finances, du prince et de sa noblesse.* Metz, 1597.

Lamont, Mr. de. *La Fonction de tous les officiers, depuis celle du sergent jusques à celle du colonel.* Paris, 1668.

La Mothe-Fénelon, François de Salignac de. *Les aventures de Télémaque, fils d'Ulysse*. Ed. Charles Le Brun. Philadelphia, 1834.

La Liberté de France et l'anéantissement des ministres étrangers. N.p., 1649.

La Noue, François de. *Discours politiques et militaires*. Lyon, 1599.

[La Rivière, H. F.] *Abrégé de la vie de M. de Courville, Colonel du Régiment d'Infanterie du Maine, & Brigadier des Armées du Roy*. Paris, 1719.

La Roque, Gilles André de. *Traité de la Noblesse, et de Toutes ses Différentes Espèces*. Paris, 1678.

La Primaudaye, Pierre de. *Academie Françoise*. Paris, 1580.

Laval, Antoine. *Desseins de professions nobles et publiques*. Paris, 1612.

Le Laboureur, Claude. *Histoire généalogique de la maison de Sainte-Colombe et autres maisons alliés*. Lyon, 1673.

Le Moyne, Pierre. *L'Art de Régner*. Paris, 1665.

Le Rebours, G. *Discours fait aux obsèques de Mgr de Medavy*. Rouen, 1618.

Lettre de M. le Marquis du P., à un gentilhomme de ses amis sur les études et sur la méthode de M. de Morbidi. Paris, 1707.

Lettre d'un gentilhomme écrite à un sien ami qui est à la Cour. N.p., 1651.

Louis XIV. *Mémoires, suivi de Réflexions sur le métier du roi, Instructions au duc d'Anjou, Projet de harangue*. Ed. Jean Longnon. 2 vols. Paris, 1923. Rev. ed., 2 vols. in 1. Paris, 1978.

Louvois, François-Michel Le Tellier, marquis de. *Testament Politique du marquis de Louvois*. 2 vols. in 1. Cologne, 1716.

Loyseau, Charles. *Traité des ordres et simples dignitez*. In *Les Oeuvres de Maistre Charles Loyseau, avocat en Parlement*. Lyon, 1701.

Malingre, Claude. *Eloge historique de la noble et illustre maison de Rantzow*. Paris, 1641.

———. *Histoire Chronologique de Plusieurs Grands Capitaines, Princes, Seigneurs, Magistrats, Officiers de la Couronne, et autres hommes illustres*. Paris, 1617.

Marois, Claude de. *Le Gentilhomme Parfaict ou tableau des excellences de la vraye noblesse: Avec l'institution des jeunes gentilshommes à la vertu*. Paris, 1631.

Mauroy, H. de. *Discours de la vie et faits héroiques de M. de La Valette, amiral de France, gouverneur . . . en Provence*. Metz, 1624.

Mavidal, M. J., M. E. Laurent et al., eds. *Archives Parlementaires de 1787 à 1860, première série (1787 à 1799)*. 97 vols. to date. Paris, 1867–.

Mayer, Charles J., ed. *Des Etats-Généraux et autres Assemblées Nationales*. 18 vols. Paris, 1788–89.

———. *Recueil des Cahiers Généraux des Trois Ordres aux Etats-Généraux*. 4 vols. Paris, 1789.

Mémoires à messieurs des Etats, pour parvenir à oster la vénalité des offices, tant de judicature que de finance, tirant gages de Sa Majesté. N.p., 1614.

Mondésir, Thiroux de, ed. *Ordonnances Militaires.* 33 vols. N.p., n.d.

Monluc, Blaise de. *Commentaires et Lettres de Blaise de Monluc, Maréchal de France.* Ed. Alphonse de Ruble. 5 vols. Paris, 1864–72.

Montchrétien, Antoine de. *Traicté de l'Oeconomie Politique, dedié en 1615 au Roy et a la Reyne Mere du Roy.* Ed. Th. Funck-Brentano. Paris, 1889.

Montesquieu, Charles-Louis de Secondat, baron de. *De l'esprit des lois.* 2 vols. Paris, 1979.

Paschal, Charles. *La vie et moeurs de m. Guy Du Faur, sr. de Pybrac.* Paris, 1617.

Pasquier, Nicolas. *Le Gentilhomme.* Paris, 1611.

[Pelletier, Claude]. *Discours sur la mort de feu M. de Souvré, Mal de France.* Paris, 1626.

———. *La nourriture de la noblesse où sont représentées comme en un tableau, toutes les plus belles vertus, qui peuvent accomplir un jeune gentilhomme.* Paris, 1604.

Perrault, Charles. *Les Hommes Illustres qui ont paru en France pendant ce siècle.* 2 vols. Paris, 1697.

Plainte de la noblesse française faite contre les Partisans & Mange-Peuples. N.p., 1651.

Le Politique étranger. Paris, 1649.

Pontis, Louis de. *Mémoires.* Collection des Mémoires Relatifs à l'Histoire de France, ed. M. Petitot, ser. 2, vol. 32. Paris, 1824.

Prefontaines, Sieur de. *Eloge de m. Henry de Matignon . . . Cte. de Thorigny . . . prononcé au parlement de Rouen, le 9 avril 1658.* N.p., [1658].

Pure, Abbé de. *La vie du Maréchal de Gassion.* Paris, 1673.

Remond des Cours, Nicolas. *La véritable politique des personnes de qualité.* Paris, 1692.

Requête de la noblesse pour l'Assemblée des Etats-Généraux. N.p., 1651.

Richelet, Pierre. *Dictionnaire Français tiré de l'usage et des meilleurs auteurs de la langue.* 2 vols. Geneva, 1679–80.

Richelieu, Jean Armand du Plessis, cardinal et duc de. *Testament Politique.* Ed. Louis André. Paris, 1947.

Rousseau, Jean-Jacques. *Oeuvres complètes de J. J. Rousseau.* Ed. V. D. Musset-Pathay. 22 vols. Paris, 1823–24.

Ruffi, Antoine de. *La vie de M. le chevalier de La Coste.* Aix, 1659.

Sainct-Julien, Pierre de. *Meslanges Historiques et Recueils de diverses matieres pour la plupart paradoxales, & neantmoins vrayes.* Lyon, 1588.

Saint-Simon, Louis de Rouvroy, duc de. *Louis XIV et sa Cour: Portraits, Jugemens et Anecdotes extraits des Mémoires Authentiques du duc de Saint-Simon.* Paris, 1863.

Sandras, Gatien de Courtilz, sieur de. *La conduite de Mars, Necessaire à tous ceux qui font profession des armes.* The Hague, 1685.

———. *Histoire du maréchal de Fabert.* Amsterdam, 1697.

Saumières, Jacques de Langlade, baron de. *Mémoires de la vie de Frédéric-Maurice de La Tour d'Auvergne, duc de Bouillon, avec quelques particularités de la vie et des moeurs de Henri de La Tour d'Auvergne, vicomte de Turenne.* Paris, 1692.

Sieyès, Emmanuel Joseph. *Essai sur les privilèges* [1789 ed.]. In vol. 1 of *Oeuvres de Sieyès.* 3 vols. Editions d'Histoire Sociale. Paris, 1989.

Savaron, Jean. *Traicté de l'Espee Françoise.* Paris, 1610.

Spanheim, Ezechiel. *Relation de la Cour de France en 1690.* Ed. Charles Schefer. Paris, 1882.

Le Tableau des tyrans favoris, et la description des malversations qu'ils commettent dans les Etats qu'ils gouvernent. Paris, 1649.

Thierriat, Florentin de. *Trois Traictez.* Paris, 1606.

Thiville, Nicolas de. *Généalogie générale de la noble, ancienne, et illustre maison de Thiville.* Paris, 1662.

Torsay, [H.T.S.] de. *La vie, mort, et tombeau de Philippe de Strozzi . . . où par occasion se voit la bonne et généreuse nourriture de la jeune noblesse française, sous les roys Henry et François second, pendant son bas aage et plusieurs notables points de l'histoire de nostre temps non touchez, ou si particulièrement déduis ailleurs.* Paris, 1608.

Très-humbles Remonstrances Faites au Roy. Paris, 1651.

Trotti de la Chétardie. *Instructions pour un jeune seigneur, ou l'idée d'un galant homme.* 2 vols. Paris, 1702. First edition published in 1683.

Turquet de Mayerne, Louis. *La Monarchie Aristodemocratique.* Paris, 1611.

V., F. F. P. de. *Tableau Historique, dans lequel sont contenus quelques remarques d'Etat: Et comment le Roy a fait Monsieur le Mal de Lesdiguières, Connétable de France.* N.p., 1623.

Vanière, M. *Discours sur l'éducation.* Paris, 1760.

Vauban, Sebastien Le Prestre, maréchal de. *Méthode Générale et facile pour faire le dénombrement des peuples.* Paris, 1686.

———. *Oisivetés.* 2 vols. Ed. Antoine-Marie Augoyat. Paris, 1842–45.

———. "Pensées et mémoires politiques inédits de Vauban, recueillis par A. de Rochas d'Aiglun." *Journal des Économistes* 18 (1882): 169–95, 329–42.

Vauréal, Cte. de. *Plan ou Essai d'Education Général et National.* Bouillon, 1783.

La véritable conduite du courtisan généreux. Paris, 1649.

La Vie de Jean-Baptiste Colbert. Cologne, 1695.

La Vie, moeurs, et généalogie de Jules Mazarin, où se voient les banqueroutes de son père. N.p., n.d.

Secondary Sources

André, Louis. *Michel Le Tellier et l'Organisation de l'Armée Monarchique.* Paris, 1906. Reprint, Geneva, 1980.

———. *Michel Le Tellier et Louvois.* Paris, 1942. Reprint, Geneva, 1974.

Anisimov, Evgenii. *The Reforms of Peter the Great: Progress through Coercion in Russia.* Trans. John T. Alexander. Armonk, N.Y., and London, 1993.

Antoine, Michel. *Le Conseil du Roi sous le Règne de Louis XV.* Geneva, 1970.

———. *Louis XV.* Paris, 1989.

———. "La Monarchie Absolue." In *The Political Culture of the Old Regime,* ed. Keith M. Baker, 3–24. New York, 1987.

Ariès, Philippe. *Centuries of Childhood: A Social History of Family Life.* Trans. Robert Baldick. New York, 1962.

Aston, Trevor, ed. *Crisis in Europe, 1550–1660.* New York, 1965.

Avenel, Vicomte d'. *La Noblesse Française sous Richelieu.* Paris, 1901.

Aylmer, G. E. *The King's Servants: The Civil Service of Charles I, 1625–1642.* New York and London, 1961.

Baker, Keith M. "Defining the Public Sphere in Eighteenth-Century France: Variations on a Theme by Habermas." In *Habermas and the Public Sphere.* ed. Craig Calhoun, 181–211. Cambridge, Mass., 1992.

———. *Inventing the French Revolution.* Cambridge, 1990.

———, ed. *The Old Regime and the French Revolution.* Chicago, 1987.

———. *The Political Culture of the Old Regime.* Vol. 1 of *The French Revolution and the Creation of Modern Political Culture.* 3 vols. New York, 1987–89.

Barker, Thomas M. *The Military Intellectual and Battle: Raimondo Montecuccoli and the Thirty Years War.* Albany, N.Y., 1975.

Bayard, Françoise. *Le Monde des Financiers au XVIIᵉ siècle.* Paris, 1988.

Béchu, Philippe. "Noblesse d'épée et tradition militaire au 18ᵉ siècle." *Histoire, Economie, et Société* 2 (1983): 507–48.

Becker, Marvin. *Civility and Society in Western Europe, 1300–1600.* Bloomington, Ind., 1988.

———. *Medieval Italy: Constraints and Creativity.* Bloomington, Ind., 1981.

Beik, William. *Absolutism and Society in Seventeenth-Century France: State Power and Provincial Aristocracy in Languedoc.* Cambridge, 1985.

———. "Celebrating Andrew Lossky: The Reign of Louis XIV Revisited." *French Historical Studies* 17 (1991): 526–41.

Bell, David. *Lawyers and Citizens: The Making of a Political Elite in Old Regime France.* Oxford, 1994.

Bergin, Joseph. *Cardinal Richelieu: Power and the Pursuit of Wealth.* New Haven, 1985.

———. *The Rise of Richelieu.* New Haven, 1991.

Bien, David D. "The Army in the French Enlightenment: Reform, Reaction, and Revolution." *Past and Present* 85 (1979): 68–98.

———. "Manufacturing Nobles: The Chancelleries in France to 1789." *Journal of Modern History* 61 (1989): 445–86.

———. "Military Education in Eighteenth-Century France: Technical and Non-Technical Determinants." In *Science, Technology, and Warfare. Proceedings of the Third Military History Symposium, U.S. Air Force Academy, 8–9 May 1969*, ed. Monte D. Wright and Lawrence J. Paszek, 51–59. Washington, 1971.

———. "Offices, Corps, and a System of State Credit: The Uses of Privilege under the Ancien Régime." In *The Political Culture of the Old Regime*, ed. Keith M. Baker, 89–114. New York, 1987.

———. "La réaction aristocratique avant 1789: L'exemple de l'armée." *Annales, E. S. C.* 29 (1974): 23–48, 505–34.

———. "The 'Secrétaires du Roi': Absolutism, Corps, and Privilege under the Ancien Régime." In *Vom Ancien Régime zur Französischen Revolution: Forschungen und Perspektiven*, ed. Albert Cremer, 153–68. Göttingen, 1978.

Billacois, François. "La Crise de la Noblesse Européene (1550–1650): Une Mise au Point." *Revue d'Histoire Moderne et Contemporaine* 23 (1976): 258–77.

———. *The Duel: Its Rise and Fall in Early-Modern France*. Trans. and ed. Trista Selous. New Haven, 1990.

Bitton, Davis. *The French Nobility in Crisis, 1560–1640*. Stanford, 1969.

Bloch, Jean-Richard. *L'anoblissement en France au Temps de François Ier: Essai d'une définition de la condition juridique et sociale de la noblesse au début du XVIe siècle*. Paris, 1934.

Bluche, François. *Les Honneurs de la cour*. 2 vols. Paris, 1957.

———. *Louis XIV*. Trans. Mark Greengrass. New York, 1990.

———. *Les pages de la grande écurie*. 3 vols. Paris, 1966.

Bohanan, Donna. *Old and New Nobility in Aix-en-Provence: Portrait of an Urban Elite*. Baton Rouge and London, 1992.

Bonney, Richard. "Absolutism: What's in a Name?" *French History* 1 (1987): 93–117.

———. *The King's Debts: Finance and Politics in France, 1589–1661*. Oxford, 1981.

———. *Political Change under Richelieu and Mazarin, 1624–1661*. Oxford, 1978.

———. *Society and Government in France under Richelieu and Mazarin, 1624–1661*. New York, 1988.

Bossenga, Gail. *The Politics of Privilege: Old Regime and Revolution in Lille*. Cambridge, 1991.

Bourdieu, Pierre. *Le Sens Pratique*. Paris, 1980.

Briggs, Robin. *Early Modern France, 1560–1715*. Oxford, 1977.

Brocher, Henri. *A La Cour de Louis XIV: Le Rang et l'Etiquette sous l'Ancien Régime.* Paris, 1934.

Brunelle, Gayle K. "Dangerous Liaisons: Mésalliance and Early Modern French Noblewomen." *French Historical Studies* 19 (1995): 75–103.

Burke, Peter. *The Fabrication of Louis XIV.* New Haven and London, 1992.

Carmona, Michel. *Richelieu: L'Ambition et le Pouvoir.* Paris, 1983.

Carné, Gaston. *Les pages des écuries du roi: L'Ecole des pages.* Nantes, 1886.

Carré, Henri. *La Noblesse Française et l'Opinion Publique au XVIIIe siècle.* Paris, 1920.

Censer, Jack, and Jeremy Popkin, eds. *Press and Politics in Pre-Revolutionary France.* Berkeley, 1987.

Chalmin, Pierre. "La Désintégration de l'armée royale en France à la fin du XVIIIe siècle." *Revue Historique de l'Armée* 1 (1964): 75–90.

Chartier, Roger. *Cultural History: Between Practices and Representations.* Trans. Lydia G. Cochrane. Ithaca, N.Y., 1988.

———. *The Cultural Origins of the French Revolution.* Trans. Lydia G. Cochrane. Durham, N.C., 1991.

———. *The Cultural Uses of Print in Early-Modern France.* Trans. Lydia G. Cochrane. Princeton, 1987.

———. "La noblesse et les Etats de 1614: Une réaction aristocratique?" In *Représentation et Vouloir Politiques: Autour des états-généraux de 1614,* ed. Roger Chartier and Denis Richet, 113–25. Paris, 1982.

———, ed. *Lectures et lecteurs dans la France d'Ancien Régime.* Paris, 1987.

———. *Pratiques de la lecture.* Marseilles, 1985.

Chartier, Roger, Madeleine Compère, and Dominique Julia. *L'Education en France du XVIe au XVIIIe siècles.* Paris, 1976.

Chartier, Roger, and Henri-Jean Martin, eds. *Histoire de l'édition française.* Vol. 2, *Le Livre triomphant, 1660–1830.* Paris, 1984.

Chaussinand-Nogaret, Guy. *La Noblesse au XVIIIe siècle: De la féodalité aux lumières.* Brussels, 1984. First edition published in Paris, 1976. Translated into English by William Doyle in *The French Nobility in the Eighteenth Century: From Feudalism to Enlightenment* (Cambridge, 1985).

Childs, John. *Armies and Warfare in Europe: 1648–1789.* Manchester, 1982.

Church, William F. *Constitutional Thought in Sixteenth-Century France.* Cambridge, Mass., 1941.

———. "France." In *National Consciousness, History, and Political Culture in Early-Modern Europe,* ed. Orest Ranum, 43–66. Baltimore, 1975.

———. *Richelieu and Reason of State.* Princeton, 1972.

Clément, Pierre. *La Police sous Louis XIV.* Paris, 1866.

Cole, Charles W. *Colbert and a Century of French Mercantilism.* 2 vols. New York, 1939.

———. *French Mercantilist Doctrines before Colbert.* New York, 1931.

Collins, James. *Fiscal Limits of Absolutism: Direct Taxation in Early-Seventeenth Century France.* Berkeley, 1988.

———. "Sur L'Histoire Fiscale du XVIIe siècle: Les impôts directs en Champagne entre 1595 et 1635." *Annales E. S. C.* 34 (1979): 325–47.

Conrads, Norbert. *Ritterakademien der Frühen Neuzeit.* Göttingen, 1982.

Constant, Jean-Marie. *Les Conjurateurs: Le premier libéralisme politique sous Richelieu.* Paris, 1987.

———. "L'Enquête de Noblesse de 1667 et les Seigneurs de Beauce." *Revue d'Histoire Moderne et Contemporaine* 21 (1974): 548–66.

———. *Nobles et paysans en Beauce aux XVIe et XVIIe siècles.* Paris, 1981.

———. "Les Structures sociales et mentales de l'anoblissement: Analyse comparative d'études récentes, 15e–17e siècles." In *L'Anoblissement en France, XVe–XVIIIe siècles,* Centre de Recherche sur les Origines de l'Europe Moderne, Université de Bordeaux 3, 37–67. Bordeaux, 1985.

———. "La Troisième Fronde: Les Gentilshommes et les Libertés Nobiliaires." *XVIIe Siècle* 36 (1984): 341–54.

———. *La Vie Quotidienne de la Noblesse Française aux XVIe et XVIIe siècles.* Paris, 1985.

Corvisier, André. *L'armée française de la fin du XVIIe siècle au ministère de Choiseul: Le soldat.* 2 vols. Paris, 1964.

———. *Armies and Societies in Europe, 1494–1789.* Trans. Abigail T. Siddall. Bloomington, Ind., 1979.

———. "Les généraux de Louis XIV et leur origine sociale." *XVIIe Siècle* 42–43 (1959): 23–53.

———. *Louvois.* Paris, 1983.

———. "La Noblesse Militaire: Aspects militaires de la noblesse française du 15e au 18e siècles." *Histoire Sociale/Social History* 22 (1978): 336–55.

Corvisier, André, et al., eds. *Histoire Militaire de la France.* 3 vols. Paris, 1992.

Cubells, Monique. "A propos des usurpations de noblesse en Provence, sous l'Ancien Régime." *Provence Historique* 20 (1970): 226–301.

———. *La Provence des Lumières: Les parlementaires d'Aix au XVIIIe siècle.* Paris, 1984.

Davis, Natalie Zemon. "Beyond the Market: Books as Gifts in Sixteenth-Century France." *Transactions of the Royal Historical Society,* 5th ser., 33 (1983): 69–88.

———. "A Renaissance Text to the Historian's Eye: The Gifts of Montaigne." *Journal of Medieval and Renaissance Studies* 15 (1985): 47–56.

Decouflé, André. "L'Aristocratie Française devant l'Opinion Publique à la veille de la Révolution." In André Decouflé, François Boulanger, and Bernard-André Pierrelle, *Etudes d'histoire économique et sociale du XVIIIe siècle.* Paris, 1966.

Dent, Julian. *Crisis in Finance: Crown, Financiers, and Society in Seventeenth-Century France.* New York, 1973.

———. "The Role of *Clientèles* in the Financial Elite of France under Cardinal Mazarin." In *French Government and Society, 1500–1800: Essays in Memory of Alfred Cobban,* ed. John Bosher, 41–69. London, 1973.

Deschard, Bernard. *L'Armée et la Révolution: Du service du roi au service de la nation.* Paris, 1989.

Dessert, Daniel. *Argent, Pouvoir et Société au Grand Siècle.* Paris, 1984.

———. *Fouquet.* Paris, 1987.

Dessert, Daniel, and Jean-Louis Journet. "Le Lobby Colbert: Un royaume, ou une affaire de famille?" *Annales, E. S. C.* 30 (1975): 1303–36.

Dethan, Georges. *Gaston d'Orléans: Conspirateur et prince charmant.* Paris, 1959.

Devyver, André. *Le Sang Epuré: Les Préjugés de race chez les gentilshommes français de l'ancien régime, 1560–1720.* Brussels, 1973.

Dewald, Jonathan. *Aristocratic Experience and the Origins of Modern Culture: France, 1570–1715.* Berkeley, 1993.

———. *The Formation of a Provincial Nobility: The Magistrates of the Parlement of Rouen, 1499–1610.* Princeton, 1980.

Deyon, Pierre. "A propos les rapports entre la noblesse française et la monarchie absolue." *Revue Historique* 231 (1964): 341–56.

Dosher, Harry Randall. "The Concept of the Ideal Prince in French Political Thought, 800–1760." Ph.D. diss., University of North Carolina, 1969.

Doyle, William. "The Price of Offices in Pre-Revolutionary France." *Historical Journal* 27 (1984): 831–60.

Dravasa, Etienne. *Vivre noblement, recherches sur la dérogeance de noblesse du 14e au 16e siècles.* Bordeaux, 1965.

Duby, Georges. *The Early Growth of the European Economy: Warriors and Peasants from the Seventh to the Twelfth Century.* Trans. Howard B. Clarke. Ithaca, N.Y., 1984.

———. *Les trois ordres ou l'imaginaire du féodalisme.* Paris, 1978.

Durand, Yves, ed. *Hommage à Roland Mousnier: Clientèles et fidélités en Europe à l'Epoque Moderne.* Paris, 1981.

Elias, Norbert. *The Court Society.* Trans. Edmund Jephcott. New York, 1983.

Ellis, Harold A. *Boulainvilliers and the French Monarchy: Aristocratic Politics in Early-Eighteenth Century France.* Ithaca, N.Y., 1988.

———. "Genealogy, History, and Aristocratic Reaction in Early-Eighteenth Century France: The Case of Henri de Boulainvilliers." *Journal of Modern History* 58 (1986): 414–51.

Fagniez, Gustave. "Fancan et Richelieu." Pts. 1 and 2. *Revue Historique* 107 (1911): 59–78; 108 (1911): 75–87.

———. "L'Opinion publique et la presse politique sous Louis XIII, 1624–1626." *Revue d'Histoire Diplomatique* 14 (1900): 352–401.

Falk, Joyce Duncan. "The Concept of the Ideal Prince in the Literature of the French Enlightenment, 1700–1780." Ph.D. diss., University of Southern California, 1969.

Fogel, Michèle. *Les cérémonies de l'information dans la France du XVIe au milieu du XVIIIe siècle.* Paris, 1989.

Forster, Robert. *The Nobility of Toulouse in the Eighteenth Century: A Social and Economic Study.* Baltimore, 1960.

———. *The House of Saulx-Tavanes: Versailles and Burgundy 1700–1830.* Baltimore, 1971.

Foucault, Michel. *Discipline and Punish: The Birth of the Prison.* Trans. Alan Sheridan. New York, 1979.

———. *The Order of Things: An Archaeology of the Human Sciences.* Vintage Books ed. New York, 1973.

———. *Power/Knowledge: Selected Interviews and Other Writings, 1972–1977.* Ed. Colin Gordon. New York, 1980.

Fréville, Henri. "Notes sur les subdélégués généraux et subdélégués de l'intendance de Bretagne au XVIIIe siècle." *Revue d'Histoire Moderne* 12 (1937): 408–38.

Geertz, Clifford. *The Interpretation of Cultures.* New York, 1973.

Giesey, Ralph E. "The King Imagined." In *The Political Culture of the Old Regime,* ed. Keith M. Baker, 41–60. New York, 1987.

———. *The Royal Funeral Ceremony in Renaissance France.* Geneva, 1960.

———. "Rules of Inheritance and Strategies of Mobility in Prerevolutionary France." *American Historical Review* 82 (1977): 271–89.

———. "State Building in Early Modern France: The Role of Royal Officialdom." *Journal of Modern History* 55 (1983): 191–207.

Godard, Charles. *Les pouvoirs des intendants sous Louis XV.* Paris, 1901.

Goodman, Dena. "Public Sphere and Private Life: Toward a Synthesis of Current Historiographical Approaches to the Old Regime." *History and Theory* 31 (1992): 1–20.

Gordon, Daniel. *Citizens without Sovereignty: Equality and Sociability in French Thought, 1670–1789.* Princeton, 1994.

Gossman, Lionel. *Medievalism and the Ideologies of the Enlightenment: The World and Work of La Curne de Sainte-Palaye.* Baltimore, 1968.

Gouldner, Alvin W. "The Norm of Reciprocity: A Preliminary Statement." *American Sociological Review* 25 (1960): 161–78.

Grinberg, Martine. "La Culture Populaire comme Enjeu: Rituels et Pouvoirs (XIVe–XVIIe siècles)." In *Culture et Idéologie dans la Genèse de l'Etat Moderne: Actes de la table ronde organisée par le Centre national de la recherche scientifique et l'Ecole française de Rome (Rome, 15–17 octobre, 1984),* 381–92. Rome, 1985.

Gruder, Vivian R. *The Royal Provincial Intendants: A Governing Elite in Eighteenth-Century France.* Ithaca, N.Y., 1968.

Guéry, Alain. "Le Roi Dépensier: Le don, la contrainte, et l'origine du système financier de la monarchie française d'Ancien Régime." *Annales, E. S. C.* 39 (1984): 1241–69.

Habermas, Jürgen. *The Structural Transformation of the Public Sphere: An Inquiry into a Category of Bourgeois Society.* Trans. Thomas Burger and Frederick Lawrence. Cambridge, Mass., 1989.

Halkin, Léon. "Pour une histoire d'honneur." *Annales, E. S. C.* 4 (1949): 434–44.

Hamscher, Albert N. *The Conseil Privé and the Parlements: A Study in French Absolutism.* Philadelphia, 1987.

———. *The Parlement of Paris after the Fronde, 1653–1673.* Pittsburgh, 1976.

Hanley, Sarah. "Engendering the State: Family Formation and State Building in Early Modern France." *French Historical Studies* 16 (1989): 4–28.

———. *The "Lit de Justice" of the Kings of France: Constitutional Ideology in Legend, Ritual, and Discourse.* Princeton, 1983.

Harding, Robert. *Anatomy of a Power Elite: The Provincial Governors of Early-Modern France.* New Haven, 1978.

Harth, Erica. *Ideology and Culture in Seventeenth-Century France.* Princeton, 1983.

Hayden, J. Michael. *France and the Estates General of 1614.* Cambridge, 1974.

Heal, Felicity. "The Idea of Hospitality in Early-Modern England." *Past and Present* 102 (1984): 66–93.

Hebbert, F. J., and G. A. Rothrock. *Soldier of France: Sebastien le Prestre de Vauban, 1633–1707.* American University Studies, ser. 9, History, vol. 51. New York, 1989.

Heinrich, Natalie. "Arts et sciences à l'age classique: Professions et institutions culturelles." *Actes de la Recherche en sciences sociales* 67/68 (1987): 47–78.

Hennet, L. *Les compagnies de cadets gentilshommes et les écoles militaires.* Paris, 1889.

Herman, Arthur L. "The Language of Fidelity in Early-Modern France." *Journal of Modern History* 67 (1995): 1–24.

Herr, Richard. "Honor versus Absolutism: Richelieu's Fight against Dueling." *Journal of Modern History* 27 (1955): 281–85.

Hickey, Daniel. *The Coming of French Absolutism: The Struggle for Tax Reform in the Province of Dauphiné, 1540–1640.* Toronto, 1986.

Holt, Mack P. *The Duke of Anjou and the Politique Struggle during the Wars of Religion.* Cambridge, 1986.

———. "Patterns of *Clientèle* and Economic Opportunity at Court during the

Wars of Religion: The Household of Francois, Duke of Anjou." *French Historical Studies* 13 (1984): 305–22.

Homans, George C. "Social Behavior as Exchange." *American Journal of Sociology* 63 (1958): 597–608.

Hunt, Lynn. "French History in the Last Twenty Years: The Rise and Fall of the *Annales* Paradigm." *Journal of Contemporary History* 21 (1986): 209–24.

Huppert, George. *Les Bourgeois Gentilshommes: An Essay on the Definition of Elites in Renaissance France*. Chicago, 1977.

Jay, Martin. *Downcast Eyes: The Denigration of Vision in Twentieth-Century French Thought*. Berkeley, 1993.

Jouanna, Arlette. *Le Devoir de Révolte: La noblesse française et la gestation de l'Etat moderne (1559–1661)*. Paris, 1989.

———. "Les Gentilshommes Français et leur rôle politique dans la seconde moitié du XVIᵉ et au début du XVIIᵉ siècle." *Il Pensiero Politico* 10 (1977): 22–40.

———. "Des 'Gros et Gras' aux 'Gens d'Honneur'." In Guy Chaussinand-Nogaret, ed., *Histoire des élites en France du XVIe au XXe siècle: l'honneur, le mérite, l'argent*, 17–141. Paris, 1991.

———. *L'Idée de Race en France au XVIᵉ siècle et au début du XVIIᵉ siècle (1498–1614)*. 3 vols. Paris, 1976.

———. "Perception et appréciation de l'anoblissement dans la France du XVIᵉ siècle et au début du XVIIᵉ siècle." In *L'Anoblissement en France XVᵉ–XVIIIᵉ siècles*, Centre de Recherches sur les Origines de l'Europe Moderne, Université de Bordeaux 3, 1–36. Bordeaux, 1985.

———. "Recherche sur la Notion d'Honneur au XVIᵉ siècle." *Revue d'Histoire Moderne et Contemporaine* 15 (1968): 597–623.

Jouhaud, Christian. *Mazarinades: La Fronde des mots*. Paris, 1985.

Kaiser, Thomas. "The Abbé de Saint-Pierre, Public Opinion, and the Reconstitution of the French Monarchy." *Journal of Modern History* 55 (1983): 618–43.

Kamen, Henry. *European Society, 1500–1700*. London, 1984.

Kantorovicz, Ernst. *The King's Two Bodies: A Study in Mediaeval Political Theology*. Princeton, 1957.

Kelly, George Armstrong. *Mortal Politics in Eighteenth-Century France*. *Historical Reflections/Réflexions Historiques* 13, no. 1 (spring 1986).

Kennett, Lee. *The French Armies in the Seven Years' War: A Study in Military Organization and Administration*. Durham, N.C., 1967.

Keohane, Nannerl. *Philosophy and the State in France: The Renaissance to the Enlightenment*. Princeton, 1980.

Kettering, Sharon. "The Causes of the Judicial Frondes." *Canadian Journal of History* 17 (1982): 275–306.

———. "Gift-Giving and Patronage in Early-Modern France." *French History* 2 (1988): 131–51.

———. "The Historical Development of Political Clientelism." *Journal of Interdisciplinary History* 18 (1988): 419–48.

———. *Judicial Politics and Urban Revolt in Seventeenth-Century France: The Parlement of Aix, 1629–1659.* Princeton, 1978.

———. "Patronage and Politics during the Fronde." *French Historical Studies* 14 (1986): 409–41.

———. *Patrons, Brokers, and Clients in Seventeenth-Century France.* Oxford, 1986.

King, James E. *Science and Rationalism in the Government of Louis XIV, 1661–1683.* Baltimore, 1949.

Klaits, Joseph. "Men of Letters and Political Reform in France at the End of the Reign of Louis XIV: The Founding of the Académie Politique." *Journal of Modern History* 43 (1971): 577–97.

———. *Printed Propaganda under Louis XIV: Absolute Monarchy and Public Opinion.* Princeton, 1976.

Kossman, Ernst. *La Fronde.* Leiden, 1954.

La Bigne de Villeneuve, Marcel de. *La Dérogeance de la noblesse sous l'Ancien Régime.* Paris, 1971.

Langer, Ullrich. "Merit in Courtly Literature: Castiglione, Rabelais, Marguerite de Navarre, and Le Caron." *Renaissance Quarterly* 41 (1988): 218–41.

Latreille, Albert. *L'Armée et la nation à la fin de l'ancien régime: Les derniers ministres de la guerre de la monarchie.* Paris, 1914.

Laulan, Robert. "Pourquoi et comment on entrait à l'Ecole royale et militaire de Paris." *Revue d'Histoire Moderne et Contemporaine* 4 (1957): 141–50.

Leclercq, Henri. *Histoire de la Régence pendant la minorité de Louis XV.* 3 vols. Paris, 1921.

Lemoine, H. "Les écuries du roi sous l'Ancien Régime." *Revue de l'Histoire de Versailles* 35 (1933): 150–83.

Léonard, E. G. *L'armée et ses problèmes au XVIIIᵉ siècle.* Paris, 1958.

Le Roy Ladurie, Emmanuel. "Rangs et Hiérarchie dans la vie de cour." In *The Political Culture of the Old Regime,* ed. Keith M. Baker, 61–75. New York, 1987.

Levantal, Christophe. "La Noblesse au 17ᵉ siècle: la robe contre l'épée?" Pts. 1 and 2. *La Science Historique* 14 (1985): 8–16; 15 (1986): 3–20.

Lewis, W. H. *The Splendid Century: Life in the France of Louis XIV.* New York, 1957.

Livet, Georges. *Les Guerres de Religion.* Paris, 1962.

Lossky, Andrew. "The Absolutism of Louis XIV: Reality or Myth?" *Canadian Journal of History* 19 (1984): 1–15.

———. *Louis XIV and the French Monarchy.* New Brunswick, N.J., 1994.

Lougee, Carolyn C. *"Le Paradis des Femmes"*: *Women, Salons, and Social Stratification in Seventeenth-Century France.* Princeton, 1976.

Lux, David. *Patronage and Royal Science in Seventeenth-Century France.* Ithaca, N.Y., 1989.

Lynn, John. *Bayonets of the Republic: Motivation and Tactics in the Army of Revolutionary France, 1791–94.* Urbana and Chicago, 1984.

———. "The Growth of the French Army during the Seventeenth Century." *Armed Forces and Society* 6 (1980): 568–85.

———. "Tactical Evolution in the French Army, 1560–1660," *French Historical Studies* 14 (1985): 176–91.

Mai, Ekkehard. *Le portrait du roi: Staatsporträt and Kuntstheorie in der Epoche Ludwigs XIV.* Bonn, 1975.

Major, James Russell. "Bastard Feudalism and the Kiss: Changing Social Mores in Late-Medieval and Early-Modern France." *Journal of Interdisciplinary History* 17 (1987): 509–35.

———. "The Crown and Aristocracy in Renaissance France." *American Historical Review* 69 (1964): 631–45.

———. *From Renaissance Monarchy to Absolute Monarchy: French Kings, Nobles, and Estates.* Baltimore, 1994.

———. "Noble Income, Inflation, and the Wars of Religion." *American Historical Review* 86 (1981): 21–48.

———. *Representative Government in Early Modern France.* New Haven, 1980.

———. "The Revolt of 1620: A Study of Ties of Fidelity." *French Historical Studies* 14 (1986): 391–408.

Marin, Louis. *Portrait of the King.* Trans. Martha M. Houle. Theory and History of Literature, vol. 57. Minneapolis, 1988.

Marion, Marcel. *Dictionnaire des Institutions de la France aux XVIIe et XVIIIe siècles.* 1923. Reprint, Paris, 1984.

Martin, Ronald. "The Army of Louis XIV." In *The Reign of Louis XIV,* ed. Paul Sonnino, 111–26. Atlantic Highlands, N.J., 1990.

Maumené, Charles, and Louis d'Harcourt. *Iconographie des Rois de France.* Vol. 2. Paris, 1932.

Mauss, Marcel. *The Gift: Forms and Functions of Exchange in Archaic Societies.* Trans. Ian Cunnison. Glencoe, Ill., 1954.

Maza, Sarah. *Private Lives and Public Affairs: The Causes Célèbres of Prerevolutionary France.* Berkeley, 1993.

———. "Women, the Bourgeoisie, and the Public Sphere: Response to Daniel Gordon and David Bell." *French Historical Studies* 17 (1992): 935–53.

Meehan-Waters, Brenda. *Autocracy and Aristocracy: The Russian Service Elite of 1730.* New Brunswick, N.J., 1982.

Megill, Allan. "The Reception of Foucault by Historians." *Journal of the History of Ideas* 48 (1987): 117–41.

Merrick, Jeffrey. "The Cardinal and the Queen: Sexual and Political Disorders in the Mazarinades." *French Historical Studies* 18 (1994): 667–99.

Méthivier, Hubert. *La Fronde.* Paris, 1984.

Mettam, Roger. *Power and Faction in Louis XIV's France.* London, 1988.

Meyer, Jean. *La Noblesse Bretonne au XVIIIe siècle.* Paris, 1972.

Morgan, Edmund. *The Puritan Family.* New York, 1966.

Moote, A. Lloyd. "The French Crown versus its Judicial and Financial Officials, 1615–1683." *Journal of Modern History* 34 (1962): 146–60.

———. *Louis XIII, The Just.* Berkeley, 1989.

———. *The Revolt of the Judges: The Parlement of Paris and the Fronde, 1643–1652.* Princeton, 1971.

Motley, Mark. *Becoming a French Aristocrat: The Education of the Court Nobility, 1580–1715.* Princeton, 1990.

Mousnier, Roland. *The Assassination of Henry IV: The Tyrannicide Problem and the Consolidation of the French Absolute Monarchy in the Early Seventeenth Century.* Trans. Joan Spencer. London, 1973.

———. "Les concepts d'"ordres,' d''états,' de 'fidélité,' et de 'monarchie absolue' en France de la fin du XVe siècle à la fin du XVIIIe." *Revue Historique* 247 (1972): 289–312.

———. "Les fidélités et les clientèles en France au XVIe, XVIIe et XVIIIe siècles." *Histoire Sociale* 15 (1982): 35–46.

———. *The Institutions of France under the Absolute Monarchy.* Trans. Brian Pearce. 2 vols. Chicago, 1979–84.

———. "L'Opposition Politique Bourgeoise à la fin du XVIe siècle et au Début du XVIIe siècle: L'Oeuvre de Louis Turquet de Mayerne." *Revue Historique* 213 (1955): 1–20.

———. "Les Survivances Médiévales dans la France du XVIIe siècle." *XVIIe Siècle* 106–7 (1975): 59–76.

———. *La Vénalité des Offices sous Henri IV et Louis XIII.* Paris, 1945.

Mousnier, Roland, and Fritz Hartung. "Quelques problèmes concernant la monarchie absolue." In *Relazione del X congresso internazionale de scienze storiche,* 1:1–55. Florence, 1955.

Neuschel, Kristen B. *Word of Honor: Interpreting Noble Culture in Sixteenth-Century France.* Ithaca, N.Y., 1989.

O'Brien, Patricia. "Foucault's History of Culture." In *The New Cultural History,* ed. Lynn Hunt, 25–46. Berkeley, 1989.

Oestreich, Gerhard. *Neostoicism and the Early Modern State.* Trans. David McLintock. Cambridge, 1982.

Ozouf, Mona. "L'Opinion Publique." In *The Political Culture of the Old Regime,* ed. Keith M. Baker, 419–34. Oxford, 1987.

Pagès, Georges. "Autour du grand orage: Richelieu et Marillac, deux politiques." *Revue Historique* 179 (1937): 63–97.

Palmer, R. R. *The Improvement of Humanity: Education and the French Revolution.* Princeton, 1985.

Parker, David. "Sovereignty, Absolutism, and the Function of the Law in Seventeenth-Century France." *Past and Present* 122 (1989): 36–74.

Parker, Geoffrey. "The 'Military Revolution' 1560–1660—A Myth?" *Journal of Modern History* 28 (1976): 195–214.

———. *The Military Revolution: Military Innovation and the Rise of the West, 1500–1800.* Cambridge, 1988.

Peck, Linda Levy. " 'For a king not to be bountiful were a fault': Perspectives on Court Patronage in Early Stuart England." *Journal of British Studies* 25 (1986): 31–61.

"Pour une Histoire Anthropologique: La Notion de Réciprocité." *Annales, E. S. C.* 29 (1974): 1309–80.

Racinais, Henry. *Un Versailles inconnu: Les petits appartements des roys Louis XV et Louis XVI au château de Versailles.* Paris, 1950.

Raeff, Marc. *The Well-Ordered Police State: Social and Institutional Change through Law in the Germanies and Russia, 1600–1800.* New Haven, 1983.

Ranum, Orest. *Artisans of Glory: Writers and Historical Thought in Seventeenth-Century France.* Chapel Hill, 1980.

———. "Courtesy, Absolutism, and the Rise of the French State." *Journal of Modern History* 52 (1980): 426–51.

———. *The Fronde: A French Revolution, 1648–1652.* New York, 1993.

———. *Richelieu and the Councillors of Louis XIII: A Study of the Secretaries of State and Superintendents of Finance in the Ministry of Richelieu, 1635–1642.* Oxford, 1963.

———. "Richelieu and the Great Nobility: Some Aspects of Early Modern Political Motives." *French Historical Studies* 3 (1963–64): 184–204.

———, ed. *National Consciousness, History, and Political Culture in Early-Modern Europe.* Baltimore, 1975.

Reinhard, Marcel. "Elite et Noblesse dans la seconde moitié du XVIIIᵉ siècle." *Revue d'Histoire Moderne et Contemporaine* 3 (1956): 5–38.

Riccomard, Julien. "Les subdélégués des intendants aux XVIIᵉ et XVIIIᵉ siècles." *L'Information Historique* 24 (1962): 139–48.

———. "Les subdélégués des intendants jusqu'à leur élection en titre d'office." *Revue d'Histoire Moderne* 12 (1937): 338–407.

Richet, Denis. "Autour des origines lointaines de la Révolution française: Elites et Despotisme." *Annales, E. S. C.* 24 (1969): 1–23.

———. *La France moderne: L'esprit des institutions.* Paris, 1973.

Roberts, Michael. *The Military Revolution, 1560–1660.* Belfast, 1956.

Roche, Daniel. *Le siècle des lumières en province: Académies et académiciens provinciaux, 1680–1789.* 2 vols. Paris and The Hague, 1978.

Rosenberg, Hans. *Bureaucracy, Aristocracy, and Autocracy: The Prussian Experience, 1660–1815.* Cambridge, Mass., 1958.

Rothkrug, Lionel. *Opposition to Louis XIV: The Political and Social Origins of the French Enlightenment.* Princeton, 1965.

Saffroy, Gaston. *Bibliographie Généalogique, Héraldique et Nobiliaire de la France: Des Origines à Nos Jours.* Vol. 3, *Recueils généalogiques généraux, Monographies Familiales et Etudes Particulières.* Paris, 1974.

Salmon, J. H. M. *Society in Crisis: France in the Sixteenth Century.* London, 1975.

Sawyer, Jeffrey. *Printed Poison: Pamphlet Propaganda, Faction Politics, and the Public Sphere in Early Seventeenth-Century France.* Berkeley, 1990.

Schalk, Ellery. "Clientage, Elites, and Absolutism in Seventeenth-Century France." *French Historical Studies* 14 (1986): 442–46.

————. *From Valor to Pedigree: Ideas of Nobility in France in the Sixteenth and Seventeenth Centuries.* Princeton, 1986.

Scott, Samuel. *The Response of the Royal Army to the French Revolution: The Role and Development of the Line Army, 1787–93.* Oxford, 1978.

Sewell, William H., Jr. "Etat, Corps, and Ordre: Some Notes on the Social Vocabulary of the French Old Regime." In *Sozialgeschichte Heute, Festschrift für Hans Rosenberg zum 70 Geburtstag,* ed. Hans-Ulrich Wehler, 49–68. Göttingen, 1974.

————. "Ideologies and Social Revolutions: Reflections on the French Case." *Journal of Modern History* 57 (1985): 57–85.

————. *Work and Revolution in France: The Language of Labor from the Old Regime to 1848.* Cambridge, 1980.

Skinner, Quentin. *The Foundations of Modern Political Thought.* 2 vols. Cambridge, 1978.

————. "Some Problems in the Analysis of Political Thought and Action." *Political Theory* 2 (1974): 277–303.

Solnon, Jean-François. *La cour de France.* Paris, 1987.

Solomon, Howard. *Public Welfare, Science, and Propaganda in Seventeenth-Century France: The Innovations of Théophraste Renaudot.* Princeton, 1972.

Sonnino, Paul. "The Dating and Authorship of Louis XIV's *Mémoires.*" *French Historical Studies* 3 (1964): 303–37.

————, ed. *The Reign of Louis XIV.* Atlantic Highlands, N.J., 1990.

Stegmann, André. "Les Juristes et le Prince (1610–1640)." In *L'Image du Souverain dans les Lettres Françaises des Guerres de Religion à la Révocation de l'Edit de Nantes,* Actes et Colloques, vol. 24, 153–68. Paris, 1985.

Stone, Lawrence. *The Crisis of the Aristocracy, 1558–1641.* Oxford, 1965.

Tatum, James, ed. *The School of Cyrus: William Barker's 1567 Translation of*

Xenophon's Cyropaedeia. Vol. 37 of *The Renaissance Imagination.* New York and London, 1987.

Thomas, Keith. "The Social Origins of Hobbes's Political Thought." In *Hobbes Studies,* ed. K. C. Brown, 185–236. Oxford, 1965.

Thuau, Etienne. *Raison d'Etat et Pensée Politique à l'Epoque de Richelieu.* Paris, 1966.

Tocqueville, Alexis de. *The Old Regime and the French Revolution.* Trans. Stuart Gilbert. New York, 1955.

Vaissière, Pierre de. *Gentilshommes campagnards de l'Ancienne France.* Paris, 1903.

Weary, William. "The House of La Trémoille, Fifteenth through Eighteenth Centuries: Change and Adaptation in a French Noble Family." *Journal of Modern History* 49 (1977): on-demand supplement.

Weber, Max. *The Theory of Social and Economic Organization.* Trans. A. M. Henderson and Talcott Parsons. New York, 1964.

Williams, Alan. *The Police of Paris, 1718–1789.* Baton Rouge and London, 1979.

Wolf, Charles. *Histoire de l'Observatoire de Paris: De sa fondation à 1793.* Paris, 1902.

Wolf, John B. *Louis XIV.* New York, 1968.

Wood, James B. *The Nobility of the 'Election' of Bayeux, 1463–1666: Continuity through Change.* Princeton, 1980.

Yardeni, Myriam. *La Conscience Nationale en France Pendant Les Guerres de Religion (1559–1598).* Paris, 1971.

Index